IN-SERVICE EDUCATION

FOR TEACHERS, SUPERVISORS, AND ADMINISTRATORS

Officers of the Society
1956–57

IN-SERVICE EDUCATION

FOR TEACHERS, SUPERVISORS, AND ADMINISTRATORS

The Fifty-sixth Yearbook of the
National Society for the Study of Education

PART I

Prepared by the Yearbook Committee: STEPHEN M. COREY (*Chairman*),
JOHN I. GOODLAD, C. GLEN HASS, ARTHUR J. LEWIS,
and J. CECIL PARKER

Edited by

NELSON B. HENRY

1 9 **NSSE** 5 7

Distributed by THE UNIVERSITY OF CHICAGO PRESS • CHICAGO, ILLINOIS

The responsibilities of the Board of Directors of the National Society for the Study of Education in the case of yearbooks prepared by the Society's committees are (1) to select the subjects to be investigated, (2) to appoint committees calculated in their personnel to insure consideration of all significant points of view, (3) to provide appropriate subsidies for necessary expenses, (4) to publish and distribute the committees' reports, and (5) to arrange for their discussion at the annual meetings.

The responsibility of the Yearbook Editor is to prepare the submitted manuscripts for publication in accordance with the principles and regulations approved by the Board of Directors.

Neither the Board of Directors, nor the Yearbook Editor, nor the Society is responsible for the conclusions reached or the opinions expressed by the Society's yearbook committees.

Published 1957 by

THE NATIONAL SOCIETY FOR THE STUDY OF EDUCATION

5835 Kimbark Avenue, Chicago 37, Illinois

The Society's Committee on In-service Education

STEPHEN M. COREY
Dean, Teachers College, Columbia University
New York, New York

JOHN I. GOODLAD
Professor of Education and Director of Center for Teacher Education
University of Chicago
Chicago, Illinois

C. GLEN HASS
Associate Superintendent and Director of Instruction
Arlington County Public Schools
Arlington, Virginia

ARTHUR J. LEWIS
Assistant Superintendent of Schools
Minneapolis, Minnesota

J. CECIL PARKER
Professor of Education and Director of Field Service Center
University of California
Berkeley, California

Associated Contributors

MARVIN L. BERGE
Assistant Superintendent, Elgin Public Schools
Elgin, Illinois

HUBERT S. COFFEY
Associate Clinical Professor of Psychology
University of California
Berkeley, California

ANNA L. DAVIS
Co-ordinator of Guidance, Pasadena Public Schools
Pasadena, California

GEORGE W. DENEMARK
Assistant Dean, College of Education
University of Maryland
College Park, Maryland

CLARENCE FIELSTRA
Assistant Dean, School of Education, University of California
Los Angeles, California

v

ROBERT S. GILCHRIST
Superintendent, University City Public Schools
University City, Missouri

WILLIAM P. GOLDEN, JR.
Associate Professor of Education, San Francisco State College
San Francisco, California

VIRGIL E. HERRICK
Professor of Education, University of Wisconsin
Madison, Wisconsin

B. JO KINNICK
Oakland High School
Oakland, California

J. W. MAUCKER
President, Iowa State Teachers College
Cedar Falls, Iowa

MATTHEW B. MILES
Assistant Professor of Education and Research Associate
Horace Mann–Lincoln Institute of School Experimentation
Teachers College, Columbia University
New York, New York

A. HARRY PASSOW
Associate Professor of Education and Research Associate
Horace Mann–Lincoln Institute of School Experimentation
Teachers College, Columbia University
New York, New York

DARYL PENDERGRAFT
Director of Field Services, Iowa State Teachers College
Cedar Falls, Iowa

HERMAN G. RICHEY
Professor of Education, University of Chicago
Chicago, Illinois

HARRIS E. RUSSELL
Director, Division of Instructional Services, Racine Public Schools
Racine, Wisconsin

CHARLES B. WALDEN
Co-ordinator of Secondary Education, Kenosha Public Schools
Kenosha, Wisconsin

Acknowledgments

The authors of chapters vi, vii, and viii wish to express their appreciation of the assistance provided by the several persons whose names are identified with these three chapters, respectively. In each case the collaborators mentioned gave the author valuable suggestions or opinions regarding specified problems related to the subject of the chapter or contributed materials for the author's use in preparation of the text of the chapter.

CHAPTER VI

Virginia Boney, De Kalb County School System, Decatur, Georgia
Elizabeth A. Huntington, Connecticut Farms School, Union, New Jersey
Robert T. Rasmussen, Roslyn Public Schools, Roslyn, New York
Shirley A. Simon, Minnehaha School, Minneapolis, Minnesota
Nicholas G. Tacinas, Horace Mann Junior High School, Denver, Colorado
Elizabeth Zimmerman, La Grange Public Schools, La Grange, Illinois

CHAPTER VII

Selmer H. Berg, Superintendent, Oakland Public Schools, Oakland, California
Mildred Biddick, Principal, Jesse H. Newlon School, Denver, Colorado
Ronald C. Doll, Director of Instruction, Montclair Public Schools, Montclair, New Jersey
James A. Hall, Superintendent, Port Washington Public Schools, Port Washington, New York
Jess S. Hudson, Assistant Superintendent, Tulsa Public Schools, Tulsa, Oklahoma
Dwight Teel, Director, Division of Curricular Services, Corpus Christi Public Schools, Corpus Christi, Texas

CHAPTER VIII

Joyce Cooper, Assistant Superintendent in Charge of Instruction, State Office of Public Instruction, Olympia, Washington

Elizabeth Donovan, Consultant, Division of Instruction, State Department of Education, Atlanta, Georgia

Jane Franseth, Specialist for Rural Education, Office of Education, Department of Health, Education, and Welfare, Washington, D.C.

Claudia Pitts, Elementary Supervisor, Arlington County Public Schools, Arlington, Virginia

Drummond C. Rucker, Director of Personnel, Springfield Public Schools, Springfield, Missouri

Editor's Preface

The present volume is the second in the National Society's series of yearbooks to be devoted entirely to in-service education. Part I of the Seventh Yearbook was planned as a sequel to earlier volumes dealing with the preparation and certification of teachers and supervisory officers. Substantively, it is the report of returns from an inquiry submitted by the Society to superintendents and principals in city school systems with the view of ascertaining best practices being utilized for the improvement of teachers in service. The report was prepared by Charles D. Lowry, a member of the Society and District Superintendent of Schools in Chicago. The author's observations on the purpose and method of in-service education are a noteworthy pronouncement on the timeliness of the National Society's first yearbook on this subject. As an interesting background for the reading of the present yearbook, Mr. Lowry's comments are presented here in his own phrasing.

"The work of making good teachers must be carried forward steadily because of the immaturity of teachers on entering the profession, the unevenness of their preparation, the singular lack of external stimulus connected with the practice of the profession, the complex nature of the work that must be intrusted to even the poorest teacher, the profound injury that results when the work is badly done, the constant change in methods and curriculum.

"The making of good teachers is accomplished in two ways, by instruction on the part of the supervision, by personal study on the part of the teacher. Instruction and study may be concerned with information, with methods, or with principles. The instruction which comes through sympathetic supervision which suggests correct methods but does not impose particular ones, which points to principles underlying methods, which shows the application of principles to schoolroom practice, which arouses a love for excellence in work and in scholarship will ever be the most powerful of the agencies for good."

In-service Education for Teachers, Supervisors, and Administra-

ix

tors reflects the advances in preservice programs of professional education since the publication of the Seventh Yearbook as well as the changes in objectives and procedures of institutional design for the improvement of educational services. It accentuates the shift from an authoritarian to a co-operative conception of school management exemplified in theory and practice of best repute at the conclusion of a half-century of extraordinary progress toward democracy in education on a nation-wide basis. It will serve the useful purpose of stimulating teachers, supervisors, and administrators to participate cordially in the development and maintenance of inservice activities calculated to insure their individual and collective attainment of the highest possible degree of efficiency as members of the school staff. The planning and preparation of this yearbook were carried on under the direction of Dean Corey, who was requested to serve as chairman of the yearbook committee at the meeting of the Board of Directors in May, 1954. At the same time, the Board scheduled the volume for publication in 1957.

NELSON B. HENRY

Table of Contents

SECTION II

Roles of Teachers, Administrators, and Consultants

SECTION III

In-service Education Programs

SECTION IV

Organization, Evaluation, Training

CHAPTER I

Introduction

STEPHEN M. COREY

This yearbook, as its title makes clear, has to do with the in-service education of professional school personnel. Attention is centered upon planned programs in some contrast to the various activities in which teachers and others might independently engage in order to improve themselves. This emphasis upon programmatic activity should not be interpreted to mean that wide reading, travel, convention attendance, taking professional courses, or anything else that teachers or administrators find conducive to professional growth is depreciated. Planned programs in in-service education are, however, in the judgment of the yearbook committee, essential to adequate professional improvement of school personnel. The demands now being made upon schools and upon the people who are responsible for the quality of schools make it impracticable to place full dependence upon preservice preparation and the initiative of the individual to better himself in service.

Need for In-service Education

That there is great need for better programs of in-service education is rarely contested. As Hass shows in chapter ii, our rapidly changing culture and its implication for curriculum change, the continuing increase in pupil enrolments and numbers of teachers, the need for improved school leadership, the continuous additions to our knowledge in general and particularly our knowledge about children and youth and the learning process, all, in cumulation, mean that professional school people need to work continuously to keep abreast of what they must know and must be able to do. They need help, too, in the form of carefully planned and creative programs of in-service education. There are many indications that such programs are becoming increasingly common; but it is also apparent that much of what goes for in-service education is uninspiring and ineffective.

More than a Century of In-service Education

Activities designed to enable teachers and other professional school personnel to improve while they are in service do not represent a new idea. Such activities have been part and parcel of American education for more than a century. Many lessons can be learned from the history of attempts at in-service improvement of instruction as Richey, in chapter iii, traces it clearly and with great insight. During most of the nineteenth century, and to a degree during the first few years of the twentieth, teachers in the common schools were generally immature, poorly educated, and superficially trained. The main purpose of in-service education was to correct such deficiencies, and teachers' institutes became the chief means of accomplishing this end. Early in the 1900's these institutes were required in about two-thirds of the states. By 1930, however, they had lost much favor, and the conception of teacher improvement as a major aspect of supervision had grown in popularity. Ideas about supervision slowly changed, too, influenced no doubt by forces which introduced greater permissiveness, shared-planning, and humaneness in classroom practices. The supervisor came to be viewed as a guide and counselor to teachers rather than a director of activities. By the late 1930's workshops had become popular for in-service education, as did the belief that co-operative work on instructional problems, in general, was the best way to assure the professional growth of the total school staff.

In-service Education as a Design for Change

The modern conception of in-service education, with its heavy emphasis upon co-operative problem-solving, is in considerable degree a result of changes in our ideas about human motivation and the way learning occurs within an institutional setting. In-service education of school personnel has always had as its objective the improvement of professional behavior. Acquiring new attitudes and learning new knowledge were but means to this end. For many years, however, it was generally believed that learning *about* ways and means of improving instruction would stimulate changes in practice that would result in these improvements. It was generally believed, too, that someone in authority in the schools—the supervisor or the administrator—could directly tell teachers how to better their instruction with the result, again, of rapid improvement.

These conceptions of desirable ways of bringing about change in professional behavior are no longer considered valid by persons who have made a special study of this kind of learning. The results of such study have, in the judgment of the yearbook committee, such relevance for in-service education that two chapters have been included in the yearbook to make the relationship clear. Chapter iv, by Coffey and Golden, summarizes what social psychologists have found out about the process of change when it represents learning of pervasive and dynamic quality and takes place within a complex institutional structure such as a school. In this chapter a great deal of attention is given to the effect which other people have upon our willingness and ability to modify our attitudes and behavior, particularly when these other people belong to groups that we belong to and value. The concept of "role" is introduced, as well as the characteristics of general institutional groups, like the professional personnel of a school system, that facilitate or hinder individual behavior change.

It is difficult, even when a report based on research and enlightened speculation is as lucid as is the chapter by Coffey and Golden, to see what the implications might be for a practical, complicated activity like the in-service education of school people. Consequently, chapter v was prepared by Parker to make these implications more explicit. This, Parker did by describing and illustrating a list of twelve guidelines or operating principles that he and the members of the yearbook committee believed were implied in chapter iv and might well give direction to the planning of programs of in-service education. In brief, these guidelines serve to define the most satisfactory kind of professional improvement program as a series of planned activities that provide a maximum opportunity for school people (*a*) to identify the instructional or other problems on which they want to work, (*b*) to decide upon ways and means for attacking these problems, (*c*) to work within an atmosphere of mutual support and permissiveness, and (*d*) to move from thought and study into action with a minimum of difficulty.

Chapters ii, iii, iv, and v constitute Section I of the yearbook and represent its basic definitional and historic and theoretic framework.

Chapters iv and v were read by all the authors of the chapters that appear in Sections II, III, and IV before they prepared the first drafts of their manuscripts. This has served to provide a degree of unity in the total yearbook which the committee felt highly desirable.

Perceptions of the Parties Involved

The conception of in-service education developed in Section I represents the yearbook committee's beliefs about what should characterize attempts to further the professionalization of the school staff. In order for these attempts to succeed, the commitment and involvement of a number of groups is required. The committee was particularly interested in the role of teachers, administrators, and consultants. In order to learn the way these three groups would see their responsibilities and would evaluate the co-operative problem-study or co-operative action-research approach to in-service education, representatives of each group were asked to prepare a chapter. The arrangements for this involved setting up separate committees of teachers, administrators, and consultants under a chairman. The latter collated and summarized memoranda prepared by his committee members.

The reaction of teachers to the kind of in-service education in which individuals and groups work in ways that they define and on problems of their own choosing is favorable, but a bit skeptical. Mrs. Kinnick and her associates write in chapter vi as if they were not quite certain how free they really were to work in this fashion. And even when there may be considerable freedom, there is little time. Apparently there have been many occasions when school administrators have urged co-operation and have talked about freedom to experiment, but things happened subsequently that made the teachers not quite certain what was meant. These teachers, too, see great promise in the informal group and the informal individual in-service activity. The "program," planned and initiated too often by some power figure, is in their judgment apt to be overvalued.

Teachers apparently realize clearly that the school hierarchy with its clear differences in power is a fact, and they resent its denial. They have rather strong feelings, too, about the necessity of in-service education for everyone—certainly including the administrators. Too often it sounds to teachers as if someone believed that they were the only ones who needed to grow in service. The classroom teachers add that they would benefit greatly in all in-service activities from a clear and early understanding of the limits within which they can make decisions, take actions, and experiment.

The administrators, comprising status leaders of the "line" in contrast with those of the "staff," recognize that their role in co-operative programs of in-service education is a difficult one. They are convinced, though, that this role must be learned and that, when it is learned, the benefits will be great. One body of knowledge and skill that the administrators recognize they must acquire, to facilitate the group problem-solving kind of professional improvement, involves their becoming quite expert in the process of productive small-group work. This means not only learning to behave constructively in the small group, which is hard enough, but learning something, too, about ways and means of teaching other people so that their behavior is conducive to productivity. The administrator knows that his most important general responsibility in the in-service education program is to provide a wide range of needed resources and to create, to the degree that he can, an atmosphere that is conducive to change.

Principals and superintendents realize, as has been said above, that they have much to learn about co-operative problem-solving. Lewis emphasizes in chapter vii that there must be in-service education unique to the special needs of such people. Much of chapter xiv describes what this recommendation means in practice.

One of the requirements of in-service education which consists largely of small groups working on a diversity of instructional problems meaningful to them is the provision of adequate human resources. The yearbook committee was particularly concerned about the role of the consultant—the man or woman who is brought from outside the institution because he has the kind of special competence the group needs to get on with its task. Goodlad and his associates in chapter viii describe the roles and problems of this consultant, especially when he works with one group for a considerable period of time. His relation to institutional and group factors that are conducive to change, as well as the importance of certain personal characteristics that are essential to the success of the consultant, are stressed. A great deal of attention is devoted to the importance of the consultant taking the time and developing the ability to assess the forces in the local situation that have a bearing upon in-service education activities.

In respect to the consultant's personal characteristics, his ability to use the internal structure of the working group to foster the potentialities within it, and his ability to help the group feel free and able to make group decisions and to accept the desired change are developed at some length. In this chapter, as in chapter vii, the need for in-service education, this time for consultants, was both admitted and urged.

In-service Education Programs

The yearbook's emphasis upon in-service education programs caused the committee to want to describe a variety of them. All of Section III is devoted to these descriptions. The illustrations do not, of course, represent a random selection but, rather, those activities which seemed to illustrate the operational principles that are developed in chapter v. The criterion that was employed to differentiate among many illustrative programs so that a chapter could be devoted to each was predominantly geographic and resulted in these two classifications: system-wide programs and programs involving areas, regions, a single state, and the nation.

There are, of course, many system-wide programs designed to engage the interest and participation of a wide variety of school personnel from all buildings and at all levels. Berge, Russell, and Walden report an original questionnaire study of such programs in chapter ix. They give particular attention to the effects of centralizing the administration of in-service education. One kind of program is highly centralized in its control; another is almost completely decentralized with most of the decision-making concentrated in the building unit. Still a third type of program includes a great deal of decentralized activity but with adequate provisions for central coordination. The authors admit that this classification system includes categories that are not mutually exclusive, but they felt they were able to capture the essence of the organizational rationale from the responses to their questionnaire made by a large number of school systems. Berge and his associates were impressed by the degree to

which the centrally co-ordinated kind of in-service education program seemed to be consistent with the principles of change developed in chapters iv and v. The highly centralized type of program seemed least likely to enable large numbers of people to work
on problems significant to them and to work in ways of their own
devisement.

Instructional-improvement programs depending upon in-service
education for their major achievements and involving teachers and
others from more than one school system are of relatively recent
origin. In geographic scope such programs ranged from the limited
area involving the co-operation of a small number of contiguous
school systems through the national type of organized activity such
as is represented by some divisions and departments of the National
Education Association. In-service education of this multisystem kind
not only faces unique and fairly obvious disadvantages but has some
decided advantages as well. Rehage and Denemark in chapter x describe a number of programs that include participants from a few
to hundreds of separate school districts. They evaluate these programs by trying to determine the extent to which they make possible the application of Parker's guidelines (chap. v).

Speaking generally, the in-service programs of broad geographic
scope undertaken outside the decision-and-action structure of any
particular school system have been surprisingly successful in their
influence upon change. In addition to describing illustrative and
highly successful state, area, and regional programs, Rehage and
Denemark comment at some length upon a national training institute
that was designed to facilitate the development of co-operative curriculum research skills. This institute, undertaken under the auspices
of several organizations interested in curriculum improvement, represented a conscious effort to exploit, in a training situation, the conception of change developed by Coffey and Golden in chapter iv
and further elaborated in the guidelines by Parker in chapter v.

In-service Education and Teacher-Education Institutions

Colleges and universities have long exercised great influence upon
in-service education, but their influence has been particularly marked
since the development of strong professional and graduate departments or schools of education. The method of instructional im-

provement that puts great stress on group problem-solving in service makes certain unique demands upon teacher-education institutions. Their programs of preservice and in-service education can support or partially block the efforts of a school staff to improve itself in service. Preservice professional courses, for example, that stress subject matter to be memorized and answers to instructional problems to be learned do not provide good preparation for independent and creative problem-solving in service.

Maucker and Pendergraft in chapter xi describe the implications for what is done in the teacher-education institution of the kind of in-service education programs this yearbook advocates. Their chapter is a rich source of specific suggestions of activities and programs which will enable institutions of higher learning to make important contributions to the in-service growth of the school's professional personnel. These two authors believe strongly that co-operative group work on school problems must constantly be supplemented by a great deal of individual initiative and activity. Teacher-education institutions, however, can and should contribute significantly to both kinds of in-service education.

Organization, Evaluation, and Training

The yearbook committee was certain that something would need to be done about the organization, evaluation, and training features of an in-service education program, regardless of its scope or its identification with a large- or small-group enterprise. Section IV concludes the yearbook and includes a chapter devoted to each of these three areas.

Organization, of course, is merely a method of making functional and visible channels for communication and decision-making and action that will facilitate whatever it is an institution or a less formalized group wants to do. Defining in-service education as getting people to follow directions requires a type of organization that will assure the clarity of these directions as well as continuous supervision to see that they are followed. The point of view toward in-service education that dominates this yearbook suggests an organization that is quite different. It must be one that will provide maximum opportunity for individuals and particularly groups to (*a*) identify the particular problems on which they want to work, (*b*) get together to work on these problems in ways that seem most productive to the group, (c) have access to a variety of needed resources, (d) try out in reality situations those modifications in practice that give a priori promise, and (e) appraise and generalize from the consequences. Organization for in-service education is considered from this point of view in chapter xii. Gilchrist, Fielstra, and Anna Davis have had varied and rich experiences in instructional-improvement programs, and their convictions about organization are persuasive.

No activity, including in-service education, can be adjudged good or bad until its effects are assessed in relation to some goal. The yearbook committee, aware of its own strong disposition to assume as good whatever seemed to be consistent with its predispositions and sentiments, wanted a strong and closely reasoned statement on the evaluation of in-service education. Herrick (chap. xiii) provides the yearbook with this kind of statement. Without trying to discourage the tentative and subjective kind of evaluation which so often is the only type that seems feasible, he calls attention to standards that must be met by any pervasive and penetrating appraisal of the over-all effects of an in-service education program. Herrick attends to what must be done to determine the effects of the program upon changes both in the practices of individuals and in the educational program itself. He notes the danger in assuming that the mere existence of a great deal of small-group activity that may be enjoyed is resulting in better classroom experiences for boys and girls.

In-service education that rests heavily upon co-operative group action and appraisal requires of its participants a host of attitudes, understandings, and skills that most of us have not adequately learned. We are insufficiently competent in respect to communication and co-operation in small face-to-face group situations as well as to the intricacies and subtleties of problem-solving and research processes. Unless we can train ourselves so as to improve our competencies on these two related dimensions, instructional improvement as a consequence of co-operative problem-solving will remain little more than a hope.

Training in small-group process and problem-solving skills is exceedingly difficult to plan and conduct. As a final chapter in the yearbook, Miles and Passow, in a highly concentrated fashion, describe kinds of training with which they have had a great deal of experience and which was designed to improve co-operative curriculum research skills. Of all the chapters in the yearbook, this is probably the one most representative of ideas that are just beginning to gain acceptance in respect to either preservice or in-service teacher education. Miles and Passow insist upon using the word "training" and define it as being concerned with skill development, with opportunities for "whole person" learning, with opportunities for practice of what is to be learned under circumstances when the "chips are not down." In this final chapter a great deal is made of the desirability of role-playing as a training activity.

Conclusion

This introductory chapter has served its purpose if it has helped the reader to understand the argument of the yearbook and to anticipate it somewhat. Most of the chapters and sections are replete with down-to-earth illustrations which help to give life to what might otherwise be sterile admonitions. In the judgment of the yearbook committee, the yearbook will be a success if it provokes its readers to experiment thoughtfully and carefully with the various procedures and activities and ideas that are described in the several chapters.

THE NEED, HISTORY, AND BASIC CHARACTER OF IN-SERVICE EDUCATION

CHAPTER II

In-service Education Today

C. GLEN HASS

Introduction

In this chapter the facts and factors which demonstrate the urgent need for the in-service education of the professional staff are reviewed and some of the typical in-service education needs of teachers, principals, and supervisors are examined. Finally, the present extent of in-service education activities in public school systems throughout the nation is noted briefly. In summarizing the chapter, consideration is given the great importance of an adequate supply of good teachers who are constantly growing professionally.

WHAT IS IN-SERVICE EDUCATION?

Broadly conceived, in-service education includes all activities engaged in by the professional personnel during their service and designed to contribute to improvement on the job. In this yearbook our attention will be focused upon those activities that are promoted and directed by local school boards and school leadership staffs. We recognize that professional growth may also be the result of activities or experiences initiated by teachers themselves, by the supervisory staff, by the public, by any combination of these, or by miscellaneous groups in the community.

PURPOSES OF IN-SERVICE EDUCATION

The major reason for in-service education is to promote the continuous improvement of the total professional staff of the school system. All teachers, administrators, and supervisors must constantly study in order to keep up with advances in subject matter and in the theory and practice of teaching. Continuous in-service education is needed to keep the profession abreast of new knowledge and to release creative abilities.

An additional purpose is to give the much needed help to teachers who are new in a particular school and to those who are entering a new responsibility or a new field of work within the profession. Such people need answers to their many questions and extensive help with the new problems which they face.

At least for the present, a third purpose of in-service education must be to eliminate deficiencies in the background preparation of teachers and of other professional workers in education. Many members of the professional staff do not have adequate preservice preparation and have not, for various reasons, continued with the work toward Bachelor's or Master's degrees, or their equivalent, which they need. An extensive study of the professional preparation of American teachers was made in 1947–48. At that time, 59.1 per cent had the Bachelor's or a higher degree: 44.7 per cent having a Bachelor's degree, and 14.4 per cent having a Master's or higher degree. The 40.9 per cent remaining had three years of college preparation or less.[1]

Of the three purposes of in-service education listed above, the most important is the necessity for all members of the professional school staff to keep abreast of the rapid accumulation of new knowledge and new professional subject matter.

The Need for In-service Education
of the Total Professional Staff

There are a number of facts and factors which make clear the need for in-service education. These are considered in the following section.

THE CONTINUING CULTURAL AND SOCIAL CHANGES WHICH
CREATE NEED FOR CURRICULUM CHANGE

The American society is not one in which the problems of government, business, and social living have been solved for all time, thus leaving to education the simple function of disseminating fixed doctrines and knowledge of the practical arts. Ours is a society which constantly confronts new issues at home and in its relations with other countries. In our society education has the responsibility

1. Council of State Governments, *The Forty-eight State School Systems*, p. 202. Chicago: Council of State Governments, 1949.

both for dealing with these new problems and for conserving and transmitting the values in our heritage.

In order to know the kind of education which America needs in the years ahead, attention must be given to the complexities of modern life and to the role of the United States in world affairs. The most important element in America's future is, of course, the quality of the American people—their character, their ability, and the degree to which talents are cultivated. The American system of public education plays a vital role in the development of human talents that are needed in facing the problems of America's future. The Educational Policies Commission has identified a number of ways in which the public schools of America must modify their offerings in order to meet the immediate and future needs of the nation. Among the areas of needs identified is the need for the "know-how" of ordinary living in our complex society which must be learned by the whole population. Another need identified is that of developing the broad foundation of education which is one of the bases for the miracle of the American industrial economy. A typical understanding of the basic moral commitments of democracy must be taught, in part through the public education program, in order to provide for a sound American future. The social effects of recent wars place special emphasis on the need for the school to give particular attention to moral and spiritual values. The United States now bears an unprecedented burden of international responsibility; our public educational system has the task of developing the nation-wide understanding necessary for meeting this responsibility.[2]

Many explicit demands for curriculum changes are constantly made on the schools by groups that are integral to a dynamic culture. Any principal or superintendent could prepare a list of these demands. They include requests for the teaching of first-aid, mental hygiene, Spanish in the first grade, international understanding, home-making, nutrition, labor relations, human relationships, the use of firearms, temperance, kindness to animals, civil defense, thrift, consumer education, the evil of narcotics, aviation education, driver education, the work of the United Nations, and moral and spiritual

2. Educational Policies Commission, *Public Education and the Future of America,* pp. 86–89. Washington: National Education Association and the American Association of School Administrators, 1955.

values. These requests and pressures grow out of the constantly shifting cultural changes which occur in society today.

Other social changes of particular significance for the school program are identified in Allen's *The Big Change*, which tells the ways in which America transformed herself during the period 1900–1950. Among the changes of great significance for education described by Allen are the tremendous increases in interest in reading, music, and the arts. The sales of paper-bound books like Ruth Benedict's *Patterns of Culture*, George Orwell's *1948*, and Norman Mailer's *The Naked and the Dead* have gone beyond the million mark. Allen also reports that there have been more sales of paintings since 1940 than in all the previous history of the United States and that there has been a great increase in the number of local museums and the sale of art reproductions. When we turn to music we find that 1,500 American cities and towns now support annual series of classical concerts, that there are 657 "symphonic groups" and a wide variety of miscellaneous amateur musical groups. In America a love of music and art and good reading is no longer a mark of the elite.[3] These increases in interest in the arts indicate needed changes and improvements in, as well as a tribute to, the program of public education.

Margaret Mead argues for in-service education "which will permit the teacher to keep abreast of a changing world," and goes on to say:

Within the lifetime of ten-year-olds the world has entered a new age, and already, before they enter the sixth grade, the atomic age has been followed by the age of the hydrogen bomb, differentiated from the atomic age in that many of those who failed to understand the dangers of the atom bomb are painfully beginning to take in the significance of the hydrogen bomb. Teachers who never heard a radio until they were grown up have to cope with children who have never known a world without television. Teachers who struggled in their childhood with a buttonhook find it difficult to describe a buttonhook to a child bred up among zippers, to whom fastnesses are to be breached by zipping them open, rather than fumblingly feeling for mysterious buttons.[4]

3. Frederick Lewis Allen, *The Big Change*, pp. 273–83. New York: Harper & Bros., 1952.

4. Margaret Mead, *The School in American Culture*, pp. 36, 33. Cambridge, Massachusetts: Harvard University Press, 1951.

Undoubtedly, the characteristics and needs of the American public school cannot be determined except with reference to the unfolding social scene. The qualities, skills, and necessary preparation of a good teacher must also be determined in this light. Because of constant social change, the preparation needed by the professional educator is continuous throughout his professional career.

PRESERVICE EDUCATION CANNOT ADEQUATELY PREPARE MEMBERS OF THE PUBLIC SCHOOL PROFESSIONAL STAFF FOR THEIR RESPONSIBILITIES

We now spend more than 8.9 billion dollars a year educating children 5 to 17 years of age in the public schools.[5] The American people will not continue to spend this and the larger sums needed for public education unless they are convinced they are buying good education. It is not enough to repeat the 1945 model of good education in 1955. As has just been noted, the changing demands and needs of society are too great to permit this to be true. Preservice education cannot develop the skills and attitudes and knowledge which are necessary. There are constant additions to our knowledge in all fields. We learn better ways of dealing with individual differences among pupils, acquire greater knowledge of how learning occurs, devise improved teaching methods, achieve greater understanding of child growth and development, and study ways in which groups can work together effectively. We will consider these and other in-service needs of teachers, principals, and supervisors in later sections of this chapter.

INCREASE IN PUPIL ENROLMENT

Since the school year 1947–48 there has been a marked increase in elementary-school enrolments, and it seems clear that for more than a decade they will continue to be high. The number of pupils of high-school age is also beginning to increase, and this increase will continue for at least ten years as the enlarged elementary-pupil population moves into the secondary school. During the thirty-year period from 1920 to 1950 the enrolment in public elementary and

5. National Citizens Commission for the Public Schools, "Financing Public Education in the Decade Ahead," pp. 8–9. New York: National Citizens Commission, December 6, 1954.

secondary schools increased from 21.5 million to 25 million. In the five years following 1950, there has been even a greater increase, to an estimated enrolment of 30,670,000 for the school year 1954–55.[6] By 1960 elementary enrolments will be 28 per cent above 1954–55, and secondary enrolments will be more than 70 per cent above the 1954–55 level. These greatly increased enrolments, together with the sharply accentuated rate of growth in enrolments, call for large increases in the number of teachers.

THE PRESENT AND CONTINUING INCREASE
IN THE NUMBER OF TEACHERS

During the period 1920–50, the number of classroom teachers in public elementary and secondary schools increased from 678,000 to 913,000. From 1950–55 there was a further increase of 150,000. This most recent increase has occurred during a period when the number of emergency teachers was also increasing. According to one study,[7] there will need to be a half-million more schoolteachers on the job in 1965 than there were in 1955. To maintain the present pupil-teacher ratio during the next ten years, the schools would have to increase their teaching staffs more than was done in the past thirty-five years. The colleges and universities would have to add more teachers in the next fifteen years than in all previous years combined.[8]

The quality of teachers in our schools is, of course, a matter of the deepest social concern. The Commisison on Teacher Education of the American Council on Education pointed out in its final report that:

The nation needs teachers who respect personality, who are community-minded, who act reasonably, who know how to work co-operatively with others. It needs teachers whose native gifts have been highly developed through sound general and professional education, whose knowledge is accurate, extensive, and increasing. It needs teachers who

6. Information furnished by the Educational Research Service, National Education Association.

7. The Fund for the Advancement of Education, *Teachers for Tomorrow*, p. 17. New York: Fund for the Advancement of Education, Bulletin No. 2, November, 1955.

8. *Ibid.*

like and are liked by children, who understand how children grow and develop, who know how to guide learning and mediate knowledge extensively.[9]

THE PRESENT AND CONTINUING SHORTAGE
OF ADEQUATELY PREPARED TEACHERS

The teacher has the crucial role in the educational process. If he is inadequately prepared and lacking in character, convictions, knowledge, and skill, he can exercise a harmful influence. On the other hand, we are aware of the powerful contributions to the development of children and to the promotion of social well-being that are made by superior teachers. To gain these advantages for our children, every possible means must be used to improve the skills and release the creative abilities of the teaching staff.

The reports on teacher supply and demand, prepared each year by the Research Division of the National Education Association, have given a clear picture during the past several years of the serious shortage of adequately prepared teachers. This shortage is one of the most serious problems facing American education. The number of new elementary-school teachers employed in the fall of 1954 was twice the number of the 1954 graduates who were prepared to be elementary-school teachers. This undersupply of newly trained teachers has obtained for several years and indicates the extent to which the elementary schools are dependent upon the return of former teachers to the classroom, the availability of graduates of liberal-arts colleges who may enter the classroom without any professional preparation, and the granting of temporary licenses to persons who may have little or no preparation for elementary-school instruction. The 1955 report also indicates that for the past few years the number of qualified graduates preparing for high-school teaching has been just about equal to the demand. This datum is misleading, however, since each year a substantial number of the members of the graduating classes preparing for high-school teaching do not enter teaching. In the fall of 1954, only 55.7 per cent of the eligible group in the 1954 class actually took teaching jobs. As

9. Commission on Teacher Education, *The Improvement of Teacher Education*, p. 247. Washington: American Council on Education, 1946.

has been noted, this report also indicates that the high-school enrolment is now entering a period of growth which within the next five years will be tremendous.[10] Another serious problem noted in this publication is the large number of emergency teachers who are employed. In 1955–56 the total was over 80,000.[11]

The problem of maintaining the necessary supply of adequately prepared teachers is not temporary. The Commission on Teacher Education of the American Council on Education has pointed out that the problems of maintaining a supply of more than a million professional workers, which is far more numerous than the members of any other professional group, is under any circumstances a considerable enterprise. Its magnitude is increased by the fact that, having entered the profession, teachers often do not continue in active service as long as the members of other professions. Marriage and the losses due to the attraction of other work opportunities which offer better salaries drain away large numbers each year.[12]

THE PRESENT AND CONTINUING NEED
FOR IMPROVED SCHOOL LEADERS

The human resources of the schools and the community which supports them are rich and varied. The yield of these resources is often insignificant when compared with what is potentially possible. Development of the kind of leadership from principals, supervisors, curriculum directors, and superintendents necessary to facilitate the use of these human resources is largely dependent upon in-service education in the form of courses taken at a college or university, experience as a competent teacher, conferences, work experience, and recreation. Training for positions of leadership in education requires continuous effort from the beginning days of teaching.

At one time it was thought that an experienced teacher who had

10. Research Division, National Education Association, *The 1955 Teacher Supply and Demand Report*, pp. 12–14. Washington: National Commission on Teacher Education and Professional Standards of the National Education Association, March, 1954.

11. Research Division, National Education Association, "Advance Estimates of Public Elementary and Secondary Schools for the School Year 1955–56," p. 3. Washington: National Education Association, December, 1955.

12. Commission on Teacher Education, *Teachers for Our Times*. Washington: American Council on Education, 1954.

acquired the technique of managing unruly children and irate parents was adequately prepared for a principalship. The possession of these skills may still be necessary for the modern principal, but they are far from sufficient. The principal, as well as the supervisor or superintendent, now occupies a well-defined professional position which presupposes specific preparation. These status leaders must have a comprehensive grasp of educational, personnel, and administrative problems which can be obtained only through the integration of continuous, careful study and practical experience. The principal, who is the status leader at the building level, should have the ability to mobilize the skills and efforts of the teaching staff to provide an effective educational program. To do this he must develop a favorable climate for staff work and co-ordinate the efforts of various staff members.

In-service education is needed for every member of the profession engaged in public education. We suggest in the following sections the many ways in which all members of the profession need to grow on the job.

Some Typical In-service Education Needs of Teachers, Principals, and Supervisors

All teachers, principals, and supervisors must continue to learn throughout their professional careers. In the following pages consideration is given to some of the areas in which growth must occur if educators are to do the job that is needed in these complex times. In each of the areas there are given only a few from among the many possible illustrations of a need for growth.

MAINTENANCE OF FAMILIARITY WITH NEW KNOWLEDGE AND SUBJECT MATTER

One of the marks of a profession is that its members seek constantly to keep abreast of the new knowledge germane to its activities. An article written by the president of the American Academy of General (Medical) Practice described one of the requirements of that group for its members as including 150 hours of postgraduate training every three years. Two-thirds of this requirement can be met through attendance at scientific society meetings or hospital staff meetings. At least 50 hours must be formal training in approved courses.[13]

Teachers, principals, and supervisors also have new subject-matter developments in their particular fields with which they must keep abreast. The English teacher must be alert to the endless stream of new books. He must take increasing notice of the mass media of communication. He must be prepared to apply the principles of semantics to classroom experiences in propaganda analysis, in creative thinking, and in problem-solving. He must keep informed on the state of our living language and the frequent changes and additions in its general and special vocabularies.

Teaching the social studies requires continuous study. Information about the world which was vital and useful during the teacher's student days frequently becomes outdated and inadequate. Therefore, the social-studies teacher must study the never-ending flow of current affairs—local, national, and international. He must do what he can to become acquainted with the mass of historical publications and the literary interpretations of the modern and ancient world. He should be aware of the many interpretations and modifications of our system of law, the changing face of the globe, and the inroads made on time and space by the genius of modern man. He must try to keep his finger on the pulse of the changing economic, social, and political scenes and experiment with new ways of communicating to his students the effect of new knowledge on man and his civilization.

Science teachers, too, must grow and study continuously. For instance, today's science teacher must structure a sound classroom program presenting scientific facts about atomic energy, its present uses and promise, in order that his pupils will be equipped to analyze the social, political, and economic issues that grow out of these scientific facts. For the science teacher to do this, he must study regularly, and he often needs work experience in industries which are making applications of atomic power.

In these subject fields and in others, today's teachers of children and youth must continually "run to keep from falling behind."

13. R. B. Robins, M.D., "Too Many Wrong Ideas about Doctors," *U.S. News and World Report,* XXXIV (April 3, 1953), 44–51.

HUMAN GROWTH AND LEARNING

The study and understanding of how learning occurs is central to the work of teachers. So many contributions are being made to this area that continous in-service education for all teachers is necessary for them to keep informed. Havighurst and others, for example, have studied and reported exceedingly useful information regarding the "developmental tasks" of childhood, adolescence, and adulthood. Knowing about these developmental tasks helps in discovering and stating the purpose of education in the schools and in timing of educational efforts. "When the body is ripe, and society requires, and the self is ready to achieve a certain task, the teachable moment has come."[14] All teachers will be helped in their understanding of the learning process if they understand the concept of developmental tasks and know which tasks dominate the striving of individuals at each age level.

Similarly, Jersild and Tasch have conducted an extensive study of children's interests and what they mean for learning.[15] Knowledge of children's interests indicates the importance of making provision in the educational program for a variety of experiences because children differ from one another so markedly.

Foshay and Wann have reported a study which increases our understanding of the way in which children learn values and how teachers may proceed to help children develop acceptable social values.[16] All teachers are concerned with the teaching of values and can do so more effectively when they know about new developments and new understandings in the important areas of learning.

Child growth and development is recognized today as one of the most important of the specialized branches of psychological research. Increasingly, professional workers in this field are telling us that what we try to accomplish through education at any grade level must be in keeping with the individual's capacity and potentialities

14. Robert J. Havighurst, *Human Development and Education*, p. 5. New York: Longmans, Green & Co.,1953.

15. A. T. Jersild and R. J. Tasch, *Children's Interests and What They Suggest for Education*, pp. 86–87. New York: Bureau of Publications, Teachers College, Columbia University, 1949.

16. A. W. Foshay and K. D. Wann, *Children's Social Values*, pp. 52–53. New York: Bureau of Publications, Teachers College, Columbia University, 1949.

at that level. Findings with respect to growth and behavior should serve as guides to practice. Such studies as those reported by Jersild should have great influence on curriculum development.[17]

Important studies are also being reported in the area of adolescence and adult development. In the latter area, for instance, Lehman's report indicates that "a very large proportion of the most renowned leaders in science and the humanities did their first important work before twenty-five; and . . . in general, the earlier starters contributed better work and were more prolific than the slow starters."[18] This study reverses our commonly accepted ideas about the age at which genius reaches its peak of contribution.

Teachers and school administrators cannot depend upon the knowledge which they gained five or ten years ago in preservice education regarding human growth and development and learning. So much new knowledge is being accumulated in these areas and the knowledge is so important that it must be widely and continuously disseminated and understood in the profession.

IMPROVED KNOWLEDGE OF TEACHING METHODS

The classroom teacher can rarely employ any teaching method or device without modifying it to fit his particular situation, the need and interests of pupils, and his own personality. School administrators seldom find it possible to deal with a problem in the same manner in which other administrators have dealt with it in another community and in a different school situation.

The problem of method in teaching can be better understood if it is applied to particular teaching fields. In language arts, for instance, special skills are needed to teach the total population of the increasingly heterogeneous modern secondary schools. How to teach writing in this age of television to five or six classes every day is one of the many puzzling problems in methods which faces every high-school teacher of English. How to individualize instruction in reading in a classroom so as to take care of the needs of the gifted and the retarded at the same time is another difficult problem.

17. A. T. Jersild, *Child Development and the Curriculum.* New York: Bureau of Publications, Teachers College, Columbia University, 1946.

18. Harvey C. Lehman, *Age and Achievement,* p. 326. Princeton, New Jersey: Princeton University Press, 1953.

All of these problems require skill in classroom management, in selecting and organizing teaching materials, and in planning group activities. Each teacher works out some way of dealing with these problems, but, without in-service education which includes counseling, supervision, and other types of assistance, these solutions may often be merely expedients.

The need for in-service education in teaching methods becomes increasingly urgent as more and more former teachers who left the profession some years ago re-enter the classrooms. The job of preparing them to resume teaching is a serious one for several reasons: the school population has changed since they last taught; the teachers themselves have changed; the courses of study are different; and in many other ways the problems of teaching are different from those with which these teachers were confronted in the past.

INCREASED SKILL IN PROVIDING FOR THE INDIVIDUAL DIFFERENCES AMONG PUPILS

The President's Scientific Research Board reported in 1947 that the ". . . future of our county lies in the undeveloped potentialities of the young people who attend our schools, no two of whom are alike. These young people differ in physical, emotional, and mental characteristics. They live under a wide variety of conditions in homes varying from assembled packing boxes to mansions."[19]

Differences among children are the result of constitutional, psychological, and cultural backgrounds. Knowledge of differential psychology is growing rapidly, and the major generalizations must be understood and used by members of the teaching profession.

In increasing numbers schools provide cumulative record folders in which pertinent data are kept throughout the pupil's school experience. Preparation of and reference to such material helps the teacher get a clearer picture of each child, including his physical condition, his native endowments, his school attendance, his school experience and achievement, his family background, the problems he has faced in meeting his developmental tasks, and his attitudes and emotional adjustment. The necessary skills for gathering and

19. John R. Steelman, Chairman, The President's Scientific Research Board, "Manpower for Research," *Science and Public Policy*, Vol. IV, p. 61. Washington: Government Printing Office, October 11, 1947.

utilizing such information are not easily learned. All teachers and other educational workers need additional study and preparation from time to time in order to develop and maintain these skills.

In addition to knowing the pupils as individuals, each teacher needs to know his pupils as members of groups. He must be able to make factual, objective, and anecdotal records of a pupil's behavior in relation to various groups in order to deepen insight into the child's potentialities. This is particularly important during the period of adolescence when peer relationships assume such great importance in personality development. All teachers as well as principals and supervisors need to learn and keep up to date with recent developments in the study of pupils as individuals and as members of groups.

Extensive developments in mental, aptitude, and achievement testing constitute much of the subject matter of the psychology of individual differences. Studies of rate of growth of intelligence and the constancy of the intelligence quotient, for example, are of importance in the planning of the school curriculum, in the placement of pupils in grades best suited to their abilities, and in vocational guidance and training. Professional school staff members should be able to use the recent findings that have resulted from improvements in our methods of mental measurement.

The earlier work on individual differences was related primarily to intelligence. Recent evidence as to the origin and nature of personality indicates that there are significant individual differences of many other kinds. People vary in personal tempo, aggressiveness, sociality, and other qualities. Teachers need to know about the continuing progress in the study of personality so that classroom procedures may be adapted to the needs of different individuals in a classroom group.

Many techniques for understanding the individual child have recently been improved. The use of behavior observation and sociometry are skills for studying children with which teachers and other professional workers should be familiar and which can often be best learned in service. Information about these techniques is constantly growing so that teachers need to continue to learn about them, even though some acquaintance was acquired during pre-service education.

The information most useful to teachers for developing competence in dealing with personality problems of pupils results from observations and ratings, daily diary records, autobiographical materials, tests, and interviews. The use of these methods of getting information requires training. Teachers must learn what to observe about students if they are to use this method. They must know how to select significant behavior for observation. The other techniques mentioned call for particular skills in their use, and these skills can usually be developed if the teacher has had experience with a number of pupils and has knowledge of the kind of problems which are faced by the teacher in trying to help pupils.

The development of good citizenship is generally accepted as one of the first goals of public education. This statement appears in conclusion to the Detroit Citizenship Education Study: ". . . the emotional adjustment of pupils is the most important factor in the quality of citizenship of boys and girls." This same study reports that "poor citizenship results primarily from an inability on the part of the child to adjust satisfactorily to the various forces playing upon him."[20] If the development of good citizenship depends upon emotional adjustment, then it becomes increasingly clear that dealing with personality problems of pupils is a part of the work of every teacher. Teachers need in-service education in this area to keep abreast of new knowledge and to develop the needed skills.

IMPROVED ATTITUDES AND SKILLS INVOLVED IN
CO-OPERATIVE ACTION RESEARCH

One of the frequently recurring emphases in educational literature has been the idea that curriculum improvement is primarily a consequence of improvement of people. To the degree that this is true, one of the very important bodies of skills needed by all educators is that required by co-operative group work. The mastery of principles of co-operative group work is not easy.[21] Any newly formed group would do well to give attention to these principles. Each year

20. Stanley E. Dimond, *Schools and the Development of Good Citizens,* p. 208. Detroit, Michigan: Wayne University Press, 1953.

21. See Stephen M. Corey, "Principles of Co-operative Group Work," in *Group Planning in Education,* pp. 130–38. Yearbook of the Department of Supervision and Curriculum Development. Washington: National Education Association, 1945.

the principal of any school and his staff will need to give attention
to their skills in co-operative group work if the desired goals in curriculum improvement are to be achieved.

In the area of co-operative group work there is a developing science of group dynamics which is teaching us ways to liberate ideas
in group discussion and how to enable groups to function efficiently.
Business, industry, government, and the military services are all
making use of this new science in in-service education programs for
their workers. Education can afford to do no less.[22]

The scientific movement in education is now about fifty years old.
This movement is based upon the idea that school practices can be
improved as a result of research. Recently much has been written
in the field of education about the importance of practitioners doing
research—studying their problems scientifically in order to guide,
correct, and evaluate their decisions. This process has been called
action research. If teachers are to engage in action research, new attitudes on the part of administrators are necessary, and there must
be a considerable change in the working environment and atmosphere of many school systems. The status leaders must take the
initiative in making it possible for teachers "to admit their professional limitations, to hypothesize creatively, to have the resources
and consultative help they need, to obtain the best possible evidence
of the consequences of change, and to derive from this evidence
generalizations that are sound and helpful guides to future behavior."[23]

Co-operative action research has clear implications for the in-
service education of teachers and all other educational workers. This
is best understood when it is applied to a specific problem facing
a school system, such as recently has been done by the committee
on intergroup education of the American Council on Education.
In a study conducted by this committee it was concluded that "Co-
operative experimentation in program-building is both possible and

22. For illustrations of the use which the Navy is making of group dynamics,
see Bureau of Naval Personnel, *Conference Sense*, NAVPERS 91139, pp. 1–30.
Washington: Government Printing Office, 1950.

23. Stephen M. Corey, *Action Research To Improve School Practices*, p. 145.
New York: Bureau of Publications, Teachers College, Columbia University,
1953.

productive. . . . A large part of this productivity can be attributed to action research as a primary method. . . ."[24]

GREATER SKILL IN UTILIZING COMMUNITY RESOURCES
AND IN WORKING WITH ADULTS

One of the important tasks of modern education is the development of intelligent civic loyalties and understandings. To an ever increasing degree it is felt that schools must be related to the life of the community if this is to happen.

The Citizenship Education Project of Teachers College, Columbia University, has developed, in co-operation with many school systems and colleges, planning resources and materials to help teachers make more effective use of their communities in the development of citizenship education. In this project an attempt is made to utilize community resources by combining an appreciation of democracy's basic premises with skill in putting them into action.

Many new understandings and approaches pertaining to the relation between schools and communities have evolved during recent years. Interviews, field trips, surveys, and work-experience activities have all been utilized by schools as methods of relating their programs of instruction to community problems. The best use of each of these methods of teaching involves skills and ways of work which teachers must learn. These skills are usually so closely related to the local community that they are best learned in the local situation. In-service education in this area is urgently necessary if teachers are to utilize community resources effectively in their teaching.

HOW TO LEARN A NEW JOB

New teachers rarely begin their teaching service at the peak of efficiency. After a few years in college, beginning teachers are often able to do little more than toddle through their new world of baffling pupil personalities and unfamiliar subject matter. Each new pupil and each new combination of pupils creates problems which could not have been anticipated in the most enlightened preservice courses.

In recent years many school systems have as many as 30 per cent

24. Hilda Taba and Others, *Inter-Group Education in Public Schools*, pp. 310–11. Washington: American Council on Education, 1952.

of their teachers either starting their professional careers or possessing less than two years of experience. This has caused school system officials to realize that they must start the in-service program with an organized orientation for new teachers so that the schools may operate efficiently from the first day and so that the new teacher may begin immediately to "belong." New-teacher orientation programs must be designed to help the new teacher with his most pressing problems—social, personal, and professional. Such programs give an introduction to the organization and policies of the school system and the routines of the respective schools to which individual teachers are assigned. In an orientation program each new teacher is helped to make a good start toward increasing the effectiveness of his teaching procedures, toward handling personal problems, and toward making friendships among fellow-workers, parents, and others in the new community. Only the teacher's most pressing problems can be given much attention before the opening of school. Everything else should be deferred. If the orientation program tries to do too much before the teacher is on the job, confusion results. After some experience in the classroom, the assistance offered can become more varied.

THE DEVELOPMENT AND REFINEMENT
OF COMMON VALUES AND GOALS

One of the major purposes of in-service education is the development of common values and goals in the staff of a school, in a group of principals or supervisors, or in any other professional group that must work co-operatively over a period of time. This can be accomplished if the work of the group is centered about problems which are considered to be important by all participants, if needed resources are provided, and if a premium is placed on the development of appropriate courses of action on which all can reach a consensus of agreement. Social psychologists are constantly telling us that, to change a group's norms and values, it is necessary for the group to experience and communicate about a common set of influences.[25] An in-service education program for teachers, principals, and supervisors is one excellent way of meeting these conditions.

25. Theodore M. Newcomb, *Social Psychology*, p. 613. New York: Dryden Press, 1950.

THE BUILDING OF PROFESSIONALISM AND HIGH MORALE

To be professional, teachers need to have a profound conviction of the worth of their work. For this feeling to exist, the individual must have a sense of greatness of his profession, of its significance for society, and its power to benefit boys and girls. The climate of professional stimulation provided by a good in-service education program can give teachers pride in their achievements and stimulation to surpass their previous best efforts. When a school system fails to provide this professional stimulation, teachers often begin their careers with anticipation and readiness for hard work and then lose their zest when they find that nothing challenges them to use their abilities to the utmost.

In-service education of all professional personnel is the major key to the building of a greater professionalism among teachers.

The Extent of In-service Education

HOW WIDESPREAD IS IT?

In-service education programs are now widely and generally planned by school systems of all types and size throughout our nation. A recent nation-wide study shows that in-service education programs are in operation in public school systems in all of the forty-eight states.[26] In 1951 the National Education Association studied in-service education practices in 1,615 urban school systems: 1,488 of these school systems reported special opportunities for in-service education and professional growth of teachers.[27] In 1952 the Research Department of the Hartford Public Schools, Hartford, Connecticut, conducted a study of the in-service education programs of 218 cities over 25,000 population: 90 per cent of the 218 cities reported that "planned" professional growth programs were being conducted in their school systems.[28] In a study conducted in

26. Federal Security Agency, *Schools at Work in Forty-eight States,* pp. 133–34. Office of Education Bulletin, No. 13. Washington: Government Printing Office, 1952.

27. Research Division, National Education Association, "In-service Education of Teachers," p. 15. Washington: National Education Association, February, 1954 (mimeographed).

28. Research Department, Hartford Public Schools, *Professional Growth Programs in 218 Cities,* pp. 1–2. Hartford, Connecticut: Hartford Public Schools, March 25, 1953.

1954, the California Teachers Association found that 155 school systems in California have organized programs of new-teacher orientation. [29] Many other similar studies indicate a widespread and increasing interest in in-service growth activities.

TYPES OF ACTIVITIES WHICH ARE GENERALLY INCLUDED
IN IN-SERVICE PROGRAMS

A wide variety of activities are included in the in-service education programs which are reported in the nation-wide studies in this area. Workshops, teacher study groups, conferences, preparation of curriculum publications, seeing other teachers at work—all are included as kinds of activities which are highly valued and in which teachers in every section of the country are engaged. In 1954 McMahon found that six school systems which she surveyed had fifty-four different types of in-service education activity.[30] The activities of these school systems varied in number from thirty to thirty-six. It is not possible in this chapter to examine any such range of in-service education activities, but several of the more widely accepted and the more widely used types are commented on in the following paragraphs.

To an increasing degree the colleges in which teachers obtain their preservice education are assuming a responsibility for the follow-up and for the initial in-service education of their most recent graduates. Some teachers' colleges have added full-time staff members to spend a major proportion of their time providing this kind of service. The purpose of visits to these beginning teachers is to observe them at work and to offer college facilities to both the former students and to the school administrators if in-service help is needed. In addition, this kind of program enables the teachers' college to become better acquainted with the school systems in which its graduates are employed so that it can do a better job of preparation and placement.

29. California Teachers Association, *Teacher Orientation in California Elementary Schools,* pp. 2–5. California Teachers Association Research Bulletin No. 78. San Francisco: California Teachers Association, November, 1954.

30. Lois G. McMahon, "Survey of a Study of In-service Education Programs in Selected California Public School Systems." Unpublished Doctor of Education dissertation, University of California, Graduate Division, Northern Section (Berkeley), June, 1954.

One of the most widely accepted types of in-service education is the new-teacher orientation workshop. This type of workshop is being made widely available because of the great need of teachers for help when they are first beginning their work.

The workshop, as a general in-service education procedure, has been carefully studied by the North Central Association of Colleges and Secondary Schools, and the study indicates widespread and general acceptance of the workshop as a major means of organizing in-service education programs.[31] Almost without exception participants seem to catch the spirit behind the workshop and feel the uplift which comes through co-operative effort and through progress made toward self-determined goals.

It is important to keep in mind that there is no one best in-service education activity, and there is no one best way to get a program started. The approach in each school must be one which fits that particular situation and should emerge out of the problems of primary interest to the teachers, principals, and supervisors in the school system concerned. To the degree that all staff members have an opportunity to participate in planning and carrying out the in-service education program, advantage is taken of their interest and resources. This is increasingly the practice in developing these programs.

Concluding Statement

In this chapter some of the facts and factors which demonstrate the need for the continuous in-service education of the total professional staff have been cited. In addition, attention has been given to a number of the typical in-service education needs of teachers, principals, and supervisors. Factors such as the rapid accumulation of academic and professional knowledge, the rapid cultural changes which characterize modern times, and the importance of making it possible for excellent teachers to make use of their creative abilities, all argue for continuous and well-planned programs for professional growth.

Other conditions which demonstrate the need for continuous in-

31. James R. Mitchell, *The Workshop as an In-service Education Procedure*, pp. 431–32. Wichita, Kansas: North Central Association of Colleges and Secondary Schools, April, 1954.

service education are the rapid curriculum changes necessitated by cultural and social changes, the inadequacy of preservice education for meeting the great increase in numbers of teachers resulting from rapidly increasing pupil enrolments, and the continuing need for school leaders with improved skills.

In-service education is necessary for all members of the professional staff of America's public schools. The reasons for this are numerous and include these important responsibilities: the maintenance of mastery of new knowledge and new subject matter, the acquisition of new knowledge about human growth and learning and teaching methods, the development of skill in providing for the needs and problems of individual pupils, the acquisition of the techniques and skills necessary for co-operative action research, for the utilization of community resources, and for working with adults.

The importance of an adequate supply of educators who are constantly growing professionally should be viewed as (a) important to the children of America, (b) important to the professionalization of education, and (c) important to society and its future. This necessary national resource can only be achieved and maintained through improved and expanded programs of both preservice and in-service education for all public school professional personnel. During the past fifty years, programs dealing with in-service education have undergone substantial change. These changes are traced in the next chapter.

CHAPTER III

Growth of the Modern Conception
of In-service Education

HERMAN G. RICHEY

Introduction

The history of in-service teacher education in the United States is complicated by the influence of various factors contributing to the gradual structuring of the total educational program, of which the promotion of continuing professional growth on the part of teachers has been only a small, although an important, part. The history of in-service education is further complicated by the fact that its development has not been uniform, either as among or within states. In the course of their development, in-service programs have reflected the differences in the educational programs of the several states, differences that arose from the freedom of each state to shape its own educational enterprise and from the efforts that were made by all states to meet the needs of different groups such as city-dwellers, on the one hand, and countryfolk, on the other.

An enumeration of the factors that have led, directly or indirectly, to the development of in-service education and that have influenced the nature of that development would include changing concepts of the aims and values of education, the nature of the learner and learning, the function of the school, and the role of the teacher. It would include the evolution of the definition of American democracy, the increasing complexity of social, economic, and political arrangements, a high and rising standard of living, and a continuing growth of knowledge. It would include related factors such as unprecedented growth of school enrolments, the expanding heterogeneity of the school population, and the consequent revisions and extensions of the curriculum (see chap. ii). For the purposes of this chapter it is sufficient to note that these forces, along with many others, have, in their operation, generally tended to increase the demand for teachers, to add to the prerequisites of teaching, and to augment the need for continuing growth on the part of the teacher. Historically, the changing program of in-service teacher education has been formulated in response to the demand for more and more teachers and the contemporary conception as to the relative importance of the various needs of teachers.

The tremendous but largely unfulfilled need for even modestly educated and professionally trained teachers set the pattern for in-service programs during most of the nineteenth century. During the late nineteenth and early twentieth centuries, the enormous need for teachers acceptably prepared to meet the vastly increasing social and educational demands being made upon them led to a remarkable upgrading of teacher education and to the adoption of other means of improving instruction. It was the attainment or approximation of professional status on the part of a majority of teachers, along with the recognition that even well-trained teachers continued to have training needs, and the acquisition of new knowledge of how changes are effected in the behavior of individuals and groups that opened the way for the development of programs based on the realization that the success of those who teach at any level or administer programs of any grade results from growth that cannot achieve maturity prior to induction into service.

In-service Education of Culturally Deficient and Untrained Teachers—the Nineteenth Century

During the nineteenth century, in-service programs of teacher-training and ideas current regarding them reflected, above all else, the prevailing and partially valid assumption that the immaturity, meager educational equipment, and inexperience of the teacher rendered him unable to analyze or criticize his own teaching, or, unless given direction, to improve it. This assumption, combined with the teacher's obvious need for a better command of the subject matter that he expected to teach and of appropriate methods of teaching it, went far to determine the purposes, content, and methods of in-service programs of teacher improvement.[1]

1. It should not be inferred that there were no educated and well-trained teachers. No period in the past has been so poor as to have been without some

THE STATUS OF TEACHERS AND PRESERVICE EDUCATION
PROGRAMS BEFORE 1890

During the period between the establishment of state systems of public education and the recovery from the effects of the Civil War, the public schools, on the whole, were staffed by probably the most indifferent, incompetent, and poorly educated teachers in the history of American education. Reports of superintendents and others of the period abound in castigations of the teaching staff and with references to the sorry state of education.

Knight, writing with special reference to southern states, concluded that it was many years after the close of the Civil War before teachers generally were markedly improved over those of ante-bellum days who, as a class, were described in contemporary reports as being ignorant, incompetent, incapable of making a living at other employment, and recommended only by their cheapness.[2]

More temperate statements, particularly in the North, acknowledged the existence of some good teachers but deplored the fact that, as a rule, teachers had no more than a common-school education, that they had "gone through" arithmetic but did not understand it, that their knowledge of English grammar was equally superficial, and that only a few considered teaching anything more than a stepping stone to a profession or a genteel activity in which to engage between girlhood and marriage.[3] More objectively, superintendents in states in which conditions were by no means the worst complained year after year that one-half of their teachers were under 21 years of age; that a sizable number was under 16; that the average age was 23, 24, or 25; that from one-half to three-fourths of

---

qualified teachers, and no period, including the most recent, has been without some inept and poorly trained ones. The program of in-service education of the period must be viewed against the background of the quality of the large majority, the needs of which were most pressing and the defects of which were most obvious.

2. Edgar W. Knight, *Public Education in the South*, pp. 294–304. Boston: Ginn & Co., 1922.

3. James H. Smart, *Teachers' Institutes*, pp. 7–8. Circulars of Information of the Bureau of Education, No. 2, 1885. Washington: Government Printing Office, 1885.

the teachers changed positions each year; and that one-fifth or more of the teachers were teaching for the first time.[4]

Although the cultural level of teachers improved gradually after the Civil War and the status of teachers came in many areas to reflect this improvement, more than a generation was to pass in the North as well as in the South before the situation came to be, especially outside of cities, in marked contrast to that of prewar days. The gap between the number of teachers needed and the number of qualified ones available remained wide in spite of strenuous efforts, particularly after 1870, to weld normal schools into the structure of the state systems.[5]

The requirements for certification continued generally to be those that permitted the number offering to teach to approximate the number of teaching positions to be filled. As late as 1877, it was reported that about 1,500 of Maine's 6,000 teachers were new each year and that among these beginners were many girls between the ages of 14 and 17.[6] And a few years later, a committee of the Vermont Teachers' Association not only complained about the youth, inexperience, and meager education of the teachers of the state but also repeated long-standing charges that the quality of teachers generally was such that public instruction was degraded, public funds squandered, and public opinion debauched.[7]

IN-SERVICE EDUCATION TO CORRECT DEFICIENCIES OF THE EDUCATION AND PRETRAINING OF TEACHERS

The conditions described, the prevailing ideas regarding education, and the temper of the people generally made it essential that programs of in-service education of the period should be directed toward the correction of the most obvious defects of teachers, i.e., inadequate command of subject matter to be taught and lack of professional skill; that they should take into account the needs of the

4. Wellford Addis, "The Teaching Force of New England from 1866 to 1888," *Report of the Commissioner of Education for the Year, 1888–89*, Vol. I, pp. 319–46. Washington: Government Printing Office, 1891; Willard S. Elsbree, *The American Teacher*, pp. 293–305. New York: American Book Co., 1939.

5. Elsbree, *op. cit.*, chap. xxiv.

6. Addis, *op. cit.*, p. 334. *See also* Elsbree, *op. cit.*, chaps. xv and xxii.

7. Addis, *op. cit.*, p. 338.

inexperienced and entirely untrained teacher; that they should be inexpensively operated; and that they should involve large numbers of teachers. Of programs suggested or devised during the period, the teachers' institute most nearly fulfilled these conditions.

The Teachers' Institute. Originating in a period in which there was a shortage of even partially trained teachers, the teachers' institute was established as a normal school and closely resembled it. It was designed not only for teachers but also for inexperienced candidates for teaching positions whose needs were not greatly different from those of employed teachers. The nature and purpose of the early institute as described by Barnard, Page, Sweet, and others was well summarized by Mann, in 1845, when he wrote:

It is the design of a Teacher's Institute to bring together those who are actually engaged in teaching Common Schools, or who propose to become so, in order that they may be formed into classes, and that these classes, under able instructors, may be exercised, questioned and drilled, in the same manner that the classes of a good Common School are exercised, questioned and drilled.[8]

The classes taught content which the prospective teachers would later teach and provided, when well conducted, excellent instruction in the approved methods of teaching.

Although the institute served a preservice teacher-training function, its value as an agency of in-service education accounted for its rapid and widespread adoption, gave it vitality to endure in recognizable form for a century, and led its proponents to exhaust superlatives in describing its beneficial effects.

An examination of the programs of early institutes reveals that, although little found its way into later ones that had not been included in some amount in earlier ones, there was a tendency toward a change of emphasis.[9] As time went on, the review of elementary subjects (the major emphasis of early institutes) gave way before or divided time with a consideration of these subjects from "the teaching point of view." This change was not too difficult to make because, it was charged, the two activities could not, in most instances,

8. Circular addressed, "To Public School Teachers," by Horace Mann, September 1, 1845. Reproduced in Samuel N. Sweet, *Teachers Institutes or Temporary Normal Schools . . . Including a Synopsis of Their Proceedings* (by Stephen R. Sweet), pp. 45–56. Utica: H. H. Hawley & Co., 1848.

9. Compare Sweet, *op. cit.,* pp. 78–104 and Smart, *op. cit.,* pp. 149–206.

be distinguished from each other. Later, the practice grew, at least in the more advanced systems, of devoting more time to methods of teaching and to school management. This instruction was generally given through lectures by normal-school teachers, the more articulate administrators, and other persons who annually traveled the institute circuit.[10]

Barnard had called the institute a temporary expedient, and others active in its early organization thought that it might soon become unnecessary. These persons were probably overoptimistic concerning the advance of preservice education and were, of course, unaware of the vastly increased demands that were to be made upon teachers in later years. Repeatedly during even the early years of the period, the hope was expressed that the institute would be able to eliminate drill in the common branches from its program and to add professional work in its stead, and, in later years, the demand was often made that such a change be no longer delayed. After noting an advance in the qualifications of teachers employed in some of the better systems, Bates boldly stated in his book, *Methods of Teachers' Institutes*, published in 1866, that "the Institute is not the place to give instruction in the elements of the sciences." However, he immediately retreated from this advanced position by stating, on the following page, that "in the township or district Institute, class-drills in forms of solution and methods of explanation are in place."[11]

In 1888, Thayer stated that the function of the institute was not to give detailed instruction but rather "to stimulate the general work of the teacher." Apparently this purpose was to be achieved by gathering "teachers at the great centres of population to listen to

10. That the change in the nature of the institute was one of emphasis rather than a result of a series of innovations is clear. Early institutes, although stressing instruction in the common branches, were often high-lighted by lectures described as "inspirational and cultural." Some offerings added an "element of elevating entertainment," e.g., a lecture on elocution accompanied by specimens of the oratory and manner of speaking of Daniel Webster, Henry Clay, John C. Calhoun, and Colonel Crockett (Sweet, *op. cit.*, pp. 88–89). Lectures on methods of teaching also were given in early institutes. Sweet lists eleven subjects of lectures, including 'Elementary Reading" and "Organs of Digestion with Practical Hints [for teaching]," given before institutes, in 1847, by David P. Page, the first principal of New York's first normal school (*ibid.*, p. 104).

11. Samuel P. Bates, *Methods of Teachers' Institutes and the Theory of Education*, pp. 12–13. New York: A. S. Barnes & Co., 1866.

lectures," by "detailed discussions of pedagogical principles and methods," and, he added, in spite of his definition of function, "the third object is to give more or less instruction bearing upon the branches to be taught in the schools."[12]

The institute changed very slowly—even more slowly than did the conditions which were the justification for its existence. Late in the century, it was asserted by normal-school principals that the reviews of subject matter were still useful in institutes held in areas not so fortunate as to be easily accessible to normal schools. They were of the opinion that the programs of institutes in areas supplied with normal schools should not include such reviews, should be shortened, and made more stimulating.[13]

Criticism mounted toward the close of the century. Many teachers, if still a minority, were rapidly outgrowing the old institute which had become formalized, embedded in legislation, and resistant to change. But what was rapidly becoming an anachronism in some situations continued to be looked upon as a necessity in others. And always there was a tendency toward organizing all institutes and their programs in terms of the needs or assumed needs of the more backward systems and the poorer teachers. However, during the last decade or two of the century, the institute underwent some change. Institutes for city teachers were modified and sometimes discontinued as teachers rebelled against a type of program which duplicated their preservice training and which afforded "cultural" opportunities that were inferior to those easily available to them elsewhere. The original concept of in-service education was being slowly modified. This modification was reflected by changes in the institute itself but, perhaps more clearly by the development of newer agencies for in-service education, agencies that had emerged in response to changing conditions. The summer normal schools, extension courses, teachers' reading circles, and certain supervisory practices reveal, in their origin and development, the changing aims and purposes of in-service education. These agencies, however, were to

12. Jesse B. Thayer, "County Institutes: What Is the Purpose of County Institutes, and How Is It Best Achieved?" in *Proceedings of the Department of Superintendence of the National Education Association, 1888,* pp. 44–45. United States Bureau of Education Circular of Information, No. 6, 1888. Washington: Government Printing Office, 1888.

13. Smart, *op. cit.,* pp. 11–12 ff.

undergo their most rapid growth and significant modification near and particularly after the close of the nineteenth century.

In-service Education and Rapid Upgrading of Teachers, 1890–1930

For the period from about 1890 to 1930 or later, the changing concept of in-service education must be viewed against the background of (*a*) the increasing demand for teachers possessing a broad culture and professional skills—a demand intensified by the rapid expansion of knowledge, the extension of the educational program to provide for a longer period of education for more children, and by other developments of a maturing social order, and (*b*) the rapid upgrading of the teaching staff in response to this demand.

THE UPGRADING OF THE TEACHING STAFF

The extent and nature of the change wrought in the status of the teaching staff in a period of some forty years may be noted in the rise of the admission requirements of teacher-training institutions, the upward extension and enrichment of the programs of those schools, the adoption of higher standards for certification, the increase in the stability of the teaching staff, and in other changes involved in the improvement and upgrading of the teaching staff.[14]

In 1890, relatively few teachers had received a high-school education.[15] Those who attended normal schools generally had received all of their formal education in rural ungraded or city elementary schools. Normal schools accepted these students for short terms and organized programs of elementary and secondary level in keeping with their educational attainments.[16] Almost two decades were to pass before any state was to make high-school graduation the minimum requirement for all licenses.[17] Universities had only begun to

14. Jessie M. Pangburn, *The Evolution of the Teachers College.* Teachers College Contributions to Education, No. 500. New York: Teachers College, Columbia University, 1932.

15. *Ibid.,* pp. 4 ff.

16. William W. Parsons, "The Normal School Curriculum," *Journal of Proceedings and Addresses of the National Education Association, 1890,* pp. 718–24. Topeka: The Association, 1890. See Pangburn, *op. cit.,* pp. 1, 16 ff.

17. Elsbree, *op. cit.,* p. 350, citing Harlan Updegraff, *Teacher Certificates Issued under General State Laws and Regulations.* United States Bureau of Education Bulletin No. 18, 1911. Washington: Government Printing Office, 1911.

develop a content of professional education and to train men to teach it.

By 1930, normal schools generally and the evolving teachers' college universally had come to require high-school graduation for admission to their programs which had been raised to collegiate level and strengthened to include general education, professional study, specialization in subject areas, and extended practice in teaching.[18] More than three-fourths of the states had provided or were soon to provide that high-school graduation should be a prerequisite for all certificates. Post-high-school work in some amount was becoming a requirement for certification in an increasing number of states. Between 1926 and 1937, the number of states making one to four years of college-level work prerequisite for the lowest certificate increased from 13 to 32.[19] By 1930, about three-fourths of the teachers had attended college two or more years. High-school teachers seldom had less than four years of college work, and an increasing number had five years of work beyond the high school. During the period, the average years of experience of employed teachers increased greatly and, except in poorer rural districts, teachers came to move less frequently from one school system to another. By the thirties, if not before, it was evident that teaching at all levels was in the process of becoming a profession.

THE PERSISTENCE OF THE TRADITIONAL CONCEPT OF IN-SERVICE EDUCATION

The improving and improved status of teachers was reflected in changes in programs of in-service education. However, the improvement was uneven as among states and types of communities, and the needs of the poorer teachers tended to set the pattern of in-service

18. Pangburn, *op. cit.*, pp. 33–96. See also W. C. Reudiger, "Recent Tendencies in Normal Schools of the United States," *Educational Review*, XXXIII (March, 1907), 271–87; "Report of Committee on Statement of Policy Regarding the Preparation and Qualification of Teachers of Elementary and High Schools," *Journal of Proceedings of the National Education Association, 1908*, p. 735 (Winona: The Association, 1908); Carnegie Foundation for the Advancement of Teaching, *Curricula Designed for the Profeessional Preparation of Teachers for American Public Schools*, par. 5 (New York: Carnegie Foundation for the Advancement of Teaching, 1917).

19. Benjamin W. Frazier, *Development of State Programs for the Certification of Teachers*, p. 73. United States Office of Education Bulletin No. 12, 1938. Washington: Government Printing Office, 1938.

education for all. This tendency plus the power of tradition and vested interests led to the persistence of agencies long after the growing concept of in-service education had reduced them, so far as teachers in the better systems were concerned, to routines of dubious value.

The Teachers' Institute. The teachers' institute is a case in point. By the turn of the century it was under severe attack. It was described as fossil of an age when other facilities for teacher-training were not easily available and when the qualifications of teachers were so low that even a mediocre program was worth while.[20] McManis, in 1903, questioned the pedagogical value of the work of institutes in which, he said, the lecturer talked on pedagogical principles but violated all the canons of modern education, in which the lecturer preached activity but assumed a strictly passive set of individuals to teach.[21] A few years later, Seerley condemned the institute as a makeshift never intended as a permanent part of the school system. The institute, it was charged, served to prevent or to dissuade teachers from pursuing the longer, better organized, and more exacting programs of the summer normal schools.[22] To these criticisms were added those of others who claimed that the institute's program provided little except an opportunity for the display of the speakers' erudition; that the institute was often captured by "hobby riders" and that it was conducted and evaluated by persons who stood to lose financially, or otherwise, if attendance was not maintained.

Reudiger stated, in 1910, that, as conducted, the institute which had served a useful purpose was rapidly becoming an anachronism. He argued that teachers' institutes should differentiate their programs according to the functions they were serving: (*a*) a professional training-school for teachers, (*b*) a meeting to inspire teachers and to acquaint them with the policies of their schools, and (*c*) teachers' conventions, largely social in nature. The differentiation,

20. John T. McManis, "Problems of the Institute," *Elementary School Teacher,* IV (December, 1903), 232–39.

21. *Ibid.,* pp. 235–36. The validity of this criticism had increased as talks on teaching supplanted actual teaching of reading, writing, elementary arithmetic, and the like in the program of the institute. *See* Mann's statement, footnote 8.

22. Homer H. Seerley, "Practical Value of the Institute System," *Educational Review,* XXXVI (November, 1908), 356–63.

he admitted, would result in the disappearance of the traditional institute.[23]

But tradition and vested interests are mighty forces. In 1910, institute attendance was compulsory in 28 states and virtually enforced in others by financial inducements or penalties of one kind or other. [24] It was true that city institutes were disappearing and that high-school teachers were seldom obliged to attend them. In rural areas, however, they continued to be the chief agency for the in-service education of teachers and, too often, to serve as an important agency of preservice training as well. In Kansas, in 1908, 88 per cent of those attending (11,255) were from rural or ungraded schools or were preparing for them. Of the total, 25 per cent were high-school graduates and fewer than 10 per cent had taken work beyond the high school. Forty-three per cent were without teaching experience.[25] In spite of criticisms of them, institutes were generally held throughout the period. In 1921, 32 of 39 superintendents questioned expressed the view that they were still valuable even though criticisms of them appeared to have more justification than previously.[26]

In 1933, the National Survey reported that the institutes were losing ground steadily and that there were unmistakable tendencies toward substituting other forms of in-service training for them. It was also noted that the general level of teacher preparation was rapidly rising.[27] It had by that time become clear that the long struggle to improve teachers and teaching had passed the stage in which superficial institute courses, lacking in continuity and offered without adequate facilities, had much, if anything, to offer the classroom teacher. Teachers were no longer elementary-school graduates to be inspired or instructed by programs such as the institute was able to

23. William Carl Ruediger, *Agencies for the Improvement of Teachers in Service,* p. 32. United States Bureau of Education Bulletin No. 3, 1911. Washington: Government Printing Office, 1911.

24. *Ibid.,* p. 13.

25. *Ibid.,* p. 27.

26. Benjamin W. Frazier, "History of the Professional Education of Teachers in the United States," *National Survey of the Education of Teachers,* V, 81. Office of Education Bulletin No. 10, 1933. Washington: Government Printing Office, 1935.

27. *Ibid.,* pp. 81–82.

provide. They had become more effective in the classroom than were the administrators and others who had previously instructed them either in or out of institutes. With each advance of the teaching staff toward full professional status, the older concept of in-service education had become less tenable. Although the name *institute* was to continue as the legal designation of teachers' meetings, orientation programs, and the like, the institute of history and tradition was rapidly disappearing from the educational scene.

Teachers' Reading Circles. Teachers' reading circles, which sprang out of the conditions of the late nineteenth century, continued to flourish throughout the first decades of the twentieth. By 1910, reading circles were organized in three-fourths of the states.[28] Cheap, easily administered, and providing statistics of astronomical size, they persisted in spite of the rapid decline in the number of teachers in service who possessed only a mediocre education and little or no training.

The work of reading circles is difficult to evaluate. From their work, as superficial as much of it must have been, many teachers were, no doubt, introduced to general books of literary merit and were motivated to continue to read such books. Also, many teachers must have acquired theoretical professional insights from the works of Hanus, De Garmo, the McMurrays, and others. Some must have acquired an increased respect for teaching and an understanding that teachers must continue to learn as they became aware that their problems were compelling the attention of some of the best minds in American universities.

However, both teachers' institutes and reading circles were agencies designed to advance the performance of teachers, generally deficient in academic attainments and professional skills, a small distance on a wide front. The lowly status of the teacher and inability to provide anything better were the only excuses for their existence. Both continued to flourish in competition with newer and more

28. Reudiger, *op. cit.,* p. 93. Teachers' reading circles, organized generally on a state-wide basis and often controlled by the state education authorities, compiled reading lists for teachers, provided individual teachers or local groups of teachers with outlines for the study of the books, and sometimes granted diplomas to teachers completing a reading course which might cover from one to four years. By 1910, the work done in reading circles could be applied in 27 states toward meeting the requirements for a certificate.

promising programs of in-service education long after the conditions which explain their origin and early development no longer prevailed.

THE TEACHER GOES TO COLLEGE AND THE COLLEGE GOES TO THE TEACHER

Although summer schools, extension courses, after-hour classes, and correspondence study had their origins in the nineteenth century, all made their greatest contribution to teacher education well after the opening of the twentieth century. Relatively young, they had not yet become bound by tradition and were able, therefore, to shape themselves more readily than the older agencies to fit the needs of teachers striving toward full professional status.

The Summer School. The rapid growth and expansion of the summer school during the last fifty years is to be attributed to its success in meeting these needs. The early summer schools of methods (of instruction) developed in the late nineteenth century as a part of the work of summer assemblies and Chautauquas and from the efforts of interested persons. They were independent of colleges and universities, offered work of less than college grade, and attempted to reach the same classes to which the old institute was intended to bring a modicum of training.[29]

As normal schools, colleges, and universities began to organize summer schools, the growth of these schools, which had been relatively slow, quickened. The Commissioner of Education, in 1887, reported only 3 such schools for the entire nation,[30] and as late as 1894, a speaker at the meeting of the National Education Association stated with the air of a discoverer that "the summer school has until now escaped discussion in any department of the N.E.A."[31] In 1903, it was reported that the number of universities and colleges

---

29. W. W. Welloughby, *"The History of Summer Schools in the United States," Report of the Commissioner of Education, 1891–97,* II, 893–959. Washington: Government Printing Office, 1898.

30. *Report of the Commissioner of Education, 1886–87,* pp. 406–7. Washington: Government Printing Office, 1888. *See* Joseph Emory Avent, *The Summer Sessions in State Teachers' Colleges.* A study made under the auspices of the Teachers' College Committee of the National Council of Education, N.E.A. Richmond: William Byrd Press, 1925.

31. Avent, *op. cit.,* p. 17.

maintaining summer schools was growing rapidly.[32] In 1908, Dutton and Snedden surmised that the summer normal school might shortly replace the institute.[33] By 1910, summer normal schools were legally established in 14 states and legally recognized in a number of others. After about 1910, the movement instituted by the University of Chicago in the nineties to make the summer session an integral part of the academic program gained ground rapidly. All over the nation, summer schools and sessions multiplied and, except for a temporary setback during the period of the first World War, enrolments mounted year by year with hardly an exception throughout the entire period.[34]

The summer school offered the teacher an opportunity to do college work—an offer his recently acquired academic status had made him eligible to accept. The education acquired was a preservice variety, but such education was still the most obvious need of many teachers. Through work in the summer school the teacher was able to advance toward a full partnership in the educational enterprise.

Extension Courses, After-Hour Classes, and Correspondence Study. Extension courses were established long before the close of the nineteenth century. The earlier ones, however, whether offered by university or other agency, were generally of secondary level and admitted anyone who, in the instructor's judgment, could profit from the instruction given. Although teachers were prominent in attendance at these courses, they made little concession to teacher needs. Extension courses of this type did provide opportunity for teachers to make good their cultural and subject-matter deficiencies.

Largely after the turn of the century, colleges and teacher-training institutions reorganized their extension programs, raised the standards for admission, and granted college credit for work successfully completed, thus permitting teachers to earn credit toward degrees without loss of salary—an opportunity accepted increasingly, particularly after about 1910.

32. *Report of the Commissioner of Education, 1903,* II, 1504–5. Washington: Government Printing Office, 1905; Avent, *op. cit.,* pp. 17–18.

33. Samuel Train Dutton and David Snedden, *The Administrator of Public Education in the United States,* p. 285. New York: Macmillan Co., 1908.

34. Frazier, "History of Professional Education of Teachers in the United States," *op. cit.,* pp. 82–83.

Also, after-hour classes were offered in increasing numbers by "practically all colleges and universities and by some normal schools located in centers of population large enough to furnish an adequate number of students."[35]

Correspondence work also dates from the nineteenth century but, as late as 1904, Dexter wrote that the University of Chicago was the only major institution stressing this work.[36] By 1910, correspondence courses were offered by ten state universities and a number of colleges and normal schools. The work offered ranged from that of the high school or even lower to that of the graduate school. Much of the work was planned to help teachers pass examinations for certification, and the secondary-school work taken was often used to satisfy entrance requirements of teacher-training institutions.[37]

Higher institutions, earlier wary of becoming involved in the training of teachers, particularly elementary teachers, rapidly organized and developed campus and off-campus programs to participate more fully in the vast movement of the period to upgrade the entire teaching staff.

IN-SERVICE IMPROVEMENT OF TEACHERS AS AN ADMINISTRATIVE-SUPERVISORY FUNCTION—TO ABOUT 1930

Supervision, in some form one of the oldest instruments for the improvement of instruction, came to be recognized in the twentieth century as the most important agency for teacher improvement. Its function as of any time had been largely determined by the prevailing conception of the role of the superintendent. This official had made his appearance as the executive officer of an overwhelmed lay board and, while discharging the responsibilities delegated to him (such as visiting the schools, inspecting the work of teachers and pupils, and examining applicants for teaching positions), came to understand the value of the supervisory function and to devote a great deal of time to it.[38]

35. Reudiger, *op. cit.*, p. 55.

36. Edwin Grant Dexter, *A History of Education in the United States*, p. 547. New York: Macmillan Co., 1904.

37. Reudiger, *op. cit.*, p. 59.

38. Thomas McDowell Gilland, *The Origin and Development of the Power and Duties of the City-School Superintendent*. Chicago: University of Chicago Press, 1935.

As the superintendent's managerial and other responsibilities increased, he was obliged to delegate more and more of the supervisory function. First, the head teachers of the schools of the system were freed from teaching responsibilities in order that they might take over supervisory duties.[39] Also by the beginning of the century new supervisory officers had become intrenched in the larger systems. These were specialists in the newer subjects—art, music, physical education, manual training, and home economics. These were subjects of the expanding curriculum which the classroom teacher was not prepared to teach nor the principal to supervise. They were, therefore, placed in the hands of specialists who taught them, gave the regular teachers "normal instruction" in them, and supervised the teachers' efforts to teach them. By the close of the period, such supervisors were to be found in most large school systems. Also during the period the appointment of an increasing number of supervisors of traditional subjects was made necessary because, it was claimed, existing knowledge and experimental data with reference to subject matter and methods were increasing more rapidly than the average teacher's grasp of them.[40] To these supervisors were added those of special classes designed to meet the needs of children formerly eliminated from the school through failure and through the lack or nonenforcement of attendance laws.[41] Near the close of the period, supervisors of research were added in number.[42] All of these supervisors were generally organized into a department of supervision under the head of a director who was, in effect, an assistant superintendent of schools charged with the responsibility of improving instruction and the teaching staff.

The development of supervision as a function of administration, the organization of supervisory staffs, the empirical nature of professional knowledge, the generally conceded superior learning of administrators and supervisors, all of these and other forces, helped

39. Paul Revere Pierce, *The Origin and Development of the Public School Principalship*, pp. 7–17. Chicago: University of Chicago Press, 1935.

40. Fred C. Ayer, "The Rise of Supervision," *Educational Supervision*, pp. 13–15. First Yearbook of the National Conference on Educational Method. New York: Bureau of Publications, Teachers College, Columbia University, for the National Conference on Educational Method, 1928.

41. *Ibid.*, p. 17.

42. *Ibid.*, pp. 19–20.

shape the concept of teacher improvement as "bringing teachers up to a standard of performance contrived out of the superior knowledge of the specialists."

Teacher Improvement as a Major Task of Supervision. Much of what had earlier passed for supervision had been directed at the protection of the public from the most incompetent of poorly trained teachers. An early conception of the administrative-supervisory role in improving the level of teaching in the schools was voiced by a superintendent who stated that "among the obstacles to the improvement in school teaching, I have thought that to get rid of poor teachers will be the most difficult to overcome."[43] He thought that the institute might save the situation in which policy did not permit wholesale elimination of teachers from the system because "many of the most useless teachers are in every other way respectable, have respectable friends, and cannot be made to believe that they are not good teachers. . . ."[44]

A somewhat different conception of the administrative role was expressed by Lowry in 1908. Noting the presence in most systems of large numbers of teachers with only a high-school education, of others with no professional training, including many young women who had rushed from "childish studies to professional discipline" without having matured emotionally, Lowry concluded that although principals and superintendents should not relax their efforts to secure better-trained teachers, they should "give more time and attention to making good teachers of those new in service."[45]

The first method for the improvement of teachers, he asserted, should be supervision, which was the most important of all ways in which the character of teaching might be improved. Lowry's conception of supervision and perhaps that of most of his contemporaries is indicated by the supervisory activities which he listed and described with approval. The superintendent should learn the needs of his teachers. Special supervisors should give model lessons in each classroom, criticize the work done, give directions for future work,

43. Sweet, *op. cit.*, pp. 28–30.

44. *Ibid.*

45. Charles D. Lowry, *The Relation of Principals and Superintendents to the Training and Improvement of Their Teachers*," pp. 12–15. Seventh Yearbook of the National Society for the Study of Education, Part I. Chicago: Distributed by University of Chicago Press, 1908.

and hold classes to instruct the regular teachers. Grade supervisors should bring the work in all schools up to their own standards of excellence, so far as the ability of the teachers permits. Subject supervisors should visit teachers, help them in the preparation of outlines and on various problems that arise, meet each group of teachers regularly, and meet small groups organized to consider special problems.[46] Hearty approval was given to Van Sickle's report on the duties of the supervisory staff in relation to five groups of teachers classified as to scholarship, motivation, training, and experience. The co-operation of superior teachers was to be sought. For the other groups, there were recommended demonstration, the exhibiting of attainable standards, and positive direction as the situation demanded.[47]

From the practices that prevailed and from those recommended, it is obvious that the supervisory staff was considered the authority that, within limits prescribed by law, should determine the curriculum, textbooks, standards, and methods of instruction. It judged the extent to which the teacher succeeded in teaching prescribed materials by prescribed methods and rated teachers accordingly.

The administrator, aware of the urgency of the task of improving instruction, was interested in developing a program and employing means that would most rapidly remedy the situation. Direction, then as now, was widely regarded as the most efficient procedure for achieving immediate improvement, particularly of the rank and file. And, although the rising qualifications of teachers, particularly throughout the first three decades of the twentieth century, were making increasingly untenable the long-accepted assumption that their meager education, inexperience, inadequate training, and immaturity rendered them incapable, except under direction, of analyzing their own weaknesses or of developing new understandings and skills, direction from above continued throughout the period to be the guiding force of most programs of in-service improvement. Teachers, long conditioned to prescription and direction, were little disposed to be critical of the direction of those in whom legal authority resided. At least, there would be little questioning of such authority until large numbers of teachers came to realize that it was

46. *Ibid.*, pp. 16–17.   47. *Ibid.*, pp. 21–22.

not always based on competence and understanding superior to their own. Teacher dependence upon established authority was perhaps more firmly fixed by the fact that administrators were generally men and generally older and more experienced than teachers. Not only their age but their sex demanded the respect of many young women teachers who were not entirely certain in their own minds that men were not their natural superiors. Under these conditions and since most superintendents, principals, and directors of supervision were helpful and kindly in their relations with teachers, questioning of the nature of their leadership was slow to develop.

In-service Education and Scientific Management. The questioning of the authority of administration that occurred during the first decades of the century was not that of classroom teachers so much as that of educational theorists who wished to supplant authority based upon position and empirical knowledge by the authority of science.

The clearest early expression of the need for the substitution of the authority of science for older forms of authority is found in the Twelfth Yearbook of the National Society for the Study of Education.[48] The administrator and supervisor were to remain the instrument of authority but they, too, were to be subjected to the authority of science which they, no more than teachers, could question.

Administrators and supervisors, said Bobbitt, should be the planners because they were best fitted for this function by the possession of a better understanding of the science.

In any organization, the directive and supervisory members must clearly define the ends toward which the organization strives. They must co-ordinate the labors of all so as to attain these ends. They must find the best methods of work, and they must enforce the use of these methods on the part of the workers.[49]

Management and the supervisory staff were to have the greater share in determining proper methods and standards because this activity constituted too large and complicated a burden to be placed on the shoulders of teachers. Teachers were to be specialists in prac-

48. Franklin Bobbitt, "Some General Principles of Management Applied to the Problems of City-School Systems," *The Supervision of City Schools,* pp. 7–96. Twelfth Yearbook of the National Society for the Study of Education, Part I. Chicago: Distributed by University of Chicago Press, 1913.

49. *Ibid.,* pp. 7 ff., 87.

tice. Administrators and supervisors were to be specialists who could scientifically order socially determined content, discover the best methods of procedure, give these methods to the teachers for their guidance, and set up definite standards for the finished product and for each stage of its development.[50] The obvious weakness in the separation of the teaching and supervisory functions, that is, the possible inability of the teacher to cope with an unexpected situation or one not covered by direction, was to be overcome by making the teacher "reasonably familiar with the controlling science in general outlines as used in the planning room." The importance of the continued training of teachers was recognized:

Full technical training before and during service together with constant contact of teacher with the representatives of the planning room will enable the management to give directions that are wholly definite and yet give them in brief general terms, leaving the teacher to the direction of his inner technical knowledge as to standards and procedures.[51]

There was to be no interference with the teacher's freedom and initiative so long as he was able to go right. If the teacher did not go right, his freedom was to be restricted, not by personal arbitrary authority but by law. However, superintendents, principals, and supervisors were still regarded as the chief discoverers and interpreters of the science.

Sixteen years later Bobbitt restated his philosophy of supervision based upon science.[52] In the meantime, supervision had made increasing use of tests, rating scales, and other products of the scientific movement. Many educators continued to envisage a rapid solution of all educational problems through the discovery of laws of learning and other behavior. Bobbitt, still the most clear-spoken and convincing champion of science, had come to a fuller recognition that some situations are not readily susceptible to rigid scientific methods and he thereupon defined science as the best vision of reality which mankind had yet been able to achieve.[53] He recognized that teachers might have a better vision of parts of such reality than others. The

50. *Ibid.*, pp. 52–53.   51. *Ibid.*, p. 93.

52. Franklin Bobbitt, "Educational Science and Supervision," *Educational Supervision,* chap. xviii. First Yearbook of the National Conference on Educational Method. New York: Bureau of Publications, Teachers College, Columbia University, for the National Conference on Educational Methods, 1928.

53. *Ibid.* p. 239.

primary task of supervision was not to tell the teacher what to do but to enlarge, clarify, and quicken the teacher's mind. Scientific management continued to be the antithesis of arbitrary personal management. In summarizing his position, Bobbitt stated:

It is expected that science shall be generally distributed among teachers, principals, special supervisors, superintendents, and others, according to their situation and responsibility; and that each shall then perform his duties as guided by the light of educational science, provided within his own understanding. . . . In such a situation teachers are not directed by principals . . . but by their own original vision of the educational realities.[54]

Supervision has continued to employ the scientific method and the new instruments that it provided. The uncritical enthusiasm for "scientific supervision" and the extravagant claims made regarding the future of measurement gave way before the development of a better understanding of the nature of learning, the problems of measurement, and the limitations of the scientific method. Supervisors and teachers, as well, made themselves increasingly familiar with the developing science to the extent that the place of science in supervision and in other types of in-service education has been one of growing importance.

In-service Growth of the Professional Staff, 1920–55

The division of the history of in-service education into periods based on the cultural and professional status of the teaching staff should not be permitted to obscure the fact that, at any time in our past, the qualifications of teachers have covered a wide range and the existing programs of in-service education have exhibited widely different aims and methods. Under such conditions, trends are difficult to trace and generally denote nothing more than changes in the number of persons who modified their practices or accepted new aims.

PROFESSIONALIZATION OF THE TEACHING STAFF

Three-quarters of a century after Horace Mann had been able to count only three or four hundred professional teachers in all Massa-

54. *Ibid.*, p. 240.

chusetts, teachers generally had achieved or were nearing professional status. By 1920, the success of the teachers' college had
marked the end of any possibility of a dual system of teacher education—university grade for secondary-school teachers, subcollegiate
normal-school preparation for elementary-school teachers. Judged
by professional and educational requirements alone, high-school
teaching had become a profession and, in the better school systems,
the number of elementary-school teachers with training equivalent
to that of high-school teachers was rapidly increasing.

By 1940, one-third of the states had taken action to require a minimum of four years of post-high-school education of all teachers in
elementary schools, urban or rural, and, by 1950, 19 states had set
four years of college work as the minimum requirement for certificates of any grade.[55] In town and city systems, professional standards were being established increasingly. In 1951, 74 per cent of
1,615 urban systems reporting required four years of college education for appointment as an elementary-school teacher. Corresponding percentages for 1931 and 1941 were 6 and 63, respectively.[56]

The qualifications of employed teachers increased of necessity as
certification and employment standards for new teachers rose. "By
1940, only 4 per cent of urban classroom teachers and 16 per cent of
the rural teachers" of the nation had less than two years of college
education. Sixty per cent of the urban and 40 per cent of the rural
teachers had received four or more years of collegiate preparation.[57]

Another evidence of increasing professionalization was the growing stability of the teaching staff. Better-trained teachers were teaching for longer periods of time. In 1920, less than half of the teachers
had acquired four years of experience. In rural areas, the average
was lower; in cities to which the experienced rural teacher fled, it
was higher. In 1940, the average number of years of experience was

55. *Teachers in the Public Schools,* p. 130. Research Bulletin of the National
Educational Association, Vol. XXVII, No. 4. Washington: Research Division
of the National Education Association, 1949.

56. *Teacher Personnel Practices, 1950–51: Appointment and Termination of
Services,* pp. 8–9. Research Bulletin of the National Education Association,
Vol. XXX, No. 1. Washington: Research Division of the National Education
Association, 1952.

57. Edward S. Evenden, *Teacher Education in a Democracy at War,* p. 48.
Prepared for the Commission on Teacher Education. Washington: American
Council on Education, 1942.

about 10, and for urban elementary-school teachers approximately 14.[58] By 1951–52, the average experience of rural elementary-school teachers had risen to 14.2 years. During the preceding 15 years the experience of the average teacher almost doubled.[59]

As pointed out by Hass in chapter ii, the present shortage of adequately prepared teachers is acute and will become even more so. It is a matter of grave concern that the teaching staff is threatened with deterioration. The relaxation of certification requirements, the increase in the number of emergency teachers, the re-employment of teachers without recent experience—all of these facts point to the need of in-service education as described. However, neither the acuteness of the present situation nor the lack of an acceptable pre-service education on the part of many, if a minority of, teachers should be permitted to obscure the fact that progress has been remarkable. Teaching, once described by Kandel as a procession, has come to approximate, during the last half-century and especially during the last 30 years, a profession. Certainly much remains to be done, but a large majority of today's teachers are, by current standards, liberally educated, professionally trained, and ready, on their induction into the service, to begin (with the help that in-service activities can provide) to put a goodly store of theory and knowledge to the test of the schoolroom situation.

THE TREND AWAY FROM ADMINISTRATIVE DIRECTION IN IN-SERVICE EDUCATION

By the middle twenties, thinking with respect to supervision, long regarded as the most important agency for in-service education, was being revised in terms of the advanced and advancing status of teachers and of a growing knowledge of the psychology of human relations. In 1923, Dunn stated that instructional supervision had, for its large purpose, "improving the quality of instruction, primarily by

58. *City Teachers: Their Preparation, Salaries, and Experience,* p. 16. Research Bulletin of the National Education Association, Vol. XXVII, No. 1. Washington: Research Division of the National Education Association, 1940. See also *Progress in Rural Education.* Research Bulletin of the National Education Association, Vol. XXVIII, No. 4. Washington: Research Division of the National Education Association, 1940.

59. *Rural Teachers in 1951–52,* p. 15. Research Bulletin of the National Education Association, Vol. XXXL, No. 1. Washington: Research Division of the National Education Association, 1953.

promoting the professional growth of all teachers, and secondarily or temporarily by correcting deficiencies of preliminary preparation for teaching by the training of teachers in service."[60] It is clear that to the extent that "promoting professional growth" replaced "correcting deficiencies of teachers," a new relationship between the supervisor and the teacher was indicated. This new relationship was slow to develop partly because the correction of deficiencies continued to appear the most pressing need and also, perhaps, because supervisors, too, needed to acquire the understandings and skills that appropriate modifications of their own previous practices required. The traditional authority of administrator and supervisor could be relaxed only as a new authority was established. Methods had to evolve for what Kyte termed "the professional liberation of the professionally trained teacher."[61] Liberty could not be established by administrative decree.

In-service Education as Guidance. A first step away from the promotion and stimulation of teacher-improvement, through "the arrangement or management of incentives" or direction, whether arbitrarily dictatorial or reasonably persuasive, was the adoption of the method of guidance. The authority of the administrator and supervisor was retained as a principle, but it was partially disguised by their growing respect for the teacher. The superintendent, as the responsible administrative and supervisory expert in the system, was to "initiate any changes in the supervisory policies and methods of applying them." He was to "delegate responsibility to assistants" in terms of well-defined functions. And the special supervisor, defined as "an authoritative specialist employed to assist constructively in the improvement of teaching" was charged with the responsibility, among many others, of "training the persons directly engaged in guiding and improving learning."[62] Fundamentally the difference between administrative direction and guidance was little except for the tendency to make the latter conform to the conception of it

60. Fannie W. Dunn, "What Is Instructional Supervision?" p. 763. *Addresses and Proceedings of the National Education Association*, Vol. LXI, cited in A. S. Barr, William H. Burton, and Leo J. Brueckner, *Supervision*, p. 5. New York: D. Appleton-Century Co., 1947 (second edition).

61. George C. Kyte, *How To Supervise*, p. 42. Boston: Houghton-Mifflin Co., 1930.

62. See Kyte, *op. cit.*, pp. 51–53.

earlier expressed by Dewey in the words, "guidance is not external imposition . . ." but rather it "is freeing the life process for its own adequate fulfillment. . . ."[63]

In 1938, Burton, after a careful examination of developing theory and practice, and after indicating newer principles and ideas that were attracting wide attention, concluded that, in practice, training and guidance continued to be the most commonly accepted principles.[64]

IN-SERVICE EDUCATION FOR THE GROWTH OF THE ENTIRE STAFF

For some time, it has been clear that a new concept of in-service education has been emerging. A partial explanation of the disappearance or modification of older aims and methods and the appearance of new ones is to be found in a number of related developments.

The continued upgrading of classroom teachers, during the period, was accompanied by a growing recognition of the expertness of an increasing number of them and of their growing capacity for self-direction. More and more teachers were becoming equipped, through extended training and lengthened experience, with knowledge and skills possessed by neither superintendent nor principal and with a body of theory equal or superior to that possessed, in some spheres, by the supervisor.

The growing complexity of the educational enterprise was making expertness at all levels and in many areas increasingly essential. The many high-level competencies required could hardly be the possession of a single person or of a single group of persons such as administrators or supervisors. To the extent that competence became general and special abilities distributed among all levels of the staff, the assumption of an inferior-superior relationship between any two levels became untenable and administratively-organized-and-directed programs to train teachers in service lost whatever meaning they may have once possessed.

Other developments were leading to a questioning of the aims and training procedures of existing programs of in-service education.

63. John Dewey, *The Child and the Curriculum*, pp. 22–23. Chicago: University of Chicago Press, 1902. Quoted in Kyte, *op. cit.*, p. 44.

64. A. S. Barr, William H. Burton, and Leo J. Brueckner, *Supervision: Principles and Practices in the Improvement of Instruction*, p. 37. New York: D. Appleton-Century Co., 1938.

New knowledge concerning the motivation of behavior was suggesting a modification of the theory that positive direction by an expert constituted the most effective means of improving the performance of the worker.[65] The newly evolving concepts of human relations and the developing principles of leadership which found their "criterion in the long-time effectiveness of individual workers" were pointing increasingly to the need for "redirecting efforts to improve the staff and its functioning at all levels."[66]

Observation of educational practice and the findings of research appeared to indicate increasingly that an attack upon an educational problem by all persons concerned with it was a superior means of clarifying the understanding of all, of obtaining a commitment to policies and practices developed to remedy the problem situation, of insuring intelligent participation in attempts to implement suggested solutions, and of promoting professional growth, in general.

The improvement of the entire staff rather than merely that of teachers was inherent in the co-operative attack upon problems as was the idea that leadership is the function of the person—administrator, supervisor, teacher, or other—most competent to exercise it in connection with a particular problem confronting the group.

Increasing use of co-operative procedures involving the staff at all levels has been reported in connection with surveys of school practices and of the community, the planning of educational policies, curriculum revision, and the like. The spirit of the concept of in-service education as expressed by a growing number of writers and in gradually developing practices is exemplified, in part or in whole, in the work of a number of in-service agencies among which supervision, workshops, and action research are excellent illustrations.

65. *See* F. J. Roethlisberger, W. J. Dickson, and Harold A. Wright, *Management and the Worker*. Cambridge: Harvard University Press, 1939. *See also* Goodwin Watson, "The Surprising Discovery of Morale," *Progressive Education,* XIX (January, 1942), 33–41.

66. Herbert A. Thelen, *Dynamics of Groups at Work* (Chicago: University of Chicago Press, 1954); F. J. Roethlisberger, *Management and Morale* (Cambridge: Harvard University Press, 1941); Schuyler Dean Hoslett (editor), *Human Factors in Management* (Parkville, Missouri: Park College Press, 1946); Burleigh B. Gardner and David G. Moore, *Human Relations in Industry* (Chicago: Richard D. Irwin, Inc. 1950 [revised edition]); Kenneth D. Benne and Bozidar Muntyan, *Human Relations in Curriculum Change* (New York: Dryden Press, 1951).

(See chap. ii for discussion of these and other activities and agencies.)

Supervision and the Growth of the Staff. As teachers came to possess the skills and understandings that the supervisor had formerly attempted to supply and as new knowledge concerning the motivation of behavior and of the role of leadership appeared, supervision stressed less its inspectorial, rating, and training functions and set new goals. Courtis, as early as 1928, foretold the later change in the aims and methods of supervision when he wrote:

Tomorrow the goal of supervision will be the facilitation of the natural process of growth of personality in teachers, a process which yields inevitably the important concomitants, sympathy with children and teaching power. It takes creative supervision to develop creative teaching.[67]

In the years that followed this expression of a hope, programs of supervision planned for the teaching staff did give way slowly in favor of an attack by teachers, supervisors, and others upon problem situations that were recognized to be of common concern. The aim of the co-operative effort was the solution of the problem; an important concomitant was the growth of teachers and supervisors in understanding and in the ability to attack and solve problems. By 1947, Barr in an extensive treatment of supervision was led to write that the "expression 'training teachers in service' is no longer in good repute . . ."[68] and, in the same volume, Burton noted the shift from the "limited concept 'improvement of teachers in service' to the broader and more fundamental one 'improvement of the staff in service,' "[69] and, he went on to add, "the 'concept of growth' is increasingly replacing that of 'improvement.' "[70]

The changing goals of supervision and the changing role of the supervisor are to be noted in the tendency to emphasize the consultative nature of supervision and in the advocacy by some educators of the change of the title "supervisor" to that of educational

67. S. A. Courtis, "A Philosophy of Supervision," *Educational Supervision,* p. 251. First Yearbook of the National Conference on Educational Method. New York: Bureau of Publications, Teachers College, Columbia University, for the National Conference in Educational Method, 1928.

68. Barr, Burton, and Brueckner, *Supervision, op. cit.,* p. 565.

69. *Ibid.,* p. 10.   70. *Ibid.,* p. 11.

consultant, technical assistant, helping teacher, instructional adviser, and the like.[71]

Workshops. In 1955, it was stated that with the exception of courses, workshops continued to be the most used form of in-service education.[72] Although the accuracy of this statement depends upon a narrow definition of "forms of in-service education," it is true that the workshop has gained wide acceptance since the title was first used in 1936 to designate a particular type of activity.[73] There is no accepted definition of a workshop, but it normally consists of a number of teachers working together, with resource persons and a director, under conditions that are designed to provide for individual growth through contact with a stimulating environment, a part of which is the group itself.[74] Claims made for the workshop resemble those made for situation-centered supervision, planning conferences, and other modern in-service agencies: It is an agency in which and through which new ideas can be found, new ways to do old things worked out, new skills developed, new knowledge acquired, and new stimulation secured for a still more effective job of teaching and administering the schools.[75] In theory, there is no preplanned or arbitrary schedule of activities; the participants work on problems they wish to work on; and leadership is a function of the workshop members.[76]

In spite of the validity of some of the criticisms of the workshop, it has qualified, not as a panacea for all the ills of teacher education,

71. *Ibid.,* p. 15.

72. Kenneth E. Anderson and Herbert A. Smith, "Preservice and In-service Education of Elementary- and Secondary-School Teachers," *Review of Educational Research, XXXV* (June, 1955), 221

73. Kenneth L. Heaton, William G. Camp, Paul B. Diederich, *Professional Education for Experienced Teachers: The Program of the Summer Workshop,* pp. 1–20. Chicago: University of Chicago Press, 1940. *See also* Charles E. Prall and C. Leslie Cushman, *Teacher Education in Service,* pp. 201–40. Washington: American Council on Education, 1944.

74. James R. Mitchell, "The Workshop as an In-service Education Procedure" (A Study Conducted and Reported by the Subcommittee on In-service Education of Teachers), *North Central Association Quarterly, XXVIII* (April, 1954), 421–57.

75. Mitchell, *op. cit.,* p. 429. *See also* Willard S. Elsbree and Harold J. McNally, *Elementary-School Administration and Supervision,* pp. 417–19. New York: American Book Co., 1951.

76. Mitchell, *op. cit.,* pp. 434–35 ff.

but as a useful agency for the in-service education of the professional staff.[77]

Action Research. Action research, defined by Corey as "research undertaken by practitioners in order that they may improve their practices,"[78] has been increasingly recognized during the last decade as an instrument for the development in teachers of the ability and desire to apply the methods of science to the solution of their own educational problems.

In broad outline, the steps involved in action research and research conducted by research specialists are quite similar. The major differences between them rise from the fact that the problems attacked by action research are, in the main, broad and complicated ones involving many variables which cannot be eliminated or entirely controlled. Admittedly providing less definitive tests of stated hypothesis, action research seeks its justification in claims for greater relevancy of its findings and in the greater possibility that the results of the research will be translated into practice. In fact, if teachers as investiagtors become entirely involved in the search for means of improving their practices as teachers, the problem of transferring the results of research to practice does not arise.[79]

The theory of action research is in accord with the evolving concept of in-service education. The research is focused upon problem situations. It generally, if not necessarily, involves participation of many persons in formulating suggested solutions to real problems, in trying out the most likely appearing methods of solving the problems, and in evaluating the results of the application of those methods. The creativeness of teachers finds an outlet in activities which it helps shape. The trained intelligence of many teachers working together to make the education of children more rational and effective serves also to promote in-service growth of teachers and to further advance teaching as a profession. Action research, no matter what

77. *Ibid.,* pp. 446–47.

78. For detailed statement of purpose, methods, and values, *see* Stephen M. Corey, *Action Research To Improve School Practices.* New York: Bureau of Publications, Teachers College, Columbia University, 1953.

79. *Ibid.,* pp. 7–12, 18. *See also* B. Othanel Smith, "Science of Education," *Encyclopedia of Educational Research,* pp. 1145–51. Edited by Walter S. Monroe. New York: Macmillan Co., 1950.

the final verdict may be concerning some of its outcomes, promises to become an important agency for in-service education.

From In-service Training of Teachers to Professional Growth of the Staff

The history of in-service teacher education must be viewed against the background of changing educational theories and practices that developed in response to or in conjunction with the changes that occurred in the aspirations of the American people and in the conditions of their social, political, economic, and intellectual life.

The early commitment of the American people to the ideal of universal literacy carried with it the obligation to make a measure of education available to all children. This tremendous burden taxed not only the financial resources of the country but the intellectual ones as well. This is true even though during most of the nineteenth century the idea was generally, if decreasingly, accepted that a common education involved nothing more than the acquisition of a few simple academic skills and of a small and prescribed body of knowledge. As long as this idea prevailed, most teaching consisted of little more than drilling pupils in basic skills and imparting to them knowledge possessed by the teacher. The need of the teacher for a degree of skill in teaching was recognized, but it was generally believed that such skill derived from experience and, to an even greater extent, from the possession of the knowledge that was to be taught. The most obvious teacher-need was proficiency in elementary subject matter. Early in-service education provided for some discussion and demonstration of methods employed by successful teachers, but this and other aspects of the program could expand only as teachers generally came to possess an elementary knowledge of arithmetic, reading, and other subjects of the elementary curriculum.

As the ideal of universal literacy gave way before that of equal opportunity for an expanded and extended education, not only more but better-educated and better-prepared teachers were sorely needed. During the last decades of the nineteenth century, it was increasingly noted that the education acquired in ungraded rural and city elementary schools, even when supplemented by short periods of normal-school training, left teachers embarrassingly inadequate to instruct the youth of a social order that was maturing and in which democracy was beginning to acquire a new definition.

Academic and professional qualifications of teachers were raised. Prospective teachers were called upon to extend their preparation, and employed teachers were left little choice but to acquire more academic education and professional training of a type that could be translated into course credits, normal-school diplomas, advanced certificates, and college degrees. For a long time, programs designed to upgrade the teaching staff overshadowed all other in-service efforts.

The rapid growth of school systems, the increase in the complexity of the educational task, and related forces led to the emergence of the superintendent and to a situation in which teachers, in spite of the general upgrading that had occurred, continued to represent widely varying degrees of competence. The superintendent, charged with responsibility for administering and improving the educational program, came to recognize the value of supervision as a means of improving instruction and staff and to devote a great deal of time to it. He and the supervisors and principals to whom he delegated a large share of his supervisory function were more experienced than most teachers and were, more often than not, superior to them in culture, education, professional training, and understanding of the advancing science of education. They, therefore, set themselves to the task of bringing teachers up to their own standards of excellence in carrying out educational plans designed by administration.

This concept of supervision was challenged during the second and third decades of the present century by persons in whom there had developed a distrust for empirical knowledge and a faith in the science of education. Their efforts toward replacing the authority of administration with the authority of science initiated a movement which left its imprint on all subsequent programs of in-service education, even after the limitations of science were more generally recognized. The concept was challenged again by the development of a better understanding of the importance of morale and of the ways in which behavior is changed and why it is changed. These understandings led to the development of supervision as a kind of guidance that accomplished administrative ends but took account of the personality and ability of the teacher.

It was not, however, until after teachers in large numbers had demonstrated that background, preparation, and experience had made them experts in areas to which the specialization of the administrator and supervisor did not extend that the earlier concept was strongly challenged and that teachers began to be freed, in large numbers, from the imposition of administratively designed programs of in-service education. The need to meet new demands being made upon the schools and the continued development of new understandings relating to human motivation and the learning process combined with other factors to establish the expertness of teachers as a resource that demanded use in planning and administering the educational program. The teacher was no longer an elementary-school graduate to be trained but a specialist to be consulted. Supervisory and administrative effort previously directed toward teacher-improvement could be more sharply focused on the promotion of pupil growth. Attempts by teachers, supervisors, administrators, and others to solve problems of common concern constituted in-service education, not of the teachers individually but of the teaching staff as a professional group. New programs of in-service education involving group activity, alternating leadership as it emerged from the staff, and freedom on the part of the teacher to experiment found expression in the organization of curriculum-planning committees and policy-making boards, in the organization and development of workshops, and in the attempts by teachers singly and in groups to apply more and more the methods of research in the solution of their educational problems.

Most teachers, by commonly accepted standards, have attained professional status but, as has been emphasized in chapter ii, inadequately prepared teachers are numerous and, for the next decade or two, may become more so. For some of these, in-service education will need to be directed toward making good their deficiencies in education and training and toward developing attitudes that compel the truly professional teacher to study and to learn, generally without direction or encouragement, until after her last class is taught. Until such time as all teachers earn and are accorded full professional status, older concepts and types of in-service education will perhaps persist. But even the poorest prepared and least competent of the unqualified that will be employed for some time must be, no matter what else is planned for them, involved in the really professional activities of the professional staff for, as Dewey said, "only by sharing in some responsible task does there come a fitness to share it."

CHAPTER IV

Psychology of Change within an Institution

HUBERT S. COFFEY

and

WILLIAM P. GOLDEN, JR.

Introduction

While there is little in the psychological literature formally classified under the heading "psychology of change," many of the differentiated fields are concerned with the conditions and processes of change. These include such fields as classical learning theory, social psychology, group dynamics, and clinical psychology, particularly as the latter is oriented to therapy. In presenting this chapter, then, the authors will draw from these various areas. We are especially indebted to the approach developed by Krech,[1] Lewin,[2] and Parsons.[3] We realize that our approach represents a particular theoretical bias, and, although there is no theory which embraces consistently every aspect of change, we believe we have selected the one which has the most usefulness to the practitioner at this time.

Characteristics of Behavior: Forces Actuating Change

TENSION AND ITS RELATION TO CHANGE

We think of ourselves in terms of what we *need*, what we are *interested in*, what we *want to do*. When we think of our "basic needs," we call to mind such universals as "hunger," "thirst," "sleep," and "sex." We know, too, that the natural drives which accompany these needs lead the organism to change its relationship to the environment so that its needs can be satisfied. Likewise, we know that

1. David Krech, "Notes toward a Psychological Theory," *Journal of Personality*, XVIII (September, 1949), 66–87.

2. Kurt Lewin, *A Dynamic Theory of Personality*. New York: McGraw-Hill Book Co., 1935.

3. Talcott Parsons, *The Social System*. Glencoe, Illinois: Free Press, 1951.

our *interests* also have the character of driving us to act in a way which accomplishes satisfaction even though they may not seem as "basic" as our needs. When we describe our relation of need to the objects of our interests and explain the behavior by which we undertake to obtain satisfaction, we use the term "motivation."

Motivation may be thought of in reference to a concept of "tension." Tension describes the state of a system which is in a process of change, and the change is in the direction of equilibrium in relation to the state of neighboring systems. Thinking of experiences or situations as "tensional" means that the environment and the person are regarded as related and interdependent systems. The concept of tension is, then, more inclusive than that of need or drive. It means not only that such "basic" needs as hunger are motivational but also that the perception of any aspect of the environment may create a tendency for change in relation to it; it may be equally "motivational."

We would all agree that a political ideology which promises subsistence to a starving Chinese peasant is likely to motivate him to accept this ideology. But we would insist that the desire of an American schoolboy to achieve acceptance in the peer group is also an example of motivation. Both motives, one of basic physiological survival, the other of social acceptance, induce tensions which are resolved by the creation of a new relationship between the individual and his environment.

DIFFERENTIATION AND ITS RELATION TO CHANGE

As we think in everyday language about needs (tension), we also think in terms of what we have learned, what we know, how we perceive, how we see something differently from the way we have seen it before. These changes we may conceptualize by the term *differentiation*. What is unknown is actually equivalent to having no differentiated psychological structure for us, as being unstructured. As we learn about something, our perception and our knowledge of it become more differentiated, more structured. Thus, a stranger in a city learns more about the city as the unstructured whole becomes differentiated into parts and subregions. He may do this by the actual experience of walking and motoring about the city, or by becoming familiar with maps of the city, or by conversation with "old timers." The differentiation may be one which is exclusively geographical or it may be one which includes sociological or social psychological knowledge.

We can, following Lewin, think of differentiation in relation to the two major aspects of the process: the differentiation which goes on *within the person,* and the differentiation which goes on *within the environment.* In some sense this is an unreal distinction; yet perhaps a necessary one if we are to emphasize that what is differentiated is learned and will, under normal conditions, endure. When the organism changes, there is a difference in its future behavior in respect to expectations and desires. We can think of this kind of learning, those changes, as differentiations *within* the person. But just as these changes within the person are brought about in connection with changes in the environment, so also do they determine how the environment itself is perceived and experienced. The small child's concept of a "table" may readily be as something upon which desirable articles are placed beyond his reach. Later when his experience with "table" includes sitting at a small table, his concept of table is enlarged and his expectations concerning his own behavior are changed. His concept of "table" is then said to be more differentiated than before, and this differentiation has behavior consequences. This implies a change in the way the child sees things and responds to his environment.

Akin to the particular use of the concept of differentiation is the more general concept of cognitive structure. We have seen that cognitive structure may be produced by increased differentiation resulting from the subdividing of regions into smaller units. But "sometimes a change in cognitive structure occurs without increase or decrease in the degree of differentiation."[4] Under some situations a change in cognitive structure is brought about by seeing a connection between areas which previously were not seen as related. Much problem-solving and "insight" represent this type of change in cognitive structure. Thus, to use an oversimplified example from therapy, the patient may be well aware of two aspects of himself, his self-depreciation and his strong need for unrealistic perfection.

4. Kurt Lewin, "Field Theory and Learning," *The Psychology of Learning,"* p. 227. Forty-first Yearbook of the National Society for the Study of Education, Part II. Chicago: Distributed by University of Chicago Press, 1942.

Through his therapy he may see a connection between his own perception of himself as unworthy and his belief that all his goals are unattainable.

Not all change is initiated by the effects of newer concepts on cognitive structure; in some instances the observed effect is related to the tension system. Thus, we may think of change in the person's own needs or interests, or a change which is induced by forces in the environment. The latter may involve compelling the individual to do an unpleasant action by the imposition of force, or through the counterbalancing of one set of needs or interests by establishing another more powerful set. For instance, a school system may require that its teachers take certain courses if they are to be eligible for promotion. The goal of promotion may be stronger than the dislike of having to spend time and money on something which, at the time of choice, may be seen as intrinsically worthless, so the teacher may choose to enrol in the course. The imposition of force by the setting of requirements does not in itself, however, decree that the activity will continue to be disliked.

In some cases where direct force is imposed, particularly in those cases where the disliked activity leads to a reward, there may be an actual change in interest or valence with a consequent change in cognitive structure. Thus, although there may be initial resistance to embarking upon the required activity, the teacher may find that the activity is one he likes. Most teachers are familiar with the change in attitude toward reading which the child experiences once he is able to master the effective techniques. The steps involved in becoming a speedy reader, for example, may meet with great resistance to learning and a negative attitude toward reading; yet, once these skills have been mastered, the child may become an avid reader. On the other hand, where force is imposed without any change in cognitive structure or without development of intrinsic interest or motivation, the desired effects are not likely to survive after pressure has been relaxed.

The impetus to do something, to learn, or to carry out a new activity, may be associated with the meaning which the activity acquires and the goals which are established. A change in interest or the awareness of a new need may give a particular activity a new meaning and, hence, a new goal and a new value. New interests, changed needs, and newly established goals are associated with new ways in which things are seen. Frequently the sources of changes in perception are related to one of the following conditions: (*a*) There is a crisis which indicates that new methods of approach are necessary if the problematic situation is to be resolved (e.g., new methods of approach may be required by some change in the cognitive structure of the particular situation). (*b*) There is a sensitization to new ideologies or goals with consequent shifts in the levels of aspiration, so that what may have been perceived at one time as satisfactory is now, in the frame of reference of a new set of values, regarded as inadequate. Under these conditions the new values set new goals, and the new goals are associated with the creation of new tensions or new needs. Thus, an adolescent boy found himself an accepted member of his group when he became adept in playing a guitar as an accompaniment to group singing. His motivation to learn the skill was related to his awareness that he could not compete with others on the basis of physical prowess because of his small size but would be accepted through the development of this skill. Another illustration might be an adolescent girl who influenced her "gang" to accept peers of different racial backgrounds after her own significant experience in an interracial camp.

The needs of an individual are to a very high degree determined by social factors. Thus, the fact that one belongs to a group, or many different groups, may induce needs which lead to change. The needs of the person are also affected by the ideology and conduct of those groups to which he would like to belong or from which he would like to be set apart. Needs may be induced by the force of another person or a group, particularly where the force is related to social status and prestige, or where the person is seen as an instrumentality for achieving a goal or as the agent for preventing the movement of others. In many ways similar to the needs induced by the force of another person are the needs or tensions the individual experiences as a result of belonging to a group or adhering to its goals. The similarity between the two is apparent if we think of the power of one person as emanating from his importance to the other person, particularly in the case of one with whom he shares goals or ideologies.

RELATIVE CONNECTION AND ISOLATION
AND THEIR EFFECT UPON CHANGE

It is a matter of common observation that some attitudes of a
person or some of the objects in his environment have greater significance to him than do others. When aspects of his environment—
what he perceives, what he apprehends—have deeper significance,
we usually think of this significance as having more emotionally
toned meanings to the person. Thus, the symbols of family, nation,
religious group, or even political ideology are likely to evoke a
more potent emotional response from him. Sometimes we say he
has "deeper" feelings about these things—that they have greater
meaning for him. If we employ a Lewinian concept, we can say
these things are more *central* to him. They are less easily expressed,
more private, more intimate, more personal. Just as some things are
more central, so other attitudes on his part or objects in his environment have less emotional significance to him. We say these latter
aspects of the person are more *peripheral*. Thus, we can differentiate regions of the person, just as we can differentiate regions in
the environment.

Concepts of tension and differentiation have a basic relationship
to any consideration of change, for they involve what might be
thought of as both the emotional and the cognitive aspects of the
relationship of the person to his world, particularly to his world of
other persons. In any relationship, both aspects—the *cathectic*, by
which we mean the feeling and emotional aspects, and the *cognitive*, by which we mean the differentiated way of seeing and knowing the world—become integrated. Change in the individual takes
place in connection with both of these characteristics. When we
use the term *cathectic*, we mean the emotional investment which
the person makes in an object or in a goal. Its importance in change
lies in its motivational significance. Rarely does change come about
without the person developing dissatisfaction with things as they
are, without his developing a new level of aspiration for himself.
But dissatisfaction or a new level of aspiration may be very threatening unless the person sees how he can change, unless it is possible for
him to understand the regions through which he must travel, psy-
chologically, in order to reach the goal. Thus, he must see himself in

relation to his world in a different way. We think of this differentiated construct as *cognitive*.

At times we see these aspects compartmentalized. An inspirational talk to teachers may have the salutary effect of bringing about dissatisfactions or raising the level of aspiration to new heights. It may, however, have a deleterious effect in the long run if there seems to be no way in which the aspiration can be realized; for without some implementation of the inspiration, the exhortation to change may eventuate in despair or in the total rejection of the briefly envisioned goal. On the other hand, when only the cognitive aspects are stressed without any attempt to arouse emotional involvement, the differentiated way of perceiving may be just another set of techniques unrelated to any felt need or deeply perceived value. The individual must want what he has not wanted before, must recognize the barriers which are to be overcome if he is to reach the new goal, and must be able to perceive the pathways to the goal.

While it is true that most persons have aspirations which would indicate dissatisfaction with their present behavior, some of their values and beliefs seem mutually antagonistic or antithetical. Thus, a person may have considerable resistance toward this goal. Becoming a better teacher may mean, for instance, that he must realize that he is not perfect, as he now thinks he is, or achieving his goal may involve changing his relationship to his principal, who seems to like him as he is now. He may be torn between his own desire to function more effectively and his desire not to impair the esteem which he feels he now enjoys in the eyes of his principal. We have all seen the internal struggle of children who try to resolve the conflict between living up to the expectations of both their peers *and* their parents.

INDIVIDUAL CHANGE PROCESS—PSYCHOTHERAPY

The psychotherapist involved in the process of producing change in the behavior of another person is essentially concerned with dealing with the struggle between different subsystems of the central regions which are in a state of tension. Thus, the objectives of psychotherapy are essentially to help the person make new differentiations, discover new meanings, see relationships anew, and correct distortions in his perception of existing relationships. Acquiring a new motor skill by learning to drive an automobile and developing more reality-oriented relationships to other persons (learning to express the way one feels) are both instances of learning. But they differ, and in the process of re-education this difference is very great in several respects: in the centrality of the tensions which the patient has, in their effect upon his perception of reality, in the relation between the individual's level of aspiration and his realistic conception of himself, and in the conflict between those subregions which are related to values he wants to achieve.

Experiences in psychotherapy have placed great emphasis upon the primacy of the phenomenological world of the patient—that is, the world as *he* sees it. What has meaning, what has value, what he honors or dishonors, what invites him to approach or frightens him into withdrawal—these are based upon the way he sees the world in which he lives, his cognitive structure. One of the prime sources of his discomfort or ineffectiveness is the extent to which his cognitive structure departs from what we might call "social reality." Thus, his level of aspiration may clearly be incongruent with what is realistic. His requirements for himself may be beyond that which can be expected for the human being. He may repress all of the impulses which normally are expressed in aggression. He may regard other persons with suspicion as threatening and destructive agents, when there is no reason to perceive them as such. He may be caught between his need to see himself ministered by others while defying their authority and a need to see himself independent beyond any boundaries of social living. In all of these typical instances the patient sees his world and himself in a way others cannot share.

What is the true basis of reality is a philosophical question, the ramifications of which we cannot pursue here. Unlike the scientifically constructed physical world, social reality depends upon the overlapping character of many phenomenological fields, and the criterion here of social reality is what Harry Stack Sullivan calls "consensual validation."[5] The patient is likely to depart quite clearly from that which is consensually validated, even though within our culture considerable range of perception is permitted. Thus, neurotic patients have been shown by studies to have a significantly different

5. Harry Stack Sullivan, *The Interpersonal Theory of Psychiatry*, p. 224. New York: W. W. Norton & Co., 1953.

perception of themselves than what is seen by others. A patient may see himself as benign, generous, loving, and giving, but others in a therapy group, for example, may see him as hostile, aggressive, and dominating. What the true characteristic of the patient is we are more likely to find in the consensus of other patients, providing there is not a collective distortion of the person. This consensus or agreement of others about a person is called "consensual validation." Providing we have no more objective measure of the reality than this agreement, we must rely upon this as the standard. Much of what we know about social standards and social perception belongs to this level of agreement.

Clinicians seem to agree that the perception of the patient is likely to be distorted because of rather central areas of tension. The clinician usually relates the way the person sees his environment to certain areas of disturbance within the "deeper layers" of the person. Probably the meaning of "deeper layers" can be equated with the concept of more minute, more central, differentiated areas of the person. Most clinicians trace disturbances to historical causes, such as difficulties with parents, sibling rivalry, or anal fixations. We would not deny the importance of the history of the individual and the effect of childhood relationships or traumatic experiences. But of greater relevance here is that, rather than dealing with these events as incidents in the life of the patient, we are encountering the consequences of these events in the impact they have made in developing certain stable valuations and perceptions.

Much of what is known about the psychotherapeutic situation has implications for effecting change. The relationship between trainer and trainee must be a permissive one, that is, it must permit the trainee to express his feelings, to indicate his needs, to communicate his tensions. It must deal with the tensions and the cognitive structure as he presents them, not in the way in which the trainer might idealistically hope that he would see them. The trainer must be willing and able to tolerate and respect resistance. The trainer must serve in many ways as the representative of reality, as the person against whom the perceptions of the trainee can be tested, and as the person who can transmit to the trainee effective methods of determining the nature of reality.

We have evidence that change takes place most significantly in a relationship which is *participative* and *collaborative*. What is transmitted to the trainee is most significantly communicated through *two-way communication*. It is a relationship which is *essentially cooperative* even though there may be a distinct division of labor. For change to be significant in its effects, it must involve the central regions of the person, the *deep-lying values* and *attitudes about the self*. For this to occur, the change must be oriented to *felt needs* and *greater sensitization* and must include *opportunities to engage in the process of interaction* which express these feelings and translate them into concrete action steps.

The Nature of Stability and Change in Social Systems

Thus far we have focused our attention exclusively on the person and on the conditions which bring about change. We have thought of the person in relation to tension systems, differentiation, and isolation, but we have tried to view him as having direct and continuous communication with his environment and as having a dynamic relationship with it. Perhaps the most influential aspects of his environment are those forces which emanate from the social system of which he is a part. These forces are particularly influential in determining individual behavior because they represent the world of human relationships.

BOUNDARY-MAINTAINING CHARACTERISTICS OF SOCIAL SYSTEMS

We can think of social phenomena as they exist apart from the person by using many of the same concepts which we have used in thinking about the person and the environment. We can think of the social system as a boundary-maintaining structure existing in relatively constant patterns, which we may think of as "moving pattern-constancies." We use the concept of "moving pattern-constancies," because the social system is always in a process of adaptation. The tempo of this moving equilibrium may vary considerably in time and place. Thus, in a preliterate society, isolated from the effects of other cultures, the tempo of change may be very slow, and such institutions as puberty rites, for example, may continue relatively unchanged from one century to another. On the other hand, our own social system is in a constant state of change largely because of the demands which our technical advances place upon social institutions. A survey of changes in attitudes, folkways, and mores brought about by the automobile would give us an excellent picture of the constant process of social adaptation to a technological innovation. And even as this is said, the example is a little quaint, for already our attention is focused on the jet-propelled and supersonic airplane.

Social systems tend to receive the impact of disruptions which go on in the physical environment. Thus, where there are significant disruptions, such as a change in economic base resulting from the disappearance of a natural resource or the invention of a new instrumentality, the social system undergoes considerable alterations. These may range from transformation of the previous patterns toward more adaptive ones to even the dissolution of the system itself and the creation of an entirely new arrangement. This is not to say, however, that social institutions are themselves "sensitive" to changes in environmental forces and that we can expect systematic and adaptive modifications as a matter of course. The phenomenon of internal stability frequently desensitizes the social system to the environmental demands. In some cases such internal stability may actually amount to rigidity, and, under these cases, the intransigence of the system itself may jeopardize survival of the inhabitants, as is notable in the extreme case of Labrador fishing villages, where the "rituals" of a particular type of fishing persisted long after they were economically effective. More typical, however, in institutional complexes, is the outmoding in one part of the system by developments in another. Semiautonomous attitudes within one part may be incompatible with technological advances in another. We think of this as "cultural lag."

We can emphasize in another way the connection of the individual and the social system when we examine the way in which the person is seen as intimately related to the preservation of the system itself, as contributing to its boundary-maintaining characteristics. The phenomena of learning and socialization, the values to which the individual is exposed, and, in spite of the apparent wide divergences in our own culture, the finite repertoire of possible behaviors, all of these are in a general sense perpetuated to support and insure the continuation of the social system. For example, in preliterate societies, child-rearing practices are designed to produce the socially desired character structure. The social system would seem in an implicit way to specify those purposes and objectives which, through the processes of socialization and learning on the part of the individual, tend to maintain the system and develop individuals which fit it. It goes without saying that the simpler the social system, the more easily is this congruence of individual and social pattern achieved.

The essential characteristics of the social system can be found in its subparts, the particular institutional forms. Thus, this yearbook is concerned with a specific context, namely, the relations of the professional personnel in the school system, and methods of effecting change in these persons within that context. It is clear that one of our assumptions is that individual change is always going on within an organizational or institutional context. There are some general characteristics in which institutional or organizational settings mediate between individual dispositions and interactional patterns as specified by the institutions themselves.

CONCEPT OF ROLE: INDIVIDUAL AND INSTITUTIONAL INTEGRATION

There are several ways in which we may view individual behavior as it appears in an institutional setting. One of the most useful of these methods involves the concept of "role." Thus the "teacher" can be thought of in terms of the role which is prescribed for teachers in the general sense of the social system and in the particular institutional subpart, "the school." Actually, the institution can be said to consist of a "complex of institutional role integrates." The institution of the school consists of a prescribed set of roles which inform the teacher of what his behavior ought to be. Within any institution there is some latitude in the way the role is assimilated; likewise, there are defined limits to the amount of deviance which will be permitted. In addition to general role prescriptions for "school people," there are differentiations made between the roles of classroom teachers and administrators. In fact, the belief and value systems of these two groups frequently differ substantially and in such a way as to result in conflict.

ROLES ARE INTERACTIONAL: INVOLVE RELATIONSHIPS

The essential aspect of the concept of role is that it is interactional and complementary. The role of the person is interactional in the sense that it always involves relations to some other object than the self, or the person. Usually, if not always, this interaction is with another person, hence the role can be said to be *interpersonal*. However, this does not mean that what is interpersonal is necessarily "face to face." It may be interpersonal because it involves a series of expectations on the part of one individual with respect to others. These expectations define how the individual should act. It is just this element of expectations which, although it involves an image of interactions, may operate as an attitude, or disposition to act, without involving others directly in a face-to-face fashion. Thus, in the role of the teacher there are certain expectancies which the teacher has concerning his behavior with students and also certain behavior which he expects from students. This role is not limited to specific educational tasks as such but includes a great deal that has to do with his total position or status as a person.

ROLES ARE COMPLEMENTARY: INVOLVE
EXPECTATIONS OF OTHERS

A second characteristic of roles is that they are complementary. By this we mean that the expectations of one person are related to the expectations of another. More properly speaking, we can think of this relationship as one which involves the *expectations* of the one and the *sanctions* of the other. Expectations are often supported and re-enforced by sanctions. What the child feels is expected of him by the parent or the teacher may often be just what is sanctioned by the parent or the teacher. It is not inevitable in a social relationship. A person may discover that his expectations, what he perceives his role to be, are quite different from what is expected or, more properly, sanctioned by others.

The role is likely to involve a feeling of approval or disapproval. From the standpoint of the social system, it involves the dimensions of conformity and deviance. Self-approval does not always mean conformity with the sanctions of the other. Frequently the person may realize his expectations through deviance from the sanctions of the other. Thus, the "bohemian" would be embarrassed by the sanction of approval from the "philistine." Of course these two contrasts do not exhaust the catalogue of possible deviance–conformity relations. While two persons might involve mutually complementary expectations and sanctions, this mutuality may be in deviance from the total social system, or some aspect of it. The deviance expectation through which the person may seek and, indeed, receive disapproval from the others is somewhat related to his feeling of approval in some other expectation-sanction relationship. Dissent from one value aspect of the social system means conformity to some other aspect.

The complex of role expectations and sanctions is not typically confined to a single act or a particular relationship. Rather, the person may very well *internalize* within his role a whole motivational disposition to conform to or deviate from the institutional pattern. This may become, through internalization, a part of the central regions of the person, a part of a more or less enduring relationship to the institutional complex. Thus, the person in a particular situation behaves in a manner consistent with his usual behavior in many interpersonal relationships. He is usually concerned that he not only perform in a manner sanctioned by the other but that his behavior in general is sanctioned, that he is, indeed, a sanctioned person.

INSTITUTIONS INCORPORATE MOTIVATIONS OF THE INDIVIDUAL

Institutional systems must incorporate, to a greater or lesser extent, the major motivational interests of the participants. Freud has described the major problems of the persons as centering around the issues of *work and love*. Both aspects of the person's relationship to society demand institutional forms which provide appropriate roles in which these needs can be fulfilled. For instance, the problem of work is likely to demand the acceptance of certain role expectations, and these vary widely in a complex society where many different types of work relations exist. Similarly, in love relationships the society institutionalizes the roles of husband, wife, parent, brother, and sister, and, because the control of sexuality is so important for the survival of society, these roles usually permit less deviance than those which are occupationally oriented.

Cultures vary greatly in the particular institutional prescriptions which define the role-behavior with respect to these central social concerns. Through socialization and indoctrination, the essential affective factors in training to be a social participant, the role expectations involved in behavior concerned with work and love are communicated and internalized. While much of what is internalized has application to the social system as a whole (sex differentiated roles, for instance), an institution within the social system, such as the *particular* occupation, develops a set of standards and beliefs which characterize it and determine to some extent the relations which its *particular* participants have with other segments of the social system. The medical profession is an excellent example of this. It goes without saying that these value standards may be codified into law or made explicit in a public body of ethical standards including permissions and taboos. On the implicit level, however, the role makes certain demands in behavior and attitudes which are role-syntonic, that is, they become an intrinsic characteristic of the person. Often the stereotypes associated with an occupation are caricatures of the actual extent to which the person internalizes his occupational role and becomes in a total way the "physician" or the "teacher."

Characteristics of Institutional Groups: Status Quo
OBLIGATIONS AND PRIVILEGES

Although social institutions are a complex of role integrations which arise historically over a considerable period of time, they tend to develop a formal, rationalized structure. The degree of organization required may well be a result of the scope and comprehensiveness of the function which a particular institution has in relation to the total structure of society. Thus, while we may think of the school as an institution which performs a function delegated to it by the larger society, the difference between the "little red schoolhouse" and the complex metropolitan school system directly reflects the greater complexity of the urban community. In addition to the highly developed institutional characteristics, the urban school reflects the increasing range of responsibilities which are thought of as "educational" and are being delegated to the school by the larger social system.

In a modern social structure, the offices of a specific organization are integrated in a manner designed to carry out the purpose of that organization. These offices usually form a hierarchy, and each office or each level of offices within the hierarchy has an established social status around which are organized certain obligations and privileges. Thus, the obligations of the principal are different from those of teachers, as are his privileges. Similarly, the obligations and the privileges of the supervisor are likely to be different from those of the persons supervised. These offices, with their corresponding obligations and privileges defined by specific rules, prescribe the competence and responsibility which their officers must have. Thus, the office of the principal demands certain competencies not required of the teacher. This is true in reverse, also. Authority involved in decision-making responsibility and power (manifest in the degree of influence) is included in the office itself as a part of the institutional structure.

Clearly defined social distance between occupants of different official levels denotes the corresponding difference in obligations and privileges. These status differences signify the distribution of power and authority within the social structure of the particular institution and serve to objectify official contacts by prescribing their modes. Moreover, explicitness in prescription of modes of relationship minimizes the friction which usually arises from ambiguity in relationship. The specific institutional roles, with their supporting expectancies, may facilitate interaction on a formal and public level. Thus, each officer is protected from the impulsiveness or arbitrariness of the others by the constraint of mutually recognized procedures and regulations.

SOCIAL STRUCTURE INVOLVES ENDS AND MEANS

The distinctive attributes of hierarchic organization in social institutions are clearly illustrated by the urban school system. The hierarchy of offices of superintendent, principal, supervisor, and teacher, together with the official sentiment which surrounds the prescription of "going through channels," is in itself a regulation which recognizes the authority of existing hierarchical status. Though usually justified, such a regulation may be a jealous guarding of power, with clarity of communication an excuse for its existence. The formalized social structure, or a particular institution thereof, is characterized by at least two essential elements. One is the culturally defined goals, purposes, and interests which indicate what is held "worth striving for," objectives which are legitimate for all members of the society and comprising sentiments and values more or less accepted by most persons. The other element is the culturally accepted modes of achieving these goals, which are defined by what is considered allowable in the sense that they are permitted by the sentiments or values of the society, not necessarily because they are efficient.

Cultural goals and institutionalized means for achieving them are not always in a close correspondence. Merton has pointed out that emphasis on cultural goals may be accompanied by little stress on the means of achieving such goals.[6] Thus, the educational goal of "educating the whole child" may represent an aspiration with little attention paid to the institutional means of achieving it. Under such conditions, aspirations are likely to be idealistic or sloganistic. An alternative to the overstress on ends, as compared to the anemia of means, is what is substantially its opposite. Thus, a school system may develop highly institutionalized procedures and, at the same time, become forgetful of the goals. Institutionalized means may become self-contained practices while institutional conduct becomes a virtual ritual, with conformity to procedures elevated to a central value.

PRODUCTION INSTITUTIONS DEVELOP EQUILIBRIUM

Both these variants from a truly productive relationship between institutional goals and institutional practices are barriers to the development of change. For we must think of productive institutional structure as maintaining an effective equilibrium between these two aspects of social structure, thus bringing satisfactions to individuals through accepting institutional goals and attaining them by institutionalized procedures.

The problem of institutional change follows directly, we think, from this analysis. Any institution is built around a set of purposes and values. Moreover, the institution develops means by which these purposes are carried out. The function of the particular institution, however, is influenced heavily by what is going on within the total

6. Robert Merton, *Social Theory and Social Structure.* Glencoe, Illinois: Free Press, 1949.

social system. Thus, if the economic structure of the society changes, this is bound to have an influence upon the institutional subparts and will demand some revaluation of goals and some reassessment of means. *The central problem of institutional change is the development of those conditions in which institutional goals and means can be reassessed for the purpose not only of adapting to change going on within the social system but also of assuming responsibility for exerting influence on the various alternatives of change which may be open to the society.*

Many of the problems of the modern school system can be seen in this frame of reference. Certainly the goals of the school as perceived by various segments of the community are in controversy. These conflicts are likely to be a reflection of conflicts about the goals and purposes of the larger society. Moreover, to defend one set of institutionalized means as against another is to force one's self to accept one set of purposes in preference to another. That these are highly charged with emotion means that the goals are based upon value premises in which the choice is bound to have threats to existing vested interests. The school administrator is in the unenviable position of having to espouse one value and reject another, each of which may be supported by powerful segments of the community. He is likely to escape into the comfort of instrumental ritualism. Thus, "the school's business is to teach" symbolizes the new focus on administrative means. But the avoidance of partisanship by this means is an illusion; escape only contributes to the status quo.

STEREOTYPED ROLES MAY CREATE STRAINS

As we analyze the characteristics of hierarchical organizations, their positive attainments and functions in emphasizing efficiency, we need also to consider some of the internal stresses and strains. In particular it has seemed to us that the efficiency of organization which contributes to the functional achievement of an educational institution may actually work against the realization of educational goals. In the general sense, hierarchical organization may develop what Veblen has called "trained incapacity," the technical skill which serves the particular end, but which, while successfully applied in the past, may be inappropriate under changed conditions. The well-trained administrator, to use a slightly expanded version of Veblen's intention, may be able to make keen discriminations in certain areas which involve his particular administrative skill (specific occupational role), but his very attention on these matters means that he develops blind spots in areas involving other perspectives. Frequently his "reliability, precision, and efficiency" become highly valued because external forces prescribe that this is what his administrative role should be. His acceptance of these sanctions often is related to his need for security and the wish to be protected from more controversial goal values.

In such situations there can develop a virtual displacement of sentiments from goals onto means, which in turn foster the vast overvaluation of means, with little questioning of ends. Concern with adherence to regulations and the propriety of procedures becomes an end in itself which is coupled with "timidity, conservatism, and technicism," and, above all, conformity. Although many aspects of the bureaucratic role could be mentioned, one of the most essential is that any attempt to personalize relationships is likely to be looked upon as graft, favoritism, "apple-polishing"—certainly as improper. Although we recognize the extent to which personal relationships in an organizational structure may indeed promote individual exploitation of that particular system, creative advances toward productive change have their genesis in the quality of interpersonal relationships within the system.

GROUP COHESION CAN PROTECT BY INSTITUTIONAL ROLES

The school organization frequently poses the conflict between what are administrative values, such as efficiency of records, orderliness, and technical excellence and what are goal values, including concern for the growth and development of the individual child and the progress of mature group relationships. The latter values may necessitate the tolerance of conditions inimical to the efficiency of a bureaucratic system. The adventure and experimentalism of a progressive approach to educational goals may be hampered by the social distance which a bureaucratic organization prescribes as the proper relationship between different status levels. Although the conflict may exist as we see it with certain deprivations to the teacher who feels a victim of the impersonal organization, we should recognize certain important secondary gains to him as possibly one reason he does not rebel against it. A well-organized structure develops an impressive solidarity which can resist intrusion from the segments of the community outside. Actually the teacher may be protected from criticism or complaints of those holding alien educational values, such as parents or noneducational groups, by the impressive *esprit de corps* and in-group cohesion which in other situations may be frustrating. For where there is a virtual monopoly of enterprise, such as in the school, protest from the outside is likely to be met with ideological uniformity, and in-group identification can occur speedily under the situation of attack from the outside, even though there be internal disagreement about the very values which are under threat.

In addition to the protection which such group cohesion gives to the erstwhile dissenting teacher, the organization, where it becomes thoroughly defensive, can resist changes which under reasonable conditions of receptivity might have been sparked by the "intruder." Organizations can develop highly specialized ways of seeming to be receptive; thus, the defense may be disarming to the intruder when it is essentially "nondirective," even though the status quo is resolutely maintained.

Characteristics of Institutional Groups: Social Change

THE METHODOLOGY OF SCIENCE

Social scientists tend to publish more concerning the characteristics of a given society than they do about the processes of change which go on within the group. The process of change is difficult to study under any circumstance, and particularly so when it is thought of in connection with the impingement of environmental conditions upon a given social system or studied with respect to the influence which one relatively autonomous part of a culture may have upon another.

Turning to the institution of science itself, we see a general cultural attitude toward knowledge and toward the social structure in which change is accepted and fostered. The acceptance of the validity of the scientific method, while widespread within our culture, is at times uneven. The approach of the scientific method to economics, to medicine, to welfare, and to education is welcomed by some but may be feared by others. Knowledge is bound to be inimical to some values and, by its nature, brings about thrusts toward change, perhaps followed by some disruption. As John Dewey pointed out, every thinker places some part of a stable world in peril. Yet the climate of opinion which so universally supports research and the pursuit of truth, usually regardless of its consequences, is not isolated from a prevailing attitude toward the encouragement of progress and the existence of deeply rooted cultural attitudes associated with rationality and experimentalism. Research of a scientific character, either basic or applied, has become a necessary part of most social enterprises, even gaining respectability in quarters traditionally hostile to scientific advance.

It seems that one can hardly view these developments without being impressed by the extent to which they imply that social change and the direction of social processes are the legitimate and necessary activity of any segment of the community. Perhaps there has been a scarcely perceptible shift in the way in which we conceive of social change. Formerly, we associated social change with cosmic historical forces, and the problem of the social scientist was to identify, describe, and interpret these forces. Today the methodology of science is being applied more frequently to the solution of specific problems and the analysis of specific situations. Empirical methods of data collection, clarification of relevant hypotheses and variables, an attitude of objectivity, and other institutionalized precepts of science are increasingly taken as moral commitments which tend to characterize the process of intelligent analysis. The aim of such analysis is almost uniformly directed toward improvement in the functions of the institution or organization, and the values that may be observed would seem to imply the recognition of planned social change.

CHANGE TYPICALLY TAKES PLACE WITHIN INSTITUTIONS

Now all of this would have little interest for us were it not for the fact that it describes the social and cultural media through which individual change most typically takes place. In a previous section, we analyzed some of the characteristic aspects of psychotherapy, with attention focused on the processes and conditions for individual change. Yet, despite its popularity, psychotherapy is not the typical situation for individual change in our society. Much more common are the situations *within organizations and institutions* where individual change takes place. This change may take place in either of two ways: (*a*) by studied arrangements as a part of organizational planning where the procedure is formal in character, or (*b*) by the induction of the individual into a new group, the change being brought about under informal pressures.

When change results from organizational planning, the person is made aware of a preconceived plan directed toward him, although it may function primarily on an information-giving level, as in orientation programs. In the second instance, there is no formal program directed toward change, but it is quite clear from studies of informal groups within more formal organizations that membership in the new groups affects the values and attitudes of the new member as well as provides him with information. In any case, even though formal attempts at directing change in the individual may be undertaken, the greater potency of the informal organization for producing change can be verified.

The person's emotional relationship to the organization, his sense of belonging, his emotional attitude toward the objects which symbolize it are much more likely to be determined by the informal or psyche-group processes than by the formal. For his membership in the informal organization immediately mobilizes his feelings, his loyalties, his values for acceptance, and his need for belongingness. The extent to which the formal organization also pulls upon these motivational attributes—tension regions or quasi-needs—depends primarily upon the closeness in communication between informal processes and formal directives and the degree to which needs which tend to be satisfied by the informal organization can be satisfied through task-oriented pursuits relevant to the purposes of the formal organization.

EFFECTIVENESS OF INFORMAL ORGANIZATION

There is no guarantee at all that the purposes of the informal organization will mesh with those of the formal. In fact, there is considerable evidence to show that the two groups may operate in undercover conflict, the one providing covert resistance to the other. Change of the individual is most effective, however, when his membership in the informal group overlaps membership in the larger organization. This is to say, the identification which he has with the subpart is closely connected with and in no significant way antagonistic to his identification with the larger organization. The factors which influence amount and direction of change in the *member of the group* can be seen as related to the extent to which the group in which he has most significant membership *is itself an agent of change.* The way in which group membership influences the direction of change will be discussed in the next section.

Group Membership and Individual Change
BARRIERS TO GROUP OBJECTIVES

As we have indicated above, much of the concern about individual change has been expressed in connection with the individual's membership in a group. To evaluate all of the studies that have been reported about the effects of this membership would go beyond the scope of this chapter. Our purpose will be to emphasize various research findings and to indicate the particular theoretical positions as they seem to apply to the problems of individual change.

We find useful the basic assumption that the problem-solving activities of groups are similar to those of the individual. A group goal is reached by overcoming barriers in the process of movement toward it. As is true for goals sought by individuals, group goals are dependent upon the character of the environment, the possibilities which exist, the difficulties to be encountered, and the limitations which are imposed by environmental demands. Thus, for example, we have seen that for any particular group, the characteristics of the organizational hierarchy itself influence the ability of the group to reach its goal.

INTERNAL PROCESSES OF GROUPS

Internal processes within the group help determine its ability to move toward the goal. This we can think of as a dimension of emotionality which characterizes the group in its problem-solving activities. Thelen,[7] following Bion,[8] has studied empirically this aspect of group functioning and has been able to quantify Bion's clinical concepts of dependence, fight-flight, and pairing, as contrasted to "work." We can think of the concept of work as being primarily goal-oriented, but the aspects of emotionality may be characteristic group tensions which either produce barriers to reaching goals or doing work or may, if organized in the direction of work, function as strong motivating forces. Groups which are dependent seek nourishment and protection by a strong member or leader; the group may mobilize forces against something, either to fight it or run away from it (fight-flight), or the group may see itself as existing to establish intimate pair relationships (pairing).

There is little doubt that the internal fabric of the group—its tensions, its ideology, and its "personality"—influences individual motivation and individual change. A work group may be characterized by a high degree of dependency, with all members sharing the same passivity, fearing the risks of incurring leader disfavor and at the same time experiencing restlessness and even intragroup rivalries because no member can realize his effective individual potential. In another situation, the internal rivalries may become so divisive as to exhaust the energies of the group in inter-clique hostilities in which alternate patterns of domination and submission drive the individual into either hyperaggression or passivity, whichever is most congenial to him temperamentally. Yet the very forces which produce destructiveness in groups are forces which may produce constructive behavior under effective leadership. Dependency, for instance, has on its positive side loyalty and identification with the group goal; conflict has in its positive dimension involvement in group activity and the development of creative alternatives. We can look at emotionality as a motivation-tension dimension of the group; it is effective if the resources for action can be directed effectively toward a goal.

7. Herbert Thelen, *Methods for Studying Work and Emotionality in Group Operation.* Chicago: University of Chicago Human Dynamics Laboratory, 1954.
8. W. R. Bion, "Experiences in Groups: I," *Human Relations,* Vol. I, No. 3 (1948), 314-20; "Experiences in Groups: II," *Human Relations,* Vol. I, No. 4 (1948), 487-96.

LEADERSHIP, DECISION-MAKING, AND STANDARDS

We are interested in the internal processes of groups because the group's internal structure is closely related to the effectiveness of both the group and the individual in the group. This structure can be thought of as related to several dimensions which, while universal within groups, vary from group to group in degree and in the manner in which they exist. The first characteristic is *type of leadership*. The well-known studies of the social climates of groups[9] indicate clearly that differences in atmospheres associated with autocratic, democratic, and anarchic leadership lead to differences in behavior of the members. It is sufficient to point out that where leadership engaged the participation of the group members in setting goals and planning work, as was done in the democratic group, the amount of co-operative endeavor and the heightened enthusiasm for the group was much greater than in the anarchic or autocratic groups.

The second characteristic affecting the group would seem to center about the *group's freedom and ability to make decisions*. The classic work here is that of Lewin and associates in the field of decisions regarding food habits.[10] Lewin showed that when group discussion was followed by a group decision regarding a course of action, the members were more likely to persist in carrying out the activities than in a situation in which the discussion did not result in a group decision. This observation is even more significant in view of the fact that the group decision was carried out, for the most part, by individuals after they had terminated face-to-face relationships with the group.

Closely related to decision-making is the *development of group standards*, a third group characteristic. A group's members develop expectations or standards which apply to the behavior, attitudes, and beliefs of all members of the group. Standards are more strongly enforced by the group the more relevant they are to the group goals and activities. This seems to be true not only when the group

9. Ronald Lippitt and Ralph White, "The Social Climate of Children's Groups," in *Child Behavior and Development*. New York: McGraw-Hill Book Co., 1943.

10. Kurt Lewin, *Field Theory in Social Science*. New York: Harper & Bros., 1951.

develops standards with respect to a common goal but also when the group emphasizes the meeting of individual needs. Here the group develops standards for "confiding." Through this process, the conflict between dealing with deeply personal problems and being unwilling to be seen by others in a self-deprecating light can be worked through. The working through of resistance in this type of group develops the freedom to view his own position without subjecting himself to punishment and ostracism. This is an important factor in co-operative activities because failure to identify is deeply feared until a group norm of permissiveness is developed and internalized.

GROUP SUPPORT OF CHANGE

The establishment of group norms in the direction of change is not inevitable. However, where change is itself a goal of the group, norms which include change can be established and function to support change in behavior or attitude of the individual within the group. The fact that a group may explore, open up channels for change, and support newly acquired behavior and attitudes is of the greatest importance. For, to the extent that the group supports change in the individual helps members see the need for change and helps them take the necessary steps in the direction of acquiring new attitudes and behaviors—to that extent the group can be said to have developed a *new culture* which in itself supports and encourages individual change. It should be noted that the individual's relation to any social system of which he is a member is such that change can scarcely take place if it jeopardizes his membership in the group or detracts from his sense of belonging. However, when change becomes a function of his membership and is a part of his group identification, then change itself becomes a valued property of the group.

While we have thought of these three characteristics of groups—*leadership, decision-making,* and *group norms,* as of especial importance in affecting individual behavior and have treated them separately, we are aware of their dynamic interrelatedness. The type of leadership in the group affects the freedom of the group to make decisions. Whether the group can make its own decisions with respect to goals, manner of operation, use of resources, planning for action, and evaluation of process depends upon whether the group can itself be permitted to assume these functions. Although the assumption of these responsibilities does not guarantee "efficiency," it is likely to enhance the group's cohesiveness and to develop the conditions under which the group exerts greater influence on its members.

STRONG SENSE OF BELONGINGNESS AIDS CHANGE

The principle of cohesiveness can be seen as one of cardinal importance in Cartwright's summary[11] of the ways in which research findings have shown groups to be of influence upon individual change. He points out that those people who are apt to be changed and those who are to exert influence toward change on the part of others must have a strong sense of belongingness to the same group. Further studies have reinforced this point by showing that discussion groups operating with participatory leadership have demonstrated greater influence toward change than these operating with supervisory leadership. The chances for change seem to be increased by the manifestation of a strong "we" feeling in the group. It is probably not amiss to point out that whenever educational aims have been directed toward development and inculcation of attitudes (character) as in the English university system, much more attention is placed upon the tutorial method (strong teacher-student relationship) than in those educational systems with a strong emphasis on information-giving.

Cartwright also points out that the more attractive the group is to its members, the greater is the influence it can exert. Attractiveness of the group is related to the degree to which it satisfies members' needs. The satisfaction of members' needs, in turn, is related to the identification of needs and the building of group experience in such a way as to satisfy these needs. Thus, a group which is formed to satisfy the particular needs of its members and in which these needs have a central focus is likely to form a cohesive base. However, we should be aware of the fact that the needs of members are not static; they emerge and change in the process of the members' becoming more aware of and more sensitive to the values of group activity.

11. Dorwin Cartwright, "Achieving Change in People: Some Applications of Group Dynamics," *Human Relations*, IV (1951), 1–71.

COHESIVE GROUP MAY BE MORE FLUID

It is important that the productive relationship between need satisfaction and group cohesion be maintained. To this end, the group members must participate in the leadership functions, the processes of goal formulation, the planning of appropriate steps to goal realization, and the evaluation of these aspects of leadership experience. Under these conditions the attractiveness of group work is not synonymous with euphoric emotionality but with a realistic relationship between the group function of establishing procedures calculated to satisfy the selective needs of the membership. Thus, the forces of attraction and cohesion enable individual members of the group to respond with greater readiness to the ideas and suggestions of others.

Cohesion is also associated with another aspect of group activity conducive to change, namely, greater fluidity. When a group develops considerable cohesion, members may function much more freely in a "trial and erorr" fashion. Verbal expression, attitudes manifested, or values exposed under conditions of greater cohesion may be exhibited without fear of retribution or personal criticism. Whatever attitude or value is expressed in the group need not have unfavorable consequences. In other words, with group cohesiveness members may send out many "trial balloons," knowing that this will lead neither to their isolation nor to any deprivation. To feel that admission of failure will have enduring effects in the eyes of others is to place a premium on defensiveness and hiding one's failures. If in the atmosphere of the group behavior there is a realization that whatever is communicated is "not for keeps," then failures as well as successes can be brought into the open. In this sense, greater cohesion and greater fluidity may be associated with some degree of "irreality."

This is one reason why individual change may frequently first be induced under conditions removed from the reality situation of everyday work. Some persons feel that the induction of change can *best* be accomplished under social and physical conditions as much removed as possible from the specific working environment. The concept of the "cultural island" carries with it the implication of the ecological and geographical conditions for greater freedom and fluidity.

The group functions to facilitate change in the individual in the following ways: by helping him meet his needs in an atmosphere in which he participates in establishing the goals and is supported by other members who are also engaged in such need-meeting activities; by encouraging his participation and involvement in a step-by-step evaluation of the process so that the group continues to be effective in helping him meet emerging need-goal relationships; by producing a situation where he can try out new behavior and express new attitudes without being threatened by the "consequences" of such behaviors; by bringing to bear on the problems of his interest new resources of information and discovery so that his behavior may have the benefit of mutual criticism and assistance.

INSTITUTIONAL STRUCTURE AND INDIVIDUAL CHANGE

Whether the change within an individual—his changed perception of the situation, his development of new goals and levels of aspiration—can be effective in any enduring way depends crucially upon the ability of the organization to facilitate and maintain individual change. In many cases where the individual or group has been stimulated to develop new patterns of behavior in response to new perceptions of what is a desirable mode of functioning, the new patterns may actually be discouraged by the other parts of the organizational hierarchy. In order for change on the part of the individual to be effectively established, he must have the opportunity of putting it into operation within the organizational structure.

One of the most interesting experimental studies of this relationship was made in connection with the training of supervisors in industry.[12] It was found that the extent to which a supervisor is successful in attempting to help employees reach their goals depends upon whether the supervisor himself is perceived as having influence in the total organizational setting. If the supervisor is recognized as an influential official of the company, the more the supervisor aids goal-achievement, the better satisfied the employees will be and the higher will be the correlation between supervisory behavior and

12. Robert Kahn (editor), "Human Relations Research in Large Organizations," *Journal of Social Issues,* Vol. VII, No. 3, 1951.

employee attitudes. But when a supervisor is perceived as being "non-influential," stronger attempts on his part to help employees cannot be expected to raise the level of employee satisfaction. Actually, employee satisfaction may even fall.

GROUP LEADER MUST HAVE INSTITUTIONAL INFLUENCE

The difference between an "influential" and a "noninfluential" supervisor in this study is of particular interest to us. The influential supervisor appeared to have a relatively high influence over the social environment in which his employees were functioning, by having a voice in departmental decisions made by his own superior, by having considerable autonomy in running his own work group, as well as by having higher general status as indicated by his salary. What is of most general importance, however, is that the influential supervisor has impact upon the organization as a whole and influence in levels above that of his face-to-face work group. It is reasonable to conclude that whatever decisions were made within his own work group were understood by the group to have been communicated by the supervisor through organizational channels and to have a good chance of acceptance. The supervisor as an effective gatekeeper of communication with the higher authorities was, therefore, able to help the group realize that its efforts were productive.

What is true of industrial organizations and supervisory groups can be applied to other hierarchical organizations as well—in particular, to the school. The gap between the inspired ideology and the possibilities for action may be in the chain of command—the supervision, the principal's office, or the "head office." What becomes a level of aspiration for improved work or what is seen in a different light through greater sensitization may actually avail nothing. For, to put ideals and ideas into practice, the co-operation of other levels of the organization must be assured.

MAJOR PRINCIPLES OF INSTITUTIONAL CHANGE

It would seem that for change in the individual or the group to be effective, it is essential that all levels of the organization be brought into the co-operative endeavor. Space does not allow us to go into detail about many of the specific ways in which the total organizational structure can be involved in the processes that lead to change.

We should like to emphasize, however, that since any institution is a dynamic system, change within the whole system can be thought of as the degree to which all parts of the system are receptive to change. There are two major principles with respect to institutional change which should be constantly observed.

1. Communication within the organization must be two-way. It is essential that needs be communicated to supervisors and also that training activities for meeting needs be appropriately announced. Likewise, policies from above should be communicated down the line with as much participation as possible. Often the difference between organizations in the degree to which participation in policy-making is present is actually the difference between institutions which are primarily custodial as compared to those which are truly educational. The challenge which is felt in a structure continuously responsive to changing needs is likely to be translated into a dynamic functioning which is truly educational in every sense; training under these conditions becomes a part of the institutional blood stream.

2. Role differences between organizational levels tend to create barriers to problem-solving within a group and resistance to change within the individual. The principal has a different set of external pressures placed on him than does the teacher, just as the supervisor in the factory has a different set of pressures than the worker. Many times the role character of the higher-level administration official makes it difficult for him to tell groups down the line what these pressures are. They seem to him static, fixed, and impenetrable. Yet when these demands and pressures are shared as aspects of the problem-solving situation, they can become channels for facilitating change rather than for instituting barriers.

PLANNING FOR CHANGE: RESISTANCE AND ASSISTANCE

Social change would be easily accomplished were there not within every social system potent resistances to change. Just as there are forces which demand change, there are counterforces which work against any change. No stable arrangement is easily changed, and particularly is this true in a complex scheme of interpersonal relations where vested interests in authority and power become highly stabilized. Change in an institution or complex organization which has provided for no orderly means of change is bound to be disrupting. The communication system within an organization is seldom equal to the demands of the new arrangements, for rarely can all employees understand the change, and the informal organization becomes rife with rumors which only serve to increase resistance and engender hostility. Furthermore, the integrity of an institution is based upon its ability to withstand some of the forces which endeavor to change its character. If there were no resistances to change, then there would be no stability or integrity.

When organizations face the possibility of change there is an aspect of resistance which is subjective and personal and which all members may share. We have a loyalty to the ways in which we have been seeing things and doing things, and we may have no internal commitments to what is new and essentially strange. Besides, we may be faced with demands that involve courses of action which are strange and essentially unknown to us. Further, the change may entail a new description of our roles within the organization, and we may be called upon to exchange our vested interest in a role which was comfortable and serene for one which, in its novelty, is anxiety-provoking.

Resistance to change is manifested in many ways. Frequently there is a denial that any problems exist, whereas, before change was suggested, there were many. There may be surface collaboration with the process of change through paying lip-service without really implementing it or by finding excuses to postpone the implementation. Sometimes resistance may be shown in excessive dependency where the individual shifts all responsibility for implementation to someone else.

Not only do we find resistance from the individual to a state of affairs, and particularly to a change in a state of affairs, but frequently it is a group phenomenon. Often the forms of resistance parallel on the group level the ways in which it appeared in individual cases. Sometimes there is a group dependency on the person in authority while covert resistance is manifest in undercover hostility.

Resistance itself usually is a symptom of the lack of recognition on the part of leadership that whatever changes come about develop most productively through collaboration and participation. Where the change is the result of an analysis of need, careful consideration of objectives, and intelligent scrutiny of the means by which the objectives are to be accomplished—and these steps are participated in by persons whom the change affects—the process of change is likely to be met with less resistance.

It is part of the great tradition of Western culture that it has built within the system a means for the critical evaluation of human needs and goals and the means employed in search of their fulfilment. This is the function of education, scholarship, and science. Such an evaluative function would have no real meaning were it not designed to achieve objectives, were it not to lead to change within the society itself. The wisdom with which this function prevails will depend on the freedom and openness of communication, undistorted by wishful thinking or the doctrinaire. Likewise, orderly change can be achieved when evaluation and problem-solving are incorporated as an ongoing process within the organization itself, allowing for the creativity which comes from freedom of expression and the responsible involvement which comes from full participation.

Summary

To summarize this chapter, the particularly significant concepts of the psychology of change in relation to programs of in-service education are briefly recapitulated in the following paragraphs.

1. The individual is motivated to change when there is a disequilibrium between the tension systems of the individual and the surrounding social field. The dynamics of the process of change are seen in the attempts to restore equilibrium within the individual or to change the tensional quality of the surrounding social field.

2. The process of change within the individual comes about through increased differentiation both within the person and within the environment. This relationship develops a cognitive structure within the person through which he perceives the world in which he lives. All differentiations result in changes within the person so that by changes in cognitive structure the world becomes more structured and more meaningful. Such changes in cognitive structure affect changes in needs, tensions, attitudes, and expectations.

3. In addition to needs growing out of physiological processes, many human needs are determined by the groups to which one belongs or the status to which one aspires. Behavior which is character-

istically human is most often in response to tensions arising in the field of social relationships.

4. In describing the process of change within the individual, it is useful to distinguish between those aspects of the person which are *peripheral* and those which are *central*. The peripheral regions, because of their proximity to the action level of the person, are more instrumental in their ability to carry out action. The central regions are more private, intimate, and personal, and their accessibility to the environment is less. Although they are less accessible to action, once there is a communication through connection of these regions, that is, through the peripheral to the surrounding social field, motivation is likely to be stronger and its effects more enduring.

5. The central regions of the person can be described as more "tensional" in character, since they involve deeply held values and beliefs. Strong feelings are the source of both sustained action and deep resistance. Psychotherapy gives us an example of the extent to which cognitive structure may be accompanied by strong affective or cathectic reactions of the person. It also illustrates the extent to which cognitive and cathectic aspects are involved in the process of change.

6. Psychotherapy frequently involves persons who are maladjusted because of cognitive distortions. These frequently are the result of not having a truly communicative relationship between the inner or central regions and the social field in which action takes place. The meaning of acceptance and permissiveness in the atmosphere of psychotherapy is that it permits tension to be released so that perception can be changed in congruence with reality.

7. The process of psychotherapeutic change comes about under conditions where the perceived needs of the patient are made the focus of attention, where the threats to his own perceptions are reduced, and where the relationship of therapist and patient are mutually collaborative. These are aspects of change situations which can be generalized to any situation.

8. In considering problems of change within an institutional setting, we need to consider the characteristics of institutions themselves. Institutions are social systems which are boundary-maintaining and tend to exist in what has been called "moving-pattern constancies." The tempo of the moving equilibrium varies considerably

in time and place. Social systems reflect the impact of environmental disruptions, just as they are reflected in the learnings and values of the individuals which they mold to support them.

9. Individual behavior within a social system is determined by the role which is prescribed by that system. Roles contribute to the functioning of the system by creating within the individual highly internalized expectancies as to how he should behave and how others will behave. Role behavior becomes highly fixed within the institution and is disrupted only under rather extreme conditions. This reciprocation in the maintenance of the status quo makes change difficult, both with reference to individual motivation and to social pressures.

10. Institutions usually develop a formal social structure as a method of performing their work. The structure is characterized by a hierarchy of offices which have distinctive responsibilities and privileges. These are exemplified in a status system which is based on differential prestige and a prescribed set of roles and procedures. Along with the formal structure are the informal functions which have much less structure, are characterized by more spontaneous flow of interpersonal relationships, and are often effective in either aiding the formal structure in reaching goals or working as a very antagonistic core and in a private way against the public goals of the institution. An institution is likely to function more effectively and with greater satisfaction to its employees if the needs which are expressed in the informal social relationships are dealt with in the formal structure.

11. The processes of change can be productive within an institution only if conditions permit reassessment of goals and the means to their achievement. The function of science is, in part, directed toward the assessment of the processes which are critical in the attainment of goals. To function in a responsive manner to the changing needs it is designed to serve, any institution must provide within its structure the facilities for objective evaluation and creative thinking.

12. The most significant barrier to institutional change is the resistance which persons express when such change seems threatening to roles in which they have developed considerable security. The process of institutional change is facilitated by a number of conditions: (a) when the leadership is democratic and the group members

have freedom to participate in the decision-making process; (*b*) when there have been norms established which make "social change" an expected aspect of institutional growth; (*c*) when change can be brought about without jeopardizing the individual's membership in the group; (*d*) when the group concerned has a strong sense of belongingness, when it is attractive to its members, and when it is concerned with satisfying member needs; (*e*) when the group members actively participate in the leadership functions, help formulate the goals, plan the steps toward goal realization, and participate in the evaluation of these aspects of leadership; (*f*) when the level of cohesion permits members of the group to express themselves freely and to test new roles by trying out new behaviors and attitudes without being threatened by "real consequences."

13. Any change within a given group must be supported by the organizational structure lest it become the storm center of ideological conflict within the institution. Therefore, communication must flow from one hierarchical level to another, and proposal for change must be sanctioned within the social structure. Resistance to change is to be expected at any level. Unless there is resistance, it is doubtful whether institutional change can endure or individual change can go very deep. Change is less threatening and, indeed, may be more validly tested if, in the beginning, while involving all levels within the institution, it can be placed upon an experimental basis to be evaluated as a part of an action-research program.

CHAPTER V

Guidelines for In-service Education

J . CECIL PARKER

Introduction

It is the purpose of this chapter to suggest guidelines for planning, organizing, and conducting in-service education activities and programs in schools and school systems.

The sources that have been utilized in the formulation of the guidelines are (*a*) the concept of in-service education presented in chapter iii, (*b*) the current growth-needs of teachers, supervisors, and administrators as described in chapter ii, (*c*) the psychology of change as interpreted in chapter iv, (*d*) recent research in the field of in-service education, and (*e*) experiences of schools and school systems with in-service education activities and programs.[1]

The processes of deriving the guidelines include an analysis of the five sources indicated above, the preparation of a tentative statement of guidelines which was presented to the yearbook committee and to a number of other individuals for criticism, and a revision of the guidelines based upon the suggestions and criticisms received.

The term "guideline" is used here to represent an operational principle or a criterion which may consistently direct or guide individual and group action in planning, organizing, and conducting in-service education activities. Considerable care has been exercised to formulate the guidelines as actions that may be taken by individuals and groups.

It is important that no "sequential-step" significance be attached

---

1. The results of the California Co-operative Study of In-service Education have been utilized extensively. The Co-operative Study was a five-year project directed by the author of this chapter and financed by the Rosenberg Foundation. The Public Schools of three California communities (Oakland, Alameda, and Stockton) were involved. In addition, considerable use has been made of the results of the California Regional Project in Secondary Education, directed by T. Bentley Edwards and supported by the Rosenberg Foundation.

to the order in which the guidelines are presented. This is true for two reasons: First, it is impossible as well as unsound to derive useful guidelines that are mutually exclusive. That is to say, practically all of the actions indicated by these guidelines are involved when a group plans how to work. Second, no two individuals or groups should proceed with the actions indicated by the guidelines in an identical series of sequential steps.

The plan of the chapter is to state separately each guideline as a basis for analysis and illustration. The material presented in chapter iv, while basic to the guidelines, is not restated here. It is suggested that the reader may wish to make his own referrals to chapter iv as he considers each of the guidelines.

Guideline I: People Work as Individuals and as Members of Groups on Problems That Are Significant to Them

The analysis of the psychology of change presented in chapter iv points to participation and collaboration as basic requisites for effective in-service education. To achieve these essential requirements, the members of a professional staff must do something. The central problem in in-service is, then, "do what?" The key to the answer, if we are to utilize what is known about change, is included in our statement of the first guideline. Whatever is done must be significant to the persons involved.

The word "significant" requires some analysis and explanation. An in-service education problem is significant to an individual when he can become involved in it emotionally as well as intellectually; when it can be seen as a basis for action; and when a solution is demanded by the exigencies of the situation as he perceives them. To pass these three tests of significance, the problem as formulated need not, of course, originate with every member of a group. Each person, including the status leader, has the responsibility of suggesting problems which may have significance for all.

An individual can often become emotionally involved in a problem if he sees its relationship to some part of his system of values. A value important to many teachers in American schools at the present time is that each child should be provided with the opportunity to learn at a rate commensurate with his abilities and achievement. There are a number of stock solutions in use in the schools to provide for differences in ability to learn. None of the solutions seems adequate to many teachers, and deep concerns persist. The leader of a recent experimental program of in-service education[2] was able to capitalize on these concerns with a number of teachers who were eager to work together for a long period of time on specific problems connected with grouping of students within a single class.

The experiment cited also met the second test of the significance of a problem. Teachers participating in the in-service activities formulated many action ideas which they tried out immediately with their own classes. The trial experiences in classrooms were then analyzed by the total group.

Another illustration will be used to show somewhat dramatically how a solution to a problem was demanded by the exigencies of the situation. One of the schools participating in the Regional Project in Secondary Education[3] decided to explore methods providing for greater articulation between the elementary and the secondary schools in the community. During preliminary meetings of the combined faculties of the two schools, a number of proposals were made. These proposals included the teaching of science to the seventh and eighth grades by the principal of the high school and the training of the high-school band by the elementary-school principal. But even with the introduction of comparable salary schedules in both the elementary- and the high-school districts, teachers in the two schools were slow to suggest further ways in which co-operation might take place.

However, a few days before school was to open for the following year, the elementary school was completely destroyed by fire. The rate of co-operation changed abruptly. Immediately, members of the high-school faculty volunteered with suggestions that made it possible for a number of elementary classes to be held in the high-school buildings. In October of the same year, when the director of the Regional Project visited the community, there was little evidence to indicate that the disaster was hampering teaching in either school.

2. Clement Albert Long, "An Analysis of In-service Education Procedures Used in Introducing Grouping Methods of Instruction in Secondary Schools." Unpublished Doctor's dissertation, University of California, Berkeley, 1954.

3. T. Bentley Edwards, *The Regional Project in Secondary Education.* Berkeley: University of California Press, 1956.

In addition to the basic idea that the success of in-service education activities depends upon people working on problems that are significant to them, there are many reasons why the effectiveness is further increased if the work is done in groups.

First, it has been demonstrated that group decisions help individuals achieve behavior change. This is in accord with the psychological findings presented in chapter iv and with other recent research.

Second, in many school situations action must be taken to implement decisions made on a subjective basis. If a number of people work on a problem, their cumulative resources result in a partial objectivity. In the absence of the kind of data which make possible an objective decision, relying upon the validity of group decisions reduces risks.

Third, activities by a group result in greater resources being available for use in all aspects of the problem-solving process. Each member of a group is superior to others in some respects. The experience and resources of all are richer than those of any one member. The group as a whole can develop a more feasible solution for a problem than can its "best" member.

There is still another reason why many important decisions should be made by a group rather than by an individual and why the decisions should be by consensus instead of simple majority vote. This reason lies in the need the school has for continuity and stability. This may seem an odd statement in a book concerned with change, but it is consistent with what has been said previously. Individuals, great or small, come and go, but the life of an institution, like a school, is usually as long as that of the community it serves. Such an institution must provide a stable platform from which new vistas can be clearly viewed. To a large extent the oscillations that characterize an individual are smoothed out when the same individual forms a part of a group. But stability does not mean rigidity, and continuity is a long way from conformity.

An implication of the proposition that people work as individuals and as members of groups on problems significant to them is the need of *all* professional members of the school staff for in-service education. This includes the top-status groups among school people; the administrators, the supervisors, and the university professors also need in-service education.

Some professional organizations are aware of this need. The Michigan Association of Secondary-School Administrators, for example, has organized and conducted for a number of years several annual workshops for status leaders engaged in teaching. Recently, in San Francisco, one hundred northern California secondary-school administrators worked in small groups for one week on problems of immediate significance to them. Some forty public school administrators and staff members of the state department of public instruction have arranged for the University of California to assist them in keeping up with educational research in regular sessions of an informal seminar.

Guideline II: The Same People Who Work on Problems Formulate Goals and Plan How They Will Work

Determination of need or identification of the problem is only a starting point for planning a course of action. Selection of the most appropriate procedures for planning demands careful consideration of the goals of the planning. Another way of saying the same thing is to say that ends and means are so intimately related that they are almost inseparable. Surely, there are instances in which means become ends and vice versa. Hence, choice of procedure is a context problem just as much as is the determination of the need. Coffey and Golden have made it clear in chapter iv that the relationship between procedures and goals is very close.

This relationship is often overlooked, and people in status positions are tempted into authoritarian statements regarding the procedures to be used in the solution of a problem. This temptation may be particularly strong when the status leader has recently attended a conference or workshop at which he has been favorably impressed by the successful use of a given procedure.

In connection with group work there is a long tradition that elaborate rules of order are essential. Some groups go so far as to elect a parliamentarian along with a chairman. Like the inexperienced traffic policeman, this official sometimes manages to reduce accidents by bringing all useful activity to a dead stop. Insistence on rigid rules of procedure often hampers the desirable psychological growth that was described in the preceding chapter.

Many productive in-service education groups plan their own procedures. For example,[4] a weekly workshop formed by the managerial staff of the Pacific Telephone Company in a southern California community was concerned with the human-relations difficulties regarding the adolescent worker just out of high school. In this workshop, the members, after identifying the problems regarding supervision and the young worker, created, under leadership, the techniques of study and the programs for each of the sessions devoted to discussion of these problems. Special surveys, studies, and projects were all conceived and carried out by one or more members of the workshop. The resulting data were utilized extensively in the workshop meetings.

Suggesting that groups determine their own procedures does not mean that the leader of a group is free of the responsibility of suggesting both goals and means of achieving goals. Often, a group will welcome a suggested procedure or a goal as being particularly appropriate. One procedure that has been found effective on a number of occasions results in the "bulge" or broken-front approach to instructional improvement. This procedure obtains when groups are encouraged to concentrate on limited goals or areas of school improvement. The school faculty is not asked in a teachers' meeting to "go to work on the school curriculum." Because of the complexities and ramifications of so broad a front, the group, even though its individual members may be highly skilled, often dissipates its energies and motivations trying to get started.

An illustration of a wise refusal to try to do everything all at once was the decision of the faculty of the Galt High School in California to begin with selected reading problems in the ninth grade. A special reading class was organized, and a committee, led by the teachers of the class, worked out new procedures for reading instruction in this class. Soon, the members of the committee were using improved techniques with their regular classes. These techniques included the use of three or four sets of instructional materials of varying levels of difficulty, the use of some free-reading time,

4. Described by Professor Donald McNassor, Claremont Graduate School, in a personal letter.

the limited development of projects so that where an interest in reading was lacking it could be developed, and especially the testing of all reading material to make sure that the level of difficulty corresponded to the reading ability of the class that was making use of the material.

In due course, this concentration on a limited objective had pervasive consequences. Teachers of other subjects became interested in reading problems, and eventually all textbooks used in the school were checked for reading difficulty. A number were found inappropriate and were discarded. Later, tests of reading difficulty were applied to selected library books.

Guideline III: Many Opportunities Are Developed for People To Relate Themselves to Each Other

The goal of any in-service education program is desirable change within an institutional system. Without doubt, the nature and quality of interpersonal relations in the system are determining factors in success or failure to achieve change. (See chap. iv.) This means that how people relate themselves to each other is a crucial dimension of any in-service education activity.

Probably the most available and effective way for people to relate themselves to each other in an in-service education program is in small problem-centered groups as suggested in the first guideline. There are other effective ways. One whose advantages are frequently overlooked makes use of the small-group approach, but the groups are not problem-centered in the usual sense of the expression. They are concerned with the development of appreciation in art, music, literature, and other related fields.

Not all persons do their best work in a relatively large-group situation. Some work most effectively as a subcommittee of two or three persons. Others are most effective if permitted to work most of the time by themselves with infrequent group contacts. Insight concerning a new solution to an old problem often comes to an individual when he is away from the distraction of other personalities.

In many schools there is a general faculty meeting only every month or two. Small faculty teams of four to eight people deal with most of the specific instructional problems—appraisal of core, student activity planning, development of work-study programs, case conferences on students with difficult problems, or planning for spring programing of students. When the total faculty meets, it usually is in a workshop dealing with some of the all-school instructional or administrative problems.

Considerable opportunity for people to relate themselves to each other occurs in completely informal contacts. Much progress toward the solution of a problem may take place when two or more people meet casually, in the hall between classes, in the cafeteria for coffee or lunch, while riding to and from school, or even during the pauses at a track meet.

Guideline IV: Continuous Attention Is Given to Individual and to Group Problem-solving Processes

The in-service program in any school system will be more productive if the staff includes one or more persons capable of providing expert help in individual and group problem-solving processes. Such help is needed to reassure and to assist the group as it experiences the confusion and frustration common to getting started and to moving ahead.

The leader of a group, especially, and all members of a group, generally, share the responsibility of helping the members keep process, content, and context related. If the activities of a group are to result in changed behavior, means and ends need to be consistent. Clearly formulated purposes must evolve for each procedure and resource.

A group that is concerned with changes in behavior will not likely succeed if it continuously keeps its feelings "under wraps." Sooner or later, if communication of deep significance is to take place, feeling as well as thinking must be expressed. Unless all members of the group develop considerable insight into the nature of communication of both thinking and feeling, there is a serious danger that not only will one or two members of the group withdraw temporarily damaged but that the entire group will break up, with permanent damage to the total school situation.

Serious emotional problems in small-group work can occasionally be traced to infection by a single individual. Retention of this person in the group after his trouble-making propensity has been diagnosed may not always be in the best interests of the group. Unless he can be provided with an opportunity to withdraw gracefully, the safest procedure may be for the group to disband and to start again. Further clues for achieving participation and collaboration by the trouble-maker must be discovered and utilized.

Just as group action is needed to take care of those members who get into emotional difficulties, it is also needed to change the member who monopolizes the discussion. There are always reasons for extreme volubility. One may be a conscious desire to thwart the group. Another may be a feeling of insecurity on the part of the talkative person. If the flow of words results only because the person feels, perhaps for the first time, exhilaratingly free from undue restraint, the group had better wait until the torrent subsides.

There is no one pattern or set of logical and sequential steps of problem-solving processes. Each group should make its own plans and possibly may not use the same procedures more than once or twice. This is true because group goals, ideals, and materials, as well as the perceptions of individual group members, are always changing. Each group and each individual must, however, include in the plan of operation continuous attention to the improvement of problem-solving procedures. Analysis and planning may well include (*a*) the creation of dissatisfaction as a result of a disparity between what *is* and what someone thinks *should be; (b)* assessment of the situation, including both the "is" and the "should be" elements; (*c*) guesses as to what may be done to bring the "is" and the "should be" together; (*d*) appraisal of the guesses and the selection of paths of action; (*e*) testing the actions selected in the reality contexts that are appropriate; and (*f*) reassessment of the situation. Each in-service group will find it rewarding to make the study of the group and its operations an integral part of its functioning. Analysis of the available research and of experience suggests that this should include critical assessment of the following more specific aspects of problem-solving:

1. Do we have realistic goals?
2. Are we working on specific problems?
3. Are we moving from identification of problems to an attack upon a problem?
4. Are we utilizing all potential resources—group members, consultants, research, facts, feelings, experience, opinions?

5. Are we planning and utilizing a variety of procedures?
6. Are we achieving variety in the role structure in the group?
7. What are our strengths and weaknesses in communication?
8. Have we agreed upon methods of making decisions?
9. Have we developed means of assimilating new members and late arrivals?
10. Are we studying the relationships of our groups to all related individuals and groups?
11. Have we perfected means of moving from decisions into action?
12. Are we making evaluation, testing, and assessment of consequences significant at all times?
13. Are we accepting the facts of differences in perceptions of group members?

Guideline V: Atmosphere Is Created That Is Conducive to Building Mutual Respect, Support, Permissiveness, and Creativeness

Individuals who are reasonably secure through their knowledge of the school system, and who are accepted by their associates, usually participate freely in the activities of the school system. Where such security is lacking, care must be taken by the other members of the staff to develop it.

Those members who already feel secure should be led to accept responsibility, to take initiative, and to provide leadership for others. The best way to make sure that they will continue to act in this positive fashion is to make sure that their initial steps bring them a feeling of achievement. Few things are more frustrating to the members of a group than to have their suggestions continually ignored by the administration. Even where a group is functioning well, on the whole, there may be an individual who attends meetings and goes through the motions but who is not one of the group. Eventually, such a person may create difficulty. He should either be drawn positively into the group or be permitted (encouraged, if necessary) to withdraw.

There are others who can upset a group. There are status people, such as administrators, heads of departments, and supervisors, who are able to keep the other members of the group from giving deference to their status. Many people in status positions function well in a group situation with people over whom they have administrative authority. But to do so is not easy. No significant discussion can be

expected unless group members feel free to express their true meanings and feelings rather than compelled to say what is expected from
them.

When a group of social-science teachers at Colusa, California,
were meeting weekly to develop improvements in the social-science
program, the meetings seemed heavily loaded with people in status
positions. The school principal, the vice-principal, and two people
from the county office were always present. Consultants from
various sources were invited from time to time. Yet, this group was
highly successful. In a sense, the status people took care of each
other. But in the opinion of one observer, part of the credit for success should go to the discussion-leader who was from the county
office. His technique was to wait for the teachers to start the ball
rolling, to pay deference to them as the real experts in the program,
and to interrupt quickly when one of the status-leaders began to
lecture. Because the agenda were being built as the meetings pro-
gressed, this technique was easily used. For example, the discussion-
leader, having himself suggested a certain film, would ask the teachers the next week how it worked, and they would tell him. Another
part of the credit must go to the principal and the vice-principal of
the school, who, over a long period of time, had developed the kind
of human relations among staff members that seems to encourage the
use of co-operative procedures.

These co-operative procedures are used to release the power of a
group and of the individuals in the group. They can be used at
faculty meetings, in workshops, in study groups, and in individual
conferences. People of widely different philosophies, educational
background, and value systems can function together through these
co-operative procedures when they are appropriately used. Basic to
the use of democratic procedures is a functioning acceptance of the
worth of each individual.

Guideline VI: Multiple and Rich Resources Are Made Available and Are Used

In almost every type of in-service education activity there is need
for three kinds of resource assistance. The first has to do with the
content of the instructional problem being considered; the second,

with human relations and co-operative group-operations skills; and the third, with problem-solving methodology.

Suggestions of a creative nature may be found in unexpected places. New teachers, students, custodians, parents, and other citizens should be canvassed for suggestions. Resource people available on a given school staff, unless they happen to be working members of a group, are often overlooked.

Upon one occasion the director of the California Regional Project in Secondary Education travelled 250 miles, much of it through winter snow on mountain roads, to find that one group was held up in its activity through the need of a resource that was available right in the school. A teacher of English wished to make use of a recording of certain symphonic music. The shop teacher, an ardent listener, had tape recorded this particular music, and much more besides.

One of the difficulties with making effective use of the findings of educational research as a resource is that, doing so, involves so much time and material. Some persons, related to the group, should be responsible for adequate summaries, criticisms, and, if need be, explanations of pertinent research. Lists of appropriate instructional materials, textbooks, reference books, films, charts, and other audio-visual material should be available in similar fashion. Other educational literature, because of its range, or because of its rarity, should also be summarized in a usable fashion. Usually a subcommittee or a single member of the committee can be assigned a task of this kind. Other individual tasks might include the checking of proposals in the light of known facts concerning psychology and sociology. A person thoroughly familiar with both method and content in man's exploration of his physical environment is often valuable. Occasionally, people familiar with classical solutions to social problems are equally useful.

Groups of teachers who have developed a useful set of procedures in one curriculum area can sometimes be used as resource persons in another area. For example, a group of science teachers who have developed new ways of meeting individual differences in the classroom might sit in with a group of social-studies teachers engaged in working on the same problem.

An excellent example of the use of elementary teachers as resource people in the teaching of reading is described by a junior high school curriculum assistant[5] in Oakland, California:

We decided that we should have a series of meetings devoted to the reading and spelling problems and knew we needed help. We felt that we must do something to learn more about elementary-school techniques since most of our faculty had not been trained in such methods.

It was through an elementary supervisor that three elementary teachers were selected to come to the first three meetings. One person from each of three grade cycles came to the first meeting, bringing with him charts and all sorts of displays for demonstrating the many methods used in building word-recognition. These teachers took us step by step through the various grades, showing how reading is approached at the different age and maturity levels. I saw people on our faculty reaching for paper and pencil and taking notes rapidly as our guests spoke. Shop-men, art and home-economics teachers, and all the others reported, both then and later, that this was one of the best faculty meetings they had ever attended.

Our second meeting was devoted to hearing a senior-high teacher tell us how she teaches high-school students to search for the main idea, the central thought of a paragraph. She used us as her class and took us step by step through a lesson based upon a selection in a literature book.

Experiences recounted by the Division of Special Services of the Oakland Public Schools provides an illustration of another way of using resource personnel in the case conference:

Consultants in the individual guidance department are specialist advisers to teachers and principals with regard to the social and emotional adjustment of pupils. They have in-service education staff-meetings with a part-time consulting psychiatrist once a month.

A consultant presents a case about which he wants interpretation as to behavior dynamics, advice as to school management, and pos-sible referral. Cases selected involve various kinds of problems and different schools and grade levels. The psychiatrist, co-ordinator, all consultants (eight on staff), a psychologist, and a school principal are present at each meeting. Where other school personnel have particular knowledge of or interest in the case and can contribute to the presentation, they are invited to attend. Frequently the teacher or counselor is invited. Usually one or more of the following are in-

5. Muriel Arends, Woodrow Wilson Junior High School, personal letter.

cluded: instructional supervisor, school nurse, speech teacher, special supervisors.

The case presented is planned and directed by one of the consultants. Facts and observations about the child, school situation, and home are presented by the consultant, principal, psychologist, and possibly others. There follows a general discussion, led by the psychiatrist, of interpretation and suggestions for follow-up. The psychiatrist then summarizes the discussion, gives interpretation of the child's problems, suggests diagnosis and prognosis, and recommends next steps in school handling and possible treatment referral.

A persisting problem in all in-service education activities is that of making existing resources rapidly available to groups in usable form. Possibly more school systems need to expand the idea of a professional library to include work "studios" as a place for groups to work together. Each "studio" could be planned for efficient and attractive organization of materials with which to work, and certain individuals could accept the responsibility for assembling the appropriate materials. Also, the possibilities of making resources accessible at every school site, rather than in central locations, needs to be explored extensively.

Those who work directly with the school as consultants are often surprised at the lack of interrelationships established among members of different educational agencies such as state departments of education, county offices of education, district offices of education, college and university faculties, and the faculties of high schools and elementary schools. In some large co-operative endeavors, such as the Illinois Curriculum Program (see chap. vi) and the Regional Project in Secondary Education in California, improved liaison between the various educational agencies has been established. Perhaps part of the difficulty grows out of the fact that administrators, teachers, supervisors, superintendents, and curriculum co-ordinators hold separate conferences and conventions.

Even though lack of communication between members of the various educational bodies may sometimes be excused, there is little excuse for a lack of close understanding between administrators and curriculum committees in a given school system. Even though administrators are unable to attend all meetings of curriculum committees, they should receive, read, and, in general, act upon the contents of detailed reports sent them by curriculum committees.

Guideline VII: The Simplest Possible Means Are Developed To Move through Decisions to Actions

This yearbook is concerned largely with the use of the group attack on school problems as a major technique of in-service education. Decisions must be made and actions taken by a group of people to solve a common problem. These operations are required in specific contexts in which people perceive themselves and other members of the group differently, when basic value systems are far from uniform, and varying degrees of significance are attached to statistically reported conditions.

To reach a shared decision, effective two-way communication is imperative. Participants must constantly test their listeners to be sure that what is understood by the listener is reasonably close to what is meant by the speaker. Such testing is much easier in a face-to-face situation than when communication is attempted by writing and reading. The gesture, the tone of voice, the smile, or the pause are often significantly meaningful, but they do not accompany the written word.

For this reason, and because the administrators need to know what goes on in in-service groups, a verbal report to the administrators by a subcommittee is desirable when the administrators are unable to attend the meetings. Still another reason for verbal reports to the administrator is the need for speedy action.

Administrators who would like to see better teaching in their schools should not only be prepared to act quickly on the basis of decisions reached by committees they have set up but they should also be prepared to encourage teachers to experiment with new methods.

Too many in-service groups have had the experience of diligent work over a period of time resulting in specific action ideas and proposals that are filed away, never to be heard from again. Frequently, this is a result of the exercise of the veto power by someone who was not a working member of the group. Group decisions must be used, or good reasons presented for not using them, to maintain the interest and active participation of the members of the group. Clear-cut understanding of the operational procedures necessary to move from decisions into action in all in-service activities is an essential condition of continuing effectiveness.

Guideline VIII: Constant Encouragement Is Present To Test and To Try Ideas and Plans in Real Situations

The major purpose of all in-service education—improvement of the teaching-learning processes—must be kept vividly in mind. In all group and individual work, the planning and decision-making must be focused sharply on school practices in context. Vividness and realism can be achieved most easily when the plans are made close to the source of a problem. The growth of individuals and their development as resourceful members of groups are facilitated materially by resorting extensively to the idea, "I'll try that out by exploring and studying it in my school or classroom." For this reason, the individual school is probably the best unit for curriculum-planning and many other in-service education activities. Complete acceptance of this idea creates numerous hazards indicated by the generalization of Coffey and Golden, in chapter iv, that "internal stability within the system frequently desensitizes it to the environmental demands."

Members of a local group can pretest a proposed plan during discussion, for they alone can be aware of the relevant local facts. Incidentally, the advantages in this multiple testing-before-action of a proposed plan is one of the major reasons why thorough group discussion should precede the adoption of any course of action. A single individual, especially an authoritarian individual, just cannot think of all the alternatives.

It is only in a *school* setting that plans can finally be put into practice and tested in action. Consequently, in-service education programs that are to move beyond the talking stage require the presence of many individuals and groups that are testing and trying ideas in a reality context. This requires constant encouragement and support. In fact, an experimental climate can be built in a school, and it will do more to encourage a trying-and-testing approach than any other factor.

At times, curriculum revision has been attempted, using the district, the county, or the state as the operational unit. Committees of outstanding teachers have been called together to spend months drawing up elaborate courses of study which the large unit proceeded to publish at considerable expense. Many of these courses of study languished, unconsidered, in the desk drawers of the teachers to whom they were distributed. They fitted neither pupils nor teachers. The reason they did not fit the teachers was partly because the teachers, generally, had not worked through or tested in classrooms the logic and reasoning that went into the preparation of the course of study. Even with a close type of supervision, the teachers could never be brought to use the prepared course of study in the manner which was intended.

All these facts should not be interpreted to mean that no value should be attached to ready-made courses of study. On the contrary, such materials as those prepared at Louisville, Kentucky, and which are nationally known, can save the members of the local group hours and months of work. The point is that there must be a local group, and considerable activity on the part of the local group must precede any attempt to choose and use ready-made resources of this kind.

There is one other important dimension of the need to encourage the trying and testing of ideas in school settings. The value of group meetings of all kinds is enhanced if the members of the group are trying things out in their schools during the times between meetings of the group. The greatest weakness of the meetings of groups is often the fact that "nothing happens in between."

Guideline IX: Appraisal Is Made an Integral Part of In-service Activities

We engage in appraisal operations in in-service education activities in order to determine what and how much is being accomplished to contribute to the ongoing activity and to identify clues for the improvement of the in-service program. To accomplish these purposes it is necessary for appraisal to be an integral part of each activity and not "something added at the end." This is made clear in chapter xiv, which deals with the evaluation of the in-service education program.

The basis of any sound appraisal is the collection of factual and descriptive data rather than the organization and expression of value judgments. Thus, an observer interested in pupil-teacher planning may approach the gathering of data in at least two ways: He may observe the teaching-learning situation and jot down a note to the effect that the teacher-pupil planning was good or poor. He may gather specific data such as the ratio of teacher participation to pupil participation, kinds of social interactions in the situation, pupil roles and teacher roles in the planning process, and kinds of decision-making. In the first instance, the observer makes a value judgment without citing supporting factual data; in the second, he gathers factual data to which value judgments may be applied.

Eliminating value judgments from the collection of data requires a new orientation on the part of many teachers, supervisors, principals, and curriculum-workers. The two basic operations, the collecting of descriptive factual data and the making of value judgments, are facilitated by making them a normal part of every in-service activity. In fact, if appraisal is to contribute in any way to significant change, the principles of participation and collaboration supported in chapters iv and x must be utilized.

Resistance to appraisal is to be expected and must be overcome. The principal means for reducing resistance are (*a*) including all who are affected in the planning of appraisals, (*b*) doing a good job in communication, (*c*) making every effort to separate descriptive data from value judgments, and (*d*) making the application of value judgments a joint enterprise of all who are involved.

Guideline X: Continuous Attention Is Given to the Interrelationship of Different Groups

Every school and school system is a network of individuals and groups performing many functions—administrative, supervisory, guiding, teaching, and others. The performance of each individual and of each group is related in many ways to the functioning of all others. Frequently, there is added to this "regular" organization and structure numerous "special" in-service education activities such as institutes, committees, workshops, courses, and research projects. This creates three distinct sets of interrelationships of significance to the effectiveness of the in-service education program. Involved are those in the operation of the "regular" organization, those in the carrying out of the "special" activities, and those in the meshing of the "regular" with the "special." Are all phases of the three sets of interrelationships moving along smoothly, with economy of time, effort, and resources? Are all of the people who are involved aware of the specific interrelationships? Are there misunderstandings concerning who is doing what and why? Is one individual or a group undoing the work of others?

In addition to the three sets of interrelationships listed above, there is another resulting from the membership of individuals in both "informal" and "formal" groups. Formal groups organized as a part of the in-service education program of a school system are made up of individuals who are also enjoying participation in a number of informal groups that may exert considerable influence for change or for resistance to change. The impact of the informal groups frequently is not communicated openly to the formal-group operation. To find ways to increase communication between the informal and the formal groups is to increase effectiveness materially.

One of the problems of interrelationships that was presented in the development of Guideline VIII needs to be emphasized here. This refers to relationships between in-service activities under way in specific schools and those conducted on a system-wide basis. The need for in-service education certainly must vary somewhat from school to school in any system. The most appropriate means of achieving growth must be, in part, a function of a specific school situation and the people who work there. This could mean that solutions for some of the problems of interrelationships between the activities operating on a system-wide basis and those in a specific school are to be found in deliberately planning the system-wide activities to support and to supplement those in the individual schools.

Guideline XI: The Facts of Individual Differences among Members of Each Group Are Accepted and Utilized

It is to be assumed that any time a group of people is assembled for a particular purpose there will be differences among the individual members. The possible differences have been catalogued in many different ways and need not be reviewed here.

The individual differences of most import in in-service education groups are probably those having to do with the values, concepts of role, attitudes toward change, skill in human relations, and knowledge of various aspects of education.

The fact that some group members seem to be categorically opposed to change is often turned to advantage. The whetstone of their criticism sharpens the eventual decision to the point where implementation of the decision is often facilitated.

Many teachers who oppose change do so because of the way in which they perceive themselves. Instead of thinking of themselves as guides to the learning of immature young people, they may think of themselves as primarily scholars. This perception of self will powerfully influence their behavior as well as that of those who are working with them.

The leader who believes firmly in co-operative processes will accept all people as they are, including their self-perceptions. Like other members of the group, he has the obligation to present his point of view, but he must not attempt to coerce nor to take advantage of any authority he may possess either from the status of his position or from the popularity of his point of view. His logic, his knowledge of the facts, or his own feelings about the matter should win its own place.

The fact that self-perceptions are apt to be vague and unrealistic provides another reason for using a group of people to reach a decision. As an individual thinks and plans a possible solution to a problem, he cannot foresee accurately the effect of the solution upon himself. As to the effect upon others, he can only guess. When a number of individuals participate in the thinking and planning, it is often possible to determine the effects upon another person.

Each member of a group must try to be aware of the self-perceptions of all members of the group, to see the problem through their eyes, and to learn from them what the effect of a decision will be upon them. Both of these difficult tasks are extremely significant as means of keeping threats to the security of each member of the group within reasonable limits.

Resistance to change is normal and is to be expected. Acceptance of individual differences in self-concept, concepts of roles, and resistance to change require nonjudgmental, supportive, permissive attitudes which will encourage individual progress through the verbalization of formal problems and stereotyped answers to real expression of feelings.

Guideline XII: Activities Are Related to Pertinent Aspects
of the Current Educational, Cultural, Political,
and Economic Scene

The importance of relating all activities of an educational nature have been urged frequently. The picture of the P.T.A. working off by itself in one corner, the teachers in another, and the principals in a third is one that must be erased from the educational canvas. Instead, the work of all service groups needs to be carefully meshed with the organization and procedures of a given school or district.

From community to community the cultural, political, and economic scene shows wide variation not only in degree but often in the basic facts. In-service activities and programs cannot possibly achieve their goals except as they are solidly based upon educational, cultural, political, and economic realities. In public education there is a continuing need for men and women who can imagine better educational, social, economic, and political conditions. This need must be accepted and provided for in a variety of ways.

We have said that the school, like the society it serves, must have effective degrees of stability and continuity. One of the reasons for the formation of groups is the need to hold fast to, and to improve, that which is good in the schools. In a discussion of several of the guidelines, the importance of having conservative members in a group has been suggested, and ways in which the point of view of such members can be used by the group have been listed. There is little danger that the point of view of those who resist change will be overlooked. The emotional needs of this group are powerful. They produce a stubborn vigor that the purveyor of new ideas can seldom match, at least not over a prolonged period. Yet the new ideas are needed. They are needed in the school and they are needed in our society as never before. The old ideas alone will neither save us from destruction nor help us achieve our goals.

The group that is ready to welcome new political, economic, or cultural ideas into the discussion can realize that all new ideas seem odd at first. Newland was howled out of the Royal Society when he first suggested grouping the chemical elements into some sort of periodical system. Lister was bitterly ridiculed when he first suggested that obstetricians ought to wash up a bit after one patient before going on to the next. Few things can kill a new idea faster than ridicule, and some people can detect ridicule in a strained silence or a lifted eyebrow. We have not time to wait twenty years while we slowly recognize a new Mendel.

On some occasions, a clash may be needed to strike the creative spark. Such a clash should be of opinion. Personal clashes are usually a negative force in the group process. At the time it must be pointed out that group participation means emotional reaction at some point. What was said previously concerning unity in the decision is true. Nothing is settled once and for all by taking a vote. Such a procedure merely indicates where people are at the moment. Sooner or later the group must agree on something.

Cherished beliefs on the part of an individual, even religious beliefs, should not be considered unassailable. For instance, the member of a group who invokes a particular religious dogma as an authority upon which to base a decision should not go unchallenged. Any value must be weak, indeed, if it will not stand up under questioning.

Many problems call for courageous and ingenious solutions. A group can provide moral support, whereas an individual may hesitate to act upon a novel suggestion all by himself. Even where the members of a group do not agree to accept a suggestion of this kind, they should protect the one who made the suggestion. The group will not stay together long if statements made under the seal of the group are "used against the contributor."

Summary—An Illustration

The following brief description of a successful in-service education activity[6] will serve the purpose of illustrating and thus summarizing all of the guidelines at work in a single situation.

Fifteen teachers from several junior and senior high schools in a large city school system voluntarily accepted the invitation of a supervisor to work together in developing the use of grouping procedures within individual classes. While participating, the teachers actually used grouping methods of instruction in at least one class, met as a total group five times, were visited on several occasions during the semester by the supervisor, were provided with minutes of

6. Long, *op. cit.*

the group meetings, were furnished with bibliographies and references, were assisted in obtaining appropriate instructional materials, and were given the opportunity to observe other teachers.

The supervisor and the teachers agreed that all of them would study continuously the effectiveness of the project as in-service education. As a result of this agreement, the project was evaluated carefully by the total group with some assistance from a consultant.

The meetings of the entire group, the teachers' use of grouping methods in their own classrooms, and individual conferences with the supervisor were the three in-service procedures most frequently mentioned by the teachers as being "extremely helpful."

The major problems which the teachers encountered in changing to a new method of instruction involved: (*a*) materials and equipment, (*b*) methodology, (*c*) insecurities on the part of the teachers, (*d*) teacher-pupil relationships, (*e*) teacher-staff relationships.

The more important conclusions reached by the group were summarized as follows: (*a*) The in-service education activities aided teachers significantly in changing their methods of instruction. (*b*) It was not necessary to know all the answers or to have unalterable goals before attempting new procedures. (*c*) A spirit of experimentation was fostered both among the teachers and the pupils. (*d*) Teachers expected to inaugurate more procedures than they could handle at one time. (*e*) The importance of morale among the teachers was evident because the reinforcement derived from belonging to a supportive group was strong enough to overcome outside influences. (*f*) There was evidence of the need of support by the school administrators and other teachers. (*g*) In-service education programs are made up of various procedures and activities with many of them overlapping. (*h*) One of the most significant factors was the face-to-face relationship which led teachers to recognize that personal elements were paramount in achieving success. (*i*) The critical factor in the success of an in-service education activity is the direct relationship of the activity to the teacher's immediate situation—the classroom. (*j*) The most successful in-service education activities are action-centered in the school and in the classroom. (*k*) It is paramount that teachers do what they feel is necessary and that they have freedom to experiment.

A Final Word

One final word concerning in-service education activities—the goal is learning, change, improvement. Someone has to learn something if the activities are to be effective. This means that guidelines for planning, organizing, and conducting in-service education programs are based, of necessity, upon sound principles of learning.

REFERENCES

This reference list is included because it represents research that influenced the formulation of the guidelines. Evidence in support of each guideline is to be found in practically all of the references listed. Therefore, it was decided not to utilize the space necessary for exact citation or quotation.

ABRAHAM, SOLOMON. "Principles of Human Relations in Curriculum Improvement." Unpublished Doctor's dissertation, University of Pittsburgh, 1952.

BACON, WILLIAM PRATT. "A Preliminary Investigation of Training United States Air Force Student Officers in Small-Group Leadership through the Study of Group Dynamics." Unpublished Doctor's dissertation, University of California, Berkeley, 1953.

BARD, HARRY. "Development and Evaluation of the Baltimore Teachers In-service Community Study Program." Unpublished Doctor's dissertation, University of Maryland, 1951.

BEAUCHAMP, MARY. "An Exploratory Study of the Effects of an In-service Education Program on Group Processes in the Classroom." Unpublished Doctor's dissertation, New York University, 1952.

BURK, R. BURDETT. "A Study of In-service Education in Public Elementary Schools in Indiana." Unpublished Doctor's dissertation, University of Indiana, 1952.

BUSH, ROBERT N. The Teacher-Pupil Relationship. New York: Prentice-Hall, Inc., 1954.

Citizen Co-operation for Better Public Schools. Fifty-third Yearbook of the National Society for the Study of Education, Part I. Chicago: University of Chicago Press, 1954.

COREY, STEPHEN M. Action Research To Improve School Practices. New York: Teachers College, Columbia University, 1953.

EDGAR, ROBERT WILSON. "A Study of the Techniques and Procedures for Curriculum Improvement in the Great Neck Co-operative Survey." Unpublished Doctor's dissertation, Teachers College, Columbia University, 1949.

EDWARDS, T. BENTLEY. The Regional Project in Secodary Education. Berkeley: University of California Press, 1956.

GOLDEN, WILLIAM PATRICK, JR. "A Study of Human Relationships and Committee Processes on School Faculties." Unpublished Doctor's dissertation, University of California, Berkeley, 1951

Group Processes in Supervision. Washington: Association for Supervision and Curriculum Development of the National Education Association, 1948.

HALVERSON, PAUL M. "Group Maturity in Co-operative Curriculum Development." Unpublished Doctor's dissertation, Teachers College, Columbia University, 1952.

HARRISON, DONALD LEROY. "Curriculum Development Practices of the Office of the County Superintendent of Schools in California." Unpublished Doctor's dissertation, University of California, Berkeley, 1953.

HENDERSON, CLARA A. "An Evaluation of the Workshop Program for the In-service Teacher Education Directed by the Ohio State Department of Education, 1944–47." Unpublished Doctor's dissertation, Ohio State University, 1948.

HOPPE, ARTHUR A. "Student Participation in Curriculum Development in Secondary Schools." Unpublished Doctor's dissertation, Teachers College, Columbia University, 1947.

LONG, CLEMENT ALBERT. "An Analysis of In-service Education Procedures Used in Introducing Grouping Methods of Instruction in Secondary Schools." Unpublished Doctor's dissertation, University of California, Berkeley, 1954.

MACKENZIE, GORDON N., and COREY, STEPHEN M. *Instructional Leadership*. New York: Bureau of Publications, Teachers College, Columbia University, 1954.

McKEE, MARGARET. "An Evaluation of the Co-operative Study Group Plan on In-service Training for Teachers." Unpublished Doctor's dissertation, University of Pittsburgh, 1949.

McMAHON, LOIS GALLUP. "A Study of In-service Education Programs in Selected California Public School Systems." Unpublished Doctor's dissertation, University of California, Berkeley, 1954.

MICHELL, FOREST C. "The Effect of Participation in a Summer Workshop upon Selected Classroom Practices." Unpublished Doctor's dissertation, University of California, Berkeley, 1951.

MYERS, CHARLES LINCOLN. "Influences on the Learning Situation of Selected and Planned Teacher-Knowledge of Students." Unpublished Doctor's dissertation, University of California, Berkeley, 1952.

PARKER, J. CECIL. "The Alameda Mental Health Institute—An Evaluation." California Co-operative Study of In-service Education. Berkeley: University of California, 1951 (mimeographed).

———. "Evaluating Improvement Programs," *Action for Curriculum Improvement,* chap. vi. 1951 Yearbook of the Association for Supervision and Curriculum Development. Washington: Association for Supervision and Curriculum Development of the National Education Association, 1951.

PARKER, J. CECIL, and GOLDEN, WILLIAM P., JR. "In-service Education of Elementary- and Secondary-School Teachers," *Review of Educational Research,* XXII (June, 1952), 193–200.

REID, CHANDOS. "A Study of Teachers' Problems Resulting from New Practices in Curriculum and Teaching Procedures in Selected Secondary Schools." Unpublished Doctor's dissertation, Northwestern University, 1943.

RICE, THEODORE D. "Co-operative Planning and Teaching in Curriculum Activities in Certain Secondary Schools." Unpublished Doctor's dissertation, Northwestern University, 1943.

SAYLOR, GAYLEN C. "Factors Associated with Participation in Co-operative Programs of Curriculum Development." Unpublished Doctor's dissertation, Columbia University, 1942.

SHANKS, ROBB L. "Professional In-service Improvement of Teachers in Missouri." Unpublished Doctor's dissertation, University of Missouri, 1952.

TODD, ROBERT BAXTER. "A Study of Changes in Specific Teacher Behaviors Concurrent with Participation on a Curriculum Committee." Unpublished Doctor's dissertation, University of California, Berkeley, 1955.

TOULOUSE, ROBERT B. "An Analysis of the Secondary-School Curriculum Improvement Policies and Practices of States and Cities." Unpublished Doctor's dissertation, University of Missouri, 1948.

WANN, KENNETH D. "Teacher Participation in Action Research Directed toward Curriculum Change." Unpublished Doctor's dissertation, Teachers College, Columbia University, 1950.

WILLARD, RUTH ARLYN. "A Study of the Relationships between the Valued-Behaviors of Selected Teachers and the Learning Experiences Provided in Their Classrooms." Unpublished Doctor's dissertation, University of California, Berkeley, 1952.

SECTION II

ROLES OF TEACHERS, ADMINISTRATORS, AND CONSULTANTS

CHAPTER VI

The Teachers and the In-service Education Program

B. JO KINNICK

assisted by

VIRGINIA BONEY, ELIZABETH A. HUNTINGTON, ROBERT T. RASMUSSEN,
SHIRLEY A. SIMON, NICHOLAS G. TACINAS,
and ELIZABETH ZIMMERMAN

This chapter has been prepared in order to report the way a group of classroom teachers react to the conceptions about in-service education as they are developed in the early chapters of this yearbook. There is no need to stress the importance of the teacher's point of view. Unless it is favorable, or quickly becomes favorable, in-service education is in trouble.

The Role of the Administrator

It is important to teachers that in-service education should be generally accepted as a program by which people engaged in education learn and grow together. Teachers tend to resent and to reject any program of in-service education which is presented as a program planned by administrators and required of teachers so that they may make up their deficiencies.

One has only to sit in on a few beginning classes of college summer-session courses engaged in discussing in-service education to discover how many school administrators believe that such education is only for teachers and is necessary only because the teacher or his professional preparation is deficient in some respect. Very often the administrator is convinced that the teacher is in need of treatment and that the main problem is to persuade him to participate periodically in the in-service education activities until he achieves a state of professional health identical, perhaps, to that which the administrator has always maintained without treatment.

An interested, sympathetic administrator is necessary to the success of all programs of in-service education. Without such an administrator, the most elaborately planned in-service experiences produce little growth in individual teachers. With such a leader, a faculty pot-luck supper or even a few minutes of conversation in the lunchroom between teachers or between teachers and principal may prove to be valuable in-service education.

In-service Growth and Attacks on Teachers

A need of teachers in connection with genuine in-service growth, and a need not touched upon in either chapter iv or v of this yearbook, is the need for peace, or at least a cessation of hostilities on the part of public and professional critics who for the past decade have waged relentless war against the schools and the teachers and have questioned everything about us from our intelligence to our professional fitness, to our morals, to our patriotism. There are no game laws to protect teachers such as those which protect the squirrel and the deer by labeling some seasons closed to those who would hunt them. The teacher is fair game in any season.

The specialist in most fields gets credit from his public at some time for something. The teacher too often is held responsible only for failures; parents usually claim credit for the teacher's successes.

The greenest recruit is aware that an army cannot fight both a defensive and an offensive action simultaneously on the same front. The sooner we can divert our energies from self-defense to the exploration of new ways to effective teaching in the classroom, the sooner the guidelines of chapter v will be put into action.

Working on Problems Significant to Individuals

How do professional problems attain significance for the individual teacher and for groups of teachers? If they gain significance because of leadership, then surely interpersonal relationships among teachers and between teachers and administrators must be friendly and understanding, and the leadership which emerges must be creative and sincere.

Unless teachers help in the identification of their problems and plan how they will work on those problems, in-service experiences presented to teachers are likely to be the same for all and of little practical help to anyone. Are the same problems significant to teachers at successive stages of their professional life or do individual differences exist among teachers as well as among pupils? If teachers' problems are somewhat developmental in pattern, and many teachers feel that they are, then schools need in-service programs which provide for this diversity of needs. Beginning teachers want in-service experiences which help them to relate and integrate ideas and ideals of teaching with the realities and the day-to-day demands of the job. They need experiences which will help them remodel their ivory towers into practical two-room apartments.

Often, in the first confusing days with a full teaching schedule, a beginning teacher welcomes the "buddy" system which enables her, without embarrassment, to discuss school administrative procedures or lesson plans with the more experienced teacher across the hall. Many times the experienced teacher, new to a particular school, enjoys the buddy system too and is more quickly and comfortably integrated into the life of the new school because of it.

Teachers agree that in-service experiences should be planned also to meet the needs of the teacher who is older, at least in terms of years of service, and who is concerned about how to maintain a fresh, vital attitude toward teaching.

What in-service experiences would help to salvage the occasional teacher who seems to feel that as soon as she gets tenure she does not need to grow any more, whose relationships with other teachers calcify, and whose teaching continues day after day in a pattern of unrelieved monotony? What can awaken such a teacher? How can she be made once more a growing, sharing member of the school community?

Surely in-service education programs should be diversified and developmental. They may include workshops, institutes, exchange visits to classrooms, lectures, panels, demonstrations, lesson-planning sessions, and school surveys. Some of these activities may be carried on as parts of regular faculty meetings.

An excellent addition to most in-service programs would be a reading program; not to train teachers in the techniques for teaching reading, necessary as such training is, but to give them the time and the environment essential for professional reading. New materials and related materials in various subject-matter fields would be circulated to schools, and teachers would be given free time in a quiet, library environment to examine those materials, to reflect upon them, and perhaps to take notes.

Teachers working together have done the best job in identifying the problems of various teacher types so that in-service experiences can be planned to help each of them. Some experiences, such as the reading program, would benefit all teachers, but many teachers need special experiences. The individual teacher is often the last to identify her special needs because, by such identification, her concept of self and her security may seem threatened.

From time to time in-service programs do originate with individual teachers as they recognize the need for change and improvement. Often, however, an individual will not recognize a school-wide problem as such, and attention will be directed to such a problem by the principal or it will be identified in group discussion. The role of the classroom teacher in any in-service program may be as originator and leader, as a participating member, or as a group consultant.

The teacher's willingness to serve in any of these roles is largely dependent upon good group relations and upon freedom of communication within groups of teachers and between teachers and administrators. The success of the teachers' participation is in direct relation to the atmosphere of mutual respect which exists within the groups and between the groups and the status leader.

From Problems to Ways of Working

How teachers may move from identification of problems to formulation of plans for working on those problems is well illustrated by a recent in-service education program undertaken in DeKalb County, Georgia.

One faculty held several discussion meetings to identify major problems. Consensus was reached that, school-wide, the greatest need was an improved reading program. The faculty suggested possible ways of attacking the problem. Following the discussions, a steering committee was set up to arrange for the needed consultants and to help co-ordinate the program. The principal attended all meetings except those of the steering committee, and he was kept informed of all plans. The steering committee worked with the county office to get personnel and other needed resources.

When members of the steering committee learned through the county office that another school had adopted a school-wide reading program, and that it had been in operation for some time, teachers from that school were invited to tell about their program and to evaluate it. When a teacher who had studied with recognized authorities on reading was called in to work with the planners, she helped devise a reading program of testing and of grouping within the classroom.

Teachers held several discussions on reading and reading problems. Primary teachers, with their special training in the teaching of reading, were a valuable resource for these discussions. The program was not rushed. There were no pressures for results or for faster acceptance of a working plan. By consensus, teachers accepted the program of grouping within grades as suggested by leading reading authorities.

The first step in the program was to administer the Kuhlmann-Fink intelligence test to each pupil in the school. The administering, scoring, and interpreting of the test results required study and problem-solving on the part of teachers. Two faculty members who were skilled in the techniques of testing helped other teachers.

Following directions of the reading consultant, teachers compiled individual reading inventories to determine the independent reading level, the instructional reading level, and the frustration level, as well as the comprehension level of each pupil in the school. The reading consultant demonstrated how to administer and to interpret the test.

By this time the school year was over, but teachers felt that they were making definite progress. Evaluation showed that teachers were still agreed upon reading as the most urgent problem in the school, and they were still agreed upon the method of solution.

At the beginning of the next year, after a short orientation of new teachers, the program was started again. Some teachers still felt insecure when givng the individual tests, so one teacher gave a demonstration test. Then all went to work. Although they were time-consuming, the tests revealed much, and they proved highly valuable in diagnosing reading problems and in providing a basis for grouping. In the tests were found implications for study skills in other areas, and the urgent need for a program of reading for meaning became apparent.

Individual reading inventory tests as well as intelligence tests were filed with the cumulative records of the pupils, and the principal now uses the compiled results as a basis for study.

Although primary teachers found grouping and the handling of groups no problem, upper-grade teachers felt insecure in organizing and in working with groups. To allay this insecurity, the county office arranged to have a consultant spend a day in the school giving demonstrations in grouping and in the teaching of reading at all grade levels. These demonstrations helped to build confidence.

After the ground work was laid and the program was in progress, periodical evaluations were undertaken. Now, each year, a period of orientation for new teachers is provided. The list of all basic and supplementary readers, prepared by teachers and placed in each child's permanent record, indicates readers which the child has studied and, from year to year, serves as a guide to assist teachers in grouping and in the selection of further reading materials for each child.

It is interesting to note that when the reading program described here reached a point of functioning in the individual classroom, teachers began to look around for another school-wide problem.

The finest testimonial to the effectiveness of strong teacher participation in the identification of school problems and in formulation of plans for problem-solving is the increased professional spirit which such participation fosters.

A number of research studies indicate that the best way to change behavior is by group decision. But what sort of group makes the decision? The question of the efficiency of informal groups versus formal groups as agents of change inevitably confronts us. We need to think seriously about the question so that we may set up groups in in-service education which will work actively to promote change.

In-service Activities for Groups and Individuals

Again we maintain that the individual differences of teachers should be respected. Teachers need to be free to choose the group in which they wish to work. This freedom implies having a part in setting up all the groups and in helping to decide when and for how long they should meet. Finally, it includes individual choice of the group of which each person wishes to be a part. More than this, teachers need freedom to participate to the extent to which they feel capable and inspired and in a manner appropriate both to them and to the group.

Right here it may be well to say that many teacher groups seem to value mere quantity of verbal participation in group discussion too highly. The contribution of the quiet group member who sorts his thoughts well before speaking and measures his words as he speaks may be the most positive and the most useful contribution. Often the candid soul who admits that he knows little about the problem and therefore asks questions which others may answer renders a distinct service in giving the group a feeling of mutual helpfulness. All kinds of teacher personalities can help the group operate more effectively, and, the greater the atmosphere of acceptance, the greater the "group" feeling, the more probability there is that the group will work with a minimum of friction and a maximum of success.

Before someone makes a little shrine before a free-form mass dubbed a "group," let's admit that as educators we tend to be a little carried away by the whole "group" idea. Suddenly alerted to the power inherent in co-operative action, we often approach it as a method or a technique and forget where the method or the technique is supposed to take us. We sometimes provide sad illustrations for chapter iv and the discussion of procedures without goals. Such procedures can be wasteful and foolish even though they are not so sinister as the totalitarian doctrine that the end justifies the means.

Granted that we recognize the significance of co-operative action and that our search for deeper knowledge about and acquaintance with it brings all the guidelines in chapter v to our attention, how then can we acquire the understanding and the skills necessary to put them into action in whatever situation we may be?

One teacher has cited as the most difficult job we face in co-operative action that of developing the skill or the sensitivity necessary to see ourselves and the situation from the other person's point of view. Certainly this is a restatement of the Golden Rule and is accepted by most people as basic to all positive human relationships. With so much of preservice training for specialized educational positions placing emphasis on only one viewpoint, in-service programs might well consider the development of sensitivity to other viewpoints as a primary purpose.

There is evidence on every hand that the group, formal or informal, may be an effective agent of change or quite as effective a bulwark against change. For a group of teachers to be given the opportunity to work out methods to seek essential facts and to gain insight in a common study means growth in sensitivity to others, growth in teaching ability, and increased interest and sense of achievement.

Learning to teach differently and to teach better by experiment is easier for a group of teachers than it is for an individual teacher. The group feeling is a feeling of security. The experimental approach challenges the best capabilities of the group and of the individuals which make up the group. The experimental method brings the need for change into the foreground, and the group works out its own best ways to meet that need. Having recognized the need and worked out ways to meet it, the group will accept and profit by its own findings. In-service education studies are most profitable when the group's findings can be put to use within a teacher's own classroom where she can experiment and make further use of her own and of others' findings and then share any new ideas and findings with other teachers. In-service education should move in interlocking circles and not in parallel lines from pinpointed beginnings to predetermined ends.

An Illustrative In-service Project

An in-service education study which utilized many or all of the guidelines dealt with in chapter v was a self-evaluation study entitled "A Qualitative Study of the School Day," as conducted by four Minneapolis schools during the year 1953–54. The purpose of the study was to help determine ways which teachers might employ to evaluate and to improve their own instructional programs. Each school chose for its study a specific problem significant to its own particular need.

A steering committee composed of representatives of each school met to discuss the objectives of such a study and what they, as participating members, thought should be the outcomes. However, the direction of the study was not predetermined by the steering committee. Each staff was encouraged to determine methods of studying its strengths and weaknesses and to modify its program in ways that would strengthen it.

The Minnehaha Elementary School chose "A Qualitative Study of the School Day in the Field of Arithmetic Readiness." The problem specifically stated was: *To promote the maximum development of every child by means of a more effective arithmetic-readiness program.* A steering committee was chosen by the faculty members to study the approach to the year's activities, but all major decisions were made by the entire faculty.

After the major objectives of the study were stated and agreed upon, teachers began to collect information to help in the development of the study. Teachers observed the children, prepared and gave informal tests as well as standardized tests. They then planned a variety of techniques and activities to take care of the needs of children as revealed by the diagnosis. The general areas of weakness throughout the school were outlined and the arithmetic program was organized to provide for the strengthening of these areas. Careful records were kept to evaluate progress made and to measure the pupil's growth in number skills and understanding. Evidence was also recorded of the improvement in the children's attitudes toward working with numbers and their increased appreciation of the importance of mathematics in the development of society. Numerous resource people were called upon to talk to the group as a whole, and lectures were attended. Parent participation was invited, and much worth-while information was gained through the work carried on by them.

The "Qualitative Study" had two major objectives: (*a*) To provide a better program of education for children and (*b*) to help teachers become better teachers. It was definitely agreed that the arithmetic program had become vastly improved so that it did provide a better program of education for children. Greater interest was shown; there was an improvement in the mental and emotional health of the children as the general class atmosphere changed. Diaries of the school kept by the pupils in three rooms revealed more flexibility in program-planning, provisions for group work with differentiated assignments, and greater integration of subject areas. Test results substantiated the general observations.

The effect of the study upon the teachers was equally revealing. At the beginning everyone felt much confusion. Teachers were slow in getting started because it required many discussions and much thought before they could get their direction. Progress at first was slow, and it was not until after one member made a report that teachers realized they had covered a good deal of ground. From then on progress was more rapid, and with it came increased enthusiasm and satisfaction.

At the end of the study one member of the group conducted private interviews with each member of the faculty for the purpose of determining his personal reaction to a self-evaluation study and this manner of conducting one in a completely democratic way. Teachers entered into the interviews willingly because they were confidential and informal.

In general, the reaction was positive. Teachers felt the study had added to their professional growth, had improved their attitudes in relation to each other, and had given them a better understanding of children. By working harmoniously in a common field they had become more closely knit, and mutual respect had been created. All agreed that they liked working out their own problems rather than having a "tailor-made" plan presented to them. In any case, no such plan could be made to fit an individual school situation. The study seemed to prove the need for teacher participation in curriculum-planning and curriculum change.

The Informal Group

Although the formal group is often the group set up for in-service education, the informal group because of its power merits the attention of all teachers working to make in-service education more productive. The informal group which was not designated but which just happened to form in the cafeteria or the washroom or the smoking room often renders everything done by the formal group ineffective. Status leaders may have appraised the in-service program as highly successful. Individuals inside and outside of formal groups which worked on the program may have thought it helpful and may have planned to put ideas they gained into action in their classrooms. But a few facetious comments made within the informal group, belittling the study itself or the resource people who assisted or the need for change and improvement as "a lot of nonsense" and "new-fangled ideas," may have destroyed the whole potential of the educational experience.

Instead of deploring the power of the informal group, there is considerable evidence that we as teachers need to utilize in our in-service programs the values of informal groups within the structure of formal organization.

The climate or atmosphere of a working group is difficult to appraise but it is often characterized by uncertainty regarding limits of authority in carrying out action decisions. This uncertainty can prevent teachers from exercising maximum effort as groups or as individuals.

The Effects of the Hierarchy

In their eagerness to be known as democratic administrators, some school principals deny that there is such a thing as a school hierarchy. But the denial does not alter the fact. Even though the superintendent prides himself on being a democratic administrator, even though he has decision-making groups within his school system and within his community, even though he has teacher-representation on many important committees and teacher-involvement in all phases of school administration and policy-making, notwithstanding all this democratic procedure, he is still the "head man" and is so considered by his teachers, supervisors, and custodians and by the people of the community. The hierarchy cannot be denied. Even if it were possible for such a superintendent or principal to throw off and to distribute all power and authority, he would continue to be looked upon as a power figure and, therefore, as something of a threat.

Most teachers feel that it is important for school administrators to recognize the existence of the school hierarchy, to look at it, to talk about it, and to be aware of its faults and values. Surely it is helpful to teachers to be able to discuss the hierarchy with those persons at all steps in it, and to give them some thought to what it means for the work we do in in-service groups as well as in our classrooms.

Setting the Limits

The boundaries of teacher-participation and decision within each school need to be clearly defined so that we may know what problems we are free to tackle. Within those defined boundaries of participation and decision, teachers should feel free to raise ideas and to consider problems which may appear small to the school administrator but which are of real concern to the teacher.

The importance of the classroom teacher's role in providing improved experiences for the learner is accorded almost universal lip-service, yet in many instances the boundary lines of roles are too sharply drawn to permit a teacher to take any steps toward improving the learner's experience. If such strict limitations are placed on the teacher's role that she has no freedom to experiment, there is little point in verbalizing about the importance of the classroom teacher and the importance of change in the teaching or in the learning process.

A brief look around almost any school brings to light the case of a teacher who really likes to teach but who sees little or no reason to increase her competence and to improve her work because, in previous efforts, the wall of role-limitation has presented a barrier against which she has fought with no result other than frustration.

On the other hand, the increasing practice of the team-idea in education provides some reason for hope that a greater flexibility in the concept of the teacher's role may be forthcoming. The team-idea gives due regard to and respect for the special and common competencies of each team-member and awards all members equal status. However, until this team-concept becomes more prevalent, we may as well realize that significant on-the-job behavioral changes in classroom teachers and teaching may be hindered by the status assigned to teachers by the remainder of the school society.

This role assigned to the teacher by the school is, however, no more likely to circumscribe individual growth through in-service education than is the role which is self-assigned.

Surely we are often hindered in our working groups by the kinds of roles we assign to ourselves. Much of this role assignment seems to be very deeply rooted. As a teacher, I am conditioned by my own ideas of what is expected of me and by what I think my capabilities are. I see a group leader or an administrator in terms of all the ideas of leadership or administration which I have accumulated in the course of becoming an adult. I cannot react to a group leader, then, in any way that does not go along with those accumulated ideas. If I like to think of myself as a nonconformist and of a leader as a demanding individual, my participation in a group will be on those terms. I will be so busy trying not to conform that my possible contributions to the group will be limited. But if I can see the leader as someone who will respect those contributions even if they turn out to be not very worth while, my participation will be positive.

The same general concept applies in terms of how we see all other members of the group, of what roles we assign to them in relation to ourselves. Certainly, then, it would seem helpful for group members to talk about the concept of role and to assist one another in recognizing its very important place in the way people work together.

Freedom to Experiment

Remembering past experiments in teaching procedures which turned out to be trial and error *with* instead of *without* reality consequences, teachers may regard guideline viii, stressing the importance of freedom to experiment, as something of a mirage. What schools actually provide constant encouragement to test and to try ideas and plans in a "reality context" but without "reality consequences," and who is provided with such encouragement? Are all teachers encouraged to test and to try new ideas, or is such encouragement given only when administrators are reasonably sure that there will be considerably more success than error?

Administrators have a real challenge here. It is difficult to convince teachers that they will have support and encouragement in trying out new procedures and new ideas, particularly if those new procedures and new ideas turn out to be somewhat unsatisfactory. Surely, impulsiveness and haste are not to be encouraged; but careful planning of procedure, careful evaluation of consequences, and thoughtful appraisals of factors involved may have far-reaching effects in the improvement of educational programs. Teachers need to feel free to try out, for example, new ways of learning about children which have been suggested by the leader of a child study group, without concern lest the principal disapprove of the whole thing. This means that good communication between all levels of the school society is imperative. It means that an atmosphere of wanting to improve and to change must permeate all levels of the hierarchy without the threat of job security or of personal lack of status. If a teacher feels that the working relationships of supervisors and administrators is a close one, that the lines of communication among them are open at all times, then that teacher will feel that the suggestions of one are likely to be approved by the others. As a result, she will feel less threatened in her efforts to send up "trial balloons" in her dealing with children or in her methods of teaching.

The Difficult Group Member

What to do about the reluctant participant or the aggressive dissenter in all in-service education experiences is a perplexing problem. In chapter v the author states that the reluctant or rebellious group member should either be drawn positively into the group or be allowed to withdraw gracefully. Either alternative presents difficulties. It is true that by remaining with the group he may hinder the study, but, if he is left out, there is a strong possibility that he, as an outsider, may hinder it to a greater degree because of other faculty members taking a stand with him.

However recalcitrant a group member may be, most teachers will find it difficult to accept the idea that he should be provided with an opportunity to "withdraw gracefully." Most teachers have had too many experiences with the reluctant or the rebellious or the embittered teacher group member to suppose he will do anything gracefully. In his meetings with the group he is getting rid of a little excess acidity of spirit. But permit him or force him to withdraw from the group and he is denied the one normalizing influence in his professional life.

Most teachers would disagree, too, with the use in chapter v of the word "infection" in the sentence, "Such problems as these [problems in human relations] can occasionally be traced to infection by a single individual."

It is hard for teachers to think of another teacher, however bitter

and however vocal about his bitterness he may be, as a sort of pedagogical "Typhoid Mary." That he influences other members of the
group with his negative viewpoints is undoubtedly true. But instead of quarantining him, many of us feel that it would be better
to vaccinate other group members with such a sense of purposeful-
ness and direction and tolerance that they can carry him along and
perhaps may even enjoy his negativism and may even examine
their own thinking more critically because of it. After all, the
essence of a democracy is a vital and a vocal minority.

Administrative Values and In-service Education Goals

As discussed in chapter iv, the conflict between administrative
values, "efficiency of records, orderliness, and technical excellence"
and goal values, "concern for the growth and development of
mature group relationships" should be faced by teachers working
in in-service programs because it is a conflict almost certain to be
present in varying degrees in all school settings. Perhaps it must be
accepted as one of the necessary boundaries, but such acceptance
will come only as the conflict is clarified and brought into the open.

Sometimes this conflict between administrative values and goal
values may serve as a cohesive force for a group. Teachers may find
it a challenge and feel that "there ought to be something we can do
about it."

There are ways in any school system for bringing closer together a concern for efficiency of administration and a concern for
children. In one child study group in La Grange, Illinois, it was this
concern of teachers for child growth and development that led
them to examine the worth of one aspect of administrative efficiency,
namely, the kinds of records which were kept. Out of the examination came recommendations for greater efficiency, as well as greater
significance in the kinds of child-accounting procedures used by
the school system.

It is reasonable to suppose that if teachers were helped more often
to see the *why* of many administrative procedures, they would find
much of what they view as red tape easier to accept. Moreover, if
given a chance, teachers might be found to have many ideas which
could be used creatively in the fusion of administrative values and
goal values. In-service education programs which look at such

problems honestly and which free teachers to be creative in thinking about the real values of education will most certainly pay dividends to the school systems which encourage them.

A positive fusion of administrative and goal values as well as an illustration of the complementary roles of individuals and of groups in an in-service study is provided by the following account of the development of the "Mathematics Curriculum Guide in Minneapolis."

A basic committee framework has been established in Minneapolis for dealing with curriculum problems. A curriculum co-ordinating council operates as a policy-forming group. One of its duties is to sponsor curriculum projects at all levels. Two large planning committees, elementary and secondary, are in turn responsible to the council, with six members from each committee represented on it. Each planning committee has one representative from each school. Also included on the curriculum co-ordinating council are two elementary- and two secondary-school principals, two central office staff members, and two representatives from the University of Minnesota.

When the need for a new guide in mathematics became paramount, 153 teachers who had indicated an interest in a new guide were called together for a discussion on the problems involved. Numerous questions were raised regarding teaching problems in the mathematics program, and three types of committees were appointed. These were: the problem committees, to study particular problems and to report findings; an advisory committee (the chairmen of the problem committees), to co-ordinate the work and make over-all plans; and a production committee, to use the findings and work of the problem committees and to write an experimental "Guide to Teaching Mathematics."

Twelve committees varying in size from six to twenty were organized from the 153 teachers who had originally expressed an interest in such a project. Two persons were designated as co-chairmen. These were the consultant in elementary education and a senior high school teacher released from classroom duty.

One problem the committees had to face was how to find time to carry on their work effectively. Arrangements were made for the teachers to be released from their class activities for various periods of time, with substitutes provided. The length of released time depended upon the work the particular committee might require.

The first session of each problem committee was an after-school meeting to review the organization and plan of the mathematics-curriculum project and to discuss ways to deal with their particular problem.

The second session of each problem committee was an all-day meeting in the library of the school administration building. This meeting was divided into four parts: (*a*) a general discussion of the committee problem; (*b*) an examination of the resources at hand; (*c*) the making of an outline for the final report, assuming that the report would be used as the basis of a chapter or section of the proposed "Guide to Teaching Mathematics," and (*d*) the selection of a subcommittee for actual production work.

Teachers representing all grade levels and many areas of the city were represented on each committee. In this way the committees were more nearly able to meet the problems of all.

The actual writing of the reports of the problem committees was also done on released time, the amount in each case depending upon the scope of the problem. Wherever possible, the released time was arranged on successive days.

When all of the problem-committees' reports had been completed and reviewed, the chairmen of the group presented them at a joint meeting of the advisory and production committees. The editing of the material for the guide was done by the co-chairmen of the mathematics-curriculum committee, and members of the production and advisory committees were asked to read the final draft.

Such a schedule could not have been maintained without competent, enthusiastic leadership, able and willing workers, and an understanding and co-operative administration.

When completed, the experimental guide was presented to principals and teachers and then put into use for one year. During that time school faculties used it, studied and discussed it, and sent in critical memoranda concerning it. In-service education courses were organized in several sections of the city to study the guide. Leaders of these courses were one of the co-chairmen of the mathematics-curriculum committee and teachers who had helped write the guide. The guide was then revised and was put in use in its final form in the school year 1955–56. A final step in the evaluation of the experimental guide was the securing of advice and suggestions from recognized leaders in the field of mathematics.

In this way a working guide to be used throughout the entire school system was formulated through the joint study and efforts of many individuals and groups within the system and was evaluated by all who teach mathematics. It is a guide to meet the needs of the immediate school system for which it was written.

Resources for In-service Education

If asked to name the two most valuable resources for in-service education, a good many teachers would name *time* and *leadership*, in that order. When will the high-school teacher, for example, already burdened by an overcrowded day of five or six classes, a homeroom, a club, sometimes two clubs, and maybe noon-supervision of grounds —when will that teacher find time to devote to in-service education? We have just mentioned what constitutes that popular delusion, "the teacher's working day." We must also consider the extra hours most teachers put in at home on lesson-plans, on correction of papers, and on the constantly needed review and extension of knowledge in their subject-matter field. Some teachers on low salaries must hold supplementary part-time positions to provide a living for their families. For them, after-school programs involve not only the time but also loss of income.

In areas where teachers' salaries are so low that many teachers must seek extra employment, it is questionable whether a teacher should be expected to give any out-of-school time to in-service programs of education. By its very nature, in-service education implies considerable emotional as well as intellectual maturity and professional dedication of a high degree in the teacher-learner. What realistic employer would expect qualifications such as these from a worker who is expected to perform as a specialist but whose annual income may be and often is exceeded by that of his plumber, his TV repairman, and the filling-station operator on the corner?

Given what local teachers deem a fair-wage scale with provisions for some recognition of participation in in-service education by upgrading on that scale, school systems and individual schools are still faced with the problem of overloading the new teacher with the insistence that he participate in too many activities. In large school systems there are many fields of study offered to the new people, and it should be the responsibility of someone to see that the new teachers participate in a limited amount of the most necessary and helpful work.

Leadership follows time as the second most important resource for in-service education. Leaders should be dynamic and positive. They should keep the study moving. They should be people who can contribute to group and to individual morale, and, when necessary, they should involve additional resource persons and should help make available such resources as funds and materials.

Foresighted leaders in many areas have partially solved the problem of resources by centralizing in one school or in one school system all the available materials so that all teachers may have access to them rather than leaving each classroom to operate as a unit. Wise planning and co-ordinated central buying eliminate some of the duplication and improve the selection of material resources.

In-service Education and the University

Interesting evidence to demonstrate how a geographical area, such as a county, can mobilize its resources to meet the needs of teachers is provided by De Kalb County, Georgia. There, a teacher who feels that she has an individual problem or feels the need for further study in any area, finds an opportunity in what is titled the Atlanta Area Teacher Education Service. This service provides formal college courses on both undergraduate and graduate level. The University of Georgia and Emory University work with the instructional supervisors to provide the courses requested by the teachers.

A county-wide survey is made each year to determine what courses are wanted. Courses in the teaching of reading, social studies in the elementary school, child study, and art and music in the elementary school are typical requests. These courses carry credit at either the University of Georgia or at Emory University and are applicable in limited amounts to a graduate degree. These courses also fill a requirement for salary increments within the system. They meet for three hours after school in alternate weeks for a school year (eighteen classes). The cost is less per quarter hour than is the cost for regular college work.

In this area, college courses in summer sessions are organized to meet the needs and expressed desires of teachers. Oglethorpe University has Saturday-morning classes for teachers needing special training. These carry undergraduate credit.

Emory University has a department of teacher-education and each summer offers a workshop where teachers may find many resources and helps for problems. The county school system offers one scholarship (three-quarters tuition) to each school each summer. In addition to professional growth for the teacher, this workshop provides necessary credit for certificate renewal and also fills local increment requirements. The county teachers as a group decide what county-wide problems need the immediate attention of the workshop. Teachers in the workshop benefit most, but definite and concrete helps with county-wide implications have come from the workshop. Such helps include curriculum guides, theory and practice in a school-wide reading program, a guidance program, enrichment for the exceptional child, compilations of available county and state resources, improvement in the teaching of citizenship, and an eighth-grade curriculum. Teachers in the county workshop spend half the day on county-wide problems and the other half-day on their own professional needs.

Appraisal by Evidence

Although questionnaires, personal interviews, and other forms of appraisal of in-service activities have their advantages and their advocates, evaluation by "evidence" will probably appeal to teachers as the most reliable. As a result of the in-service experience, what improved teaching practices occur in the classroom?

Much attention still must be given to the evidence-type of appraisal to discover why and how teachers change their perceptions and whether these changed perceptions are being used to provide better learning experiences for students and, if they are not, why not?

The guidelines of chapter v seem readily adaptable to the teacher-learning process in classrooms at all levels. Teachers should be able to develop many insights into co-operative procedures in the classroom through experiencing these procedures in in-service activities. The development of such insights should not be left wholly to chance, however. Readiness should be provided for them by directing attention during the experience to the similarity between the in-service activity and the classroom situation.

The difficulty of obtaining and evaluting evidence related to many of the desired or anticipated outcomes of group in-service programs, or of co-operative procedures in the classroom, points up the need for a constant pooling of such evidence in workshops, in conventions at state and national levels, and in professional journals.

Summary

In summarizing positive facts and some possible pitfalls brought out in this consideration of the teachers and the in-service education program, we submit the following generalizations:

1. In-service education means a program by which *all persons* engaged in education learn and grow together and not a program for making up teacher deficiencies.
2. An interested, fair-minded administrator is essential to the success of any in-service program.
3. The emotional climate which prevails in the in-service program is as important as the goals sought and largely determines the goals attained.
4. Teachers should have some part in setting up programs of in-service education, if only the privilege of voting on several plans, preferably more than two.
5. Individual differences among teachers should be recognized in setting up in-service education plans. Sometimes recognition of these differences will supply different learning experiences for beginning teachers, for teachers new in a school system or a school building but not new to teaching, for teachers in various subject-matter fields, for teachers at the same grade level, for teachers at all stages of professional growth who need and want in-service programs of extension, that is, programs presenting their subject-matter fields in new dimensions.
6. A primary purpose of in-service programs should be the development in every participant of a sensitivity to the viewpoints of others.
7. Whenever possible, in-service programs should utilize the values of informal groups within the structure of formal organization.
8. The boundaries of teacher participation and decision within each school need to be clearly defined so that in-service groups will know what problems they are free to tackle.
9. Good communication at each level and between all levels of the

school society are necessary for the maximum success of the in-service guidelines in action.

10. Conflicts between administrative values and goal values are more easily solved when discussed frankly by teachers and administrators.
11. Time is the most pressing resource problem in in-service education. In areas where the level of teachers' salaries makes it necessary for family heads to undertake supplementary jobs, in-service education should not involve after-school time. Such education should be an opportunity, not a penalty.
12. Evaluation of in-service programs by "evidence" of improved classroom teaching is the best evaluation, but we need many studies to help us discover why and how teachers change their perceptions and how those changed perceptions result in improved learning experiences in the classroom.

CHAPTER VII

The Role of the Administrator in In-service Education

ARTHUR J. LEWIS

assisted by

SELMER H. BERG, MILDRED BIDDICK, RONALD C. DOLL,

JAMES A. HALL, JESS S. HUDSON, and DWIGHT TEEL

Introduction

This chapter is based upon the reaction of a group of principals, curriculum co-ordinators, and superintendents to the following two questions:

1. How do the ideas presented in chapters iv and v compare with your experiences with in-service education as a school administrator?
2. What implications do you see in these chapters for the role of the administrator in in-service education?

The term "administrator" was used to designate principals, superintendents, and other personnel with system-wide responsibilities for in-service education, such as curriculum co-ordinators, directors of instruction, and assistant superintendents in charge of instruction.

The chapter starts with a statement of assumptions, based largely upon chapters iv and v, that help to determine the role of the administrator in in-service education. This is followed by a discussion of some of the responsibilities of administrators for the in-service education program. The chapter concludes with a statement of the need for in-service education of administrators.

Basic Assumptions

The role which the administrator plays in an in-service education program is determined in part by his concept of the nature of in-service education and in part by his understanding of the psychology of change and his attitude toward group work.

THE PURPOSE OF IN-SERVICE EDUCATION

Chapters ii and iii make it clear that the purpose of in-service education is to improve the quality of learning experiences. This improvement will come about as all personnel concerned with the education of children and youth become more effective in their work. An in-service education program, therefore, must be concerned with helping professional personnel develop the attitudes, understandings, and skills that will enable them to provide a better program of education.

IMPLICATIONS OF THE PSYCHOLOGY OF CHANGE

Chapter iv includes many suggestions for administrators as they attempt to understand the complex nature of change. Change and the means to change are intimately related to feelings and emotions. These feelings and emotions are an integral part of the basic needs, interests, and desires of individuals. Until these needs are met or the desires satisfied, a tension exists within the individual. This tension leads to change and is, in a very real sense, a prerequisite for change.

How does this relate to the responsibility of the administrator? How can this psychological information assist in motivating change? Chapter iv suggests two different ways in which the tensions leading to change may be brought about: (a) Tensions may be induced by external pressures in the environment, and (b) tensions may be produced as a person sees his needs or interests in a new light. In order to determine the extent to which these two approaches should be used for an effective program of in-service education, it is well to examine the implications of each.

Tensions induced by external pressure are of two types: In one the individual is compelled by an external force to take an undesired action; in the other, one set of the individual's needs or interests gives way to a more powerful set. Fortunately, the first type, the use of raw force, is becoming increasingly uncommon. It is, in essence, the method of a dictator. The other method of inducing tensions through the manipulation of forces is much more common. For example, a teacher may be very much interested in summer travel; but the need for additional income outweighs this desire. An institutional requisite for salary increase is attendance at summer school. The teacher "chooses" to go to summer school in order to move up on the salary schedule. Probably this method of associating institutional requirements with more personal needs is the most common way of encouraging change in teachers. Early conceptions of supervision were based in large part on this method of inducing change.

Often when the motivation for change results from this type of manipulation of forces, the change is not a lasting one. As soon as summer-school attendance, for example, is no longer a requisite for salary increases, summer school will not be attended.

In contrast to the tensions induced by external manipulation of forces are those that come from within a person as a result of a shift in his interests or an awareness of a new need. These shifts in interests and awareness of new needs give new meaning to an activity and, as a result, may create a tension that leads to a new goal. Because the individual sees things in a new way, he may want what he has not wanted before. If, in addition, he understands the barriers that must be overcome to achieve this new goal and perceives the pathways to the objective, there is a strong likelihood that change will take place leading to the accomplishment of the goal.

How does one gain these additional insights, new interests, and new needs? Chapter iv suggests two different methods. One is through what might be called a "crisis." In this situation the individual is forced to realize that the old ways of doing things will no longer suffice. Social forces within the community, for example, might demand a change in the curriculum offerings within a school system or even in the methods used in instruction.

The other method that brings about this change in interests and needs is through a sensitization to new goals or ideologies. What was satisfactory to a person at one time is no longer satisfactory, because he has new values; and because of these new values he sets new goals for himself. These goals create tensions that exist until the goal is achieved. For example, a high-school English teacher who has gained a better understanding of youth develops a new aspiration to help youth with their personal problems. With this new goal he becomes dissatisfied with his present teaching method. The resulting tension leads to experimentation and change.

It is not easy to differentiate tensions leading to change which are the result of external or internal pressures, but it is assumed in this chapter that a more effective in-service education program results from the latter.

In considering how changes take place within the individual as a result of new interests, new needs, and new goals, it is important to realize that in in-service education these changes occur within an institutional setting. We must understand the nature of the group in which the change takes place, for this group can either accept and facilitate change, or can make the change very difficult or even impossible.

Because of the evidence that groups can be a real asset in helping individuals change, we are assuming in this chapter that in-service education should be approached and conducted, largely, on the group basis. Specifically, the group should participate in (*a*) identifying the needs, (*b*) setting the goals, (*c*) planning ways of working, (*d*) developing materials, (*e*) putting recommendations into action, and (*f*) evaluating results. These groups should focus on ways to improve the instructional program, thus avoiding some of the personal tensions that may arise when the emphasis is on changing the teacher.

Responsibilities of Administrators for In-service Education

The preceding assumptions suggest, among other things, that in-service education should be a co-operative program. If there is a desire for improvement on the part of the staff—a desire arising from an interest in meeting needs—and if given an opportunity through an organization which permits change, the staff will change to meet the needs. If there is no desire to improve, the finest in-service education program will be futile in practice.

The question may be asked, "Is there a need for a status leader in a *co-operative* program for in-service education?" Actually a higher degree of skill is needed in providing leadership for a co-operative program than for the type that results from administrative directives. For the administrator to work co-operatively with the staff, not only in in-service education but in all phases of the school operation, and for him to have respect for the individual, requires unusual characteristics. He serves more as a facilitator and co-ordinator than as a guiding and directing genius. This concept of leadership is still uncommon, in practice, but it is not a new one:

> Of the best leaders
>   The people only know that they exist;
> The next best they love and praise;
>   The next they fear;
> And the next they revile.
>   When they do not command the people's faith
> Some will lose faith in them,
>   And then they resort to recriminations!
> But of the best, when their task is accomplished,
>   Their work done,
> The people all remark,
>   "We have done it ourselves."
>
> LAO-TZE (c. 600 B.C.)

If the administrator is to serve as a facilitator and co-ordinator in in-service education, there are certain specific tasks that he must perform. These include: (*a*) providing inspiration, (*b*) encouraging development of good organization for in-service education, (*c*) facilitating the work of groups, and (*d*) creating a climate for growth.

PROVIDING INSPIRATION

Chapter iv indicates that the perceptions of an individual may be changed as he becomes sensitized to new ideologies or new goals. A shift in the level of his aspirations causes tensions which produce change. In view of this, one of the real contributions an administrator can make is inspirational. Every administrator has certain responsibilities to "fire up" the staff and help it develop visions of what the organization might be doing that would be better than what it is doing.

To provide this inspiration, the administrator must demonstrate that he, too, has higher levels of aspiration. These he develops, in part through his study of society and the role of the school in it; in part through a study of the community in which he serves and the needs of the youth within the community; in part through familiarity with research findings in child psychology and in techniques of teaching.

In short, the administrator must be actively engaged in an in-service education program to improve himself.

There are, of course, real limits to the extent to which one can encourage people to change their professional behavior through inspiration. Too often the comments fall on deaf ears. This is frequently true because the staff does not share the goals held by the administrator. The gap between the staff's present level of aspiration and the one suggested may be too great.

It is important, therefore, that the administrator have an appreciation of the present level of aspiration of staff members. Only as he knows the present goals of his co-workers can he help them to raise their sights. The skilful administrator gains this insight as he listens to what staff members say, as he analyzes their questions and concerns, and as he observes what they do in their work.

It is unfortunate when the administrator assumes that he alone can provide inspiration to the staff and fails to recognize that other members of the staff are able to raise the aspirations of the group. The sensitive administrator makes it possible, through free expression of ideas, for any member of the staff to provide inspiration for his co-workers.

ENCOURAGING THE DEVELOPMENT OF A GOOD ORGANIZATION
FOR IN-SERVICE EDUCATION

One of the assumptions made earlier in this chapter was that organized in-service education should make use of groups. The basis for the development of these groups becomes, then, one of the central problems of organization for in-service education. Organizational arrangements influence considerably the effectiveness of the in-service education program.

The administrator who attempts to develop or modify an organizational plan for in-service education by himself is making a mistake. If in-service education is to be based on co-operative group work, the development or modification of the program must be co-operative. Some communities have used system-wide elected committees, composed of teachers, principals, and consultants, to plan for an in-service education program. Other systems have used elected curriculum-planning committees for this purpose. Principals have found it effective to have an elected committee of their teachers plan in-service activities.

There is no single organizational blueprint which can be applied to all in-service education programs. However, there are certain questions, such as the following, that the planning group should consider:

1. What should be done at the local building level and what should be the relationship of this program to system-wide programs?
2. What kind of system-wide program should be planned?
3. What is the relationship between the administrators—principals and curriculum co-ordinators—the consultants, and the teachers in the in-service education program?
4. What resources are available, either within or outside the school system, to aid in the in-service education program?

The group planning an in-service education program should strive for a suitable balance between local building and system-wide activities. This can be approached through a separation of the problems that can best be worked upon at the building or system-wide levels.

There is a strong trend toward local faculty in-service education programs. Certain implications from chapters iv and v may indicate the reason for this trend. These chapters show the value of the group-approach toward in-service education and suggest that informal groups are often very potent in affecting the values and the attitudes of their members. Informal groups are more apt to form within a particular school staff. Even the more formal groups growing out of the in-service activities of a single faculty are more conducive to close interpersonal relations than are the typical system-wide committees. Such relations exert a strong influence on feelings, loyalties, values, need for belongingness, and acceptance of the individual.

Chapter iv also suggests that an individual is more susceptible to change when his membership in the informal group overlaps his membership in formal groups. The faculty group is more likely than is a system-wide group to overlap in membership with the informal groups. It is probable, therefore, that a kindergarten teacher will identify more closely with the local faculty group than with other kindergarten teachers throughout the system.

It is important to have one's new ideas accepted by the group of which he is a member if these new ideas are to result in new practices. Group standards are such that a member is usually reluctant to risk the ill will of the group by going against its standards and interjecting new ideas. This often makes it difficult for teachers to put into practice in their individual schools the ideas they have gained from in-service education meetings on a system-wide level, or ideas they have gained from recent workshops or college courses they have attended. There is a greater likelihood of faculty support for the individual as he applies ideas he has developed through participation in a local faculty study group.

Another reason the local faculty may provide for effective in-service education is that this group can probably better meet the needs of the individual than can a system-wide group. As was indicated in chapter iv, the better a group can meet the needs of the individual, the more potent it will be in facilitating change. Group cohesion in the local faculty encourages teachers to function in the trial-and-error kind of fashion that is necessary to try out new ideas and to improve methods of teaching.

Although there are sound psychological reasons for using the faculty group as an important means of in-service education, there is no guarantee that such faculty groups, when formed, will work productively. The administrator must work with the faculty in such a way as to capitalize on the values mentioned above. He must encourage an overlap between the informal groups and faculty groups through a variety of informal social activities. He must encourage the group to accept change in others by his own attitude toward change in others and in himself. He must help the group plan and share ideas in such a way that the needs of individuals are met.

An in-service education program based entirely on local faculty effort would be inadequate. Opportunities should be provided for both formal and informal system-wide group activities. Informal activities should make provision for personnel to come together in self-selected groups interested in similar problems.

System-wide groups planning in-service education should also consider more formal types of programs. The workshop is one such organization that seems to meet many of the psychological requirements for producing change. The workshop is characterized by individual choice of problem, opportunity to plan the attack and to seek resources from varied fields, an informal atmosphere, relaxation of some of the barriers, and the opportunity for exploring ideas out of the "for keeps" situation. All of these help to explain the fervent enthusiasm of many workshop participants.

The values of a workshop will be gained only if there is group and institutional support to reinforce changes resulting from the workshop. Lack of this support may well be the cause for much of the frustration and loss when workshoppers go home and feel that they are unable to practice any of the things they have worked on. The administrator should recognize the importance of group support and encourage a team from a local building to participate as a team in a workshop. An opportunity should be provided for the workshop participants to share their experiences with other staff members.

Several cities are providing system-wide in-service education programs for new teachers to give them an opportunity to work together on problems and concerns that they hold in common because of their newness to the situation. The new teacher, whether he is a beginner or experienced, is emotionally involved because he is faced with meeting certain psychological needs of belongingness, of participation, of status, and of security in his new professional relationships. His motives are powerful, because he sees the problems related to his becoming a successful teacher as a threat to his acceptance in the professional group. His problems are significant and very real because they can be seen as the basis for immediate action. Moreover, the beginning teacher has fewer old, conflicting values that he must discard in order to change to newer and better ways of teaching.

One type of organization for system-wide in-service education involves having a number of small special-interest committees. These groups are responsible for promoting system-wide interest in such areas as aviation education, conservation, and international understanding. Occasionally such groups become so attractive to their members that the group sets itself apart. This may be due to an unwillingness on the part of the members to move from the trial-and-error phase of their program to the realities of actually putting their idea into practice. It may also be caused by the development of a strong friendship clique. As a result, the committee has little chance to exert a positive influence on the entire school system and may even develop hostility toward other members of the staff. The administrator needs to encourage the group creating such a committee to guard against this danger by helping the group (*a*) be specific regarding its task; (*b*) provide for adequate communication from the committee to other personnel; and (*c*) provide rotation of its membership.

The group developing the total program of in-service education should see the local building and the system-wide activities dovetailing in such a fashion that the two supplement each other. Provision should be made for an effective means of communication so that there will be no unnecessary overlap of function or conflict in purpose.

In-service education programs sometimes collapse because they are too unwieldly and complex. Often teachers are kept so busy with in-service activities that they have insufficient time to work on the problems that are of more immediate concern to them. The administrator has the responsibility of seeing the over-all picture of in-service education. He needs to be aware of the activities in which staff members are engaged. Sometimes he may need to protect teachers from themselves, lest they in their eagerness attempt more than they can accomplish. Staff members are discouraged when so many committees are organized that time and effort is wasted. Needless multiplicity of committees may be avoided by the use of a central planning or steering committee with other committees being established by the central group for specific projects.

Over-all plans for in-service education involve a careful co-ordination of the efforts of teachers, administrators, and consultants. The various roles must be defined and agreed upon in order to have effective working relationships. More effective ways of working out these relationships must be found than the usual charts or written announcements.

Since the roles of the various persons involved in the in-service education program are complementary, interrelated, and interpersonal even though not always face to face, the process of defining roles needs to begin on a very broad, institutionalized, cross-section basis. This yearbook shows a recognition of this need at a rational level. The process, however, is complicated by the reality that each administrator, consultant, and teacher is both fulfilling a role or two and at the same time is being himself. Therefore, the relationships must always be rebuilt in terms of the actual individuals who are to work together. This means that the process is never-ending and must proceed at every level continuously so that, as persons grow and change, there may be room for new interpretations of their roles and their relationships with others.

Probably no amount of talking about roles can substitute for operation. Yet, just as in building any attitude with children, we begin by living the way that makes the desired attitude natural; but then we come to the time when it is important to lift the desired attitude to consciousness and to verbalize and generalize about it. So there would seem to be a place for a direct attack upon related role expectations at the local level and within the school system. However the roles of the various individuals are defined, they should share a real responsibility for facilitating the work of groups.

FACILITATING THE WORK OF GROUPS

When it is assumed, as it is in this yearbook, that group work is a very important aspect of an effective in-service education program, the responsibility of the administrator to facilitate group work takes on great significance. His ability to do this depends in part upon his attitude toward groups and group work, his skill as a member of a group, and the resources he can make available to the group.

The administrator who favors a group approach in the solution of school problems does so because of certain attitudes. He has faith in people and in the ability of the group to cope with instructional problems. This faith is sufficient to cause him to accept the group decision even though it may be at variance with his own ideas. He realizes that group work takes time and requires patience.

The administrator's attitude toward the group and its way of working is often apparent. When his attitude is "let's get the job done and here's the way to proceed" and he then manipulates the group toward acceptance of his own solution, he effectively stops co-operative group work. Sometimes, after a group is asked by the administrator to work on a problem, the group solution is vetoed and, unfortunately, with little explanation. The administrator, when using group procedures, has a responsibility for defining at the beginning of the group's deliberation the limitations within which its members must operate. This "setting of limits" is very important to teachers (see chap. vi). The administrator must also help the group get the needed facts. Once these things are done, the group's decisions must be honored. Administrators should be members of the in-service education group and should contribute their ideas and thinking during the process of working out plans rather than vetoing plans already accepted. Because of the power inherent in his status position, it is easy for an administrator to dominate most groups. When he does so, other group members are kept from making their resources available.

The administrator should recognize that a faculty does not automatically constitute a group. Often a school staff is a number of individuals working at similar jobs under the same roof. The teachers may be pulled among different loyalties: loyalty to the faculty subgroup, the whole faculty, or the downtown central office. Before a faculty can become an effective working group, it is necessary for members to come to know one another as persons as well as teachers and to come to feel a real sense of having chosen to work together. Much of the frustration related to in-service education occurs because we have not recognized the difference between a collection of people and a group.

The administrator can encourage the development of a group feeling and minimize competition between staff members by recognizing and commenting on group achievement. Most administrators are quick to comment on the achievement of individuals; the same should be done for groups. Within most school systems, for example, many people are selected for promotion because of some individual achievement. Group work could be encouraged if the good team members in group endeavors were also selected for promotion.

Some principals have been able to encourage group activity through the use of a policy committee elected by the staff. This gives the entire faculty a feeling they are represented and encourages them to speak freely to their representatives. The faculty sees that the administration is interested in its opinions as policy-committee recommendations are given fair consideration. A similar type of steering committee selected from the entire staff will help the

curriculum co-ordinator work out realistic policies regarding curriculum and in-service education programs.

The faculty steering or policy committee frequently serves as a
springboard for an in-service education project. This may come about
when the group identifies a problem in the school that needs the
considered effort of the staff. The solution to such a problem may
have implications for the curriculum. Faculties that have had an opportunity to work democratically in the solution of administrative
problems profit from this experience in considering instructional
problems that may contribute to the in-service education of the staff.

The administrator should realize that whether or not a collection
of individuals becomes a group depends upon how attractive the
group is to its members. This attractiveness depends to a large degree
upon how well the group satisfies the professional needs of its members as well as their personal needs for friendships and acceptance as
persons. The more attractive the group is to the members, the more
potent it will be in supporting change. These facts have important
implications for organizing groups. If the group is to meet the needs
of the individual, the members of the group must be active in setting
group goals. After goals have been established, group members
should plan the steps necessary to realize the goals and to evaluate the
success of these steps. This was emphasized in chapter v. Effective
groups are attractive because they meet the needs of their members.

To further the effectiveness of the group, the administrator needs
to be skilled in group process. He needs to have an understanding of
group dynamics and be aware of the factors that are necessary for
productive group work. One principal spent a great deal of time becoming well informed about the teaching of arithmetic in order to
help a staff committee but subsequently admitted she could have
helped more had she spent her time learning about methods of group
work.

The administrator may wish to serve in the group simply as one
of its members. This often is difficult because various persons on the
staff expect the administrator to play a certain role. They often
assume that the administrator should be the group chairman. Gradually as teachers and administrators gain more and more confidence,
and as the administrator learns and demonstrates that he can play
many different roles in a group, this difficulty is reduced.

Not only does the administrator face problems in group work because of the expectations of staff members but the expectations of people in the central office can also cause complications. When he must pass on a number of edicts or rules from "headquarters," it becomes difficult for him to participate in co-operative group problem-solving. These difficulties are reduced, of course, when the administrators in the central office attempt to work co-operatively with principals in their buildings the same way a principal is expected to work with his teachers.

Whether or not the administrator is a member of a particular group, he should be sensitive to some of the fundamental principles of group work. For example, the selection of a leader should be made by the group itself. This should happen even though it may be necessary, at times, for the administrator to appoint a temporary leader in order to get started. When this is done, the appointed leader should be an individual who is seen by the group as being influential, although it is sometimes difficult for the status leader to identify these persons.

The group, as it moves into the stage of identifying and proceeding to solve the problem that it faces, follows a procedure similar in nature to that used in individual problem-solving. The administrator may expedite the work of the group if he helps it become more conscious of the aspects of problem-solving. It is important, too, that the group be helped to realize that it is more effective when it tackles a small problem than when it "bites off more than it can chew." It takes time to identify really important and significant problems. Too often the administrator, in his hurry, mistakes a so-called respectable problem for the real problems of individuals. It takes some time and a strong "we" feeling within a group before the individuals are ready and willing to identify the real problems that need consideration. The administrator or curriculum co-ordinator should feel a responsibility for helping the group clarify the problem and distinguish between those problems that deserve group consideration and those that require individual handling.

As the group moves ahead in its problem-solving, it is important to evaluate constantly the ideas that are presented, the processes used by the group, and the results. The more the group and the members within the group feel a responsibility for evaluating the ideas suggested, the better the ideas will be and the more freely they will be presented. Group consideration of ideas will be encouraged when suggestions made by members are treated as group property rather than the property of the individual presenting the idea. If the status leader assumes the responsibility for evaluating the ideas presented, for the processes used in arriving at ideas, and for the results, it is likely that the ideas will stop coming very soon.

It is a stimulation to a group to check on what they have done. One faculty, engaged in an in-service education program, felt they were making little progress. Their representative to a system-wide planning group was asked to summarize the progress made by the faculty. In order to give an accurate picture to the planning group, she first discussed with the faculty the report she was to present. The faculty reacted by being surprised at its accomplishments. Its members took new heart in their project and proceeded with considerable dispatch to arrive at worth-while results. Because it is stimulating to a group to review what it has done, the administrator has a responsibility to encourage this kind of group activity.

In addition to assisting the group directly, the administrator should do what he can to make available the resources of other individuals within the school system. It has been customary for some time to bring in various specialists when certain areas of the curriculum were under consideration. Consultants are also needed who can help in conducting action research and in analyzing the results of informal group research. Consultants can also assist in improving the group process by helping members evaluate somewhat systematically the roles they are playing and the effectiveness of their working together.

Sometimes it is helpful to have a consultant from outside the school system come periodically, meet with the faculty, hear their plans, challenge their thinking, inject some new ideas, and depart. Much of the resentment that follows the challenging of one's ideas is directed toward the departed consultant, and the local administrator and group pick up the pieces and go on from there, but with something new added. In due time the consultant comes again to repeat the process at another point or on another level.

Careful planning by the staff should guide the administrator in the use of consultants from outside the school system. Sometimes, for example, the administrator has rendered a consultant ineffective by insisting that he speak to the whole staff before he has been informed as to the problems being considered and the work being done by the local staff.

One other resource that can be helpful is the layman who is an expert in a certain field. For example, there may be a layman in the community who is a scientist or a successful businessman and who could be a valuable resource to some group. We need much more information about how to make it possible for him to bring to the group new understandings and new ideas.

The administrator has a responsibility for providing resources for effective group work other than consultative help. Professional books and magazines can contribute much to the in-service education of teachers. The physical facilities available for teachers in their meetings can also assist in in-service education. The provision of a coffee break at the close of the day and prior to in-service education meetings can help to create the kind of atmosphere that will promote effective working together. Tape recorders are valuable instruments to record group discussions in order to assist the group in analyzing its progress. Groups may bog down if they try to look after all the details of securing these resources. The administrator should serve as the executive for the group in getting the needed aids.

Another type of resource that is important for the administrator to provide is time for teachers to do the work. Teachers consider time a very important resource (see chap. vi). There are many ways of making time available for in-service activities. Employing substitutes enables teachers to attend conferences or workshops as part of their in-service education. Some systems are dismissing school at intervals for an entire day or half a day, and others dismiss an hour early once a week for in-service education work.

Citing inadequate time as a deterrent to in-service education may not reveal teachers' real objection. Lack of time is a respectable reason for what may actually be a resistance to change. When this is the case, providing more time will accomplish little.

CREATING A CLIMATE FOR GROWTH

One of the greatest contributions the administrator can make to a program of in-service education is to develop a situation in which the growth of individual teachers will be encouraged. As chapter v makes clear, this means an atmosphere in which a teacher is not afraid to admit that he has a problem, or that he does not view the problem in the same fashion as others, or that he has made a mistake and wants help. This atmosphere reduces the fear of being judged adversely because of an opinion and contributes to the individual's sense of his own worth. This implies a setting in which both the individual's and the group's needs may arise.

How can an administrator encourage the development of such an atmosphere? One important way is to have positive feelings toward the staff. The administrator should believe in his staff members. He should look up to them rather than consider them inferior.

One trait of the administrator who has real respect for his co-workers is humility. It is easier to develop this trait as the administrator recognizes that every member of the staff excels him in one or more different ways. This may be done consciously as the administrator looks for strengths in others. His recognition of the superior qualities in his co-workers will not only give him a better perspective on himself but will also improve his relations with the staff.

The effective administrator realizes that teachers generally are interested in children. They chose their profession for the most part because of a desire to help children. As a result, teachers are interested in doing a good job, and, therefore, they are eager to improve their professional performance. The results of a spelling experiment in the Minneapolis schools support this point. This experiment involved additional time and effort on the part of teachers. Recently the teachers were asked to evaluate the experiment by responding anonymously to questionnaires. Overwhelmingly they felt that through the experiment they were getting better results. They also stated that the experimental method required more teacher preparation and energy than the method previously employed. However, their response was almost universal in stating that they would not wish to return to the former method of teaching spelling. They wanted to go on with the experimental method, in spite of the fact that it took more time and energy, because they felt it was more beneficial to boys and girls.

The administrator who demands deference from others because of his position often upsets groups. If he is to get at real needs and problems, he should make it possible for teachers to think of him as a peer rather than as a person of superior status. There are hazards here. As a result of an increasing awareness of the importance of good human relations, there has been a growth of a good-fellow, first-name informality, let's-get-acquainted pattern, which is often superficial and does not involve changes in the way basic decisions are reached or the way persons are regarded vis-à-vis status.

The administrator's understanding of the problems faced by individual staff members will help him create an atmosphere for growth. Adults, just as children, face certain developmental tasks. These include (a) adjustment to a marriage partner, (b) adjustment to children in the home, (c) adjustment to aging parents in the home, (d) making new friends, (e) adjustment to the realization that previous goals have not been met. Many of the problems faced by teachers are personal and center around these developmental tasks.

Problems also arise, of course, from an individual's professional work. Some of these problems stem from the fact that most older persons are very "status conscious." They are afraid of making fools of themselves in front of others, much more so than children, generally. Change for the adult is frequently accompanied by a sense of anxiety.

Whereas an understanding of the general problems that staff members may face is helpful, the administrator should establish personal relationships that enable individuals to discuss their special problems and needs with him. To do this, the administrator must develop the ability to listen with patience and sympathetic understanding. The administrator can do this best if he can put himself in the position of the speaker as he tries to see the problem through the other person's eyes, as he attempts to understand the reasons behind the other person's feelings. He needs to be readily accessible to people. He should have the kind of interest in staff members that will make him approachable.

The administrator also gains an understanding of individuals' problems as he visits them in their place of work. The principal gets into classrooms and sits through the "stuffy-heat" and "the glare." He gets onto the playground in the dust. The central office worker, likewise, would get out with the principal.

As the administrator gains an understanding of the problems faced by staff members, he should attempt to help the individual with the problem. A real effort should be made to eliminate the annoyances, no matter how small. The suggestions of individual teachers of the faculty group should be given careful consideration. Although it may not be possible to accept and put into effect all of these suggestions, they should never be ignored by the administrator.

Growth of staff members can be stimulated as the administration gives constant encouragement to try new ideas that are related to a practical classroom situation. Actually administrators are the real gatekeepers to experimentation. The principal or a curriculum coordinator can sabotage an experiment by a little ridicule. Often what the administrator fails to do to encourage is more significant than what he does to discourage.

All creative ideas are not equally good, and some may not be good at all. Consequently the person advocating such ideas must look critically at what he is proposing. The administrator has the responsibility for helping teachers assume this critical attitude. He should give help when needed on means of appraising ideas before action is instituted as well as during and after action.

It may be well for status leaders in education to look to some of the forward-looking leaders in industry for some of the ways they encourage creativity on the part of their employees. Industry spends large sums of money on research laboratories in order to discover new products and new and better ways of producing present materials. Recently the vice-president who was responsible for the development of new products in his large corporation told of his formula for encouraging creativity. He has developed the motto, "Celebrate the idea." Any time a man working in the research laboratory comes up with any idea it is immediately celebrated. When he was asked, "Supposing the idea is no good, do you still celebrate it?" his reply was that they did. He added that whether or not the idea is good is determined by all the men in the laboratory, not by the administrator. "Actually," he said, "the individual proposing the idea tends to be most critical of the idea." He stated that the alternative, that is, having the administrator in the laboratory decide whether an idea was good or bad, would result in a drying-up very quickly of any ideas coming from the staff.

Teachers have commented that too often administrators are inclined to oppose new ideas. That is, some teachers feel that the first reaction of the administrator to any proposal is that it will not work because . . . , and then he proceeds to explain the faults in the plan. Administrators put blocks in the way of good teaching or of experimentation by appealing to the propriety of an institutionalized set of procedures. Again, industry has learned in its research that projects that fail must be accepted along with those that succeed. Education must take this same attiude toward research with necessary protection and safeguards for the welfare of children. Education can move in this direction as administrators and teachers feel more freedom to try out ideas.

In-service Education for Administrators

At one time the administrator was presumed to be a highly skilled teacher who could tell teachers how to teach. Much of the training and experience of administrators has been based on this concept of the status leader. This kind of leadership is not adequate for the type of in-service education proposed in this yearbook.

This chapter has indicated that the effective administrator in an in-service education program must be one who can work co-operatively with the staff in all phases of the school operation and with real respect for the individual or human personality. To achieve this kind of leadership, there is a need for in-service education programs for administrators.

Any program of in-service education for administrators should be designed to meet the needs for leadership in a particular situation and should be designed in terms of the individuals involved. This chapter, by describing the responsibilities of administrators, has indicated some of the needs for effective leadership in an in-service education program. The following summary of some of these needs provides a partial basis for the in-service education program for instructional leaders that is developed in chapter xiv.

The effective administrator needs the following knowledge:

1. An understanding of the psychology of change.
2. Knowledge of possible types of organization for in-service education.
3. Knowledge of how to use available resources for in-service education.
4. Understanding of the role of education in our society.

The effective administrator needs the following skills:

1. Ability to work co-operatively with staff.
2. Expertness in group process.

The effective administrator needs the following attitudes:

1. Faith in teachers.
2. Respect for individual or human personality.
3. Recognition of the importance of working with groups.
4. Faith that a group can find reasonably sound solutions to problems.
5. Patience in working with groups.

CHAPTER VIII

The Consultant and In-service Teacher Education

JOHN I. GOODLAD

assisted by

JOYCE COOPER, ELIZABETH DONOVAN, JANE FRANSETH,
CLAUDIA PITTS, and DRUMMOND C. RUCKER

Introduction

Schools and school systems are increasingly using consultants for assistance with the significant problems of education. The word "consultant" is here used as a name for the person who (*a*) is brought from outside the institutional group that is to be immediately affected by any change contemplated; (*b*) is a resource in the sense that he appears to have an "answer" to a particular problem under study, is able to provide specific information that permits more intelligent selection from alternative procedures, or is skilled in helping people see and work through their problems; and (*c*) maintains a relationship of such length and involvement that the outcomes have personal significance to him.

Consultants come from federal, state, and local education offices, from colleges and universities, and, more recently, from professional organizations. Bringing on-the-job assistance to teachers is rapidly becoming recognized as the primary function of local supervisory personnel. It is of interest to note that the service most desired by school superintendents of Kentucky in 1949 was consultative service,[1] although the term "educational consultant" did not appear in *Education Index* as an index title until 1948.[2]

1. Harold P. Adams, *An Approach to the Development of a Program of In-service Education of Public School Superintendents in Kentucky*, p. 51. Bulletin of the Bureau of School Service, Vol. XXII, No. 2. Lexington, Kentucky: College of Education, University of Kentucky, December, 1949.

2. Woodson W. Fishback, "Improving Instruction through Consultative Service," *Educational Administration and Supervision*, XXXVI (October, 1950), 374.

In-service education is concerned with change—the phenomenon through which new knowledge, skills, and attitudes are acquired. The value of in-service education depends on the kind and amount of these changes that are produced. The intelligent use of consultative help and adequate consultant performance are closely related to an understanding of the conditions that are conducive to change as they are developed in chapters iv and v. The present chapter seeks to apply these ideas about the facilitation of change to the work of the consultant.

This is done by first analyzing and interpreting what seem to be the key ideas of chapters iv and v so as to indicate possible significance for the educational consultant. Then, examples of practice are presented with the intention of showing more specific, concrete applications. Finally, consultative tasks, roles, and techniques thought to be called for are examined.

Concepts of Change and the Consultant

Careful analysis of chapter iv reveals, among other ideas, a number of penetrating insights regarding factors thought to impede or facilitate change in an institutional setting. Some of these insights have to do with the character of institutions themselves, particularly educational ones. Others pertain to the individuals who work in such settings and to their group associations. These insights are arbitrarily grouped below and applied to the consultative role.

INSTITUTIONAL FACTORS AFFECTING CHANGE AND THE CONSULTATIVE ROLE

One of the basic assumptions in chapter iv is that individual change may take place within an organizational or institutional context. Since feeling and emotion always are involved in change and since these, in turn, are affected by identifications as well as perceptions, the consultant cannot operate effectively without comprehending the dynamics of the institutional setting. In other words, the conditions under which the teacher works and his perception of those conditions profoundly affect his readiness for change. The consultant serving a school system which uses merit-rating scales in teacher promotion may find his efforts to promote change quite ineffectual when these same teachers perceive other concerns to be more directly related to their advancement.

As mentioned above, emotional relationships are involved in any lasting change of individuals. Because of this, every effort must be made to relate the personnel comprising temporary or informal groups to the membership of the larger organization. When change reinforces rather than threatens these dual memberships, it becomes more acceptable to those to be affected by that change. In applying this principle, several alternatives appear open to the consultant seeking to work with teachers employed in a system using merit-rating scales. He can help the administration see the total effects of the merit system in operation. He can bring "status personnel" into the child study sessions for the purpose of reassuring the teachers regarding the close relationship between the activity undertaken and institutional aims. He can help members of the group see this relationship by repeatedly emphasizing the possible benefits of increased understanding of children in improving teacher effectiveness. Obviously, these alternatives are closely related, and all three might well be included in the consultative effort.

Individuals operating in an institutional setting are expected to play roles. The teacher, for example, promoted to the principalship of the school where he previously served and anxious to maintain a "buddy" relationship with his colleagues finds his role to be "sus-pect" in some quarters. His former colleagues feel more comfortable when he "acts like a principal." Many principals who said, as teachers, that they would be different if they ever became principals find themselves playing—and often enjoying—the roles they once deplored. The consultant who ignores or deliberately plays down the status differences between teachers and principals may be resisted by both groups, at least early in his relationship with them.

Most consultants know from experience the various role-expectancies likely to exist in a school or school system. If the consultant's function is not likely to be impeded by the status roles and expectancies that exist, it probably is wise for him to support them. Sometimes, however, existing perceptions are such that it becomes necessary for the consultant to deal with these roles if he is to affect the desired change process positively. In such instances, it probably is best for the consultant to seek to establish nonthreatening situations in which individuals may see themselves more clearly and get some perception of the roles others perceive for them. Thus, a little role-playing of different ways of conducting faculty meetings may help principals see how they really operate, without the consultant having to take the initiative in more threatening ways. It is important, however, that groups hold their first efforts of this kind among their own peers. There often is some guilt attached to seeing one's self as he really is. The guilt created in a situation such as the one described may be almost too great to bear if incurred by a principal when his own teachers are present.

It became apparent from the Coffey-Golden analysis of the change process that the administrative or supervisory personnel identified with in-service activity contribute to the success of that activity. Teachers come to regard certain people in the hierarchy as "strong" or "weak," in the sense that what these persons endorse is or is not likely to gain ultimate top-level approval and be translated into action. Consequently, they come to know that whatever Mr. Brown gets involved in is likely to come to fruition, whereas Mr. Smith's actions are likely to be abortive. The consultant seeking to work through Mr. Smith may soon discover that he simply is not getting any place; nothing ever seems to come of what is planned, regardless of the time and care put into the enterprise.

Effective consultants recognize that institutional arrangements such as hierarchic organization frequently are established as much to maintain the existing power structure as to facilitate communication and administration. Such arrangements often provide a sense of security for many people because roles are clarified. Not only does one see what is expected of him but, in addition, he has considerable assurance that his perceptions are shared by others and that his actions will not appear bizarre to others within the structure.

The consultant who views structure always as being intimately related to function, and who is naïve about the emotional, human attachments so often accompanying existing structure, may be doomed at the outset. His normally sound proposals regarding curriculum change may fall on deaf ears because these ideas simply are too threatening to existing organization and status to be tolerated. Knowledge of local conditions and careful analysis of them in relation to needed changes frequently clarify an approach that is relatively nonthreatening and yet in line with desirable ends.

The role of the consultant is complicated perhaps most of all by the realization that "the central problem of institutional change is the development of those conditions in which institutional goals and means can be reassessed for the purpose not only of adapting to changes going on within the social system but also of assuming responsibility for exerting influence on the various alternatives for change which may be open to the society."[3] The consultant finds himself the one called upon to clarify alternatives for change that may be threatening to local administration, for example, because of potentially dangerous factional disagreements in the community. Creating tension toward change by expressing ideas regarding "what might be" threatens what now exists, and the consultant finds himself the scapegoat for resolving conflict.

A situation in point is where a superintendent and members of his board are in disagreement over the need for additional tax funds to provide new services. A consultant may be useful in describing trends over the country and the relation of local conditions to these trends.

It becomes apparent that the consultant who ignores the realities of the consultative setting will be ineffective, if not actually dangerous. The nature of the problem, the degree to which the school or school system attracts or repels individual teacher loyalties, the institutional hierarchy, the role-expectancies of personnel, the relative status (in the eyes of the teachers) afforded leadership personnel, the support or lack of support provided by the board, superintendent, or principal—all these and other factors operate constantly to impede or facilitate desirable change. No single consultative approach will ever satisfy the demands of all situations. Each situation will be unique, no matter how extensive the consultant's experience may be. But one broad, general guideline can be spelled out: *The first step toward successful consultative performance is careful study of local-setting dynamics.* What are the controversial issues? Being aware of them, the consultant knows when to deal with an issue directly and when to postpone discussion of it, if possible. Where are the sore spots, and where are the comfortable

3. From Coffey and Golden in chap. iv, p. 84.

places regarding compatibility of school system and teacher interests? What are the power structures which, even if remotely threatened, will block change in a spirit of self-preservation? What is the relative acceptability of leadership personnel to teachers? Has the consultant been brought in to do a job that no local person would dare to do?

It becomes apparent that both those using and those giving consultative help have mutual responsibilities in regard to proper understanding and interpretation of local conditions. Some of these responsibilities are enumerated below in the form of guidelines for both consultants and employing personnel.

1. If the basic problem is friction among personnel in the administrative hierarchy, this fact should be faced directly. The consultant may perform a worth-while service as disinterested "third party" in such a setting, but, if the facts are disguised and he is brought in ostensibly to serve another purpose, the chances for worth-while services are slim, indeed.[4]

2. The nature of the problem and the circumstances surrounding it should be clarified at the outset. The consultant may be able to save himself time and the system money if he realizes early enough that he cannot make a worth-while contribution to a solution. Even if the problem is bitterly controversial so far as local authorities are concerned, the consultant, knowing all its ramifications in advance, may assist local personnel to achieve planning and satisfactory performance.

3. It is well for the consultant to have "local knowledge," as the golfer calls it, relative to personalities and perennial friction spots in the school system. It is difficult for any one person in the local setting to provide all information needed, just as it is difficult for the consultant to know what confidence to place in the information that reaches him. But it is at least reassuring to receive an invitation from both a committee of teachers and an administrative officer when a system-wide problem is involved.

4. If a board or chief administrative officer is committed to a certain framework that must be maintained, it is best to clarify this

4. See Kansas Council for the Improvement of School Administration, *Consultative Services for Kansas School Administrators,* p. 7. Topeka: The Council, 1953.

fact at the outset. It is a cruel waste when officials permit or even encourage efforts to change, knowing full well in advance that they are committed to a certain policy or procedure regardless of the change ultimately to be recommended.

5. As has been said, most consultants know from experience the various role-expectancies likely to exist in a school or school system. The relationships are more likely to be comfortable when these expectancies are recognized from the beginning. It is well, therefore, that the consultant be informed in advance of any deviations or peculiarities existing in the setting where he is expected to assist. Readjustments may take place readily afterward, growing naturally out of initial adherence to protocol. Even a simple familiarity such as "Bill" instead of "Mr. Brown" will be resented in some settings and approved in others.

6. Local authorities should be most careful in their selection of personnel designated to work with the consultant in the change process. Selection of a noninfluential or nonacceptable person may well doom the effort in advance.

7. Consultant and administration alike should strive for some kind of administrative recognition of what has been accomplished. Change is distasteful to many people. It is easy to turn back the clock when the halfhearted administrative attitude is sensed. Change is more likely to "stick" when sanctioned by top-level authority in the administrative hierarchy. Also, consultative support of a forward-looking administration often provides the necessary "spine-stiffening" to administrative personnel at a most vital time.

GROUP FACTORS AFFECTING CHANGE AND THE CONSULTATIVE ROLE

An analysis of chapter iv reveals many insights appropriate to the consultant in his major work—namely, helping individuals change their behavior in group settings. We have discussed the importance of recruiting emotional involvement for the cause of desirable change by bringing individual goals and group goals into the closest possible agreement. It must be pointed out that the very necessity for emotional attachment to what now exists produces the phenomenon of resistance to change as an ever-present force. The consultant, then, must accept as normal any initial readiness to resist change. The greater the satisfaction with existing conditions or the larger the number of personal needs that are met by what now exists, the greater this resistance will be. Strange though it may seem, the consultant often must encourage dissatisfaction with the change he helped produce if still other changes are to be contemplated. As Coffey and Golden point out (chap. iv), new values set new goals and new goals create new tensions or needs.

The readiness of a group to move forward or to resist change stems in part from the following roots:

1. The individual or group simply does not perceive the proposed line of action as "good" and resists it on this basis.
2. Although the proposed change appears "good" in the abstract and may even be approved vocally, it threatens present values and, therefore, is not internally accepted as good.
3. Inner tensions are such that the view of reality is grossly distorted and cannot be "consensually validated" (see chap. iv, pp. 74–75). That is, the individual or the group has a viewpoint that does not line up with what is generally accepted as reality.

The consultant's problem is different in each of these three instances. Resistance rising from the first cause presents a situation and suggests procedures that are familiar to most of us. Some kind of research, study, or other means of securing increased intellectual insight is called for. In the second instance, however, no amount of increased intellectualization is likely to change anything. In fact, deepening insights may lead only to increased frustration. "I don't want to know any more," says the teacher to himself, in effect. "I'm guilty enough as it is about my inability (or lack of freedom) to act on the basis of what I know." The consultant's role becomes one of helping to modify the setting or that of building up self-confidence and courage. Either the value structure must be changed or those striving for change must be encouraged and protected as they seek to defy existing structure. The third cause presents a still more complex consultative problem. Neither intellectualization nor modification of the structure is likely to help. Individuals whose perception of reality is distorted must be helped to gain self-understanding. Role-playing, psychodrama, and sociodrama are frequently helpful in creating a nonthreatening environment within which important insights into self may be gained.

The Coffey-Golden idea that belongingness within the group precedes constructive planning for change within the group is a significant one for the consultant. This idea helps him to accept with more equanimity the possibility that group cohesiveness may develop through focusing upon the consultant as a threatening element. The consultant may then be able to redirect this cohesiveness to a significant problem.

This raises the whole problem of what Lawler calls "problem definition."[5] It becomes apparent that the impingement of institutional setting upon particular individuals, the degree of emotional attachment to what now exists, and what individuals have internalized as values, are significant factors in the complex and highly important steps of problem census and delimitation. On first consideration, it would appear that the problem should rise out of the group rather than be introduced by the consultant or someone else outside the situation. This would appear particularly sound when group cohesion has developed in part as resistance to the consultant. There is little evidence on this point, however, and Lawler's studies suggest that the source of the problem is not a crucial factor in problem definition.[6] Perhaps more important is that the group recognize and accept the significance of the problem. Does it enhance compatibility of institutional goals and individual goals? To what degree does it threaten present emotional attachments to what exists? Is the problem perceived as important, as compatible with present value structures, or, for that matter, as a problem?

Since the presence of the consultant frequently is initially threatening and, therefore, disruptive of group progress, early entry into the situation by the consultant appears imperative. In Lawler's analysis, the factor which did seem to make a difference to progress was the point at which the consultant began to work with the group. The project seemed to move forward when consultants participated to a great extent in initial exploration of the problem, assisted in the delineation of it, and participated with the group in setting up plans for working.[7] Groups using and consultants pro-

5. Marcella Rita Lawler, "Work of the Consultant: Factors That Have Facilitated and Impeded His Work in Selected Elementary Schools of the Horace Mann–Lincoln Institute of School Experimentation," p. 177. Unpublished Doctor of Education Project, Teachers College, Columbia University, 1949.

6. *Ibid.*, p. 48.

7. *Loc. cit.*

viding consultative help should recognize, then, *that such services are likely to be most beneficial when consultants who will subsequently participate are identified with the group at the very beginning of problem definition.*

A significant sign of the group cohesion necessary for problem definition is the group's willingness to send up many "trial balloons." The consultant works toward this willingness by encouraging and accepting ideas, by making it clear that there are few pat answers to problems in education, and by making it easy for participants to abandon ideas that no longer appeal even to the contributor. This can be done by getting out alternatives first and exploring their potential usefulness later, when individuals proposing them no longer are identified with the suggestions. In this way, a member of the group feels free to criticize and even discard an idea for which he once held a fond attachment.

The kind of wholesome group cohesion that enhances individual belongingness and supports the trial efforts of all to contribute to a worthy solution is not developed by a few magic words. Group harmony cannot be bought, begged, or bullied. Individual tensions cannot be constructively resolved and individual perceptions automatically changed by persuasion or the use of sound logic alone. This fact is a most difficult one for many people to accept. Something is so, they believe, and, therefore, should immediately guide action. *The useful consultant, then, is one who is conscious of, sensitive to, and competent in guiding the dynamics of groups at work.*

THE CONSULTANT AS A PERSON AND THE CONSULTATIVE ROLE

Performance is the end product of combining what one knows and how one feels with certain skills of execution. In addition to factors in the setting and in groups or individuals, there are certain factors in the consultant himself that determine the success of his operation. Reviewing the ideas of the Coffey-Golden chapter and Parker's suggestions, additional interpretations may be pointed out for the consultant that relate more to him as a person than to the dynamics of a particular setting or group.

First, the consultant cannot separate his understanding of the psychology of change from his own involvement in change and, therefore, from the very dynamics with which he is seeking to deal. The consultant has his own perceptions of reality, his own differentiations, his own tensions rising out of need. Because of this, he must from time to time "square" his own perceptions with reality. In effect, he too needs in-service education in order to be reasonably sure that he is alert to new ideas and not overly infatuated with a few pet notions that have little validity. In addition he must prepare himself intellectually and emotionally to accept instances of conflict between his own perceptions and those of others. The consultant who simply cannot permit others to disagree with him is not likely to further any process of change. Not only must he accept differences but he also must develop techniques for maintaining rapport with others even in the face of divergent perceptions of reality.

One of the difficult problems facing many consultants is that of accepting the individual differences that exist among people seeking to change their perceptions. Therefore, the consultant must seek to relate his own intellectual maturity to that of others. Otherwise, he will not start where people are but where he thinks they ought to be. Similarly, he must seek to understand the *process* through which people change their perceptions. They differentiate meaning out of experience. Unless he recognizes this fact, the consultant is likely to tell what is known or what he knows about the problem in such way as to stifle the thinking of others.

Perhaps the most difficult task of all for the consultant is that of recognizing the possible effects of his own emotional attachments upon others and upon his own performance. He must, therefore, seek to gain insight into the nature of his own attachments and his reactions when these are threatened. Sometimes, he may even have to withdraw from the consultative situation, if it appears threatening beyond the threshold of personal tolerance. Unless he can face honestly his own motives for remaining in the situation and also accept as honest the motives of others, his position soon becomes untenable.

The successful consultant brings to the situation a value system related to change that is recognized and accepted by those seeking his help. Broadly conceived, such a value system embraces belief in institutional planning as the basis for significant and permanent change. He is not likely to be helpful, for example, if he possesses a cynical attitude toward educational institutions as potential agents for change. Similarly, he must obviously consider himself an equal with others in the group, brought into it because of his potential contribution rather than status at home. And, of course, his value system must include faith in the involvement of those to be affected as guarantee that what is best for them will result from their plans and actions.

The consultant's usefulness depends in large measure upon his possession of certain personal qualities and abilities directly related to the demands of the group and the setting. Research to date has not been too helpful in identifying those personal characteristics deemed essential to successful performance of an educational worker. The points enumerated above do imply, however, a kind of internalization that necessarily must find expression in personality. Enumeration of the group leadership skills necessary for successful consultative performance is not the function of this chapter. Briefly, however, a consultant's success with a group appears to depend upon:

1. His skill in using the internal structure of the group to foster the potentialities within it—e.g., skill in recognizing and using leadership abilities already emerging from group structure.
2. His ability to help the group feel able and free to make group decisions, even if significant later choices are to be made individually.
3. His ability to help the group accept change—both individual and group—as a desirable goal.

Promoting social change and determining the direction for change are the necessary and legitimate activities of any segment of the community and, in the abstract, at least, are accepted as such by most segments of the community. Change is heavily dependent upon knowledge. And knowledge, therefore, is threatening since it sets in motion parts of what many would like to see remain stable. The consultant, then, virtually personalizes threat. In that situation, the seeming dichotomy between individual acceptance of change as idea and individual fear of that which changes creates a serious morale problem for the consultant. He may come to think that he is a kind of ogre, condemned in advance by the role seemingly demanded of him. Because of this, it probably is unwise for most people who perform in consultative capacities to remain in them for too long a period. Their perception of reality is likely to be restored by returning frequently to a kind of home-base where nothing more than a normal participatory role is demanded of them. Their outlook is thus refreshed and their consultative tool-kit replenished.

The consultant, too, has in-service education needs which are described in some detail in chapter xiv. It can be said here, however, that these needs are met in part by participating in a variety of educational activities. The danger is that the consultant may come to depend more and more on techniques long since learned (and thus comfortable to him) but decreasingly useful for meeting new situations. The danger is less when the consultant engages in a self-evaluative process that provides cues to the techniques most likely to be appropriate. This danger is reduced even more when the home setting is rich in problems and programs that keep the consultant constantly involved as a participant. Such involvement provides the sense of reality requisite to all effective consultative performance.

Using and Giving Consultative Help: Illustrative Practice

The two illustrations summarized and analyzed in the pages that follow are drawn from real-life practice in American education. Several changes from the original have been made in order to disguise identities.

EXAMPLE A: THE SETTING AND THE CONSULTANT

The elementary-school supervisor of a consolidated system felt that her energies and those of teachers were being dissipated because of inadequacies in the existing curriculum structure. After several refusals by the school superintendent, she was successful in getting him to free the teachers for the three-day conference they wanted. His only concern was what it would cost.

A committee then drew up a conference framework that provided an opening address by an authority on child development. This talk was to be followed by discussion sessions led by consultants from the university, supervisors from neighboring counties, and consultants from the state department of education. A final session designed for planning next steps on a system-wide basis was put into the schedule.

Throughout the planning, the superintendent attended no meetings even though he was invited to all of them. He was not known to discuss the impending conference with anyone. The conference was held in the school where the superintendent maintained his office. On the morning of the first day, he welcomed the participants to the conference. For the balance of the three days, he remained in his office and was neither seen nor heard from in any of the group sessions. He made no inquiries about the success of the conference following its termination.

The supervisor's subsequent efforts to carry through with follow-up plans were greeted with little enthusiasm. Attendance at committee meetings gradually fell off. Several teachers introduced a different approach to art or arranged to get additional reading materials, but classroom practices remained essentially the same. Efforts to set up a continuing relationship with one of the consultants were discouraged by the superintendent. A one-day conference on the same theme was held the following year, the original speaker and several of the consultants returning. It was a discouraging affair. The following year the supervisor transferred to another system.

This situation scarcely needs analysis. Whatever else may have contributed, it is obvious that the complete failure of the superintendent to endorse changed instructional practices or, for that matter, to initiate plans to produce change stifled progress. The consultants received no invitation, acknowledgment, or communication of any kind from the superintendent. They had no opportunity to secure the superintendent's perception of instructional conditions in the system and what might be expected of them and the conference. The superintendent's presence in the building but absence from the conference created in the minds of many the impression that he actually was hostile to change, to the conference, and to those who had been brought in to help set direction for change.

An important question about the role of consultants and supervisor naturally arises out of this situation, a fairly common type, unfortunately. In this instance, the superintendent was elected and not appointed. He had not come into the position through recognition of his professional leadership abilities. No doubt he was terribly threatened by the corps of "experts" camping on his doorstep. Since the superintendent obviously played the key role in endorsing educational change, perhaps the change process would have been more successful if initiated by him.

The consequences of an alternative approach are worth considering. Suppose, for example, that the supervisor had begun by playing up her own inadequacies and had requested that a consultant work with her. In a few luncheons and casual chats, superintendent and consultant would have become acquainted. These contacts, in turn, would have given the consultant a chance to provide the superintendent with ideas for instructional improvement. The superintendent's self-confidence would, perhaps, have been built up to the point where he would have personally approved and initiated the desired study program. From here on, planning might have proceeded just as it did in the example above—but with a quite different top-level endorsement and with different results.

EXAMPLE B: SETTING, GROUP, AND CONSULTANT

A college embarked upon a year of self-study with a view to bringing about certain organizational changes, curriculum revision, instructional improvements, and changes in emphases. Funds were made available for securing continuing consultative help in specific areas. Several of the consultants were selected by the president, one or two by the project co-ordinator, and some on the recommendation of other administrative officials. All were officially invited by the president, and all received considerable background information from the project director.

Each consultant visited the institution at least twice during the year, staying several days on each occasion. The first visit was spent primarily in talking informally with individuals and groups to gain familiarity with the problems. The next visit was spent in meeting with groups and individuals to help solve some of these problems. Continuing correspondence was maintained with the co-ordinator.

Before his second visit, each consultant received reports from the groups with which he was to work, summarizing what had been done since his last visit and pin-pointing specific areas in which help was wanted. Many of these reports included summaries of divergent viewpoints existing among group members and queries regarding possible conflict between individual and group goals and desires of the administration.

After his arrival for the second visit, each consultant had opportunity to talk with individuals involved and to chat informally with subcommittees before formal group sessions were convened. By the time such sessions began, the consultants knew at least some of the threatening forces at work, some of the conflicting viewpoints, and at least several possible alternatives.

Group sessions were arranged so that there was a minimum of conflict with other demands. Members were able to stay together on problems for several hours at a time. Alternative solutions to problems were presented in considerable detail and, at the consultants' suggestion, their respective merits were not discussed until all alternatives appeared to be before the group. Then, the possible consequences of the various proposed solutions were examined.

The consultants avoided personal pronouncements regarding their own preferred alternatives. From time to time, they recounted the experiences of other groups facing similar problems. Their chief role was to sharpen the issues involved and to assist the group in seeing the consequences of various lines of attack contemplated. The groups were left to make their own decisions at a later meeting, to which the consultants were not invited. The consultants had, in effect, worked themselves out of a job.

At first glance, it might seem that the various committees should have selected their own consultants. There was some feeling that several consultants represented the administrative viewpoint. But, as is often true in cases of this kind, groups admitted that they would not have been able to agree on persons. Nevertheless, even the opportunity to decide on *how* consultants were to be selected might have helped.

Many commendable aspects of the entire arrangement are readily identifiable. Consultants were thoroughly briefed on the setting, previous accomplishments, sources of conflict, and the demands to be made of them. Ample opportunity was provided for consultants to become personally acquainted with personnel and to gain first-hand reports on the views they represented. The most favorable environment possible was established for the group sessions. The consultants moved with some assurance into these sessions, using their first-hand information and general knowledge of successful group work to best advantage. The consultative roles were associated with a minimum of threat in that final decisions did not rest with consultants. Their job was defined and maintained as one of helping to clarify issues and work through the possible consequences of embarking upon the various alternatives. In this setting, the consultants were effective change agents.

Tasks and Roles of the Educational Consultant

It becomes evident from the preceding sections that whoever offers himself for consultative service should anticipate facing a wide variety of situations and performing an almost unlimited array of tasks. Lawler, studying the performance of educational consultants of the Horace Mann–Lincoln Institute of School Experimentation, found the following to be useful ways of working: (a) classroom visits followed by individual conferences, (b) small-group conferences involving two or three teachers, (c) large building-wide meetings, and (d) suggestions regarding materials submitted by teachers.[8] James and Weber, in turn, identified the following specific situations in which such ways of working were involved: (a) meeting with faculty representatives, (b) meeting with supervisory and/or administrative personnel, (c) meeting with system-wide faculties, (d) meeting with segments of school faculties, (e) meeting with school boards, (f) meeting with lay advisory groups, (g) holding individual conferences with administrative personnel, (h) participating in social-professional functions such as luncheons, etc., (i) participating as a member of a consultative panel, (j) inspecting practices in existence, and (k) meeting with administrators from a variety of school systems.[9]

In these work settings, consultants play a great many different roles, as the occasion demands. James and Weber observed sixteen consultants in seventeen consultative situations over a period of thirty-eight days. Sixty-two per cent of these consultants assumed at one time or another at least half of the following roles: answer-giver, listener, ex-officio suggester, interpreter, reassurer, stimulator,

8. Lawler, op. cit., p. 177.

9. Edward W. James and Robert A. Weber, School Consultants: Roles Assumed and Techniques Employed, p. 15. Southwestern Co-operative Program in Educational Administration. Austin, Texas: University of Texas, n.d.

advisor, fraternizer, and public relations representative. Thirty-eight per cent or fewer performed one of the following roles: synthesizer, evaluator, organizer, information gatherer, school sight-seer, demonstrator, or criticizer.[10]

Obviously, successful role-performance in such a variety of situations is dependent upon a great many variables found in the setting, in those served, and in the consultants themselves. As has been said, the ideas presented in this chapter for the purpose of analyzing these variables are not new to the volume and may be found, in different form, in chapters iv and v. They have been merely interpreted and re-presented here as they relate or appear to relate to the particular task of the consultant, his use, and performance.

Summary: The Key Ideas

The consultant comes into a setting to promote educational change. His efforts may become dissipated because of the complex array of forces already at work or ready to be set in motion that come to be associated with organized education. For the consultant to be ignorant of these forces, either as they operate in a general way or as they influence the local setting, is to limit his usefulness. Consequently, the consultant has a responsibility for acquainting himself as thoroughly as possible with the implications of the psychology of change and with the dynamics of the local setting. Likewise, local personnel have an obligation for briefing the consultant on local conditions, for clarifying what is expected of him, and for providing moral and material support throughout.

The consultant's really significant activity is his ongoing work with the groups and individuals involved. Again, there are mutual responsibilities. The consultant is most useful when he understands the basic principles of group work, when he is a thoughtful student of individual human behavior, and when he is able to work skilfully in the process of problem definition and solution. Individuals and groups, in turn, do much to help when they brief the consultant in advance regarding what is expected of him, when they are honest about their conflicts, when they provide effective communication

10. *Ibid.,* p. 21.

between sessions and among status levels, and when they provide a follow-up relationship.

The consultant as a person changes the situation into which he comes because of his very presence in it. It is essential, then, that he have some understanding of what can happen as a result of the kinds of influences exerted by his presence as a consultant. Knowledge of his own limits of tolerance helps him to make wise decisions regarding both the kinds of consultative commitment assumed and the degrees of freedom within which he can safely allow himself to operate. His essential kit of tools consists of rather extensive knowledge about himself and others in relation to the dynamics of change, certain specific skills in human relations and group work, and a value system that accepts people as they are and change as the legitimate enterprise of societal groups.

REFERENCES

ADAMS, HAROLD P. *An Approach to the Development of a Program of In-service Education of Public School Superintendents in Kentucky.* Bulletin of the Bureau of School Service, Vol. XXII, No. 2. Lexington, Kentucky: College of Education, University of Kentucky, December, 1949.
ALBRIGHT, A. D., and HOPKINS, GEORGE W. *What about Services of State Departments of Education?* Bulletin of the Bureau of School Service, Vol. XXVII, No. 4. Lexington, Kentucky: College of Education, University of Kentucky, June, 1955.
BLAHA, MARION J. "When and How a Consultant Can Be Used Most Effectively," *Educational Leadership,* X (November, 1952), 96–101.
FERNEAU, ELMER F. "Role Expectations in Consultants." Unpublished Doctor's dissertation, University of Chicago, 1954.
———." Which Consultant?" *Administrator's Notebook,* Vol. II, No. 8. Chicago: Midwest Administration Center, University of Chicago, April, 1954.
FISHBACK, WOODSON W. "Improving Instruction through Consultative Service," *Educational Administration and Supervision,* XXXVI (October, 1950), 374–76.
JAMES, EDWARD W., and WEBER, ROBERT A. *School Consultants: Roles Assumed and Techniques Employed.* Southwestern Co-operative Program in Educational Administration. Austin, Texas: University of Texas, n.d.
KANSAS COUNCIL FOR THE IMPROVEMENT OF SCHOOL ADMINISTRATION. *Consultative Services for Kansas School Administrators.* Topeka, Kansas: The Council, 1953.
LAWLER, MARCELLA R. "Raising the Level of Consultant Service," *Educational Leadership,* V (April, 1948), 445–50.
———. "Role of the Consultant in Curriculum Improvement," *Educational Leadership,* VIII (January, 1951), 219–25.
———. "Work of the Consultant: Factors That Have Facilitated and Impeded His Work in Selected Elementary Schools of the Horace Mann–Lincoln Institute of School Experimentation." Unpublished Doctor's Project, Teachers College, Columbia University, 1949.

LITTLE, WILSON. "Making the Consultant's Service Serve," *Educational Administration and Supervision,* XXXVIII (December, 1952), 480–85.

SAVAGE, WILLIAM W. *Educational Consultants and Their Work in Mid-western State Departments of Education.* Chicago: University of Chicago, 1952.

———. "Making the Most of the Consultant," *Administrator's Notebook,* Vol. I, No. 3. Chicago: Midwest Administration Center, University of Chicago, October, 1952.

———. "The Value of State Consultative Service," *Administrator's Notebook,* Vol. IV, No. 3. Chicago: Midwest Administration Center, University of Chicago, November, 1955.

SECTION III

In-service Education Programs

CHAPTER IX

In-service Education Programs of Local School Systems

MARVIN L. BERGE, HARRIS E. RUSSELL,
and
CHARLES B. WALDEN

Introduction

The responsibility of this chapter is to discuss in-service education programs in city school systems, to attempt to discover patterns in the various approaches used, and to evaluate these approaches against the guidelines set up in chapter v.

As a means of identifying actual practices in the in-service education programs of today, a survey of a number of city school systems was made. Three criteria were used in selecting the school systems to be studied: (*a*) geographical location—to collect practices and patterns from all parts of the United States; (*b*) size of system—to secure illustrations from all sizes of school systems; and (*c*) the suggestions of members of state departments of education, professors of education in colleges and universities of the country, and other authorities on city school systems—to identify those having outstanding programs of in-service education. Applying these criteria provided a list of 314 school systems to be included in the survey.

A comprehensive questionnaire dealing with all facets of the in-service education program was sent to appropriate officials of these school systems. Completed questionnaires were received from 145 of them. While responses came from all sections of the country and from school systems of different size, we realize that these cannot be viewed as fully representative of *all* in-service programs in this country. Nevertheless, for the purpose of this chapter, namely, to determine the kinds of program patterns now in use in the in-service

education of teachers, the number of respondents was deemed sufficient. The questionnaires were analyzed in order to describe the
procedures employed by the school systems reporting. Each of the
patterns identified was then evaluated in relation to the guidelines
presented in chapter v.

Patterns of In-service Education

A preliminary inspection of the questionnaire data indicated that
almost all of the programs could be grouped under three headings:
the centralized approach, the decentralized approach, and the centrally co-ordinated approach. The centralized approach "is based on
the conviction that curriculum development should be initiated,
managed, frequently conducted by persons in the central office of a
school system."[1] The decentralized approach results from a conviction that curriculum improvement can best be achieved when major
responsibility for it rests with the individual school staff. The centrally co-ordinated approach is a combination of the other two in
that, while there is a great amount of responsibility for curriculum
improvement residing in the local attendance unit, there is also a
professional responsibility of the central staff for problems which
cut across the total school program and for bringing some unity to
the entire system.

In order to classify the 145 systems reporting into the three categories mentioned in the preceding paragraph, independent sortings
were made by each of the authors. When there was disagreement
about placement, which happened in a number of cases, the report
was thoroughly studied and discussed until a consensus was reached.
This resulted in placing thirty-six systems in the centralized pattern.
Eighty-three were considered centrally co-ordinated, and twenty-
six fell into the decentralized category. In the following pages, the
writers will analyze practices carried on in the systems and indicate
how they believe each approach to in-service education meets the
guidelines suggested in chapter v of this yearbook.

Assigning each of these 145 school systems to its category was a

1. See Ronald Doll, A Harry Passow, and Stephen M. Corey, *Organizing for
Curriculum Improvement,* p. 2. New York: Bureau of Publications, Teachers
College, Columbia University, 1953.

difficult task, for there were few clear-cut cases. Most of these few seemed to fall into the centralized or decentralized approaches rather than the centrally co-ordinated category.

The first criterion used to identify the centralized approach was the answer to the questionnaire item, "Who in your school system assumes the *chief* responsibility for leadership to the system-wide in-service education program?" If the replies indicated that someone on the central office staff, whether it be superintendent, curriculum director, assistant superintendent, or supervisor, was assuming this responsibility, this was judged to be one indication of central control.

The second criterion used was the question concerned with the general faculty meetings. If these meetings were planned by the administrative staff of the central office and used as the *chief* vehicle for in-service education, this was interpreted as another indication of centralization.

The third criterion was the reply to the question, "Who assumes the chief responsibility for the planning of the in-service education program?" If the response to this question indicated that this responsibility resided wholly in the hands of the administrative staff, this was taken as another strong clue that the program was centrally controlled.

Most of the 36 systems classified as following a centralized pattern met all of the above criteria. Each, however, exhibited, to some degree, an individual pattern of its own, differing from the others in the amount of central direction exercised.

How does the centralized approach to in-service education meet the guidelines set up in chapter v? Under the centralized organization, the central office assumes the chief responsibility for the initiation of the program and, in most cases, sets up the organization with the view of achieving some preconceived kinds of action. This raises the question fundamental to all curriculum improvement, namely, "How do people learn?" If curriculum improvement and in-service growth are to be achieved through re-education of the teacher, then the organizational pattern must take cognizance of the fact that individual motivation is one of the important factors in the learning process. This motivation is strengthened when groups are permitted to select their own problems to work on and may also plan ways of working on them.

It is interesting to note that in the 36 schools which fell into the category of the centralized approach, there were 14 which submitted no evidence that they were working on a particular problem in their school system. Half of the remaining 22 listed problems suggested by the administration. The majority of the problems listed by these 22 schools had their chief focus on the subject-matter offerings of the school system. Under the centralized approach, problems chosen for committee study seem to be selected because of their significance to central-office personnel rather than to the members of the teaching staff. This practice contradicts two of Parker's guidelines, namely, that change in individuals is more likely to happen when they work on problems which are of significance to them and when they share in determining the ways in which they are to work.

Fourteen of the 36 systems utilizing the centralized approach have a professional staff of 75 or less. Seven of these 14 report that their chief vehicle for improving the educational program is the general faculty meeting. It is understandable that in the smaller schools there is greater reliance on the general faculty meeting, but again it is questionable if reliance on the general faculty meeting as a chief vehicle for in-service education will provide sufficient opportunity for small-group face-to-face relationships. It is in this kind of situation that there is both an active interchange of suggestions, ideas, and proposals and a maximum opportunity for the individual and the group to see at least some manifestation of the consequence of their action.

As the size of the staff of the systems increased, there was less reliance on the general faculty meeting as the chief vehicle for in-service education. Only one of the schools having a professional staff larger than 75 teachers stated that the general faculty meeting was the chief vehicle.

There was little evidence from the questionnaire as to how well these school systems created a working atmosphere that was conducive to building mutual respect, support, permissiveness, and creativeness. It is difficult to secure this kind of evidence from a questionnaire. However, it would seem that when committees are drawn from several schools and members are not too well known to each other, it is difficult to establish these working relationships. The job is even harder when the staff member is requested to participate and finds himself working on a problem which is of little concern to him.

There was evidence that the systems in the centrally controlled category used multiple and rich resources. Workshops were sponsored in 30 of the 36 communities, but in only 20 of the systems was there any relationship between the problems of the workshops and the work of the regularly established curriculum committees. The tendency to involve many kinds of resource personnel was noticeable in all systems in this category. But the evidence suggests that the involvement stems more from a decision from the central office that outside resources would be helpful than from a request for such personnel expressed by members of a committee working on a particular problem.

Nine schools in this general centralized-control category reported they spent no funds for in-service work in 1955–56; 18, or 50 per cent of the group, spent less than $200.00. One system spent $3,500.00. These figures are hard to interpret. To ascertain the cost of an in-service program is difficult. The budget procedures used in school systems vary and, in some cases, may hide in-service expenditures.

The questionnaire asked for a list of changes which had been made in the school program. Most of the changes reported by "centralized" programs had to do with new approaches to subject-matter areas or changes in subject-matter offerings or in administrative procedures such as time schedules. There was little indication that these changes resulted from a preliminary testing of plans in a reality context or that the simplest possible means had been developed to move from decision to action. It seemed more often that changes were made on the basis of the judgment of the few who had worked on the problem.

In the category of school systems under consideration, appraisal was made a part of in-service activities but usually was undertaken by the small group which makes decisions on changes to be effected and not by all those who are affected by the decisions made. It is interesting to note that, of the 36 systems 22 indicated that they made an evaluation of their in-service program; 13 replied that they did not; one gave no reply. Only nine of the 22 schools evaluating their program, however, used unsigned questionnaires to get evidence as to the values of their programs. This suggests some questions with respect to the type of evidence obtained.

There is little to be inferred from the questionnaire data regarding interrelationships among working groups or whether individual differences among members of each group are accepted and utilized. Perhaps the centralized approach results in more interest in production by committees than in interrelationships and is more inclined to select personnel who can make production contributions.

The centralized in-service program seems to operate within a framework where the problems have their origin in the administration and committees of teachers are appointed to find some solution. Several schools report they are working on problems related to subject-matter areas of the curriculum. These problems were suggested by the principal or superintendent although in some cases teachers were also mentioned. Sixteen of the 22 schools in this category reported the results of their study to the administration.

It would appear from the evidence submitted by these schools that the central office dominates the in-service activities and that little attention is given to the psychology of change (see chap. iv). It would also appear that the centralized in-service education program contradicts many of the guidelines developed in chapter v.

CENTRALLY CO-ORDINATED APPROACH

The centrally co-ordinated approach to in-service education is characterized by a variety of activities embracing the efforts of either a single school or several individual schools operating independently and certain city-wide activities carried on through organizational patterns such as grade-level, subject-matter, or over-all committees. The common factor running through this variety of activities and organizational patterns is co-ordination by the central office to foster the achievement of some commonly accepted system-wide goals. This co-ordination is often effected through the involvement of central-office personnel at various points in the ongoing program. Such involvement frequently includes sharing with others of the professional staff the responsibility of planning procedures to be followed in problem-solving, serving as resource people or consultants during the study phase of the program, facilitating necessary communication, and serving as members of the body authorized to translate committee recommendations into action.

Frequently a central planning committee is used to achieve the desired co-ordination of effort. Central planning committees often perform functions such as these:

1. Listing problems needing attention
2. Establishing an order of priority among problems
3. Selecting problems to be studied in a given year
4. Setting up the organizational pattern best suited to the study of a given problem
5. Making certain recommendations as to procedures to be followed in study
6. Hearing progress reports
7. Hearing final reports and recommendations
8. Passing on recommendations or forwarding them to the final authority with recommendation for favorable consideration

Fifty-seven per cent of the school systems studied were judged to fall in the category of the centrally co-ordinated approach. Key questions which formed the basis for this judgment were those having to do with the breadth of the program of in-service education and the involvement of central office staff, administrators, and teachers working together in planning and carrying on in-service education activities. These systems representing the centrally co-ordinated approach actually represent, in most cases, a combination of all three approaches. Some few indicate a degree of central control, while a limited number seem to lean quite heavily in the direction of decentralization. All, however, exhibit some indication of central co-ordination of the varied activities which characterize their system-wide programs.

A careful examination of the 83 questionnaires from school systems in this category indicated that the centrally co-ordinated approach provides ample opportunity for implementation of most of the guidelines for effective in-service education programs as developed by Parker. This statement is based on direct evidence from questions specifically related to about half of the guidelines and on inference drawn from responses to other portions of the questionnaire related less directly to the remaining guidelines.

The data reveal quite clearly that it is either committees of teachers or committees composed of a representative cross-section of the total school or school system staff which actually work on problems. Either the teachers themselves, or the total school, or the school system staff, or the committees which are engaged in actual study choose the problems on which they will work. In only eight of the 65 responses to questions related to the choice of problems for study was it suggested that school administrators had the sole responsibility for such choice. If, as is often assumed, the real problems of a school system are best identified by groups composed, at least in part, of classroom teachers, it is surely evident that school systems employing the centrally co-ordinated approach to in-service education are working on problems of high significance, not only to those who are working on them but to the school system itself.

Further evidence comes from responses indicating that much of the participation in committee study activity is on a voluntary or at least a semivoluntary basis. The semivoluntary classification in this case includes combinations of volunteering and election by fellow-teachers, appointment by committee chairmen, or appointment by administrators after volunteering. Less than 15 per cent of the returns indicated membership in groups due to appointment by committee chairmen or appointment by the administrator exclusively. This reveals a freedom of choice which is wholesome and may well mean that people participate because of an interest in the problems to be studied and the activities undertaken in the study of those problems. If this is the case, and the evidence so suggests, it is likely that conditions are conducive to effective problem-solving. Since administrators and/or central office personnel are frequently involved with teachers in the selection of problems for study, co-ordination of efforts without undue central control or domination would seem to be assured.

Responses to the questionnaire indicate quite definitely that the people involved in the study of problems significant to them at least share in planning how those problems will be studied. Sixty-five of the school systems in this category say that the superintendent or some other administrative officer has chief responsibility for planning the program of in-service education. In most instances he shares that responsibility with others, frequently with teachers. In some few cases members of boards of education, members of P.T.A. groups, or other lay people are involved. This sharing of responsibility between administrators and others who are involved in the process is apparent in staff meetings of one or more buildings as well as in the general faculty meetings concerned with the over-all program of in-service education. The involvement of those who will be on the working committees or participate in the faculty or building meetings in planning the procedures to be followed is important to the success of either venture. The fact that the administrative and central office staff are also involved in co-operative planning, and as resource people, insures a degree of central co-ordination that should be characteristic of in-service programs which fall in this category.

One of the most significant aspects of in-service education in school systems subscribing to the centrally co-ordinated approach is that many opportunities are afforded for face-to-face, small-group work. For example, most of these systems engage simultaneously in such varied activities as general faculty meetings, building meetings, grade-level committees, subject-area committees, and comprehensive, over-all committees concerned with all areas of the curriculum and the different levels of education. Such a breadth and variety should offer the opportunity for everyone to find an activity suited to his interest and his level of responsibility, providing this variety is associated with a considerable degree of freedom of choice. With the number of in-service education activities which involve less than the full faculty—and this number is proportionately large—together with the simultaneous operation of many activities, one can safely assume that much of the work is in small groups in face-to-face relationships. This assumption is further supported by the fact that 40 per cent of the school systems have staffs of 150 or less. Over 60 per cent have staffs of less than 300.

With the many and varied activities characterizing in-service education in the school systems which fall in this category, one might predict the need for many rich resources. Responses on the questionnaire indicate that such resources are made available and used. Most of the school systems provide a budget for this purpose. The amounts range from $15.00 a year in one of the smaller systems, which sum was used to defray the travel expenses of resource people, to the rather large amount of $12,500.00 provided by one of the middle-sized school systems. Most of the budgets include no more than $500.00 for this purpose. It is important to remember that this represents money clearly budgeted for in-service education. It is entirely possible that other expenditures for resources are hidden in other places in the budget.

One of the most interesting practices revealed was the extensive use of resource people who might be termed nonprofessional. Sixty-six per cent of the schools with staffs of 75 and less and all of the schools with staffs of from 76 to 150 make use of such people. In larger school systems, percentages range from 73 to 82. The non-professional people used in this capacity were not identified further than to indicate that they were members of P.T.A.'s, members of boards of education, or other lay people. This rather extensive use of lay people in this respect is a strong indication that educators are beginning to recognize the need for all concerned with the educative process to be involved in the solution of the very real and acute problems facing education in this day.

One community reports what seems to be a very promising practice, in view of the rather widespread use of lay people in group study projects as revealed in the preceding paragraph. It is a practice aimed at training lay people in group process, with special emphasis on training for effective lay leadership. School personnel, in co-operation with the parent-teacher council, have developed a nine-week seminar with two-hour meetings weekly for interested lay people. The objectives of the course are to acquaint lay persons with techniques which can be used in group situations. In structuring the seminar to demonstrate group techniques, it was necessary to find some content which was interesting and important to parents. Since most of those enrolled were parents, child development was the selected content. Beginning with the preschool child, each session followed the child through his growth patterns. The final two sessions were devoted to the role of the school and the role of the home in the child's development.

Each session was staffed by school personnel, who were specialists in the particular area of child development being discussed. Each session demonstrated some techniques of group process and some specific technique of group leadership, such as exploring interests of a group, role-playing, skits, panels, and evaluation techniques. In addition, pamphlets dealing with the specific topics were presented to the parents for their personal study and to keep in their home libraries.

This course has resulted in a noticeable improvement in P.T.A. programs and parent-teacher study groups. A very strong feeling of mutual respect and understanding between participating parents and the schools has also resulted.

A wide use of professional consultants, with little distinction among the schools of different size, was indicated in the questionnaires for school systems in this category. College and university professors were used more than any other single group. One of the interesting revelations was the extensive use made of local members as consultants and resource people. While many of the local people so used were supervisory and central office personnel, there was some tendency to use members of the teaching staff in this capacity. This indicates an awareness of the contributions which can be made by members of the local staff and undoubtedly helps to create an atmosphere of mutual respect and support. Extensive use was also made of resource people coming from publishing houses, from other schools, and from the community itself. Less use was made of consultants from regional study groups and from national educational organizations. This may indicate that these school systems feel that better assistance can be provided by people who are relatively close to the situation in which they will be working. On the other hand, it may be that people from regional study groups and national organizations were simply less available to the school systems used in this study.

Over half of the school systems falling in this centrally co-ordinated category indicated that experimentation is one of the important aspects of their programs of in-service education. School systems with staffs no larger than 75 experimented less than those of greater size. There is no evidence as to the nature of the experimentation, the degree to which it was carried on, or its relative importance in the total program. There are clues, however, which suggest that a climate favorable to experimentation exists in most of the smaller school systems. The degree to which teachers were involved in both leadership and planning roles, the number of instances in which opportunity was provided for face-to-face, small-group, problem-solving experiences, and the number of resulting changes in school practices imply that experimentation, or something very much like it, was encouraged to a considerable extent. Of course, it is entirely possible that changes resulting from the recommendations of study groups became an accepted part of the school program without continuing appraisal and evaluation. There is nothing to indicate that trial and testing run concurrently with group study. In the words of one reporter, however, "Our system is constantly under dynamic change—our personnel policies are being revised this year—our curriculum design is new—our workshop emphasis on 'Curriculum in Action' is new."

On the basis of our data, it is apparent that evaluation is a part of the in-service program in over three-fourths of the school systems in this category. In 38 per cent of them such evaluation is composed entirely of oral reactions to the program of in-service education. Seventeen, or 20 per cent, of the school systems use the unsigned questionnaire exclusively, while thirty-seven, or 45 per cent, of the systems use it in conjunction with other evaluation techniques. Forty-eight per cent of the school systems combine oral reactions with other means of evaluation. While the part of the questionnaire designed to probe the area of appraisal was slanted toward the evaluation of the over-all program, the replies of two school systems indicated that some effort was made at appraisal of the group process, as such.

It is apparent that all school systems with centrally co-ordinated programs recognize that keeping the staff informed of the progress of various working groups is a vital part of in-service education. Considerable attention is paid to setting up lines of communication between and among various groups and individuals. Such communication is in the form of written minutes or oral reports, or through some combination of the two. These minutes or oral reports go to the entire staff in most instances. In some cases they are sent to only those staff members concerned, to building representatives, to principals, or to varying combinations of these people. Whether or not these methods of communication lead to smoothness of operation, economy of time, effort, and resources, an awareness of specific interrelationships, mutually supporting action, and the elimination of misunderstanding cannot be inferred from the questionnaire evidence. The most that can be said is that avenues of communication exist.

While there is rather direct evidence that the guidelines mentioned in preceding paragraphs are operative in a positive fashion in the centrally co-ordinated type of in-service education program, the evidence is not so clear and direct with respect to some of the other guidelines. There is little evidence, for example, to indicate any attention to group process. This cannot be construed to mean that such attention is completely lacking. It was indicated on two responses that one of the changes noted as a result of the program of in-service education was more extensive and effective participation in group study activities by members of their school staffs. One might infer that, with the extent of small-group activities revealed by the questionnaires, it would be difficult to avoid considerable concern for the process itself.

A report came from one midwest community of 45,000 inhabitants, with a school staff of 385, describing the development of a series of nine sessions which were devoted to a better understanding on the part of the leadership of the school of the processes of group work. In collaboration with the department of education of a university, the administrative staff, which includes all who had responsibility for giving instructional leadership, developed a seminar around the processes of group leadership. While the content of the nine-session seminar had to do with instructional problems within the local system, special attention was given to group process itself. This proved to be very helpful to the leadership group. As a result of this experience, the teaching staff requested that a course in "Group Dynamics and Its Relationship to Classroom Instruction" be offered in the fall of 1955. Such a course has been conducted on a credit basis by a person who has had considerable work in the field.

Again, the questionnaire does not provide evidence regarding the presence or absence of an atmosphere conducive to building mutual respect, support, permissiveness, and creativeness. It would seem reasonable, however, to infer that sharing of the leadership function, involving all people concerned in the planning process at each step from the selection of the problems for study to incorporating accepted recommendations into practice, voluntary participation in many aspects of the program, and seeing to it that a study of problems results in changes in the school program are all factors which are basic to the creation of such an atmosphere. All of these practices are present, to a large degree, in the school systems with which this section of the chapter is concerned. If one cannot assume that the atmosphere itself exists in these school systems, it is apparent at least that conditions are favorable to it.

The questionnaire again provided no direct evidence as to the provision of simple methods for translating thought and decisions into action. Since many definite changes of policy and practice have resulted from these programs of in-service education, such methods must have existed. Most school systems indicated that the recommendations of committees working as a part of the program were reported to administrators. The superintendent and the board of education were mentioned most frequently. Other systems reported to a co-ordinating committee, to administrators and teachers together, or to the director of instruction. The inference would seem to be that these recommendations were made to those with the power to make them a part of the school policy and practice.

One aspect of the program of in-service education in the public schools of a highly industrialized community of 60,000 affords an illustration of a method of translating decisions into action. The general area of guidance services was selected by the professional advancement committee for emphasis on a city-wide basis starting in 1952-53. A series of four general faculty meetings was planned. These meetings consisted of presentations by individuals and by panels accompanied by general discussion. Such questions as "The Teacher's Role in a Program of Mental Health." "Constructive Discipline and Atypical Behavior," "Why People Succeed," and "What Can I Do about Children's Problems?" were dealt with by such professional people as psychiatrists, a director of a guidance clinic, a pediatrician, and university professors in related fields. This was followed the next year by a university course for those who wished to stress mental health in the classroom.

At the same time, an existing guidance committee was expanded to include not only counselors, teachers, and administrators but also representatives of various community service agencies and organizations such as Family Service, State Employment Service, the

P.T.A., and the Board of Education. During the first year, this committee became most concerned with the organization of the guidance program. Through a study of the literature in the field, a survey of organizational patterns in comparable schools, and a survey of local guidance services by a team of experts from the state university, certain recommendations evolved. These recommendations included the creation of a department of guidance and pupil personnel services in the central office to be staffed by a director, a home visitor to replace the present truant officer, and adequate secretarial help. These recommendations were presented to the board of education through the superintendent of schools. After presentation, discussion, and deliberation, the recommendations were adopted and incorporated in the central office structure.

Of even greater importance than approval of the groups with power to initiate action is a thorough understanding and acceptance of the recommendations by all of the people whom they will affect. This requires well-defined lines of communication between and among working committees as well as between the working committees and the professional staff and lay citizens of the community. Most school systems indicated that such lines of communication had been established and were used. Lay people informed of the progress of the various working committees were limited to those serving on committees so far as could be determined from questionnaire responses.

One might make certain inferences with regard to the recognition of individual differences in many schools in this category on the basis of practices in co-operative group planning, voluntary participation, utilizing members of the teaching staff as leaders and resource people, and the provision of many opportunities for face-to-face, small-group, problem-solving experiences. These activities, it would seem, must be based on recognition of the uniqueness of the individual and his contribution to the solution of problems which face the group. To the degree that this is true, it can be said that school systems in this group recognize and accept the facts of individual differences and utilize them to achieve desirable ends.

All guidelines considered up to this point have been found, on the basis of either direct or indirect evidence, to operate positively with respect to the programs of in-service education in school systems with centrally co-ordinated programs of in-service education. One guideline seems to be uninfluential in such programs in that there is nothing which indicates any real concern over the relation of the public school to currently significant cultural, political, and economic problems and conflicts. There was no mention, for example, of any attention to problems of intergroup relations, the role of public education in the growth and development of the American social order, or the defense of our freedoms. These schools seemed to be busy defending themselves against current attacks leveled at their beliefs and practices rather than devoting time and effort to issues basic to the society in which they existed. To the extent this was true, there was a neglect of one of the unique functions of public education in a free society, namely, to develop the kind of educational program which leads to the continuous improvement of that society.

DECENTRALIZED APPROACH

Doll, Passow, and Corey define the decentralized approach to curriculum improvement as one which "maintains that curriculum development is primarily the responsibility of the individual school, its staff, and its patrons. Curriculum improvement activities should be centered in the local building unit. Decisions regarding the selection of problems, the methods to be used for attacking them, and the personnel to be involved are all made in individual schools. The central office may be advised or may know of such activity going on in the local school unit, and it may also provide consultant service, but it assumes a minimum of responsibility for initiation, direction, or co-ordination of the program."[2]

Using the above criteria, the authors of this chapter identified 26 of the 145 systems responding to the questionnaire, or 18 per cent, as characterized by many decentralized practices. Such systems indicated that they relied upon building meetings as chief vehicles for in-service education and that the building principals exercised considerable leadership in planning in-service work. Many of these systems utilized general faculty meetings, grade-level meetings, subject-area meetings, and committees representing all areas and all levels, but they all double-checked building meetings as the chief

2. *Op. cit.*, p. 5.

vehicle in the organization of their in-service education programs. Some systems identified themselves through their descriptive statements. A city system in Michigan reported that it encouraged "considerable building autonomy" and that each principal gave leadership to his building in working on problems at both the building and system-wide levels.

Another questionnaire item used in identification of tendencies toward decentralization asked for the in-service problems being studied, by whom they were suggested, who was working on them, and to whom reports were to be made. Systems classified as decentralized worked mainly on building-level problems suggested by teachers and principals. Committees of teachers from the building studied the problems and reported their results to their principal and colleagues.

Size of school system made no difference in the percentage of decentralization found until the number of professional staff exceeded 500, when the percentage more than doubled. Six of the 15 systems of over 500 staff members used the individual building as a center of in-service education. These data suggest that the larger systems seem to put more emphasis on individual building activity than do the smaller systems.

Again it must be kept in mind that classifying school systems as decentralized, or otherwise, is a relative rather than an absolute matter. The 26 systems so classified all had many elements of central co-ordination and some of centralization. No case of "pure" decentralization was found. No system declared it used building meetings and individual building direction of in-service education alone. All systems used some combination of building meetings with grade-level groups, subject-matter area meetings, general faculty meetings, and committees representing all areas and all levels. Certain systems seemed to be moving in the direction of greater decentralization, others toward more central co-ordination. A Washington community reported, for example, that building meetings had been and will continue to be "most important" in its program, but that it had started in 1955 a system-wide in-service education project.

The guidelines of chapter v apply to the decentralized systems in varying degrees. Seventeen systems declared that they had made an evaluation of their in-service program; nine said, "No." Oral reactions of the staff and unsigned questionnaires were most often used. As the systems approached more complete decentralization they replied, as did one in Michigan, that evaluation was conducted "not as a total program of in-service activity—however, each activity is evaluated as it progresses." Teacher reactions on evaluation were varied; a Georgia city-county unit reported returns which were 75 per cent enthusiastic, 20 per cent lukewarm, and 5 per cent critical.

Working on the decentralized pattern would seem to offer the following strengths in making appraisal an integral part of in-service work: ease of including all who were a part of the planning, maintenance of good communication, and making application of value judgments a joint enterprise of all who are involved. Using the individual building as the work center should also make easier a day-by-day and over-all evaluation of both process and results.

Attention to the interrelationships of different groups is simplified on the decentralized level, since system-wide groups are eliminated or kept to a minimum. Meshing of "regular" and "special" activities must still be handled at the individual building level but would involve fewer groups. Most of the communities studied have developed a somewhat similar pattern for co-ordinating the efforts of system-wide groups through the creation of a committee of teachers and administrators to work with the assistant superintendent or curriculum director who has the direct responsibility for planning the in-service program.

Provision of opportunities for people to relate themselves to each other would seem to be facilitated by decentralization, since the need for co-operative problem-solving in each building would be so immediate and pressing. A New York community indicated that much can be done this way, reporting:

> It is probably fair to say that as much in-service education is done through day-by-day contacts of capable staff members with our teachers as is done by planned activities of a workshop character. Further, a great deal of in-service education is done here with all the appearance of informality, but much planning was involved to make this experience a worth-while one.

A midwest system describes its use of small problem-centered groups as follows:

Some study groups have been organized on a system-wide basis. These, however, were initiated solely by teachers and are representative of their interests. They are not representative groups in the sense that members represent various buildings or grade levels. They are study groups organized for the purpose of increased understanding on the part of participants rather than for the purpose of offering recommendations to the larger staff group.

Three such groups were studying human relations, camping, and industrial arts at the elementary level.

Systems carrying on in-service education only at the local building level might develop better relationships among individuals and groups within the building but might also lose benefits from inter-relationships among the individuals and groups of the total system. Only one of 26 systems classified as decentralized had no system-wide faculty meetings. All systems studied used, in some degree, grade-level meetings, subject-matter area meetings, or committees representing all areas and all levels in addition to their emphasis on the individual building.

The scope of the problems which decentralized systems report they are working on would indicate that individuals and groups are studying issues of significance to them. Almost all of the subject areas are under study, as are materials of instruction, teaching techniques, records and reports, and so on. Child study, guidance, and human relations were mentioned most often. Changes brought about as a result of in-service activities include an equally wide range. New guides and courses in subject areas, improved services to students, better student achievement, revised reporting systems, improved practices in unit teaching, grouping, and long-range planning of class offerings are listed along with such less tangible items as improvement of professional attitudes, better understanding of children, exchange of ideas to make for better teaching, and closer co-operation of faculties.

It would seem, also, that with in-service education focused on the individual building level, the same people who work on problems would plan how they work. Domination or control by forces outside the building would be reduced or eliminated.

Evidence on the attention given to group problem-solving processes is slight. A Colorado system, however, reported that one of the changes resulting from the in-service work was an "improving quality of meetings by having teachers help plan them."

Responding systems indicated, generally, a clear-cut and simple pattern for moving from study of a problem to reporting on it, and then to appropriate action. The use of the individual building as the center of study gives the faculties the opportunity to react, face-to-face, with the group making the study and presenting recommendations for change. Participants can also test their listeners and improve communication in the reporting process. An Alabama city presented the following flow chart showing progression from identifying a problem, to studying it, and to reporting recommendations to the group which had the power to act:

PROBLEM	WORK GROUP	REPORT TO
Understanding child behavior	Representative group of teachers	Individual faculty
Reporting pupil progress	Cross-section group of all concerned	Staff and board
Guidance in high school	Teachers, principals, and others	High-school faculties
Citizenship education	Cross-section groups	Faculties, P.T.A.
Teaching of language	Teachers and supervisors	Faculties

Parker emphasizes in chapter v the importance of trying out ideas between group meetings and of encouraging and supporting experimental climate. The individual school unit would seem to be best for such purposes. Teachers and study groups can make their plans close to the sources of their problems, and, under the sympathetic guidance of their principal, try out ideas in their own classrooms and school between meetings.

In some situations difficulties may arise from too much decentralization. There is the possibility that an individual school unit might set itself apart from the rest of the system and become encapsulated. Members of the building unit could lose contact with the rest of the system and become so engrossed with their own way of doing things that they no longer are much interested in what is going on outside their building. This may develop because of inherent satisfactions of a psychological nature which transform the group [individual school] from a work group to a tight friendship clique. If one building becomes conspicuously individualistic, interbuilding rivalries and jealousies are apt to develop. Parents, teachers, and patrons then become more interested in defending their ways of doing things or in attacking the ways of others than they are in examining together how all may improve the total educational program.

It would appear, also, that some problems cannot be considered solely from the individual building point of view. Systems of pupil accounting and record-keeping can be operated more economically and efficiently in a large system if kept somewhat uniform among the various buildings. Parents and teachers feel a sense of security if pupil-reporting practices do not vary too widely in a system. Methods of handling instructional materials, selecting, purchasing, distributing, and storing must often be done on a similar basis because of the business office. Securing this kind of system-wide agreement would be difficult or impossible under the completely decentralized plan.

Rich resources are available and in use in some decentralized school system communities. It is common practice to provide some school time for building meetings. Parents, students, and/or community organizations are involved in all but four of the responding systems, three of which employ less than 75 teachers. Resource personnel, including university faculty, consultants from publishing houses, and educators from other systems are used in all but two responding systems, both of which employ less than 75 professional workers. Resource-material centers which are developed in each building are more readily available to staff when needed.

Decentralized systems provide annual budgets for in-service education costs which vary with the size of the system. Cities and counties employing 300 or less staff provide amounts ranging from $100.00 to $1,000.00, with a median figure of $500.00. Larger systems have a median amount of $1,000.00—a Louisiana county reports budgeting $12,000.00 during 1955, and one in Maryland, $15,000.00.

Unless some plan of sharing resources, both human and material, is developed, it would be difficult under extreme decentralization to provide equally rich resources to all individual buildings in a large system. Many systems in which the in-service education program is centrally co-ordinated are developing instructional material centers where professional and instructional materials are housed for distribution to all buildings and individuals. When centrally co-ordinated systems utilize visiting consultants, they can justify large budgets for such services if a large percentage of the staff benefit. If, however, only one building—especially a small one —were to request expensive materials or helps, the problem of defending and paying for such helps would loom large.

A study of the practices being carried on in decentralized systems reveals some procedures which are not so directly related to the guidelines, perhaps, but which are quite common to all. The organizational structure for in-service work is a similar one—the superintendent delegates his responsibility to an assistant or to the director of curriculum, who in turn shares his responsibility with a group of principals and teachers. Sometimes that committee is further dignified with a title such as the "curriculum steering committee" or the "curriculum planning council."

All systems studied, except one, utilized workshops as a part of their in-service work. Most common practice was to hold the workshops for a two- to ten-day period prior to the opening of school. However, many workshops were held during the school year, and a few directly after the close of school or during the summer.

Orientation programs are held for new teachers in all but three of the responding systems, two of which employ less than 75 on their staffs, the other less than 300. This work is done prior to the start of the school year; some systems combine the preschool period with work held shortly after school begins. Few systems give extra pay for the extra days asked.

Most systems used a variety of approaches to their in-service efforts. Attendance at conventions is encouraged, one system providing a budget of $5,000.00. Experimentation ranked high as another kind of activity, as did visitation, travel, and the development of professional libraries. Professional writing was also mentioned frequently.

Less common was the granting of credit for curriculum work. Only ten of the 26 systems polled reported this plan in effect. The largest percentage occurred in the largest systems. The most common type of credit allowed is local professional credit, although five systems arranged for granting university credit, either with or without local credit. One system articulated its in-service program with state certification; in other cases the receiving of credits was an optional matter.

Some Generalizations

Although the writers felt that they could sense the basic philosophy of the systems through their responses on the questionnaire well enough to classify them, as being primarily centralized, decentralized, or centrally co-ordinated, there was much overlapping in practices in each system. Nevertheless, the categories were helpful in pointing out major differences in approaches to in-service education and in illustrating various applications of the guidelines of chapter v.

An initial generalization to be drawn from this study is that most of the comprehensive and well-planned in-service activities are consistent with a great majority of the guidelines. A typical example is the following institute program on evaluation conducted and reported by a Wisconsin public school system.

In the fall of 1954 the teachers of the system, working through their curriculum council, which is the curriculum and in-service education advisory and planning body, and through their education association, decided to study the theme of evaluation during the annual Friday and Saturday institute held in February. This theme was selected because of its appropriateness to the ongoing curriculum program. The elementary schools were working through their first year with a new program of reporting pupil progress. The junior high schools were in the midst of a study of reporting practices, and the senior high schools were making extensive changes in the high-school curriculum which involved questions of evaluation.

The improvement committee, representing teachers, consultants, and administrators, was given full freedom and a budget of $500.00 to plan how it would like to organize the institute. Early in the fall, the committee secured the services of the headmaster of a private school from a near-by city as visiting consultant and held several planning sessions with him in the fall and early winter. The following plans were announced to all teachers several weeks in advance and carried out during the institute.

The visiting consultant opened the session with an address calculated to stimulate teachers' thinking on such questions as:

1. What basic growth lines does the school system have for its children?
2. What data do we need to determine whether this growth is taking place?
3. Is the school system collecting and using the data, and how can these processes be improved?

Following the opening address, all of the professional staff met in cross-section groups, including teachers, consultants, and administrators ranging from kindergarten through high school, to discuss the application of the questions to current practice. Each group was under the leadership of a team of teachers who had been given special training in group processes by the visiting consultant. At noon, participants ate lunch together in the school cafeteria. In the afternoon, the staff met as grade-level groups of Kdg.-III, IV–VI, VII–IX, and X–XII to continue the discussions begun on a cross-sectional basis in the morning. The following morning, teachers met as building groups under the leadership of their principals to summarize their discussion of the day before, to make recommendations for studies which needed to be made system-wide, to improve evaluation processes, and to translate into action at the building level their thinking of the previous day.

Recorders kept a careful record of each session. Before the following session each participant received a copy of all the minutes of the previous sessions. The improvement committee studied the reports of the cross-section, grade-level, and the building groups and made a summary report of the entire institute which was placed in the hands of each staff member and made the subject of study by the curriculum council as it planned for curriculum and in-service education for the following year. Besides the action taken in the buildings to improve evaluation practices, a program of system-wide study of the record-keeping system was instituted in the fall of 1955 to make necessary changes for the improvement of evaluation processes at all levels.

In planning for, carrying out, and following through this one in-service education activity, application was made, in some degree, of most of the guidelines of chapter v. The staff worked on a problem which it selected as of significance to the entire system. Representatives of all professional groups made plans for working on the problem. People interrelated themselves through cross-section, grade-level, and building groups as well as through a general faculty meeting, a noon luncheon, and an intermingling for a period of two days. Considerable attention was given to group problem-solving techniques through leadership-training and through experience in participation in three types of groups during the institute. While atmosphere is difficult to measure, post-institute evaluations seemed to indicate that feelings of mutual respect, support, and permissiveness were created. Resources in the way of released time from classroom responsibilities, the services of consultants, clerical help in the duplication and distribution of minutes, etc., were available and used. From the work of the institute came action in the study of the problems agreed upon as important by those participating.

Teachers came to the institute directly from the reality of their classrooms and returned there after their two-day conference. They were encouraged to relate all they said and did in the course of their meetings. Appraisal was a part of each session of the institute. A final appraisal by the planning committee was distributed to all persons in attendance. Communication channels were provided and the interrelationships of the different groups were strengthened through the records which were made of each session and given to all participants. Facts of individual differences were accepted and utilized in the selection of leadership and recorder teams, in the assignments to discussion groups, and in the utilization of individual backgrounds and contribution by the discussion leaders and groups.

Another generalization from our questionnaire study is that most communities are following the centrally co-ordinated approach. Of the 145 school systems, 83, or 57 per cent, are listed in that category according to the judgment of the writers. Twenty-five per cent showed strong centralized tendencies, while 18 per cent were classified as being in the decentralized group.

Almost all communities surveyed were using a variety of techniques and procedures in their programs of in-service education. Mention was made of many kinds of group work, travel, attendance at conventions, professional writing, and experimentation. There seems to be no one golden road to successful in-service education, but rather a need for a multiple approach using a great variety of activities.

If any common denominator exists among the 145 systems studied, it was their use of many individuals and many groups along with multiple and rich resources. Groups of teachers, administrators, central office personnel, parents, citizens, and combinations of these persons are busy at work on local problems. They are organized in a variety of ways—as grade groups, subject-matter specialists, voluntary study groups, building staffs and subgroups, cross-section groups representing various levels and interests in a system, etc. Involvement of a large number of people seems to be one characteristic held in common by all.

The authors of this chapter have tried to reach some conclusions as to which approaches to in-service education best illustrate the guidelines of chapter v. It is their judgment that the centrally coordinated approach offers the best possibilities of meeting all of the guides. Each approach has its strong and weak points; no one approach offers a magic solution to the problem of the best application of the guidelines.

It would appear most difficult for a strictly centralized system to provide opportunities for individuals and groups to work on problems that are significant to them. As in-service activities are initiated, managed, and conducted from the central office, the opportunities for large numbers of staff to see significance in these activities, to participate in them, and to plan how they will work on them would decrease. It would also appear difficult to create an atmosphere of mutual respect, support, permissiveness, and creativeness under highly centralized operations, because without a feeling of the significance of the problems on which a group is working, it would be difficult to release the creativeness inherent in the group. By central office suggestion or decree, the centralized approach might try to direct attention of workers to the need for interrelationships, communication, appraisal, testing and trying ideas, and acceptance of individual differences. It is to be expected, however, that without the spirit of mutual respect, support, permissiveness, and creativeness, central office control would remain ineffectual. Again, centralized control might provide large budgets for resources, but unless the resources were utilized by workers who saw and felt the need for such helps, they would be of small value.

The decentralized approach would seem to possess the most strength in the very spots centralized operations appear to be the weakest. As in-service efforts are focused on teachers and their daily problems in their classes and buildings, work should increasingly be carried on in terms of problems significant to the workers. Opportunities for people to plan how they will work and the creation of respect, support, permissiveness, and creativeness should increase. Opportunities for relationships at the building level, attention to group problem-solving processes, to continuous appraisal, communication, tryouts in "reality contexts," and regard for individual differences should all increase. However, if decentralization proceeded to the point that relationships, exchange of ideas, and co-operation with other buildings and the central office were eliminated, it would seem as though decentralization would become impractical and defeat itself.

For these reasons, a wisely managed system of central co-ordination would combine the advantages existing in both the centralized and decentralized approaches and, at the same time, avoid most of the dangers that exist in each.

CHAPTER X

Area, State, Regional, and National In-service Education Programs

KENNETH J. REHAGE
and
GEORGE W. DENEMARK

The problems of definition, delimitation, and selection are especially complex in seeking to report upon in-service education programs at area, state, regional, and national levels. One means of limiting the field is to consider only those programs which involve face-to-face relationships of groups of in-service personnel. This criterion, while not excluding in-service programs which utilize printed materials as a part of their activity, does eliminate the many which depend solely upon the effects of books, pamphlets, magazines, and other printed materials. A second criterion establishes the requirement that at least two days be allowed annually for face-to-face, co-operative activities of different classification groups of employees. Still a third means of limiting the field is to exclude programs focused primarily upon groups other than educators working at the elementary- and secondary-school levels or in teacher-education programs related to those levels. The belief of the writers that more than vicarious knowledge is needed about programs under examination led to the adoption of a fourth selective factor, namely, the opportunity for the authors to observe the program in action. These four delimiting factors were used in making the selections of illustrative programs described in subsequent sections of this chapter.

The reader should recognize, therefore, that the accounts of in-service education programs which follow are not intended to constitute an extensive survey of the field, nor even a representative sampling of activities at the area, state, regional, and national levels. They are, instead, intended principally to provide illustrations of the twelve in-service education guidelines presented in chapter v. The programs discussed are those which have at certain points unique qualities which may be of special interest and help to persons having leadership responsibilities for planning and conducting in-service education activities.

Area Programs

The term *area programs* is used to denote in-service education projects involving more than one school system, but not operating over a wide enough area to be properly classified as a state program. Typically, an area program would include projects intended to serve school personnel in adjacent or neighboring systems.

A CO-OPERATIVE ACTION RESEARCH PROJECT

The Metropolitan Detroit Bureau of Co-operative School Studies has sponsored area programs of this kind. We report here briefly upon activities carried on under the auspices of the Bureau's Elementary School Improvement Committee. In its biannual conferences and through frequent one-day demonstration clinics, the committee has endeavored to promote improvement in the instructional programs of participating schools. One of the outcomes of the committee's various activities was the generation of considerable interest in organizing a co-operative study of significant educational problems. The steps taken to initiate the study extended over a considerable period of time and were carried on largely through the activities of a subcommittee known as the Co-operative Action Research Committee.[1] Among the major problems confronting the subcommittee were (*a*) the selection of a central focus of sufficient significance to appeal to staff members in several schools, and (*b*) the location of resources that could provide needed help.

A major difficulty was that of defining a problem area which could serve as a framework for co-operative activity among several schools and yet provide sufficient latitude for the separate staffs to work on matters of direct concern to them. After much deliberation

1. Paul Carter, Daniel Nesbitt, and Mary Harden (chairman), "Co-operative Action Research of the Metropolitan Detroit Bureau of Co-operative School Studies," in *A Look at Co-operative Action Research in Michigan*, pp. 51–69. Lansing: Michigan Education Association, 1954. The account here is based largely upon information contained in this bulletin.

it was felt that the problem of providing for children the kinds of learning experiences which facilitate continuous and sequential growth would serve as a suitable framework within which a variety of separate inquiries could be undertaken.

On the matter of locating resources, the subcommittee made provision for consultant help, the members of the committee agreeing to serve in this capacity as needed. In addition, the committee arranged for consultant help from the Midwest Administration Center of the University of Chicago. As part of its studies of leadership for the improvement of instruction, the Center was interested in following closely the developments of the several projects where both teachers and administrators were involved.

Eight school systems sent representatives to a workshop where the central purpose was to explore ways of getting started on action research projects. Here teachers and administrators from the various schools began the process of locating and defining problems which were of concern to them and which could fit into the larger enterprise as well. The specific problems identified included the following:

1. Will continuity and sequence of learning be increased for children by using some form of the kindergarten-primary program?
2. How can we bridge the gap between kindergarten and first grade with emphasis placed on an extended reading readiness program?
3. How may schools help children develop self-direction?
4. Can an elementary school improve learning experiences of children through flexible classroom organization by giving children opportunities to work in large groups, small groups, and as individuals?
5. What ways can be developed for gathering data which indicate the opportunities within a classroom for an individual to assume the role of leader, follower, or equal?
6. How can a school help children grow toward social maturity?

Final reports have not yet been made on all projects, since some were planned to continue for at least two or three years. The subcommittee has met regularly and has sought to help the various groups by suggesting bibliographies, arranging meetings, procuring consultants, giving general direction, and encouraging the participating teachers and administrators.

With this brief description as a background, we may now examine the developments in this project more specifically in terms of our guidelines. It is clear that those responsible for the development and general direction of the project were deeply aware of the need to encourage individuals and groups to work on problems "significant to them." This was not easy to accomplish, for the committee also desired to have the separate projects "add up" to something. The initial, extended search for a common focus reflected this concern. In general, the practice was to attach primary importance to the significance of the problem to members of each group and to look secondarily at the matter of its relationship to the general inquiry for the co-operative study.

The project demonstrates also the application of the principle that those involved in a project should plan how they will work upon it. The efforts of the co-ordinating group were consistently directed toward this end. However, the research emphasis in the project presented difficulties in those groups where individuals felt inadequately prepared for such work. One of the consequences was a considerable dependence upon local leadership and outside consultants who were presumed to have some experience and competence in carrying on research. This was particularly true in situations where new means for collecting data had to be devised and where difficulties were encountered in summarizing, analyzing, and interpreting such data.

It was early recognized that one of the important sources of motivation for continuing work is the satisfaction one gets from participation in an effective working group. Attention was, therefore given to developing and maintaining the kinds of working relationships in each group that would maximize its effectiveness. A workshop was planned for the chairmen and recorders of all groups. At the periodic conferences of the Elementary School Improvement Committee further study was made of ways of facilitating effective group work. There was considerable variation from project to project with respect to emphasis upon improving individual and group problem-solving processes. In general, it is probably fair to say that the working groups paid less attention to this matter than did their representatives at the various conferences where such problems were considered at some length.

It was clearly the intent of the co-ordinating subcommittee that the whole study be conducted in such a way as to encourage the development of mutual respect, support, permissiveness, and creativeness. Similarly, the committee recognized that individual differences would exist within and between groups and would need to be utilized. Since the major responsibility in this regard rested with the leadership in each working group, there was undoubtedly variation from project to project. The extent of this variation cannot at present be documented, although some data on this point have been gathered and are presently being analyzed by representatives of the Midwest Administration Center.

Two major resources necessary in such a project, in addition to those represented by the participants themselves, are time and consultant help. The efforts to provide the latter have already been described. The work on most of the projects was done by participants after regular school hours, and in addition to their already heavy programs. In some of the schools, administrators found ways of making time available during the school day, as well as ways of releasing at least some of the participants to attend conferences and workshops. In general, however, the co-ordinating committee found that "few schools have a workable program for releasing teachers to work on projects within a school day."[2]

Within each separate study group the difficulties of moving from decision to action seemed to be minimal, for action tended to follow rather easily once the decision to act was made. The operations of the co-ordinating committee illustrated the problems of moving from decision to action at another level, where the situation was much more complex. On this committee were people in administrative positions in each of the participating school systems. Because each system was in a different stage of readiness for participation, it was easier to secure action in some projects than in others. The factors which contributed to this situation were not always evident. One source of difficulty was the fact that the committee could make decisions but often was not the group to take the actions required by its own decisions.

This project was pointed toward the identification and testing of new ideas. But new ideas do not come easily, and they may come even more slowly if there is an expressed intention of submitting them to a more or less rigorous "test." The project encountered all of the difficulties familiar to those who set out to test ideas where

2. *Ibid.*, p. 68.

precise means of making an appraisal are neither readily available nor easily produced. In practically all of the projects, therefore, much work had to be done by the participants to develop suitable means of appraisal. One of the major tasks of the local leadership was to give support and encouragement to participants in formulating problems to be studied, in developing ways of attacking these problems, and in appraising the consequences of particular solutions that were tried.

Several efforts were made to gather data necessary for the appraisal of the in-service growth of participants. The co-ordinating committee, for example, secured evaluative comments from both participants and visiting consultants with regard to the various conferences and workshops and used these materials in planning subsequent conferences. Local leaders frequently made efforts, mostly of an informal sort, to check on the progress of the various projects and the reactions of the participants to their work. An effort to collect anecdotal records from participants produced some interesting material, but the procedure for gathering this material proved to be too cumbersome and was finally discontinued. Perhaps the most comprehensive effort at appraisal was made by representatives of the Midwest Administration Center, who secured various kinds of data from a considerable number of participants when the projects had been in progress for a little more than a year. The experience with all these efforts to make appraisal an integral part of the in-service activities points up a problem which is commonly encountered. It is not a simple matter to secure the kinds of data needed to assess the nature and extent of changes taking place in the participants.

The central purpose of this co-operative project was to test the feasibility of a variety of ideas for improving instruction. There was also the implied purpose of providing situations in which all participants—teachers, administrators, and consultants—could become more proficient in the skills necessary for successful co-operative study of significant educational problems. We have indicated the points at which the experiences of this study group illustrate the applicability of some of the principles contained in the guidelines proposed in chapter v. It seems clear to us that the guidelines are most easily applied when one is describing a particular school.

An "area" project of the kind described here presents problems of organization and co-ordination which complicate the process of making decisions and taking action. The conditions under which this kind of in-service activity is carried on are almost certain to vary from one school to another, and marked variation limits the extent to which generalization in terms of our guidelines is possible for the enterprise as a whole.

ANOTHER TYPE OF AREA PROGRAM

One other type of area program will be briefly noted here. It has been developed by the superintendents of the three adjacent school districts of St. Charles, Geneva, and Batavia in northern Illinois. With the help of the county superintendent of schools, these superintendents have arranged for in-service activities which each year focus upon some aspect of the instructional program. For example, in one recent year, attention was centered upon instruction in social studies.

The decision to work on social-studies instruction reflected the considered judgment of the superintendents after informal contacts with teachers. Within the limits of this initial decision there was opportunity for teachers to work on problems of significance to them. Very early it became apparent that a rather widely shared concern among the elementary-grade teachers related to unnecessary duplication in the social-studies program. The decision to focus upon this particular problem served to delimit the inquiry still further. We have here, then, an illustration of how a perfectly appropriate desire to give explicit direction and focus to an in-service program can be realized by decisions to limit the scope of the enterprise. While such decisions did reflect a general concern, as was true in this case, they do inevitably restrict in some way the opportunities for individuals to work upon problems of greatest significance to them.

This project was of relatively short duration, and it soon acquired a very specific focus. Partly as a consequence of these two facts, relatively little attention was given to some of the practices implied by our guidelines. Explicit concern was not developed, for example, for increasing individual and group problem-solving skills, although some such growth may well have taken place. Neither was there a systematic effort to make appraisal an integral part of the program, although every participant surely had private judgments as to the effectiveness of the program. There were very genuine attempts to encourage creative approaches to the problems identified and to plan various modifications of existing practices. There were extended opportunities to exchange experience and ideas and to see local problems in a broader context. But the groups were not really "action" groups, except as agreement to make certain recommendations to the separate school systems could be regarded as action. Nevertheless, area programs of this type seem to be thoroughly practical and worth while.

State Programs

THE ILLINOIS CURRICULUM PROGRAM

One of the most widely publicized state curriculum programs is that carried on since 1947 under the auspices of the office of the Superintendent of Public Instruction of the State of Illinois. Generally known as the Illinois Curriculum Program, this co-operative enterprise has been directed toward the improvement of instructional programs in public schools. The principles upon which the program is based, and the six major purposes which define the scope of its activities, do not explicitly mention the term "in-service education."[3] However, curriculum improvement has been clearly an "end in view." Local studies basic to curriculum revision, local curriculum improvement projects, and state-wide workshops for administrators and teachers have been encouraged. Publications helpful in curriculum development projects have been prepared and distributed. Because of this emphasis upon assistance to local schools desiring to bring about curriculum change, the Illinois Curriculum Program has had a strong impact upon the in-service education opportunities available to teachers in participating schools.

While the in-service education facet of the Illinois Curriculum Program is of primary concern to us here, it is desirable to comment briefly upon how the policies and plans are developed for the program as a whole, for this is an important factor in setting the

3. Vernon L. Nickell, Charles W. Sanford, Eric H. Johnson, Willard B. Spalding, Harold C. Hand, and Edward C. Weir, "The Illinois Curriculum Program: Its Organization and Operation," *Illinois School Board Journal*, XIX (September–October, 1952), 132–34.

context within which the program operates as a state-wide venture. Policy determination rests with a large steering committee, members of which act as liaison officers between the committee and the various professional and lay organizations or agencies they represent. The committee discusses and approves all policies before they are adopted, reads and passes upon all publications, receives and develops suggestions for changes in and improvements of specific plans, examines proposals for basic studies and suggests desirable modifications before recommending that they be carried out.[4] The responsibility for seeing that policies and programs are carried out rests with the director of the Program and his staff.[5]

Decisions to participate in the various activities of the Illinois Curriculum Program have been made locally also. The consistent emphasis on local decision-making reflects a conviction that it is important to deal with problems of concern to the participants. The workshops sponsored by the Program have consistently been organized around such problems.

The Illinois Curriculum Program has not specified how any participating school should approach the problems it chooses to study. It has endeavored to make certain, however, that schools wishing to take part are prepared to make some contribution of their own in return for the resources made available to them under the auspices of the state program. For example, schools are expected to make available enough of the time of teachers concerned so that reasonable participation is possible. They must be willing to provide funds that will enable the teachers involved to spend a number of days each year in workshops and in meetings with teachers in other schools. The schools must agree to serve as observation centers.[6]

The Illinois Curriculum Program has encouraged schools to collect facts regarding local conditions prior to making decisions as to curriculum change. It has urged that basic studies of holding power, hidden tuition costs, and pupil participation in extra-class activities

4. *Ibid.,* p. 134.

5. Dr. C. W. Sanford, presently Associate Dean of the College of Education, University of Illinois, was the director of the Program from its beginning until 1954. The present director is Dr. Eric H. Johnson. These men supplied information upon which the present report is based.

6. Charles W. Sanford and Willard B. Spalding, "The Illinois Secondary Program," *California Journal of Secondary Education,* XXVII (January, 1952), 29.

be undertaken, as well as follow-up studies of graduates and a series of "local area consensus studies." The Program has made available to schools throughout the state a fund of technical "know-how" which has enabled local faculties to carry on such studies. What use would be made of these data, and indeed whether the data would be gathered at all, were matters of local decision. The response of school systems to this offer of help suggests that assistance in developing plans for gathering information locally is much needed and greatly desired.

The Illinois Curriculum Program has sponsored county-wide and state-wide workshops and has co-operated in the development of programs for workshops sponsored by local schools. During the first six years of its existence, the Program sponsored 86 workshops, which were attended by more than 36,000 teachers, administrators, and citizens from all parts of the state. The workshop program has served a variety of purposes, such as the development of new and improved materials and methods, the launching of new projects, the development of skills and attitudes basic to effective group work, and the stimulation of interest in the improvement of local school programs.[7] The practice of bringing representatives of various groups together for workshops extending over several days has served to develop a greater measure of understanding among individuals with quite different points of view, even though the differences may not have been entirely resolved.

Another service of the State Program has been that of mobilizing needed resources. Materials relevant to problems to be studied at workshops have been provided in abundance. A roster of competent consultants has been developed. From this roster is assembled a staff of consultants who can be helpful to participants in dealing with problems to be studied at each workshop. Serving without charge, these consultants have come from the office of the Superintendent of Public Instruction, from the institutions of higher learning in the state, from public school systems, as well as from various lay organizations. Through the co-operation of these agencies a considerable amount of consulting service has also been made available to

7. Vernon L. Nickell *et al.,* "The Illinois Curriculum Program: The Basic Studies—Aids in Securing Needed Local Facts," *Illinois School Board Journal,* XIX (November–December, 1952), 165, 166, 167.

participating local school systems without charge. All publications of the Program are similarly obtainable by local schools at no cost.

In a state-wide program it is never easy to contrive simple means for moving from decision to action. The Illinois Curriculum Program has met this problem by its insistence that action taken at the local level is the action that counts. It has done what it can (chiefly through the instrument of consultant teams) to assist local schools to develop appropriate means of implementing local decisions. So far as state-wide action is concerned, the steering committee has seemed to provide a satisfactory mechanism for reaching decisions. Placing responsibility for implementing decisions upon the program director has facilitated the taking of action at the state level.

The Illinois Curriculum Program has consistently nourished the idea of testing new plans and programs. Its workshops have tried to stimulate interest in developing ideas which can be tested out locally in a variety of situations. Its consultants have repeatedly been called upon to help local school systems and individual teachers in the development of such ideas. While it is obvious that participation in a state-wide program of this kind lends support to local schools and individual teachers in their exploratory and experimental efforts, the more crucial factor in this connection appears to be the climate of opinion toward innovation in each locality. A good deal of attention has been given in Illinois Curriculum Program workshops to the problem of developing a climate favorable to curriculum change.

The problem of continuous appraisal has been recognized through efforts to encourage both the evaluation of the effectiveness of local curriculum change and state-wide activities. From time to time, consultants have met to see how they might serve more effectively in the participating schools. Efforts have been made to conduct fairly systematic appraisals of the workshops sponsored by the Program. Consultants have frequently been asked to help local school systems develop means of appraising their programs of in-service work and have assisted in the analysis of the results of such appraisals.

It is essential, in a state-wide program, that co-ordination be obtained. The Illinois Curriculum Program serves an important function here, chiefly through the work of the steering committee and the director. The organizational structure has been flexible enough to permit considerable expansion beyond that originally contemplated. Although first conceived as a program for secondary schools, in due course the Program was dealing with elementary-school problems as well. When a nation-wide project in citizenship education extended its efforts to Illinois it did so under the general auspices of the Program. The director and his staff have helped to plan several workshops on economic education in the state. The Program has co-operated in the development of the Allerton House Conferences on Education in Illinois, a series of meetings growing out of an increasing amount of criticism of practices and policies in education. The fact that the Illinois Curriculum Program has been called upon to assume these and other responsibilities suggests that the mechanisms it has developed for co-ordinating the efforts of different state groups have served their purpose well.

Finally, we may note the ways in which the Illinois projects have concerned themselves with various aspects of the current educational, cultural, political, and economic scene. In the first place, it has encouraged local schools to make a careful assessment of conditions in the local community as a means of gathering data basic to curriculum change. Secondly, its sponsorship of the series of inquiries that culminated in the publication of *The Schools and National Security*[8] represents an effort to assess the probable impact of significant national developments upon the schools and to suggest ways of taking that impact into account. Thirdly, its participation in inquiries into the basic issues of private and public education at all levels (particularly through the Allerton House Conferences) symbolizes its interest in joining with both friends and critics of the schools to seek ways of improving the conduct of the educational enterprise.

OTHER STATE PROGRAMS

For purposes of merely suggesting some of the other types of in-service programs carried on at the state level, we shall turn to brief accounts of activities in other states. In Wisconsin a Co-operative Educational Planning Program has been in operation since 1945. Some two hundred individuals, representing various phases of the

8. Charles W. Sanford, Harold C. Hand, and Willard B. Spalding (editors), *The Schools and National Security*. Circular Series A, No. 51, Illinois Secondary School Curriculum Program Bulletin No. 16. Springfield: Office of the Superintendent of Public Instruction, 1951.

educational enterprise in the state, are organized into a dozen committees. Each committee meets frequently during the year to study a variety of educational problems. Surveys of relevant research and expert opinion are undertaken. The committees ultimately develop recommendations which are published by the office of the State Superintendent of Public Instruction. For the committee members involved, this program provides rich opportunities for in-service education. The publications include pronouncements on broad questions of educational policy (*The Task of the School, What is the Job of Public Education?*) as well as reports containing quite explicit recommendations for practice with respect to the various subject-matter areas in the school program. The work of the Program is directed by a "guiding committee," which is chaired by the state curriculum co-ordinator. The latter serves as a kind of executive secretary for the entire program.

Other state-wide programs in Wisconsin, conducted under the auspices of the State Department of Public Instruction, include an annual workshop for beginning principals. This workshop is carried on in co-operation with the School of Education of the University of Wisconsin. Local school boards underwrite the cost of workshop attendance for newly appointed principals. One of the major purposes is to provide opportunities for administrators to become acquainted with the services of the state department. A similar opportunity for in-service training is provided for rural and city elementary supervisors. In this instance, state-wide meetings of a workshop nature are held twice during each school year. Study groups have been organized among the supervisors for giving continuing attention to a variety of educational problems throughout the school year.[9]

Similarly, in Missouri, a variety of in-service opportunities is provided on a state-wide basis for teachers and administrators under the general auspices of the state department of education. Among these may be noted especially the annual summer workshop for school administrators, area workshops for administrators during the fall, county-wide conferences for elementary-school teachers to

9. This report is based upon information supplied by Walter B. Senty, Assistant Superintendent of Public Instruction, and the late Elton Nelson, who was State Curriculum Coordinator for Wisconsin.

consider most advantageous ways of utilizing the newly published elementary curriculum guide, and special meetings for board members and superintendents in newly reorganized school districts.[10]

A program of somewhat different sort in Michigan can be cited as an illustration of an approach to in-service training that is getting increased recognition throughout the country. We refer to the efforts to encourage curriculum research in local schools. Reacting to a suggestion from some members of the Michigan Association for Supervision and Curriculum Development, the State Superintendent of Public Instruction authorized the establishment of a state Committee on Curriculum Research. This committee endeavors "to maintain a continuing survey of needs and efforts in curriculum research in the state and to give leadership and direction to curriculum research activity in Michigan."[11] Under the auspices of the Michigan ASCD and the Michigan Education Association a bulletin describing several local co-operative action research projects was prepared. These various activities are more appropriately considered from the standpoint of local or area projects, but it deserves to be noted that support and encouragement have been forthcoming at the state level.

Again reminding the reader that this brief discussion of state programs of in-service training is intended to be illustrative rather than representative of practices throughout the nation, we may conclude with observations suggested by our preceding descriptions and analyses. It seems clear that state-level programs are advantageously carried on through having some connection with the state department of education, and in the instances we have cited that department was either an initiator or an active sponsor of the program. Within state programs, however, much would seem to depend upon the success of parallel efforts at the local level to meet the criteria suggested by the guidelines described in chapter v, for the changes anticipated in any in-service program are most likely to be observed in local school systems and in individual classrooms. One of the important functions to be performed through state programs,

10. This report is based upon information supplied by Irwin F. Coyle, Missouri Department of Education.

11. Michigan Association for Supervision and Curriculum Development, *A Look at Co-operative Action Research in Michigan,* p. 2. Lansing: Michigan Education Association, 1954.

therefore, would appear to be that of illustrating through their organization and operation how the various criteria can be met, thus providing participants with experiences which are supportive and encouraging to their own efforts to bring about desirable changes locally.

Regional Programs

In this section we are using the term "regional" to apply to in-service programs which draw their participants from an area larger than a single state. We have chosen to report on (a) a program serving primarily elementary teachers, (b) a program of especial relevance to those engaged in supervisory work, and (c) a program designed to bring about improved instruction in high schools in four southern states.

CLASSROOM TEACHERS STUDY ECONOMIC EDUCATION AT
AN ELEMENTARY LEVEL

A recent study of economic education in elementary schools provided opportunities for in-service growth for about sixty teachers from twenty-six different school systems in Illinois, Iowa, Wisconsin, and Minnesota. Funds to support the study were provided by General Mills, Incorporated, a business firm which had been interested for some time in the general problem. Scholarships enabled interested teachers to attend summer workshops at the University of Chicago and the University of Wisconsin. Provision was made for a follow-up study in the school year immediately following the workshop.

Among the specific inquiries to be undertaken in the workshops were the following:

1. What are the basic economic concepts essential to an understanding of our contemporary society?
2. Which of these concepts, if any, have direct relevance to the lives of boys and girls in the middle grades of the elementary school?
3. What kinds of experience do boys and girls normally have, and what kinds of experience could appropriately be provided, that will help them begin to acquire an understanding of some of the economic aspects of contemporary life?
4. How can these experiences be made an integral part of the school program?

5. What kinds of resource material are presently available, and what additional materials are needed?
6. How can the results of efforts to work with children in this area be appraised?

These questions were formulated as a result of preworkshop contacts with participating teachers. So far as these teachers were concerned, the program offered opportunity to strengthen their knowledge of the field of economics and to deal with the complex curriculum problem of developing suitable instructional plans for intermediate-grade children. The first of these represented a need common to practically all workshop participants, and, accordingly, a considerable segment of workshop time was devoted to the study of economics. The second task called for considerable individualization, since participants came from widely varying school situations. Because of this diversity, and because of the great need for exploration of a variety of approaches to the particular curriculum problem under consideration, the workshop staff urged participants to define the problem in terms appropriate to the situation existing in their own schools. Each was urged to work out plans that he felt would be practicable in that situation. Thus, within the limitations imposed by the task set for the workshops, there was a considerable measure of freedom for participants to select particular aspects of the problem upon which to work and to work on these problems in a manner best suited to the requirements of their own situation.

Much of the workshop experience was a search for ideas which could be tried and tested by individual teachers in their classrooms. A major responsibility of the staff was to establish and maintain an atmosphere which would encourage genuine inquiry and support creative planning. Moving from decisions made in this planning phase to taking appropriate action posed no great difficulties, for the decisions were almost wholly made by the individual teacher who, in turn, would take the action required by his own decisions. In almost every instance the teacher felt quite free to make these decisions, for he had come to the workshop with the assurance that the local administration would support him where plans had been carefully worked out. In most instances teachers were able to anticipate the difficulties they might encounter and to plan appropriate courses of action.

The problem of appraisal in this in-service program had at least two major aspects. For participating teachers the central question was "To what extent will the plans I have worked out prove to be feasible in the classroom?" They would want to know whether the children would be able to learn economic concepts more effectively from the fresh approaches to a basic curriculum problem which these teachers have developed than from their previous practices. The workshop staff helped participants plan an appropriate program of appraisal geared to the objectives which guided each individual's work. The participants and staff together worked on the problem of developing specifications for a test of general economic understanding appropriate for use with middle-grade pupils. Such a test was ultimately developed and administered as part of the follow-up program.

For the project generally there was another type of appraisal to be made. In this case the central question was "To what extent was the workshop experience an effective means of developing interest in, and workable plans for, economic education at the elementary level?" In order to guide the thinking with respect to subsequent efforts to stimulate and encourage work in the area of economic education, it was necessary to learn whether an in-service program of this type would produce significantly greater changes among participants, and in the instructional programs on which they were working, than would activities of another sort where no workshop was involved.

Sufficient interest was developed in both these aspects of appraisal so that there was considerable participation in the follow-up program during the school year immediately following the workshops. Practically all participating teachers kept records which they were able to use in supplying answers to questionnaires regarding their classroom activities. Many went to great lengths to provide additional information in the form of diaries, logs, unit plans, and similar materials. The test of general economic understanding, developed from specifications drawn up in the workshops, was administered twice during the 1954–55 school year to pupils of practically all workshop participants as well as to pupils in many other classes where the teachers had not had workshop experience. In these ways, then, appraisal was made an integral part of the plans for the project as a whole.

We may comment finally upon the relationship of the activities of this project to other aspects of the current educational, cultural, and political scene. Discussions during the workshop meetings inevitably turned to matters of broad social policy. Even when efforts were made to focus primarily upon accurate descriptions of contemporary economic phenomena it soon became apparent that political issues were involved. It was clear that choices made in dealing with economic problems are often greatly influenced by noneconomic factors such as political beliefs and ethical considerations. In addition to attempting to gain a better understanding of complex relationships of this kind, the workshop participants were faced with the difficult problem of ascertaining the extent to which it was educationally sound to make economic concepts the objects of concern for pupils in the middle grades of the elementary school.

THE SOUTHERN STATES WORK CONFERENCE

In the activities of the Southern States Work Conference we may find another illustration of a regional program of in-service education. Organized in 1940 under the auspices of the state departments of education and the state teachers associations of fourteen southern and border states, the Conference meets for one week each year to consider the various projects it has under way. Representatives to the Conference are sent by participating states. An executive committee co-ordinates the work of the Conference.

R. L. Johns, the present executive secretary, writes as follows in describing how the Conference operates:

The Conference sponsors region-wide studies by regional committees which are supported by a state committee for that project in each of the states. Before the Conference sponsors a project, a great deal of investigation is made throughout the South in order to determine the need for the project. When it has been ascertained that there is general interest in the region, the Conference will take over the sponsorship of the project. Any person in the South who has an interest in a problem can present it to the executive committee for consideration. When the project is approved by the executive committee, each state organizes a state committee for that project and does work on it between meetings of the general conference at Daytona Beach. A project is studied for three to four years before materials are published. When a project committee is organized, it spends the first year in outlining and exploring the project. The second year is spent in intensive study and sometimes experimentation. The third year is spent in pulling materials together for publication.

The group process is used by all committees. The membership of the committees includes all types of professional employees. A typical committee will include classroom teachers, supervisors, principals, superintendents of schools, college professors, members of the state departments of education, and frequently school board members.[12]

A recent report entitled *Educational Supervision—A Leadership Service*[13] affords an example of the kind of product resulting from the process outlined above. Other committees are presently at work on a project dealing with the improvement of rural education.

This brief description of the manner in which the Southern States Work Conference operates suggests interesting illustrations of the practices implied by some of the guidelines in chapter v. We may note first that an effort is made to locate problems of general interest in the region and that suggestions of such problems are received from any who care to make them. Individuals become associated with a project committee because of their general interest in the problem area identified. The period of exploration, through which each project committee goes, permits individuals and groups to identify aspects of the general problem that are of special significance to them. The attention given to the "group process" suggests that groups work out their own methods of attacking problems. Interim meetings of state committees, as well as the general meeting of the Conference each year, afford many opportunities to exchange experiences.

Not all in-service projects culminate in the same type of action. In the case of this Conference the appropriate action appears to involve studying, describing, and analyzing significant problems and practices and, ultimately, reporting the findings coming from these activities. As suggested by Johns, a logical and orderly progression of activities is outlined by each project committee to carry it through

12. Personal letter, September 27, 1955.

13. H. Cliff Hamilton (project chairman) *et al., Educational Supervision—A Leadership Service.* A Report of the Southern States Work Conference on Educational Problems. Gainesville, Florida: Southern States Work Conference, R. L. Johns, Executive Secretary, 1955.

the steps leading to publication of its report. The educational supervision project may be regarded as an effort to bring together the
results of various enterprises which have already been undertaken to
test the validity of ideas and practices relating to supervision. Thus,
one finds in the report references to studies of a rather rigorous and
systematic sort as well as statements based upon informed judgments
of experienced people who have made less formal studies and observations. The activities of the project committee, and of the Conference generally, may also be viewed as a means of encouraging
others to test ideas. A reader of the report on supervision will find
its descriptions and analyses helpful in anticipating consequences of
the application of these ideas in other situations.

IMPROVING INSTRUCTION IN HIGH SCHOOLS

   In four southern states college consultants are working with faculties of neighboring high schools to develop improved programs of
instruction for Negro youth. This program was initiated in 1954
under the general auspices of the Phelps-Stokes Fund, which under-
writes a considerable portion of the expenses.[14] In an explanatory
meeting of principals, college teachers, and supervisors from several
southern states participants expressed the belief that improvement of
high-school instruction was one of the region's most urgent needs. A
decision was subsequently made to limit the Project to four areas of
instruction—communications, mathematics, science, and social studies
—and to work in four states. In due course, arrangements were completed, with the help of officials of the state departments of education, to involve fifteen colleges and fifteen secondary schools in
Alabama, Georgia, Mississippi, and North Carolina.

   We see here another illustration of how a decision, taken relatively
early in the program, has defined the scope of operation in terms of
four curriculum areas. Given restrictions in available funds and other
considerations, such a delimitation is undoubtedly wise, for it provides a central focus that would otherwise be missing. Nevertheless,
the mere fact of a decision to work within these four areas serves to
introduce a kind of structure which places some limits upon the extent to which participants can work as individuals or groups on prob-

   14. This account is based upon information furnished by Dr. Aaron Brown,
Project Director, Phelps-Stokes Fund, 101 Park Avenue, New York 17, N.Y.

lems significant to them. A major question, then, would appear to center around the issue of when such decisions are made, and by whom. In this instance, those responsible for the Project secured informed judgments as a basis for defining the scope of the project. At the same time it is fully anticipated that the effort to delimit will be counterbalanced by the kind of flexibility that will permit individual schools and teachers to define the problems to be studied in their own terms. Considerable care is being taken also to encourage consultants and faculties to develop their own patterns of working together.

In a project such as this, there are always complex relationships because of the fact that representatives of various agencies are involved. It is difficult, for example, for any one individual to get a clear perception of his own role as well as to see precisely what others are expected to do. Teachers may ask, "Do the consultants have some particular program, or point of view, which I am expected to accept as a participant in this project?" Consultants, on the other hand, may often wonder, "At this point am I really expected to offer explicit solutions in response to problems raised, or do teachers expect me to help them think through the problems?" In this project there is clearly great sensitivity to the difficulties arising out of such questions. In an early statement of policy, for example, it was pointed out that "although the Project seeks to be unique, creative, and imaginative, it is not visionary and will attempt to relate itself to local realities." Again, it was stated that "activities designed to develop and maintain mutual respect and co-operation should gain the objectives quicker than aims of criticism, competition, and comparisons." A final statement asserted that "the Project Director and Consultants can render greater service if looked upon by the participating schools as 'friends' and 'resource persons' rather than as 'experts.' "[15]

It is apparent that the Project is trying to bring major resources to bear upon an extremely difficult problem. There is a great concern for getting to the action stage as quickly as possible, and a corresponding desire to remove obstacles that will interfere with reaching that stage. In all preliminary discussions the testing of new ideas has been systematically encouraged.

15. These comments are taken from the summary of a planning conference at Tuskegee, Alabama, January 14–15, 1955.

At each meeting held thus far, a considerable portion of the time has been given to the problem of appraisal. It is clear that those responsible are seeking to develop among all participants a sensitivity to this important aspect of in-service training. Part of this interest grows out of the belief that existing instruments for appraisal may be neither appropriate nor comprehensive enough to give an adequate picture of student growth. But there is also a feeling that various outcomes may be anticipated from the project and that an adequate assessment of its achievements will require data of different sorts. While improved instructional programs may result in significant growth on the part of pupils in participating high schools, it is also possible that the co-operative efforts of high-school teachers and college consultants may result in significant changes on the part of high-school and college faculties. It is not inconceivable that these may be reflected in improved programs of teacher preparation and in expanded opportunities for continued in-service education for both high-school and college faculties. All this is to say that the Project has a primary preoccupation with one purpose, but at the same time it is anticipating the fact of multiple outcomes and is presently planning to make its evaluation program sufficiently broad to reflect at least some of these other types of change.

National Programs

It is easy for the meaning of the term "in-service education" to become less clear in the context of broad national programs of professional organizations and community agencies than in relation to individual schools and school systems planning, organizing, and conducting educational activities for their own staff members. Indeed, the experience of some with the programs of national organizations might well lead them to believe that large segments of such programs are only incidentally concerned with the systematic provision of educational experiences for those who participate in them. It should be recognized, of course, that numerous meetings of professional organizations on the national level are centered largely upon conducting the business of those associations as it relates to finance, legislation, broad policy-making, and other such activities.

However, there are a number of organizations—and it is encouraging to note that the number seems to be increasing—whose conference and other meeting activities are being planned deliberately and specifically to meet the in-service education needs of the group's membership. While there are many limitations in developing effective in-service education programs at the national level, difficulties which arise largely out of the distance between the problems and the activities designed to aid in their solution, there are also some important advantages associated with such national programs. Perhaps chief among these is the rich range of resources in personnel available to those planning national programs. Many experienced educators whose services may be obtained only at considerable expense to individual schools and school systems are generally willing, even pleased, to participate in programs planned in conjunction with a conference or workshop of an important national professional organization.

The problem of reporting on national in-service education programs is an increasingly complex one because of the marked growth of such organizations and their conference and workshop activities in recent years. One need only look at the National Education Association with its twenty-nine departments, many of which schedule conferences, workshops, and other activities associated with in-service education goals, to see that such a report as this can serve only as a brief commentary on those programs which seem to best illustrate some of the guidelines for in-service education established in chapter v.

With this much of an indication of the special difficulties associated with adequately reporting in-service education activities at the national level, let us turn now to brief descriptions and evaluations of four national programs, each of which provides good illustrations of some of our guidelines and each of which has certain unique qualities which should be of interest to those with responsibility for planning in-service education activities.

ASSOCIATION FOR SUPERVISION AND CURRICULUM DEVELOPMENT

The first of these is the annual conference of the Association for Supervision and Curriculum Development, a department of the National Education Association.

ASCD conference programs at several points seek to provide opportunities for many people to work as individuals and as members of groups on problems that are of significance to them. Perhaps the study-discussion groups, long seen as the "heart" of ASCD conferences, provide the best illustration of this point. These groups, consisting of between twenty and thirty educators who meet together for a total of approximately ten hours, are planned around a large number of rather specific topics. At the Association's 1955 annual conference, for example, seventy-six groups were organized around thirty-six different topics, providing each participant with an opportunity to pursue problems of particular interest and concern to him.

Each of the groups has a leader, a recorder, and from two to four resource persons appointed well in advance of the conference. One of the important responsibilities of these special personnel, and particularly of the group leader, is the carrying on of preconference correspondence among themselves to help them co-operatively determine how best to proceed at the time of the conference. As the percentage of group participants who preregister well in advance of the conference increases, opportunities for further planning with a large segment of the group's total membership also increase. Within the last two years this percentage has grown from one-half to approximately two-thirds of the persons attending the ASCD conference, a measure of encouraging progress in the Association's attempt to build the conference experiences upon the needs of those who attend.

It has been pointed out that effective in-service education programs should provide many opportunities for people to relate themselves to one another. Such an objective becomes increasingly difficult to achieve in a national meeting as the size of the conference increases. ASCD's need for rooms to accommodate the seventy-six small group meetings poses a major housing problem in many cities. Such small meetings, however, continue to be a major element in the provision of an environment in which individuals may work together closely and informally for a substantial portion of the conference. As a result of the study-discussion group plan for conference organization, no person should leave an ASCD conference without having had a rather direct and extended opportunity to get to know the twenty or thirty persons in the study-discussion group to which he was assigned. It is, of course, important that competent and skilled leaders and resource persons are assigned to these groups, for without considerable sensitivity toward the objective of individuals relating themselves to each other, such groups can easily become small lecture sessions organized around the theory that one or two people are to give the answers to the others.

It is also important that an emphasis be placed upon creating an atmosphere conducive to building mutual respect, support, permissiveness, and creativeness. Care in the selection of leadership personnel, a large segment of time budgeted for small group sessions, a deliberately minimized emphasis upon status factors in identifying group leadership personnel, and considerable thought given to the orientation of new personnel, both with respect to the broad philosophy of the Association and to the kinds of behavior appropriate to different facets of the conference schedule, all combine to help develop a good conference environment for learning. During the past several years, space in ASCD's printed conference program has been allocated to a clarification of leader and member roles in the study-discussion groups. Also, the issue of the Association's journal, *Educational Leadership*, published in the month preceding the conference, is utilized as an orientation device, particularly in terms of the broad content issues which relate to the conference theme. It is believed that this practice helps a large number of conference participants feel some sense of involvement in the topic and its various facets prior to the conference itself.

Clinic sessions, a relatively recent innovation in ASCD, provide another element specifically designed to give persons opportunities to deal with problems of special significance to them. The majority of the fifteen or sixteen clinics are job-centered; that is, organized around special problems of each of the major professional status levels represented among the participants of the conference. The format of these sessions provides each participant with opportunities to raise questions and ask advice of a resource panel especially experienced in this field.

The clinic sessions are also another measure designed to help individuals relate themselves to each other. The structure of these clinic sessions provides for bringing together groups such as elementary principals, special-subject supervisors, and directors of instruction in large city systems with other members of their own professional job-groupings for the purpose of sharing experiences and asking rather specific questions of the resource panel. The agenda of such meetings are based entirely on problems and concerns drawn from the daily work of the participants.

Attention to individual and to group problem-solving processes is evident in ASCD conferences at several points. For a number of years the Association regularly assigned group observers to its small study-discussion groups for the purpose of helping them become rather deliberate about their consideration of factors which facilitated or impeded the thinking of the group. Such assignments were abandoned two years ago, largely as a result of the feeling that group members were becoming sufficiently sensitive to and skilled in group-discussion procedures so that nearly every group could be counted upon to assume this as a co-operative responsibility of all members.

Perhaps the richest resources available in the ASCD conferences are those of the participants attending. Each conference involves over 450 people in some special responsibilities for one or another of the types of sessions. In addition to this large number having program responsibilities, several hundred more are involved actively in planning or carrying out the conference through their work on local conference committees. These committees carry important responsibilities such as the planning of school and community visits, the solicitation and display of curriculum bulletins, or the preparation of a conference summary.

Another rich resource already mentioned relates to the utilization of school field situations and community visits. Approximately one-third of the study-discussion groups scheduled at each of the last two annual conferences of ASCD spent half of their time in a field situation deemed appropriate to the topic under discussion. Thus, these groups do more than talk about a subject; they have an opportunity to observe persons in a real situation meeting the problems of special concern to the group and then have further opportunity to discuss and evaluate alternative solutions to such problems.

One of the difficulties facing national organizations concerned with in-service education is that of translating discussion and decision into action. In recognition of this objective, ASCD has attempted to encourage the attendance of teams of persons coming from the same community in order that they may be in a position to reinforce one another when attempts are made to translate discussion into action on back-home problems. An attempt has also been made to increase the likelihood of action following discussion by promoting and encouraging follow-up meetings of state and regional groups both at the conference and in back-home situations. It is felt that by developing strong roots in state and regional groups the foundation for activities which should be carried on through the year may be established.

One of the most effective measures taken to encourage testing and trying ideas in "reality context" has been the utilization of school and community field observation in conjunction with some of the study-discussion groups. A major objective in using such field experiences was the provision of a common basis for discussion which would help to keep such conversation rooted in the realities of an existing school or community situation and would facilitate agreement upon common meanings of terms employed.

Careful appraisal of the conference has been developed in recent years through the assignment of this responsibility to a committee on conference orientation and evaluation. This group has the task of developing the procedures and instruments for evaluating the conference, as well as planning and conducting orientation measures for new conference participants and for leadership personnel in the study-discussion groups. For the past several years approximately 10 per cent samplings of conference participants have provided valuable data relevant to the various types of experience provided in the conference. At the last annual meeting of the Association five additional sources of data were utilized. They included: (*a*) check lists from all newcomers attending the orientation session on the first day of the conference, (*b*) follow-up cards to these newcomers after the close of the conference, (*c*) evaluation forms distributed to leadership personnel at orientation session (115 returned), (*d*) a special questionnaire relating to adequacy of hotel accommodations (804 responded), (*e*) summaries of study-discussion group evaluation experiences received from forty-six group recorders. Data from such sources are tabulated and presented to the Association's executive committee by the conference orientation and evaluation committee at the time the executive committee is examining recommendations of the conference planning committee for the structure and organization of the next annual conference.

It would appear that at many significant points the conference activities of the Association for Supervision and Curriculum Development illustrate the guidelines for in-service education suggested in chapter v of this volume. ASCD and an increasing number of other professional organizations have come to realize that many departures are necessary from the typical convention pattern for annual meetings to make these meetings effective devices of in-service education for professional workers in education. The serious limitations associated with seeking to provide adequately for in-service education through an annual conference are, of course, obvious. Yet, much of promise has been done and much more remains to be done in capitalizing upon the potentialities of such conferences for effecting desirable change in the persons who participate in them.

ASSOCIATION FOR CHILDHOOD EDUCATION INTERNATIONAL

Another interesting national program which illustrates a number of our in-service guidelines is the annual study conference of the Association for Childhood Education International.[16] This meeting attracts between 2,000 and 3,500 persons, a high percentage of them being classroom teachers, most of whom pay their own expenses and, many, the cost of their substitutes. At the 1955 ACEI conference in Kansas City, Missouri, for example, approximately two-thirds of the total attendance was composed of classroom teachers, ranging from nursery-school through intermediate-grade levels.

As is the case with ASCD conferences, considerable emphasis in the ACEI study conference is placed upon small study groups. A wide range of topics and a high percentage of preconference registration for these groups makes it possible for conference participants to select a group dealing with a problem area of special interest to them.

The use of appropriate resources is evident in ACEI conferences at several points. Numerous opportunities for school visits and visits to museums, industries, and other points of community interest are provided as a regular part of the conference program. On several

16. Based on an interview with Frances Hamilton, Executive Secretary of the ACEI, 1200 Fifteenth Street, N.W., Washington 5, D.C.

occasions the school visits have been related to the work groups as well as being available to members on an individual basis. Approximately 80 per cent of the participants at the 1955 ACEI study conference availed themselves of the opportunity for school visits. Most of the visits to community resources are done on a group basis through plans made in the study groups, although, of course, such opportunities are available informally to individual conference participants. One interesting indication that effective use is made of community resources in personnel can be noted in the fact that 275 participants in the last study conference were listed in the "community workers and other occupations" category and that forty-two lay parents were included among the conference participants.

Another major indication of this Association's concern over the availability and use of helpful resources can be seen in its functional display of instructional materials. The display includes a wide range of art media, science materials, records, toys, children's books, and professional publications for examination and trial by conference participants. The materials displayed are those which have been tested in use and approved by one of the committees which performs this function at various test centers across the country. Teachers who are considered to be outstanding are asked to use the materials in question in a regular classroom situation and then to evaluate these materials, on a form provided for the purpose, with regard to the safety, suitability in terms of difficulty and maturity levels, and real learning opportunities provided. In the case of printed materials, their inclusion in the display depends upon whether or not they have been reviewed favorably in the Association's journal, *Childhood Education*. Books to be reviewed are selected by a committee. Materials of other organizations and agencies which may be helpful are also displayed. Conference members are encouraged to browse and to select materials which promise to be of value. The provision of adequate space for examining these materials of instruction, as well as the scheduling of considerable time to do so free from any "pressure to buy," makes this an important activity of the conference which deliberately emphasizes instructional materials that may be used to support certain educational objectives.

The evaluation practices followed in conjunction with the ACEI conference lend support to the feeling that these conferences are serious attempts to provide in-service experiences of a meaningful nature to those who attend. Evaluation sheets are included in the regular conference program which each registrant receives at the time he completes his registration. The evaluation form organizes a series of questions into sections which reflect the major types of conference activities, i.e., general sessions, functional display, study groups, branch meetings, etc. These materials are printed on different colored stock from that of the remainder of the program, in order to call particular attention to them, and may be detached easily from the program. Frequent reference is made to these evaluation forms at various sessions of the conference, and persons are urged to fill them out on a day-by-day basis rather than waiting until the end of the entire meeting. In 1955 approximately 400 out of 1,800 persons who attended the conference on a continuing basis returned such questionnaire forms. These forms are collected by the Association's headquarters staff, organized rather quickly into the major divisions to which the comments relate, and viewed by the Association's board of directors and headquarters staff immediately following the conference for the particular purpose of discerning trends or broad generalizations concerning the conference. The evaluation data are tabulated in detail later, and this material is used at the August meeting of the Association's executive board in the planning of the next year's conference. Ideas for themes, group topics, leadership personnel, reorganization of the conference, and other matters are obtained from these evaluation report forms.

CO-OPERATIVE CURRICULUM RESEARCH INSTITUTE

Up to this point in our discussion of national in-service education programs we have been concerned entirely with large conferences. We have attempted to point out that promising modifications of typical convention-conference patterns have resulted from a growing awareness within many organizations that the typical, formal speaker-listener pattern of meeting is relatively ineffective in modifying the attitudes or behaviors of those who participated. A second and perhaps even more striking development has been that of the laboratory and workshop approaches to in-service education. Instead of depending upon a didactic type of presentation which seemed to place its faith in change taking place largely as a result of listening, the laboratories and workshops experimented with by a constantly increasing number of organizations have sought to provide many opportunities for discussing implications of what participants have seen or heard and for practicing the skills necessary to effect change. Such approaches are based upon the assumption that participants come with important problems on which they wish to work, rather than coming simply to a tightly predesigned, rigidly planned program.

A laboratory or institute of this type and and one which operates at the national level is the Co-operative Curriculum Research Institute, held at East Lansing, Michigan, in 1955[17] and at Grafton, Illinois, in 1956. The 1955 institute was co-operatively planned and staffed by representatives of a number of organizations such as the following: the Association for Supervision and Curriculum Development, NEA; the Horace Mann–Lincoln Institute of School Experimentation, Teachers College, Columbia University; the Center for Improving Group Procedures, Teachers College, Columbia University; the School of Education, New York University; the Bureau of Educational Research, Ohio State University; and the National Training Laboratories, NEA.

The purposes of this institute were to provide training for curriculum leaders in co-operative curriculum research, attitudes, understanding, and skills. These institute purposes were made more explicit in a brochure mailed out in advance of the conference. They were as follows:

1. To further the *insights* of curriculum leaders into the co-operative research process.
2. To further the ability to *diagnose* human-relations problems in curriculum research.
3. To practice and evaluate some *skills* in co-operative research, leadership, and planning.
4. To relate the learnings of the institute to specific curriculum development problems faced in the *back-home* situation.

The institute was planned for a maximum number of fifty participants. Forty-three persons were registered and participated in the 1955 sessions, in addition to the ten staff members involved. Three

17. A detailed report of the Institute was prepared in dittoed form by Stephen M. Corey and Matthew B. Miles of the Horace Mann–Lincoln Institute of School Experimentation, Teachers College, Columbia University.

major kinds of group experiences for the institute were planned: (*a*) large meetings, (*b*) intensive laboratory-type work groups, and (*c*) special-interest groups. The institute included a total of nine general sessions. These involved all institute participants and used many different kinds of large-meeting procedures to elicit audience participation. The general sessions were designed to aid conceptualization, to increase sensitivity, and, in some instances, to provide skill-training. The content of these general sessions was as follows: (*a*) orientation, (*b*) helps and hindrances to group work, (*c*) group reports and choosing special groups, (*d*) characteristics of groups at work, (*e*) institute self-study, data analysis, and interpretation, (*f*) hidden agenda, (*g*) co-operative curriculum research as social change, (*h*) design of co-operative curriculum research, (*i*) summary and closure. A conscious effort was made by the staff to have general sessions illustrate different approaches to training in their organization, as well as to provide training through the content with which they were concerned.

Each of the basic work groups included sixteen group members, plus two trainers having competencies and experience in human-relations training and co-operative curriculum research. The groups were made maximally heterogeneous as to job status, geographic representation, and other such factors. Their purpose was to provide training in the human relations and research sensitivity and skills needed for co-operative curriculum research. The agenda and activities were established by the group members themselves to study their own experiences in a laboratory-type approach.

The special work groups were planned in advance by the staff for the purpose of giving instruction for either two or four hours on a number of specific topics. An enrolment criterion of at least three for the organization of these groups was set. The choices made by conference participants on the second day of the institute resulted in the scheduling of such groups on the following topics:

1. Getting and analyzing data about children
2. Quantifying and analyzing unstructured data
3. Introducing innovations, getting experimentation under way, risk-taking
4. Design for action research
5. Questionnaire and inventory construction

6. Role of the consultant
7. Getting involvement and shared leadership
8. Efficient treatment of numerical data
9. Diagnosing a troublesome school situation
10. Problems of working within a school organizational structure
11. Role-playing for diagnosis, training as a source of data
12. Projective tests as sources of evidence
13. The use of published tests in action research

The fourth type of situation provided for "back-home" consultation periods of one hour on the last two afternoons of the institute intended to facilitate consultation with participants regarding applications of the training to back-home problems. These conversations were scheduled in twenty-minute units. Many of them involved teams of persons.

Since the 1955 institute was experimental in nature, the staff desired to get data regarding it before, during, and after the week, both for the purpose of improving the immediate quality of planning and the execution of the training experience and also to assess the longer-term effects of the week's work on the behavior of the participants as a basis for improving the quality of future similar institutes. In addition to the usual data on the application form relating to professional position, address, and previous experience, information was requested relating to the needs and expectancies of those applying to attend. A sentence-completion form was utilized to get data on participants' conceptual understanding of co-operative curriculum research. An inventory was also used to get data on participants' attitudes, beliefs, and ways of behaving as well as on skills and techniques that are useful in co-operative curriculum research. In addition, participants were asked to analyze a case problem for the purpose of getting some measure of their ability to diagnose a school situation and to plan effective action with respect to it.

During the institute much additional evidence was gathered. Post-meeting reaction sheets were filled out by the participants after every group meeting. Anecdotal records were kept by staff members of all group sessions as a way of recording the sequence of activities. Brief comments were also made by staff members on the growth and change of individuals in the work groups. Another measure of growth was the repetition of an analysis of a role-played demonstration of a school situation for the purpose of noting changes in the diagnostic sensitivity of participants after the week's experience. Gathering of follow-up data was also an important part of the evaluation plan of this institute with a repetition of much of the original sentence-completion, case-analysis, and inventory material at a point about six months after the conclusion of the institute. In addition to this, a number of follow-up interviews of a sampling of the participants were scheduled.

The Co-operative Curriculum Research Institute seems to have been a particularly interesting attempt to examine consciously some of the approaches to promoting and encouraging research on curriculum problems. The institute also illustrates well the principle that appraisal be made an integral part of in-service activities.

Of special interest in relation to the structuring of the institute is the blending of a considerable degree of preplanning on the part of staff members with a large amount of flexibility involved in the program itself for the purpose of providing many opportunities for individuals to identify and work on problems of special concern to them. The experience of the East Lansing institute would seem to suggest that much more time for preplanning than we ordinarily give to this activity is desirable and necessary if the best use is to be made of the time persons spend together in such a situation. It would seem that the shorter the time available for the training experience the longer the time necessary for preliminary planning and exploration of interests and expectations.

JOINT COUNCIL ON ECONOMIC EDUCATION

Another in-service education program operating at the national level is of special interest because of its direct and established lines of relationship to programs of regional, state, or local origin. This is the program of the Joint Council on Economic Education, a nonprofit educational organization composed of representatives from business, labor, agriculture, education, and other community groups which was created to assist school systems and teacher-education institutions to improve the quality of economic education through curriculum research, workshops, seminars, in-service education programs, and the preparation of materials for teachers and pupils.[18]

18. Joint Council on Economic Education, *Handbook for Regional Councils on Economic Education,* p. 4. New York: Joint Council on Economic Education, 2 West 46th Street (mimeographed).

One of the major functions of the national organization has been to provide stimulation and encouragment to persons and groups interested in the formation of organizations to promote economic education at the regional, state, and local levels. Each of these groups, however, is free to plan its own organization and to operate its program in a manner appropriate to the needs and resources of its area. Local, state, and regional councils are thus completely autonomous, though bound to the Joint Council by a common philosophy, mutual interest, and an agreement of affiliation and cooperation.[19]

Among the many services which the Joint Council provides for regional and local groups are the following:

1. Advice to groups in the initial steps of stimulating community interest and getting a program set up.
2. Assistance in locating and contacting key people from business, agriculture, and labor.
3. Assistance in planning economic workshops, conferences, and "pilot projects" through prepared planning materials and staff visits.
4. Provision of teaching guides, bibliographies, resource materials, bulletins, and brochures prepared by the Joint Council and its regional affiliates.
5. A clearing-house for activities in economic education, through newsletters, conferences, pamphlets, etc.

An interesting service of the national organization is a carefully planned *Handbook for Regional Councils on Economic Education* which makes available to persons interested in the formation of such groups the experience of national staff members and of the leadership of other successfully initiated councils.

Documentation of the interest in establishing such organizations may be found in the steady growth in the number of them from the Joint Council's beginning in 1948 to a point where there are now on-going programs being carried out by twenty-four regional councils and sixteen local councils affiliated with the national organization. These groups in turn sponsored thirty-six workshops on economic education during 1955. The considerable spread of these workshops across the country since the first was held at New York University suggests the possibility of a growing feeling of need on

19. *Ibid.*

the part of educators for developing economic competence in our students and those who teach them. The *Handbook* of the Joint Council lists the three major purposes of these workshops as follows:

1. To help school leaders understand our American economy—how it operates, what it produces, how its products are distributed, what its motivating forces are, and what major problems it faces.
2. To develop leadership in the profession for local programs in economic education.
3. To develop instructional materials and teaching techniques for improved economic education in the schools of the country.[20]

The *Handbook* continues by pointing out that "no less important than these purposes, and basic to them, is the further purpose of providing, through the best possible learning-working situations, continuous experiences in problem-solving, in democratic processes, in group discussions, and in good human relations."[21]

One of the major strengths of these workshop activities has been the extent to which school leaders have been able to enlist broad community co-operation. Extensive representation from business, labor, agriculture, government, institutions of economic research, school boards, state departments of education, and from such civic groups as the Better Business Bureau, the Rotary Club, the Chamber of Commerce, the League of Women Voters, and the Taxpayers Association has been emphasized. The Joint Council has attributed much of the success of its program to this deliberate planning of school-community contact and communication. A problem associated with such broad representation, however, and particularly when this involves specialists from the various areas listed above who are employed as visiting consultants, is that it tends to necessitate more extensive preworkshop scheduling without the benefit of participants' reactions and results in a somewhat less flexible program than is frequently found in curriculum workshops.[22]

Because the workshops on economic education associated with the Joint Council have ranged from two to six weeks in length and have frequently been located in physical settings which made it possible for participants to live and eat together, many fine oppor-

20. Joint Council on Economic Education, *Handbook*, p. 2. New York: The Council (mimeographed).
21. *Ibid.*   22. *Ibid.*

tunities for these persons to relate themselves to each other have been provided.

We have already mentioned the centrality to the workshop programs of broad involvement of representatives from community agencies and institutions. In addition to these resources in personnel, the workshops have attempted to assist in the cataloguing of community resources (natural, capital, organizational), in the provision of well-stocked libraries of printed and audio-visual materials, and in the development of bibliographies of free and inexpensive materials relating to economic education. Two recent publications of the Joint Council, *Teachers Guide to Community Resources in Economic Education* and *Bibliography of Free and Inexpensive Materials for Economic Education* indicate the interest of the organization in adequately utilizing such resources.

One of the most interesting and perhaps most unique aspects of the in-service education activities of the Joint Council on Economic Education may be seen in the extent to which the program, while national in scope, has emphasized activities conducted at regional, state, and local levels. A new project of the Joint Council which documents this is one devoted to curriculum development in economic education. Ten school systems from across the country are going to participate in the program which will involve the co-operation of the state council and a near-by university. It would appear that one of the great strengths of such an approach is its facilitation of means for moving from decision to action. Another potential advantage of such an emphasis on local or area programs is that the more immediate proximity of the training activities to the problems to which they relate tends to encourage the testing and trying of ideas and plans in reality context.

While our discussion of the in-service education activities of the Joint Council on Economic Education has necessarily been brief, we believe that it has illustrated the concurrence of these programs at a number of points with the guidelines for in-service education enumerated in chapter v. It should be pointed out that a number of other national organizations have made similar promising progress in translating a national interest and stimulus into activity at local, state, and regional levels. The workshops on consumer education sponsored by the National Committee for Education in Family

Finance of the Institute of Life Insurance (another program in economic education) and the Citizenship Education Project provide other good illustrations of this tendency.

We have been able to report upon only four *national* in-service education programs. Two of these have illustrated the annual-conference type of activity; one, the laboratory- or institute-type of activity, involving a much smaller number of people; and the fourth, a series of small workshop activities in states, regions, and local communities. Obviously many other significant and interesting programs of each type could have been reported were there space to do so.

There seems to be a most promising national trend in the direction of a greater recognition of the in-service education potential of the activities sponsored by such organizations. There also seems to be apparent a far sounder recognition of the principles involved in learning and in changing behavior and of the intimate relationship between individuals and their social environments. These trends, however, are comparatively new. There still remains great room for improvement in the development of national programs of in-service education which illustrate creative and continuing applications of our growing insights into the principles of how people learn and change.

Summary

As stated at the outset of this chapter, the in-service education programs described and analyzed are not intended to be representative of area, state, regional, or national programs currently in operation. Nor are they necessarily to be regarded as models of best practice. It should be clear also that our descriptions are by no means sufficient, and, indeed, our knowledge of the detailed operation of each program is too limited to permit anything like a systematic evaluation. We believe, however, that each program described has met with a measure of success in terms of its own purposes. The brief analysis of each has been made to illustrate the application of some of the generalizations about effective in-service education found in earlier chapters of the yearbook. We believe that our analyses tend, in general, to support these generalizations.

We do not find in these programs, however, equally good illustrations of all the generalizations. It is indeed difficult to identify in area, state, regional, and national programs all the characteristics suggested by the guidelines formulated in chapter v. Part of the difficulty arises because analysis in terms of these guidelines requires information not readily available. Whether new ideas are actually tested out can be ascertained only if one knows what occurs in local situations. To be sure, new ideas regarding the in-service activity itself may be used, as in the case of small study groups in national conferences.

Similarly, the problem of evaluation presents difficulties. In-service activities typically envision some kind of change taking place in the participants, which change presumably will be reflected in changed practices in connection with their work. Here again the data needed to assess the extent to which changes have actually occurred are not easily obtained in area, state, regional, and national programs. There are, of course, many assertions that changes do occur. It is chiefly a belief that this, indeed, is the case which justifies the continued enormous expenditure of time and energy in programs of this nature. One of the encouraging aspects of most of the programs we have examined is the increased attention being given to the problem of evaluation, in spite of the difficulties involved.

Our illustrations suggest that in-service education for teachers and administrators at the area, state, regional, and national levels are frequently focused upon the improvement of some aspect of the instructional program. In the degree that this is true, the problem of moving from decision to action often presents difficulties. Action of the kind involved here must typically be taken at the local level, and decisions made by area, state, regional, or national groups cannot always be readily implemented in the local situation. This fact is clearly recognizable as one of the central problems in in-service projects with a particular focus. A related difficulty occurs because such a focus restricts the freedom of individuals and groups to work on problems significant to them and to work in ways they regard as appropriate.

It appears that the clear-cut applications of some of the generalizations regarding effective in-service programs become increasingly difficult as one moves from a consideration of local school programs to a consideration of area, state, regional, and national activities. But there are some respects in which the application of other guidelines are better illustrated in the latter case than in the former. For example, it is apparently somewhat easier for the programs involving a larger geographical area to mobilize a wide range of resources, both in terms of personnel and materials. Participants, thus, have somewhat greater opportunity to come in contact with a wider assortment of ideas. Participation in programs involving teachers and administrators from different localities affords an opportunity to gain new perspectives. Some people derive greater encouragement to try new ideas through taking part in these programs than they receive locally. For some there is a considerable satisfaction to be obtained from association with a significant enterprise that is engaging the attention of people in a wide geographical area.

It may be noted finally that merely because it is difficult to find applications of certain guidelines to in-service programs at the area, state, regional, and national levels does not justify the conclusion that practices implied by those guidelines are inappropriate in such programs. Quite to the contrary, it may be observed that these programs could be substantially more effective if those responsible for their direction were able to contrive means of introducing practices consistent with the guidelines. As we have seen, this is no easy task, but it would appear to be one well worth the effort to accomplish.

CHAPTER XI

Implications of In-service Education Programs for Teacher-Education Institutions

J. W. MAUCKER

and

DARYL PENDERGRAFT

Introduction

This chapter is written to develop the implications of the ideas expressed in the early chapters of the yearbook for the program of colleges which prepare teachers and other school personnel. It is addressed primarily to the faculties and administrative officers of teacher-education institutions.

It is assumed that most, if not all, teacher-education institutions recognize an obligation to devote some of their energies to the in-service education of personnel in elementary and secondary schools. This point scarcely seems worth laboring, since extension and field-service programs for this purpose exist in such profusion. That colleges and universities might profitably attempt in-service education of their own staff members is not so thoroughly accepted—but more of that later.

Running throughout the following discussion is a dual emphasis on the use of *group processes* and the encouragement of *individual self-improvement* as basic approaches to in-service education. The rationale is stated below.

GROUP WORK

The burden of most of the preceding chapters may be summarized in the sentence: Experimentation has shown that lasting improvement in professional practices of teachers may be brought about by encouraging and assisting them to make a co-operative attack on professional problems of common concern.

The implication seems clear that teacher-education institutions ought to be equipped to assist in making this type of activity effective. We shall attempt to enumerate some specific suggestions to this end.

INDIVIDUAL SELF-IMPROVEMENT

There is a danger, however, that, by reason of the yearbook's overwhelming emphasis on group work, the basic importance of facilitating individual efforts for improvement in service may be overlooked.

As an educated citizen, and certainly as a member of a learned profession, the teacher has an obligation to keep up with his field, to strive for improvement of his teaching, to adapt his work to new circumstances. Members of all other professions—be they physicians, lawyers, dentists, architects or engineers—are expected to read current professional literature and adapt their practices accordingly. While they may secure assistance through specially arranged clinics, short courses, and meetings of professional associations, they are expected to learn much on their own through independent study and a certain amount of careful experimentation. Similarly, even the beginning teacher may reasonably be expected to be, to a rather considerable degree at least, scholar as well as instructor.

In the special case of those who have not, through their preservice education (in some cases limited to a few weeks of college work), achieved sufficient competence to enable them to carry on through independent study, the most urgent need may well be for specific, formal courses of instruction comparable to those usually taken as part of preservice education. Acceptance of this viewpoint has implications for teacher-education institutions at least as important, it will be claimed, as those stemming from concern with group process.

With this dual emphasis in mind, we will consider, in turn, implications for: (*a*) preservice training of school personnel; (*b*) services to professional school personnel; and (*c*) in-service training of college staff members.

Implications for Preservice Training

PROGRAMS FOR CLASSROOM TEACHERS

The first obligation of the colleges is so to educate students who are to become teachers that they will accept the professional *obli-*

gation to continue *to learn on the job* and will be equipped with the requisite abilities and skills to do so. The college which turns out a teacher who feels that he has "arrived," that his pitcher is full and he need only draw from it thereafter without replenishing it, or who wants to improve his work but does not know how to go about it, has made a negative contribution to in-service education, regardless of how many experts and consultants it may send into the field to facilitate group work among teachers. It should be accepted as part of the task of undergraduate education to instill a desire for further learning and a recognition of the fact that the professional teacher is a scholar-teacher whose task is a creative one—who, as a matter of course, expects continuously to be building units of study, incorporating new content into courses of instruction, using newly developed instructional materials (films, textbooks, references, tests, etc.), and trying to find better ways to challenge and stimulate students and to guide their learning efforts.

How is the college to accomplish this? By continuously holding the concept of the professional scholar-teacher before the eyes of prospective teachers and encouraging and rewarding creativity, independent study, and original thinking and problem-solving.

There is, of course, no single course pattern or formula for achieving such a goal. We would, indeed, be presumptuous were we to attempt a prescription. It may not be amiss, however, merely to suggest that in making the inevitable choices among the less-than-ideal alternatives open to an institution in a practical situation, those responsible for teacher-education programs ought to recognize the value of such approaches as are listed below. In stressing such prosaic matters as these, they may make a vital contribution to the ability of teachers to carry on their own personal programs of in-service education.

1. Placing increasing responsibility on the learners in the undergraduate program—just as rapidly as they can take it—through such means as seminar experience, library projects, term papers, recitals in music, and self-evaluation.
2. Using comprehensive examinations at strategic points in the undergraduate program, thus leading students to accept responsibility for synthesizing their knowledge, relating the work of various individual courses, striving systematically to "make sense" out of the many isolated items in their educational experience.

3. Encouraging students to "test out" courses in order to secure opportunity to take more advanced work or to elect courses in other fields—or in some cases to shorten the period of undergraduate preparation. Most colleges have scarcely scratched the surface with respect to this potential stimulus to independent study and improved scholarship. In this connection it will be interesting to watch carefully the School and College Study of Admission with Advanced Standing, examinations for which are being prepared by the College Entrance Examination Board.[1]

4. Providing direct instruction in use of the library and other tools of research and independent study; encouraging students to build their own personal libraries. Recent publication of relatively inexpensive editions of important books makes the latter economically feasible to a much greater extent than in previous years.

5. Making long-range assignments which lead students to secure information from a wide variety of sources, use standard reference materials, become familiar with current professional journals.

6. Striving to assure for students sufficient scope and depth in their teaching fields so they are able to pursue study on their own—so that they will "know their way around" in one or more of the subject fields in the elementary- and high-school curriculum.

7. Requiring students to gain experience in building units of instruction and utilizing materials appropriate for elementary- and secondary-school students.

In addition to striving to develop a self-reliant teacher, capable of independent study and creative adaptation to local circumstances, colleges should strive so to educate students who are to be teachers that they will develop at least a modicum of insight into the psychology of change (along lines described in chapter iv) and the dynamics of group process. This can, of course, be done through direct study within the framework of such subjects as human growth and development, the psychology of learning, and mental hygiene. Equally important is direct experience in group activity under skilful guidance such that the student comes to accept the group approach as perfectly natural and becomes increasingly sensitive to the factors which facilitate and those which impede effective group action.

The extra-curricular program offers many opportunities for di-

1. See *Bridging the Gap between School and College,* chap. iv (New York: Fund for the Advancement of Education, 1953), and *Advanced Placement Tests, 1955–56* (Princeton, New Jersey: College Entrance Examination Board Bulletin of Information, 1956).

rect experience in team work—to produce a play, put on an initiation, conduct a forum, sponsor an all-school election, hammer out a recommendation for school policy, or reconcile opposing views regarding a social activity. But the college ought not to rely on extra-curricular activities only; as part of the undergraduate instructional program itself, students should learn to work together in preparing instructional materials and in seeking co-operatively to find solutions for professional problems and to evaluate work accomplished. Such experience may most appropriately be provided in courses concerned with effective use of materials of instruction, since a great deal of the in-service education of these teachers when they get on the job will ordinarily be concerned with curriculum problems.

Finally, the college ought to familiarize its prospective teachers with the kind of services they may, as teachers, expect from educational institutions. Prospective teachers should be encouraged to attend conferences held on the campus for teachers in service, for example, so they will know first hand what kind of help teachers can get from such meetings.

TRAINING OF ADMINISTRATIVE AND SUPERVISORY PERSONNEL

It is abundantly clear that the teachers and school administrators who have spoken in the earlier chapters of this yearbook, particularly in chapters vi, vii, and viii, believe strongly that the chief administrative officer and his supervisory staff must necessarily play crucial roles in the development of effective programs of in-service education. In chapter iv, for example, it is stated categorically that change within an individual is apt to be abortive unless it is supported by the institution of which he is a part. Much stress is placed on the transition from discussion to action (involving administrative support) and on the importance of administrative arrangements for placing adequate resources at the disposal of school personnel engaged in curriculum projects. *All* levels of organization, it is urged, should be brought into the co-operative endeavor aimed at effecting change.

The implication is clear, it would seem, that educational institutions which provide specialized training for administrative and supervisory personnel should make a point of stressing these matters to insure that such personnel will recognize their responsibilities and be competent to discharge them effectively.

Since, in chapter vii, Lewis and his collaborators have suggested the kind of knowledge, skills, and attitudes relative to in-service education which should be emphasized in the training of administrators, no attempt will be made here to catalogue such items in greater detail, but perhaps the following three comments are pertinent:

1. The educational institution which prepares administrators and supervisors should assume responsibility for providing, as a part of the basic preparation of these people, *before* they accept administrative and supervisory positions, specific training for leadership of any in-service education program beyond that expected of the classroom teacher as such.
2. This training should include analysis of relevant theory and something of the experimentation on which it is based as well as accounts of successful practice in current programs of in-service education—the kind of thing found in this yearbook.
3. The superintendent is not expected to be a specialist in group dynamics, but he should be able to recognize the importance of group processes, know how to secure, and when and where to use, expert services and how to evaluate outcomes. Likewise, not every supervisor need be an expert in group process (although it certainly would be desirable to have in each school system one or more staff members with considerable skill and insight and with the intensive interest which leads one to keep up with the field), but, again, he should certainly have developed sufficient familiarity within the field as to be conscious of the barriers to successful group work and the conditions which facilitate group action.

It scarcely need be said that the program of the educational institution to accomplish the above-stated ends should include first-hand experience with effective group process, through observation of, and participation in, co-operative attacks on professional problems, preferably in the setting of a school system or an individual school building where conditions are found reasonably similar to those in which the administrator or supervisor expects to find himself as he assumes positions of greater responsibility.

Implications for the In-service Education of School Personnel

The pattern of in-service education in the schools is determined to a very considerable extent by the degree to which the teacher-education institutions have been successful in preparing beginning teachers so that they can take an effective part in an in-service program. If the colleges have not taught the proper attitudes toward in-service education or developed the understandings and techniques necessary for active participation in in-service education projects, much of the efforts of school administrators will, of necessity, be exerted to the building of these desirable attitudes and the development of the necessary skills.

Just as the need for both more and better in-service education programs has possibly never been greater, the need for teacher-education institutions to expand their programs of in-service education among the schools in their area and to seek to improve the quality of these programs is immediately urgent.

This growing need for the institutions of teacher education to render assistance in the in-service programs of the schools comes at a time when colleges and universities are faced with rapidly increasing enrolments and a growing difficulty in obtaining sufficient numbers of adequately prepared staff members. It seems clear that if teacher-education institutions are to expand and improve their programs of in-service education among the schools, they need to be alert to the research being done in this area and willing to experiment with new ideas.

What, then, are the implications of the research and experimentation reported in this yearbook for the in-service education programs of teacher-education institutions? From the evidence presented in chapter iv and supported by the conclusions in the succeeding chapters, changes in both the individual and the institution, in many instances, can most effectively be brought about if school personnel at all levels work together as a group.

Common sense should show, however, that there is much value in at least some of the older methods of in-service education discussed in chapter iii. This is particularly true, and the point needs to be emphasized, when many of the teachers or administrators in a school system are quite inadequately prepared for the work they are doing. A school superintendent, for example, who has very little understanding of the problems of the elementary school probably should take some formal college courses in this area so that he will not have to rely entirely upon his elementary teachers for facts and ideas in attempting to participate as a peer in a group interested in improving the elementary-school program. Similarly, the classroom teacher who has the bare minimum amount of education required for a substandard or emergency certificate simply cannot leave the matter of in-service growth entirely to informal group work.

The psychology of change described in chapter iv, the guidelines suggested in chapter v for the proper organization and effective functioning of groups, and the testimonials in subsequent chapters regarding the efficacy of in-service education founded upon the philosophy of chapters iv and v suggest to the writers that teacher-education institutions may improve their in-service education programs materially by attempting to incorporate these ideas in such ways as are indicated below.

1. *Educational Conferences:*

a) Have school personnel participate in the planning.

b) Devote a greater proportion of the time available to group problem-solving processes.

c) Link conferences with current in-service education projects known to be under way or contemplated in the area.

d) Ask in-service education groups known to have been particularly successful to participate in college conferences for the purpose of sharing their experiences with others.

e) Attempt to have each conference appraised by participants in terms of their personal gain from the conference and practical use of the ideas in their instructional program.

2. *Workshops* (no college credit involved):

a) Solicit the advice of teachers and school administrators as to the fields in which workshops seem to be needed. The workshop program can then be organized so that the individual teachers may work on problems of specific concern to each.

b) Before the workshop begins, see that the workshop leader has ample opportunity to become familiar with the problems of the teachers or administrators who will be involved.

c) Encourage both supervisory personnel and teachers from the same school to participate in the workshop so they can work together on a common problem.

d) Have workshop participants co-operatively appraise the value of the workshop.

3. *Extension Classes or Workshops* (college credit possible):

a) Organize classes or workshops as a result of the request of the school personnel in a given community who feel inadequate in a particular area.

The following is perhaps typical of how this takes place. Mr. A., a social-studies teacher in the high school, while eating in the school cafeteria, mentioned that he deplored the inability of so many of his students to read the subject matter of his courses. Several other teachers at the table expressed their concern over this problem and felt that the need for instruction in remedial reading was urgent. All in the group, however, confessed their lack of understanding in this area, and it was agreed that Mr. A. would write to a teacher-education institution to see if an extension course might be offered in the community to help the teachers with this problem. The class was organized; the teachers enrolled; and, even before the course was completed, the teachers, with the help of the instructor of the extension class serving as a consultant, were able to launch a well-planned remedial reading program.

b) Relate the class or workshop wherever possible to an in-service education project of a group of school personnel.

c) Provide each individual teacher opportunities to concentrate on areas of particular interest.

This, of course, must be done without lowering the standards of the institution. In many instances, the class can advantageously be divided into groups, with each group studying some particular aspect of the over-all problem and responsible to the other groups for doing its specific job well. At Mason City, Iowa, for example, at the request of some 28 junior high school teachers and principals, an extension class was organized for the purpose of helping them in their efforts to improve instruction in the junior high schools. The group submitted the specific problems in which they were interested some weeks before the class began, and the instructor and the members of the class arranged these under the following headings: "Psychological characteristics of adolescents and their implications for curriculum development"; "Guidance activities and programs for junior high school students"; "Functions of the junior high school"; "The general-education program for the modern junior high school"; "Exploratory programs and activities for junior high school students." Groups of five or six people chose to work on each topic. Each group used films, recordings, books and articles, and, in some instances, local resource people in the investigation of the particular topic. The group members pooled the results of their investigations and formulated a report to the other groups. Each group attempted to tailor its report to fit the local school system, and each report made specific suggestions for action programs for the improvement of the junior high schools of Mason City. The school superintendent, while not a member of the class, gave encouragement and made resources available to the groups as requested. The complete reports were mimeographed and distributed to all junior high school teachers and to the members of the Board of Education in the city.

The quantity of work done and the quality of the work presented are amazing in a project such as this where group tends to compete against group.[2] An extension class organized in this manner and closely related to the local school system may provide the stimulus for a series of long-range efforts for the improvement of instruction.

d) Encourage supervisors, principals, and superintendents to join the class, since the participation of school administrators in such classes or workshops is highly desirable if a successful action program is to result. This may include the modification of rules so that administrative personnel can take part in the class activities on a noncredit, nonfee basis.

e) The instructor of the extension class or workshop whose objective is the improvement of the instructional program should devote considerable time to becoming thoroughly familiar with the school system and to serving as a consultant to individual teachers and groups of teachers.

For example, Professor B. has an extension class in the teaching of

2. Peter F. Drucker, "The Way to Industrial Peace," *Harper's Magazine,* CXCIII (1947), 391–92. Industry has long known that production can be considerably increased and employee morale improved by having group compete against group rather than individual against individual or against a set standard. The work of Elton Mays in the cotton mills, with Western Electric, and with the West Coast aircraft companies "all bring out the profound importance of teamwork for human satisfaction, emotional and physical balance, and productivity. . . . No one finding in the whole field of industrial relations is as well documented as the one that men spontaneously, and by their nature, work in groups, and that any policy or organization that disturbs or tears apart the team is bound to cause severe trouble. . . . Management should consciously try to encourage the workers' natural tendency to work as a team."

elementary-school arithmetic for three hours each Monday evening. He remains in the community overnight and, on Tuesday, visits the classrooms of members of his class, observing, giving a demonstration perhaps, and consulting with the teacher or administrator about specific problems. Furthermore, the instructor should be made available to the school system as a consultant long after the termination of the class.

f) The rules regarding course prerequisites to which the undergraduate students are expected to adhere should ordinarily be less rigidly enforced for teachers in service.

Common sense will frequently indicate that a teacher, as a result of teaching experience and greater maturity, should be permitted to enrol in a class whose purpose is that of instructional improvement, even though he does not meet the specific course prerequisites. If, however, the teacher's lack of the usual background courses would impede the progress of the class or jeopardize the quality of the work, the teacher should not be permitted to enrol.

g) In such improvement-of-instruction courses the customary college requirement for grades to be recorded for each student in the class may imperil the effectiveness of the group process and cause the teachers to be more concerned with the language of the subject and other things that are easily measured than with the application of the educational theory to a particular classroom or school. Group work implies a co-operative team effort; the typical college grading system tends to be based upon the degree to which an individual's achievement varies from the average or from a predetermined norm.

This does not mean that examinations should not be given. In fact, it would be wise for the instructor to administer examinations fully comparable in number and quality to those he would expect to use if the class were taught to preservice students. The standards of high-quality instruction should be maintained irrespective of where a class is taught or the nature of the students in the class. The instructor may be tempted to lessen the amount of work required in an in-service class out of sympathy for the busy, well-intentioned teachers in the class. If this temptation is not resisted, the class may be so watered down that it bears little resemblance to the same course when taught on campus. In determining whether to record a "Satisfactory" for a given student, however, the instructor in an in-service education class may not need to rely so completely on the results of the examinations as he does with resident undergraduates since, as a result of his visits to the teacher's class, he might have considerable additional evidence on which to base his judgment.

b) Thus far we have been concerned with classes or workshops related to school problems or the improvement of instruction. To help the schools with such programs is indeed important, but perhaps of even greater significance is the responsibility all institutions of higher learning have of stimulating teachers to keep abreast of social, economic, technological, and political changes and to understand their implications. Samuel M. Brownell, former United States Commissioner of Education, has said:

> As the professional life of teachers increases, the necessity of their having intellectually stimulating experiences increases. If this need is not met, teachers, working with immature though alert children, lack the familiarity with significant contemporary developments which pupils have a right to expect, and pupils are deprived of association with intellectually stimulating teachers.[3]

The group approach has been used quite successfully as a technique for keeping teachers abreast of the rapid changes in our society; it can also be used to deepen their knowledge and widen their understanding in other areas of general education and in fields of specialization. However, much of teachers' in-service growth will have to result from the individual's willingness to make the necessary sacrifices to improve himself as a person and a scholar.

> The end of education is the human being himself, the simple perfection of his own nature. It is not the means of transforming the world but rather of transforming ourselves. It is a conversion, an exaltation of the individual from what he is into what he would like to be, and if this conversion is attended with pain (as all learning is, according to Aristotle), it is a pain that we willingly suffer for the sake of the quality which in our suffering we achieve.[4]

3. Samuel M. Brownell, "Teacher Education: A Look Ahead," *Eighth Yearbook of the American Association of Colleges for Teacher Education,* p. 24. Oneonta, New York: Edward C. Pomeroy, Exec. Secy., AACTE (11 Elm St.), 1955.

4. A. Dwight Culler, "The Imperial Intellect," *A Study of Newman's Educational Ideal,* p. 226. New Haven, Connecticut: Yale University Press, 1955.

Therefore, it would be a mistake to feel that all conferences, workshops, extension classes, consultant services, research, experimentation, and publication should be concerned *only* with the *strictly professional* aspects of teacher education. Teachers and other professional school personnel need to have the opportunity to hear addresses by learned people in all areas—the humanities, the sciences, and the social sciences; they need the opportunity to listen to a nationally-famous symphony orchestra, to attend a good dramatic production, or to view an outstanding art exhibit. If at all possible, events of this type should be a part of an educational conference. Similarly, a workshop or extension class that has for its primary objective the deepening of one's knowledge or keeping one abreast of new ideas in a subject-matter area can be very helpful. The Radio-isotope Workshop, conducted by Iowa State Teachers College in the summer of 1955, is an example of this. In this two-week workshop, high-school science teachers from several states developed a better understanding of atomic physics and learned specifically through laboratory experience how radio active isotopes may safely be used in high-school science courses.

Extension classes, it would seem, should be in the academic or subject-matter fields at least as frequently as in the field of professional education. Because they generally apply to all teachers and will, therefore, enrol greater numbers, there is a strong temptation for the teacher-education institutions to offer only professional courses and thus collect sizable amounts from the fees paid for such courses. The institution should feel the obligation to offer courses in literature, history, and science, in order to provide the opportunity for the teacher to grow as a person and as a scholar as well as a teacher.

A consultant may render a great service merely by correcting misconceptions or errors of fact that he has observed. The consultant, the extension class, the conference speaker, the television program, or the college publication which helps teachers to think more clearly, to be more open-minded, or to have a greater appreciation of nature and of man are all serving the cause of in-service education.

4. *Consultant Services:*

a) Thoroughly orient the college staff member who is to serve as a consultant. This should include specific instruction in effective in-service education, such as is suggested particularly in chapters v and viii of the yearbook.

b) Have the consultant maintain contact with an in-service education project from the point of formulating the problem until the project has been completed and evaluated. This means that the teacher-education institution must allow adequate time and a sufficient number of return trips for the staff members in each school.

c) Require the consultant to make a rather comprehensive report of each in-service education project with which he has been connected. This report should be helpful to all future consultants to the same community and to those working on similar topics in other communities.

d) Give the consultant ample opportunity to comprehend the local situation before he is asked for suggestions concerning the in-service project.

e) Tell the consultant that, although it is important that he be able to assist the teachers and administrators with group-process techniques, it is even more vital that he be able to answer the specific questions related to the area of his specialization. It is highly desirable for the consultant to get the local teachers to declare what they feel should be done about a given problem, but it is equally essential that he be able to explain, in concrete language, what the recognized authorities advise, what research and experimentation have revealed, and how other school systems have successfully attacked the problem. According to a recent study, teachers and administrators want definite answers to questions and specific advice concerning existing problems from the consultant and not merely stimulation for local in-service groups to work out their own solutions to school problems.[5]

f) Advise the consultant that he should not hesitate to caution school administrators against overburdening the teachers with in-service education projects having for their objective the improvement of the school program.

When there is an abundance of things about the school program that need to be changed, there is always the temptation on the part

5. William W. Savage, "The Value of State Consultative Service," *Administrator's Notebook,* Vol. IV, No. 3. Chicago: Midwest Administration Center, University of Chicago, November, 1955.

of the administrator to expect more of the teacher's time to be devoted to in-service education than the teacher has available. The teacher needs ample time for his own scholarly growth, for recreation, and for the multitude of professional, community, and family obligations. The group approach to in-service education is time-consuming; for the typical teacher the days are seldom long enough to do the things that should be done.

g) Select consultants with care in order to insure that they are well suited for the work to be done. The qualifications of adequate education and teaching and administrative experience in a school system are important, but of even greater significance is the personality of the consultant.

Above all, the college instructor who is to serve as a consultant must be adaptable; he must believe in the group process; he must expect to find teachers and administrators whose views differ from his own and who cannot be convinced that they should change their views simply because he can quote eminent authorities and research evidence in support of his own theories; he must be a good listener, a shrewd observer, and a humble "outsider" in whom both teachers and administrators can confide. He must be as tactful as a diplomat, as patient as Job, and as optimistic as a politician running for reelection. He must feel that there is at least a reasonable chance that his efforts as a consultant will be productive of worth-while changes.

h) Assist local groups with the planning and carrying out of adequate programs of evaluation of their work.

This is an area where the consultant's advice ordinarily is especially needed. In some instances, the consultant may call on a specialist in evaluation on the college staff to assist him in this phase of the project. Sometimes it may be desirable to organize an extension class in order to develop among local school personnel the necessary understandings and techniques for evaluating educational outcomes.

5. *Research, Experimentation, and Publication:*

a) Compile a record of successful in-service education programs and make these available to any school system interested in launching a program in the same general area.

b) Assist in-service education groups with their research needs.

c) Publish materials relating to in-service education that might be of help to the schools.

d) Engage in experimental programs of in-service education.

One of the more interesting possibilities is the use of television for the improvement of instruction and of the individual teacher. Several teacher-education institutions have been televising programs primarily for teachers; many others are currently planning to experiment with this medium of communication as a means of extending their in-service education programs.

Implications for the In-service Education of College Staff Members

Not only does this yearbook have implications for teacher-education institutions in regard to their programs of preservice and in-service education of teachers and administrators but also many ideas are suggested for the in-service education of the college faculty and administrators. The principles described in chapter iv concerning the psychology of change and the guidelines for effective in-service education suggested in chapter v are applicable to people in higher education just as they are to elementary- and secondary-school teachers and administrators. Few would question the need for continued improvement of teacher-education programs and modification of the viewpoints of many college administrators and instructors.

If such changes are to be brought about, it would be wise for college administrators to understand the values of the group approach. For effective curriculum improvement, the involvement of the total staff, both teaching and administrative personnel, seems essential. A curriculum change brought about by administrative edict or by an administration-dominated curriculum committee may produce a change in name only. As this yearbook points out in several places, it is seldom possible to transplant, intact, a program of instruction from one school system to another or even from one school to another in the same system. Similarly, the staff of one teacher-education institution ought not to be expected to adopt as its own the curriculum of another. Certainly it can profit by a thorough study of the curriculums of other colleges and, possibly, *adapt* many aspects of a specific curriculum to fit its own needs. Lengthy and time-consuming consideration and discussion by the faculty is apparently a necessary prerequisite to the adoption of any significant, far-reaching curriculum change.

Moreover, each institution should provide the means for group consideration of matters affecting faculty welfare or the interests of the college. This may take the form of a faculty council or senate, or of an educational policies commission. Whatever the name, the members should ordinarily be elected by faculty vote, and it should be a group to whom any staff member who feels that some change in policy is needed could go for a hearing. After investigation and discussion of the matter, if the group felt that a change would be desirable, it would formally propose the change to the administration or total faculty. Changes proposed in this manner should be welcomed by the college administrative staff; in fact, such procedures should be encouraged.

Another implication would concern the committee system in the institution. The evidence presented in the yearbook would indicate that the committees dealing with policy matters should be (a) faculty selected and responsible to the faculty; and (b) composed chiefly of members of the instructional staff, but with the administrative point of view represented. For the effective operation of such committees, it is implied that the faculty and administration should delineate rather carefully the functions of each committee. By doing this the committee will understand the framework within which it may operate and will not labor for weeks to prepare certain policy changes only to find that these are "not administratively feasible."

For an effective in-service program within the teacher-education institution, the college must provide the necessary resources. This includes funds for visits by the staff to other institutions; for bringing consultants to the campus; for research and experimentation; and for secretarial help, supplies, and mimeographing or printing. For an in-service project of considerable scope, it means, too, that committee members immediately concerned should be given a considerable reduction of teaching load and other duties.

Just as most public school personnel need to understand group dynamics and need training in the techniques of this process, college professors and administrators are frequently in need of instruction if the group process is to work effectively. Hence, the teacher-education institution may feel the need of having a workshop for its own staff in order to develop leadership techniques and understanding of the group process.

A growing number of institutions have been holding workshops prior to the opening of college each fall for the purpose of orientation of new staff and for the consideration of college and departmental problems. It is at such precollege workshops that the pattern of co-operative group action can best be set. The informality that usually prevails, the participation of the chief administrative officials of the college, and, particularly, the lack of pressure from routine duties make a most favorable environment for the launching of in-service education projects. At these workshops the college staff members usually do not spend all their time on broad institutional problems or projects but meet, part of the time, as members of the same department and as small groups within a department. The teachers of Freshman English, for example, may have a series of meetings for the purpose of bringing about more uniformity in the correcting and grading of themes. In some instances, it may be that a group from one department will meet with a group in another to eliminate undesirable course duplication.

For the effective functioning of an in-service education project based upon the teamwork of members of the faculty and administration, the college must be certain that the lines of communication among the faculty and between the faculty and the administration are adequate. Faculty meetings are, of course, one avenue of communication, but, in an institution with a sizable staff (say 75 or more), it is perhaps essential that faculty meetings be supplemented by periodic newsletters. It should always be possible for a relatively small number of staff members to bring about the calling of a faculty meeting either to initiate a desired change or as a referendum on some proposed action.

The college that has adopted the policy of using the group process for curriculum improvement and has solicited the co-operation of the instructor in policy formation in regard to many matters cannot expect to exclude the participation of the faculty in such things as salary scales, fringe benefits, retirement policies, and promotional policies. An elected faculty group to work with the president or dean of the institution in shaping the college policy in regard to such matters has proved invaluable in some institutions.

The college administrator, like the superintendent of schools or principal, must remember that the individual professor on his staff needs to keep abreast of the new developments in his field and in the social system. The time that each member of the faculty has available for in-service education must be divided between his personal and scholarly needs and the institutional changes for which his abilities and efforts are needed. The institution becomes stronger and better through the growth of the staff individually and as a team, as well as through improvement in the instructional program.

The teacher-education institution should have a policy such that staff members are encouraged to attend state, regional, and national meetings devoted *either* to problems of education (or teacher education) *or* to the matter of helping the instructor keep up with his field. Liberal travel funds should be provided for such purposes.

The institution should include in its library the things needed for the growth of the staff member as a scholar in his special field, just as it should have the publications that would be helpful to groups of staff members working on institutional improvement. Similarly, the professor should be encouraged to do research and experimentation both in the area of his subject-matter specialty *and* in new ways of teaching in this area. This encouragement may take the tangible form of released time, financial aid, visits to distant libraries or laboratories, and aid of specialists in research.

For effective in-service education, the co-operation between the administrative staff and the instructional staff and among the members of the various departments of the college *must extend* to matters other than in-service education. An administrative policy that unfairly restricts the professor's *freedom to teach* can scuttle all efforts to develop a co-operative approach to the improvement of the college program. The professor may reasonably feel that the administration does not have confidence in his judgment and ability if he is not given the *academic freedom* (as defined by such groups as the American Association of University Professors) necessary to enable him to do a good job in his classroom. If his freedom to teach is limited unduly by the college administration, he will be likely to consider a request that he serve on a group working to shape college policy and improve instruction as a sham and a delusion whereby the administration is merely giving lip-service to democracy.

ORGANIZATION, EVALUATION, TRAINING

CHAPTER XII

Organization of Programs of In-service Education

ROBERT S. GILCHRIST, CLARENCE FIELSTRA,
and
ANNA L. DAVIS

Introduction

This chapter presents some guiding principles for organizing in-service education programs which give individuals the maximum opportunity for growth and describes representative programs that have been successfully operated in well-established school systems. Though special emphasis is given programs in city school systems, the implications of the practices exemplified apply to in-service education in general.

Several organizational principles are presented. They are consistent with the guidelines given in chapter v, many of which have clear implications for the organization of a good in-service education program. They suggest that a good program will permit teachers to work on the problems that interest them, to be a part of the group which works out plans for solving these problems, and to evaluate the results of their efforts. The guidelines in chapter v further emphasize the importance of utilizing resources and of developing an environment in which teachers feel comfortable in working on their problems. One guideline suggests the importance of relating in-service education to the on-going program of the school so that the conclusions of in-service activities may be tested in actual classroom situations.

Enabling Individuals To Work on Their Own Problems

IMPORTANCE OF PARTICIPATION IN PLANNING THE PROGRAM

The gist of chapters iv and v seems to be that in-service education programs ought to be organized and developed with a complete recognition of the same principles of learning that are appropriate to classroom practices. It is an accepted principle of learning that one grows in insights and skills as he works on problems of genuine concern to himself. This means that those who participate in an in-service program should (a) be involved in identifying the problems on which they are to work, (b) have an opportunity to share in the planning, and (c) take part in determining the degree of success of their efforts.

Methods must be devised to get the problems of individuals out into the open. The school principal, supervisor, or curriculum co-ordinator, in informal interviews with faculty members, can discover their problems. These individual conferences can be supplemented by small-group discussions. The informal-interview technique should be used continuously and not merely when "looking" for problems in order to have an in-service program. A systematic procedure of jotting down problems as they are mentioned by teachers as individuals or as a faculty over a period of months or years proves helpful.

One interesting illustration of an involvement procedure based on data-collecting is an in-service project in an elementary school. In this school great dissatisfaction was expressed with spelling results. As a first step of their study, teachers were asked to keep a tabulation of words misspelled in the written work of the students. Thus, the spelling needs of the children in the school were found to be very different from those the teachers had supposed. As the study proceeded, teachers worked with a great deal more feeling of personal interest because they themselves had identified the needs of the children.

A committee studying the education of the gifted child is progressing in much the same manner. A careful identification of the children who fall in this category and a study of what they are doing in terms of school accomplishment has done much to alert committee members to the personal responsibility of all teachers for individual children of superior ability.

The role-playing technique was used effectively to motivate participants in one study group on discipline. A large number of elementary-school teachers, concerned with problems of classroom controls, were organized into groups of not more than twelve or fifteen persons. Each group prepared a role-playing situation centered on one problem of classroom control. A number of these were presented to the total group, and the implications were discussed. Every member of the large group felt a very personal interest in the techniques being discussed.

Another study group procedure stimulates actual participation on the part of the members in the preparation of course units, handbooks, or other materials needed for their own work. A committee that felt a great need for a counselor's handbook has been working in this manner: The total group met and planned an outline for such a handbook. In groups of two they then chose to work on the parts of this outline for which each pair felt greatest need. The subcommittees bring in their materials and present them to the whole group for analysis and criticism. While the procedure will result in a counselor's handbook, the discussions also provide a very fine in-service education activity as the group becomes involved in thinking through their own procedures in these various areas.

From these illustrations it would seem simple and easy to set up a sound in-service program. The system would merely have to involve all personnel and set up activities to meet the needs. Actual experience in a school system suggests the problem is not so easy.

TEMPTATION TO MAKE A SHOWING

Central office administrators and principals are often tempted to make a showing in their in-service programs. A program may sound more impressive if it is organized around one or two major topics in which everyone in the system participates. No one or two problems, however, can be found which are of immediate concern to all teachers in a city school system. If the in-service program is designed to permit each individual to work on problems which are important to him, considerable time will be needed to get the program under way. There must be a variety of activities to meet the individual requirements of a large number of people. It is not possible to describe the program in a quick, easy manner. Plans and projects must continue indefinitely. The first principle to recognize is that each teacher should have time and resources available to work individually and in informal group situations. Care must be exercised not to overorganize and to provide so many system-wide

and building-level activities that a teacher does not have time to
work by himself and to keep a perspective concerning his classroom
duties. Leadership personnel in a school system should emphasize
that a teacher is not expected to overengage in in-service activity.
Some systems have found that their most conscientious teachers
participate in more activities than is reasonable.

BUILDING-LEVEL VERSUS SYSTEM-WIDE EMPHASIS

One of the most complicated problems to be faced in trying to
organize an in-service program centered on actual concern of the
teachers is to determine the emphasis to be given problems to be
dealt with on the building level as contrasted to the system-wide
level. In many city school districts, principals are given primary responsibility for the program of the schools they administer. If this
point of view is sound, it seems reasonable to give the principal a
major role in helping to develop the in-service activities in which
his teachers are to participate. Initiating activities at the local
school level will help to insure that the program is centered on
problems significant to teachers. This type of organization also provides opportunity to adapt the program to the peculiar needs of a
given school. In any fairly large school system different sections of
the city are likely to have quite different types of students and,
consequently, quite different student needs. The over-all framework of a city-wide curriculum should be flexible enough to permit
a given faculty, in studying the needs of the students of its school,
to adapt the program to student needs. In this type of organization,
the superintendent says, in effect, to each principal and the faculty,
"This is your school. You are the ones who will study your program.
Change it as seems good, and improve your skills as you find need to
do so. In the final analysis, provide for this school as effective an
education program as possible."

The superintendent who emphasizes the autonomy of the individual school in in-service education does not thus relieve the central
staff of responsibility. To make the local school program effective,
rich resources must be available to every building at all times. The
consultant services of curriculum leaders, school psychologists,
school doctors, and others must be available to help in analyzing

problems and in planning. Good audio-visual and professional library facilities should be at hand.

The system-wide administration has responsibility to see that principals, both in groups and as individuals, have opportunities to improve their insights and skills. How to promote co-operative action on problems, how to involve all teachers in defining what seems significant to them, and how to use resources effectively—these are skills they will wish to cultivate. A recent bulletin[1] describes the in-service organization of the Avondale, New Jersey, School District. In this district the greatest emphasis on in-service work is at the individual school level. The central office staff spends most of its time in assisting teachers in the committees and study groups of individual schools. The principals are key persons in initiating the activities in their schools and work in many ways to facilitate the efforts of faculty groups. However, wide differences are reported in the effectiveness of the program from school to school. Some of these differences are attributed to the kind of leadership provided by principals, others to the "readiness" of a staff, and still others to the peculiar demands of a particular school community.

Some needs are difficult to meet when the emphasis is at the local school level. There are usually not enough resource people available to serve in all of the schools simultaneously. The leadership ability of principals varies, making it difficult for some faculties to get under way. It is desirable, too, that the city school system have an over-all unity of purpose and philosophy and not be permitted to become merely a collection of separate units. To cultivate this unity, there must be opportunity for teachers to work together on common problems on a city-wide basis as well as in the local school.

DESIRABILITY OF A COMPREHENSIVE PROGRAM

A combination of both building-level and system-wide activities seems desirable. Certainly individual needs of teachers should be assessed at the building level. Where there are common needs within a building, building-level activities are appropriate. However, a few teachers in one building, together with teachers of other buildings, will often have common problems which can best be met by

1. *The Work of the Curriculum Co-ordinator in Selected New Jersey Schools,* pp. 4, 5. New York: Teachers College, Columbia University, 1955.

area study groups. An analysis of individual problems usually suggests that there are certain common needs which can best be met by emphasis at system-wide level. What starts as a concern of one building gradually expands into an interest shared by many on a city-wide basis.

For example, in one school system, teachers expressed a desire to learn better ways to enrich their reading and oral-language program. Such a study was initiated at the building level in several of the elementary schools. Before long these elementary faculties had identified specific needs on which they wished expert help. For a period of time a consultant from a university was brought in to work with study groups in the elementary schools in setting up experimental situations. In these, the teachers tried out the newer practices they had been studying. While the consultant was in the community, however, he also worked in system-wide meetings in which many teachers from other schools were able to profit by his suggestions.

At another time in this same community, a city-wide program became the basis for many building-level activities. The curriculum co-ordinators found teachers expressing a desire for help with their elementary-science program. Some city-wide meetings were held in which stimulating science programs were presented by persons skilled in this area. Individual schools followed these city-wide meetings with further work-study groups at their own levels, using the ideas presented to develop materials adapted to their own needs.

It does not matter so much whether in-service education activities are concentrated at the building level or at the system-wide level. The critical point is whether the activity involves the teachers, and whether they are given an opportunity to follow through, not only in suggesting what to do but also in how to do it and in deciding at the end how effective the activity has been. Whether the emphasis is on problem-solving, whether there are useful resources available, whether there are many opportunities to work together, whether the atmosphere is permissive, and whether individual differences are recognized—all these are conditions that do not depend so much on the level of the activity as upon the concept of leadership held by the various individuals who work with teachers in a school system. At least one point seems completely clear, namely, that a system must offer a variety of opportunities for in-service education. Otherwise, individuals will find themselves "strait-jacketed" into the one activity which the system has decided upon even though it does not meet their individual needs.

The Pasadena schools have an in-service organization which attempts to provide a comprehensive program. The principals and supervisors who have the responsibility for instructional leadership meet together bi-weekly. The in-service program is the direct responsibility of the assistant superintendent in charge of instruction, who works with a co-ordinating committee including the elementary curriculum co-ordinator, the secondary curriculum co-ordinator, and the co-ordinators of the various subject fields. To avoid conflicts, the co-ordinator of guidance assumes the responsibility for expediting the program, clearing the requests for outside consultants, and co-ordinating the scheduling of activities. Principals are responsible for initiating in-service programs at the building level. Supervisors from the central office do not initiate programs but, rather, work with principals in organizing and carrying out projects that seem to meet teacher needs. Typical projects at the building level are a junior high school study group on the improvement of parent conferences, an elementary-school faculty study of role-playing and sociometrics, an elementary-school faculty study of test interpretation and use of test results, and a secondary-teacher group working on guidance problems.

Whenever similar local school needs are found in several schools, consideration is given to system-wide activities. Principals and supervisors determine these common needs by several methods. Sometimes a needs-census is taken at a leadership meeting, with principals reporting for their schools on the basis of local surveys. At other times, supervisors have been responsible for checking needs through going to buildings and personally interviewing teachers. Questionnaires are sometimes used. As common needs are discovered, city-wide committees are formed for consideration of such areas as communication skills, education of gifted children, and health education. Grade level or subject-field meetings are scheduled when teacher needs suggest the desirability of holding them. Outside consultants are employed if local leaders do not seem to have the time or the ability to help on the problem being considered. For example, because of the interest of so many teachers in the study of children and how they develop, a child study project was organized four years ago with the University of Maryland providing the leadership. Teachers in this program pursued a study of children throughout a three-year period. To date, approximately half of the teachers in the Pasadena system have participated.

VOLUNTARY VERSUS REQUIRED PARTICIPATION

Should in-service activities be on a voluntary or a required basis? How about institute credit and salary-increment requirements? Mention has already been made of the fact that individuals will work more enthusiastically on projects in which they have a role to play. Those who are responsible for organizing in-service education will be stimulated to think through their decisions more completely when the program is on a voluntary basis. When activities are required, it is easy for leadership to exercise its authority. When a school system develops an environment that is stimulative and permissive, then individuals work vigorously on activities which they feel will help them most. This is especially true if sympathetic guidance by individuals in leadership positions is available.

Individuals in groups will often set their own requirements about the work done so that the desired ends may be accomplished. Institute credit and salary-increment requirements are no longer prerequisite to professional motivation after a co-operative environment has been established throughout the school system. The fact should be emphasized, however, that proper provision does need to be made for evaluation of professional growth. Self-evaluation supplemented by appraisal of classroom teaching by administrators will help the individual identify his in-service needs. When educators accept the assumption that improvement of instruction is possible only through continuous attention to curriculum development, and when here is an appraisal program by which teachers can determine their needs for in-service education, formal requirements are no longer so important.

Some readers may be concerned that this point of view does not recognize the teacher who never faces any problem—the one who has taught the same way for twenty years and says, "In-service education is a lot of nonsense!" This kind of teacher will not be forgotten, however; he is invited to take part. Though it may take several years, the administrator who consistently tries to help teachers regardless of the nature of their problems will find that the vast majority develop more and more concern for their skill in teaching. If there are a few who refuse to accept responsibility for professional growth, perhaps they should not be permitted to continue teaching.

Utilizing the Regular Administrative and Supervisory Organization of the School System for In-service Education

Two of the guidelines in chapter v—"The simplest possible means are developed to move from decision to action," and "Constant encouragement is present to test and try ideas and plans in reality context"—suggest clearly the importance of making the in-service education program a part of the regular administrative and supervisory organization. Otherwise, in-service education may become an activity outside of the "main stream." In the past, some school systems have set up in-service education apart from the regular organization partly because administrators and supervisors were not sensitive to the needs for change and progress. Such an arrangement generally results in sharp clashes at the point where teachers wish to put into practice some of the ideas they have developed in their in-service education programs.

IN-SERVICE EDUCATION, CURRICULUM DEVELOPMENT, AND INSTRUCTIONAL-IMPROVEMENT PROGRAMS

A curriculum-development program is designed to insure appropriate learning experiences in the classroom. A program to improve instruction centers its attention on helping teachers provide the most effective teaching possible. A program of in-service education, likewise, is planned to give teachers and other instructional personnel an opportunity to grow professionally so that they may provide children with the best possible learning environment. To be of value, a curriculum-development program must take into account human development, learning processes, and the demands of a democratic society. Certainly instructional-improvement programs rest on the same solid bases. As teachers participate in in-service education, the same broad areas—human development, learning processes, and the demands of a democratic society—must be given consideration.

It is difficult to conceive of a functional in-service program which is not an integral part of the over-all curriculum-development program. In-service lectures or courses which are not closely integrated with the ongoing problems of the school itself are usually sterile. Many of the activities set up for the purpose of curriculum improvement offer rich opportunities for teachers to grow in service. The writing of teacher-guide materials for a learning unit in the course of study is an illustration, as are the examination of materials used in instruction, the study of classroom environment and classroom organization, or the grouping of pupils for work in the classroom or in the school, and classroom controls. The principles of pupil growth and development and those of the learning processes become more meaningful when considered as a means of solving such problems.

In one city school system in California, for example, many of the social-studies teachers of the junior high school felt that the study materials in their courses needed revision. Some teachers from each junior high school volunteered for a planning committee to get the project under way. This group of representatives, working with the curriculum co-ordinators and the junior high school principals, decided that in order to have new materials which would be useful, there must be the greatest possible teacher participation. The steering committee proposed that teachers in each school form a committee to examine the course content and make recommendations for the city-wide revision. First, however, it seemed desirable to train the leaders for these local meetings and to develop some resource materials for these groups as they studied together. For one semester, under skilled leadership, the members of the steering committee studied "how to lead a discussion group," in which they explored resources to be made available to the teachers. The following semester, members of the steering committee served as leaders of study groups within their own junior high schools. After examining their practices, these local groups made recommendations on various aspects of the program. Step by step the central steering committee reviewed the recommendations which came from the school groups, summarizing and relaying to the school groups materials for further teacher reaction.

At the close of the year a number of worth-while objectives had been accomplished: The new study materials were developed and ready for use. All teachers who were to teach from this outline had already become familiar with it and understood why certain content was included; consequently, they were better prepared to use the materials than they could possibly have been had they had no part in the planning. Finally, all of the participants in the study groups had had a fine experience in group work under carefully planned leadership.

In a junior high school district in Southern California, the staff of approximately 125 teachers, administrators, and the superintendent held a conference before the opening of school to plan their in-service projects for the year. They invited as consultant a curriculum professor from the University of California at Los Angeles. As a result of the conference, five study groups were formed, and every staff member associated himself with one of the groups. The study groups were formed to work on the following topics: (a) characteristics, needs, resources, and opportunities of our high-school students; (b) more effective techniques of teaching in the classics, fine arts, social studies, and English; (c) more effective techniques of teaching in mathematics, health, applied science, and shop; (d) co-ordinating and using auxiliary agencies—library, health, attendance, and audio-visual; and (e) improving guidance and counseling services.

To gain additional inspiration and guidance, the staff planned a meeting at which the consultant from the University spoke on "group dynamics" and on "some promising techniques of instruction." Also at this meeting the study groups convened and planned their next steps.

Each of the groups, during ensuing months, carried on research with the assistance of the school administrators and consultants. The findings, conclusions, and recommendations growing out of the research were shared with the total staff in meetings called for that purpose. Five such faculty meetings were held, and laymen as well as student leaders were invited to take part. The use of charts, slides, and other audio-visual materials did much to make presentations interesting and useful. Throughout all meetings, the "imperative needs of youth" as stated by the Educational Policies Commission were used as criteria in evaluating the findings presented.

A final total staff meeting of the year was devoted to an evaluation of the work accomplished and to looking ahead. It was generally agreed that the activities had been useful in revealing strengths of the school program and in sharing effective techniques of instruction. It was also agreed that at least two of the "imperative needs" were not being well met by the program and that unified faculty action should be taken to overcome the lack. Various other problems of curriculum and school-community relationships were pointed out, and plans to work further on these were given top priority as next steps. Most of all, it was agreed that through the experiences of the year, teachers had come to know each other better, both personally and professionally. An interdepartmental approach to in-service education and to curriculum improvement had become highly desirable and successful. The participation of outside consultants, as well as of laymen and pupils, had paid large dividends.

On the basis of the favorable evaluation of the outcomes of the "experiment," the staff decided to continue with a similar approach the following year. Thus, in this school the team-approach to in-service education gained major emphasis. Departments were still concerned with departmental problems and improvement; individual teachers were, of course, concerned with their personal growth; but all of these objectives were related to the over-all job of meeting, as a total faculty, the established needs of boys and girls of their community.

These two examples illustrate the close relationship between activities which are concerned with curriculum development or instructional improvement on the one hand and in-service education on the other. In fact, the programs can and often do lose their separate identities. It can probably be said that in-service education at its best is secured in projects which have a definite value for curriculum development and instructional improvement.

RESPONSIBILITY FOR CO-ORDINATION AND PROMOTION OF THE PROGRAM

Whoever is responsible in the school system for co-ordinating the instructional program should be responsible for the co-ordination of in-service education activities. In a smaller system, this person is generally the superintendent. In a large system, an assistant superintendent in charge of instruction, or someone with a similar title, has the responsibility for instructional co-ordination. Choosing the person to co-ordinate the in-service program is a heavy responsibility. Whoever is selected should get his major satisfactions from the results achieved by others rather than by being constantly in the limelight himself. He must be willing to let change occur slowly and to measure efficiency by changes in people rather than by surface results. Such criteria as the number of meetings held, the number of people in attendance, or similar standards are largely superficial.

If the administrator of in-service education is one who himself believes that all school personnel must continue to grow and improve on the job, he will want each member of the staff to contribute his share to the program. In the first place, his own conviction of the importance of the program will encourage and support the leadership staff in creative planning.

Often this individual may need to delegate to another person a specific responsibility for co-ordination of the in-service program. Delegation of this co-ordination to some one individual whose major responsibility is to promote in-service activities is questioned by some because of the possible danger that the in-service plan will develop as a separate, rather than an integral, part of the over-all program of instructional improvement. Certainly this person should be one whose interests and responsibilities relate him very closely to the whole program.

Where a school system has a curriculum council, this council should be closely related to the organizational scheme for in-service education. In fact, the council can, and often should, be the group which co-ordinates the in-service program with curriculum development. Some one person, of course, will need to administer the decisions of the group, but the council can be the body to which he reports and from which he gets his directions.

NECESSITY FOR ADMINISTRATIVE PARTICIPATION

If recommendations and conclusions pertaining to in-service activities are expected to result in action, the administrators, both principals and central office personnel, will have to be included in the planning and carrying out of the in-service program. In the same sense, supervisors or consultants will be more ready to help activate a decision if they have been parties to making it. Certainly few things arouse more in-service interest among teachers than the feeling that their administrators stand ready to work with them in carrying out plans that have been approved. Likewise, if principals, consultants, and teachers all attack a problem together, the use of teachers' classrooms as laboratories to test out new ideas will be a natural outcome. Experiments can be set up with full understanding on the part of all persons affected and, consequently, can be carried on in an atmosphere free from defensiveness or bias. For the same reasons, evaluation of the effects of the program will be more acceptable if the in-service education is a part of the over-all instructional program of the school.

Whatever the arrangement for co-ordination, it is important that all instructional leaders participate both in setting up in-service projects and in deciding what should be done with recommendations which emerge. For example, a principal of a school certainly must be acquainted with the plan by which teachers in his school can participate in a system-wide study group. As far as possible, he should have taken part in setting up the plan while it was being formulated. Likewise, the school organization should be such that, through progress reports and interaction with participating individuals, the principal keeps in touch with the findings of the study groups. In most school systems principals and central office personnel meet to consider their common problems. In other words, all of the professional staff who are to be concerned with the results of a given study should participate in planning and working it through.

NEED OF ADMINISTRATORS AND SUPERVISORS TO
DEVELOP LEADERSHIP SKILLS

Administrators and supervisors are usually cognizant of their responsibility for facilitating the work of teachers. They often discover the need for instructional-leadership skills such as those needed to lead discussions effectively. For the performance of such duties, it is fortunate if they have the ability to help a group think through a problem together and arrive at consensus.

School superintendents understand that they are captains of administrative teams of central office and local school leaders. In the same sense, in the larger sytems, assistant superintendents in charge of instruction find that their primary responsibility is the co-ordination of the work of instructional leaders in the school system. At the school level, the same trend is taking place. Principals are recognizing that their role is that of a co-ordinator rather than a line administrator whose sole job is to make decisions and to pass them on to subordinates. Within large schools the same development is taking place—department heads are becoming less and less administrators of departments and more and more individuals who provide leadership for the work of the teachers in their area. In fact, it seems that the position of department head is becoming less popular. In its place we find more curriculum co-ordinators at the school level. Often these co-ordinators are responsible for working horizontally with teachers in addition to working in the vertical organization where a subject field is the basis for considering sequence of curriculum experiences.

The organization of an in-service program which is otherwise sound will undoubtedly fail to accomplish its goals if the individuals in instructional-leadership positions lack skill in working with others.

ARRANGEMENTS FOR LEADERS TO WORK ON THEIR OWN PROBLEMS

In addition to the need for working with teachers on various projects, individuals in leadership positions need opportunities to develop skills required in their roles as leaders. Those in the same school system can band together to work in whatever areas seem most pertinent and thus capitalize on their regular meetings for consideration of the problems of instructional leadership. If they truly feel that leadership problems should be given priority on an agenda, they can see to it that time is available for such discussions. Administrators and supervisors who need outside resources will generally find that the financial arrangements necessary to bring in someone who can make a contribution to the group on the current problem will be approved.

Often when a problem becomes clearly defined, a group of instructional leaders can devise a procedure by which answers can be found through the insights gained by working together. In one school system, the elementary principals met to discuss their problems without anyone in a "line" position being designated as leader. They chose their own chairman and set up their own agenda. The discussions generally centered on ways for putting into practice the instructional policies already agreed upon. In another system, elementary principals, together with the central office supervisors and the assistant superintendent, decided that they should establish more consistent procedures for use in their evaluation of probationary teachers and in their program of working with beginning teachers. The group arranged a series of four half-day visitations. On the first half-day they visited a first-grade teacher from 9:00 until 10:00 a.m., then talked with the teacher from 10:00 to 10:30, and, between 10:30 and 11:30, discussed the results of their observations. This group found that their discussion took on much more meaning when it was based on observations of the same teaching situation by the entire group. People were able to understand each other's ideas concerning the quality of teaching observed. They also learned points of view much better and how to profit from an interchange of procedures by which a teacher can be helped to develop better methods. Here again, if top leadership gives a backing to the instructional-supervision program, the job is easier. In one system the superintendent of schools co-ordinates the efforts of principals in such group visits. Any group, however, can capitalize on the leadership within itself to move ahead on the solution of a common problem.

Most supervisors and principals are on duty before school starts in the fall and after school is dismissed in the spring. These periods, before the teachers arrive in the fall and after teachers leave in the spring, may be utilized by school leaders for meetings in which they come to grips with their instructional problems. Where the system is too small for such a group to function to good advantage, individuals from neighboring school systems may be invited to join them in work on common problems. During the summer months, teacher-education institutions offer workshops and conferences which are often of inestimable value to an individual in a position of leadership.

The School System Must Insure Time, Facilities, and Resources To Stimulate and Strengthen the Program

TIME

Administrators should help define the different activities which are to be regarded as part of the daily work of the teacher. Actual classroom instruction, plus conferences with both students and parents, plus sponsorship of activities, plus preparation for the work of tomorrow and next week, plus the long-range curriculum-development activities constitute the heavy program of the typical teacher. Besides the specified number of hours a day assigned for classroom instruction, it must be recognized that there are other responsibilities to be taken care of at times over and beyond these hours.

If the teacher's work day is defined as starting at 8:00 or 8:30 A.M. and continuing to 4:30 or 5:00 P.M., study groups can be scheduled at regular intervals for the first or last hour of the day. Some systems have found a regular teacher-planning period at the beginning of the day a satisfactory method of stimulating co-operative work on the problems of the school.

It is important to schedule in-service experience in such a way that conflicts are minimized and activities fall into their proper relationship. Without thoughtful scheduling of in-service activities, some teachers become heavily overloaded in trying to participate in everything offered; others find themselves but lightly involved, if at all. One useful technique for avoiding frustrating conflicts is the practice of setting up a basic calendar in the school system, designating certain days for city-wide activities and other days for local school activities; for instance, city-wide meetings on Tuesdays and Thursdays, building meetings on Wednesdays, meetings of teacher organizations and education organizations on Mondays.

The length of time that educators work during the year also has implications for in-service education. School systems which require teachers to report for duty a week or two before school starts have found that much planning can be completed before the rush of opening school. Likewise, school systems, which have organized workshops and other in-service activities after the close of school, have found that teachers are enthusiastic about the opportunity to work on curriculum problems during a period when they are not under the strain of teaching. The ideal plan may be that teachers be employed the year around with a month's vacation during the summer.

Whatever the administration and board can do to convince teachers that curriculum development and in-service education are vital phases of the total school operation will pay dividends. An appropriation for employment of substitutes so that teachers may be released to visit other teachers, to attend committee meetings, or to engage in curriculum projects may cause the teaching staff to develop an entirely different outlook on the in-service program. They know then that the program has importance and dignity. The same reasoning applies to the length of time that administrators and supervisors work during the year. School administrators who recognize the importance of professional leadership by providing adequate time schedules in which group leaders can plan their work have reported that the additional money required has been well spent.

FACILITIES

Teachers, supervisors, and administrators who have had the privilege of working in buildings with adequate conference rooms will attest the fact that facilities make a difference. Over and above the need of appropriate rooms in which to carry on in-service activities, the accessibility of resource material is important. A library in a school building can well have a section for professional materials on education as well as learning materials for students. The librarian who keeps abreast in the field of curriculum can often be of great help by making available to staff members materials on problems being considered. The central office building of the school system can well have curriculum-laboratory facilities where groups can meet to investigate grade-level subject fields and special interests. Here again, materials and equipment should be readily available.

Films, slides, and recordings should be included as well as books and magazines on curriculum and other fields of study.

With small appropriations of money, a school system can provide cameras, recording machines, flannel-boards, and other kinds of equipment that contribute to the success of in-service education activities. In one school system, for example, staff members were asked to make several presentations explaining various phases of the junior high school program. The group decided to use records and slides to tell their story. A teacher with artistic talent and one with ability in taking good pictures were available to help. As the group worked out their presentations, using the slides and an accompanying explanation recorded on tape, they were able to clarify in their own minds many questions regarding the philosophy and procedures of their program. Everyone connected with the project agreed that the availability of both physical and human resources to develop the audio-visual materials, and the willingness of the school system to spend a little money for the project, contributed greatly to the success of their project. Otherwise, the group would probably have developed a few talks which, without audio-visual aids, would have fallen far short of conveying their message.

RESOURCE PERSONS

In the main, the human resources needed for in-service education can usually be provided within a school system from among the teachers themselves, the supervisors, and the administrators. Many times the laymen in the community can be enlisted as resource persons. There should, however, be provision for the employment of outside consultants. Sometimes local leadership will not have time for a particular project. Often the problem is of such a nature that no one locally has the necessary background or ability to give complete leadership. Frequently the employment of an outside consultant will insure not only the success of a particular in-service activity but also will be the means by which local leaders can gain insights into the area under consideration. They will then be able to guide comparable projects in the future.

Several practices in the Pasadena (California) schools illustrate how one system tries to meet the problems of time, facilities, and personnel resources. Each year for the last seven years summer workshops have been held for teachers who wish to work on instructional problems at a time when the pressure of regular teaching is absent. To meet the needs of several teachers who wished to get credit for their summer workshop, an arrangement was worked out three years ago with the University of California at Los Angeles to co-sponsor the workshop. A university professor supervises the participation of individuals who desire credit. Approximately half of those who attend the workshop enrol for credit.

To underwrite financially the in-service program, the Pasadena schools' budget provides for expenses of the summer workshop as well as for allowances during the school year for teacher visitation, half-day committee meetings, and the release of teachers for a period of a week or two so that they may work intensively on curriculum projects. All beginning teachers and approximately a third of the entire staff are able to visit for a day during the year. Enough half-day committee meetings can be held to enable committees to move ahead on their work. Two or three half-day meetings during a year seem to make a considerable difference in the amount of work a committee can accomplish. The budget also provides for the employment of consultants during the regular year.

The element of time has been given careful consideration in the Pasadena in-service program. The school week has been defined to recognize the need for a teacher to spend approximately 35 hours per week at school and a minimum of 5 hours in activities at home that are directly related to the teaching load. Lay people, as well as teachers, have been encouraged to realize that a teacher's load includes not only instructing children in groups but also individual guidance, sponsorship of activities, and preparation for the work of the next day and the next week as well as long-term planning for instructional improvement or in-service education. In the junior high schools the school day for many years has included a daily planning period from 8:15 until 9:00 A.M. each morning. This daily period provides time for subject-area, grade-level, faculty, and committee meetings.

In Pasadena, the importance of facilities has been recognized in planning buildings. In new buildings workrooms and conference rooms have been provided. An addition is being built for the administration building to include a professional library with connecting meeting-rooms where teachers, principals, and supervisors will find it possible to confer in pleasant surroundings, with resource material readily available.

The Program Must Provide for Communication and Interaction among All Persons in the School System

INTRODUCTION

A school system is a complex organism. Internally there are various levels—preschool, elementary, secondary, and adult. There are different building units, grade levels, and subject fields. In addition, the specific responsibilities of various personnel differ tremendously—teaching, building-level administration, system-wide administration, secretarial work, and maintenance work. Some persons are concerned primarily with the financial aspects of the system, others with public relations, some with building problems, and many with instruction. Another variation which ought to be recognized is the range in ages and in numbers of years of service of people working in the system. Some teachers received their training many years ago when an entirely different kind of psychology of learning was taught in the colleges, and some are in their first year in a school system and on probationary status.

The problem of communication and interaction would still be reasonably simple, however, if the only people who needed to be considered were those employed by the school system. But the public also has a vital stake in any developments that affect the learning environment in the classroom. If misunderstandings are to be avoided, laymen and educators, alike, must understand the bases on which sound education can be built. Educators, therefore, have an obligation to help laymen recognize problems and issues that should be resolved. School people should also make available to laymen the necessary factual information and research upon which citizens can rely in making up their minds about the kinds of schools they want for their children.

The pupils must be taken into account, too. Boys and girls are valuable interpreters of the educational program upon which the schools rely. Confused students, however, make it difficult to carry on effective education. Plans for necessary communication and interaction must take into account the need for pupil participation and understanding. Obviously the nature of the participation will vary with the maturity of the pupils.

EMPLOYEES OF THE SCHOOL SYSTEM

No simple plan will suffice to insure adequate and effective communication and interaction. Internally the school system will certainly need to provide sufficient opportunities for the teachers of a certain grade or subject field to communicate with each other, and some grade-level and subject-field meetings must take place through the system. A committee in which representatives from each building get together can readily provide for two-way communication. These people bring problems from their building to the committee for clarification and take the findings back to their colleagues. Opportunities for vertical interaction will be needed, though many systems fail to provide them. It stands to reason that elementary and junior high school teachers need to understand what is happening at levels other than their own. A kindergarten teacher must have some understanding of the senior high school program if she is to be an adequate representative of the schools when she talks with parents. Some school systems have arranged for classroom visitation at various levels. Other systems have divided their total staff into cross-section groups for discussion purposes. The areas where information and understanding are needed are first identified. The leaders then bring back to their groups the information and background materials. In addition to planning appropriate kinds of meetings, school systems have found that a house organ helps, especially if teachers and others are given an opportunity to participate in deciding what goes into it. An atmosphere of permissiveness in which each person finds that his questions are respected helps assure effective interaction and communication. Leadership can do much to establish such an atmosphere. Administrators and supervisors who sense the important role which teachers should play in curriculum development and who have faith in democratic processes will succeed in building up an effective system of in-service co-operation.

Classified or noncertificated employees, as they are often called in a school system, are also important to the instructional program. A system will do well to plan in such a manner that these noninstructional people are involved sufficiently in the instructional program and its planning to understand it and thereby make their most effective contribution to it. In one city school system a luncheon meeting is held in early September each year for all employees of the system. At other social events during the year, all employees without exception—instructional, secretarial, and maintenance—are invited. In many schools, meetings primarily of a curricular or instructional nature include representatives other than the teaching staff. When, for example, a faculty meeting schedules an item to which secretaries or custodians may have a contribution to make, they are included in the planning. The same plan is followed in committees assigned for particular jobs. For example, if arrangements are made to enable high-school students to secure actual experience in secretarial work, certainly some of the secretarial staff of the school are in a position to make valuable contributions. In the same manner, when the student council considers problems concerning the campus and the building, custodial-staff members may be extremely helpful in assisting the students to arrive at sound answers.

CITIZENS

Citizen participation in developing the educational program is the surest guarantee of community understanding and support. If a school staff understands and appreciates what parents and other adults are doing in relation to children, it will be in a much better position to decide on the most appropriate experiences in school. Contacts with laymen, therefore, serve to make for better two-way communication. Perhaps the single most important way in which parents and schools can communicate and interact is in the individual parent-teacher conference. Many systems have rather well-developed plans for such conferences at the elementary level and a few have extended the practice into secondary schools. The individual conference can well be supplemented with room meetings where the teacher of a group of children talks with parents about the work of her classroom. Grade-level and school meetings for parents and system-wide meetings on specific subjects should supplement the smaller group meetings and the individual conferences but should never be used as the sole means for parent contact. In such gatherings, the group is too large, and parents often do not feel that the discussion applies to them personally. Special study groups, where parents explore a phase of the education program in which they are particularly interested, are very helpful. Sometimes teachers and parents of children in the primary grades often analyze together research findings on child development. School systems which rely on advisory committees of laymen to help solve problems often find that the laymen not only help to find a good solution to the problem but also gain a much keener insight into the program of the school.

The publication of annual reports by the superintendent and news bulletins of information which many systems issue periodically are of real help. The sympathetic and active co-operation of the newspaper of the community in writing up school news is essential as a means of communication. It must be emphasized, however, that written communication at its best should merely supplement face-to-face oral communication, and that there should be many opportunities for individual and small-group conferences rather than a reliance on big meetings.

STUDENTS

The way to insure understanding on the part of pupils is to provide appropriate classroom experiences. If boys and girls are to learn most effectively, they must work toward goals of their own. They must also understand why they engage in certain activities if they are to profit from their experiences. For best results, too, they must take part in the evaluation of their own accomplishments. Teachers who take time to have boys and girls clarify for themselves what they have learned find that they, in turn, help the parents understand better what is going on in school. Representative students can well have a significant part to play in the development of the in-service program. They can help educators determine the values of the instructional program.

Conclusion

For the most part, a good organization for in-service education in the single school or in a small school district is good for a city school system as well. The large school system, however, faces some problems which are peculiarly its own and which become increasingly serious as the number of separate school units in the system increases. In the first place, the problem of identifying the concerns of teachers and of enlisting the aid of large numbers of them in the planning of activities becomes increasingly difficult. At the same time, as a city system grows, there is increased need for an in-service program that will promote common purposes throughout the system. The greater the number of people involved, the more difficult it becomes to arrive at common understandings of goals and the methods of reaching them.

The city or county school system must work on two fronts. It must develop an in-service program that promotes teacher-initiated activities, while at the same time it must provide adequate direction and co-ordination to insure common system-wide basic purposes and practices.

Most systems try to provide opportunities for teachers and administrators to keep growing professionally. Systems with in-service programs can probably be classified in their organization on a continuum, with one extreme type dominated by the central office, and complete local autonomy at the other extreme. In the former, an individual or a few people in top-level positions decide what they think the system needs. They then, as far as possible, persuade those next in line of authority. The decision finally reaches the classroom teacher. Such a program may be characterized as the "drip down" system. It often looks good on paper; the organization can be logical, everyone engaging in a particular study and then moving on to another the next year. In the local autonomy type, each school is a law unto itself. The schools might just as well be in different systems since few interrelations exist.

An organization which recognizes the need for local and individual initiative, and at the same time capitalizes on the strengths provided by a democratically organized school system, is the ideal toward which to strive. Such a plan permits each individual faculty to develop activities that meet the common needs in their building. At the same time, when needs cut through several units in the school system, a system-wide project can be organized. Such a local and system-wide combination permits effective use of resources available in the system and the community. It enables those in charge of the in-service program to identify budgetary needs in a more effective manner since a budget is always managed at the system level.

The proverb that the whole is greater than the sum of its parts undoubtedly applies to in-service education. Several healthy building-level programs will be stronger if joint efforts are made where the nature of the problem suggests that procedure.

The special form of the organization which a school system develops is not nearly so important as are the attitudes of those in positions of leadership. If instructional leaders believe in people and their ability to see and solve problems, they will create the opportunities for teachers to work on problems significant to them. Administrators, too, will themselves be eager to learn how to be helpful to teachers as they engage in in-service activities. An organization can and will be developed to provide wholesome plans for in-service education if leadership is allowed and encouraged to emerge. No one sequence of steps insures a desirable program. The best policy, as this chapter seeks to show, is to understand guiding principles and their implications in practice. Any particular system should start at the point which seems most promising for its own situation and needs.

CHAPTER XIII

The Evaluation of Change in Programs of In-service Education

VIRGIL E. HERRICK

Most programs of in-service education in schools exist for the dual purpose of helping the members of the staff become more competent to deal with their professional roles as teachers and administrators and of improving the quality of the educational program of the school system. It follows, therefore, that the evaluation of change in programs of in-service education should consider the nature and quality of changes in people as individuals and as professional persons and the nature and quality of the changes made in the educational program itself.

In dealing with the psychology of change in individuals, the authors of chapter iv present four areas within which it is important to understand the conditions and processes of change. These areas have particular significance for the problem of evaluation in that they mark out the kinds of change a staff should consider in trying to evaluate programs of in-service education. These four areas of change have to do with: (*a*) knowledge and skills, (*b*) attitudes and values, (*c*) the relation of the individual and the group, and (*d*) the internalized feelings, motives, and aspirations of the individual.

As one examines and thinks about the nature of possible changes in individuals, the nature of the problems serving as organizing foci in programs of in-service education, and the nature of the organization and structure of various programs of staff study from the point of view of their implications for the evaluation of these programs, the following propositions seem to become clear:

1. There is a relationship between the changes in the individuals, the problems used as the organizing focus of the program of in-service education, and the nature of the approach or over-all plan being

used to implement such programs. Evaluations of changes in the individual staff member will need to consider the problem and institutional context within which these changes take place.

2. Evaluations of changes or lack of change in personal behavior should be related to evaluations of changes or lack of change in problem development and to evaluations of changes or lack of change in program organization. It is just as important to study factors which determine resistance to change as it is to examine those which promote change. The direction of attention in evaluation and the seeing of relationships among evaluations can move either from changes in personal behavior to changes in problem content to changes in organization, or vice versa. Since the improvement of people and the educational program are of primary importance, changes in organizational structure and program probably should be related to them.

3. The relationships which exist among changes in people and instructional programs and problems indicate the importance of seeing clearly the basis upon which the value of change at any one point is being determined. The change in the personal behavior of an individual must be related to the value of this change for his professional behavior as a teacher; the change in the behavior of a teacher must be related to the value of this change for the educational behavior of the children and youth with whom he works. The change in the working relationships of a group of teachers must be related to the value of this change for the development of the educational problem being worked on. This suggests evaluation based on judgments of relative rather than absolute value of changes in people and in programs of in-service education.

Nature of Changes Desired in Programs of In-service Education

In general, the changes that are desired in programs of in-service education have to do with adequacy. We desire those changes that enable people to become more adequate as persons, as teachers and administrators, and as members of a school staff. We desire those changes that contribute to more adequate educational programs for children and youth in individual classrooms, in specific school programs, and in the total educational enterprise of a city or state. We desire, also, those changes that insure more adequate understanding and support by a community of its educational program.

Adequacy of change, however, is not synonymous with amount of change. Adequacy has more to do with knowing the goal or purpose to be achieved and with its efficient and economical accomplishment. Adequacy judgments are usually judgments of the *degree* of worth-whileness and are not based on concepts of absolute goodness. These value judgments are dictated, in the main, by the nature of the goals desired and the value positions held. It is the purpose of this chapter to describe how such evaluations can take place in programs of in-service education.

Determining Change in Programs of In-service Education

Before changes in programs of in-service education can be evaluated, the presence of changes in the program or in the behavior of individuals has to be detected. This is the special problem of this section.

The determination of the presence of change is essentially the problem of determining differences over time in the phenomena being observed. These differences can only be determined when repeated or continuous observations are made of the phenomena considered. Such differences or evidences of change can be determined more adequately when it is possible to determine clearly either a beginning point or a goal toward which behavior is directed. Change under these conditions can either be determined by the difference that exists between the starting point (first observation) and the present position (second or last observation) on a behavior continuum or the difference that exists between successive observations of behavior and the goal to be achieved. In the first, the amount of information a teacher has about children is observed before a program of child study is undertaken and then is observed after the program is over. The change in knowledge about children is determined by the nature of the differences that exist between these two observations. In the second, the goal is defined in terms of what there is to know about children, and change is determined by comparing the differences that exist between repeated appraisals of teachers' knowledge and this goal.

In programs of in-service education where the problems being worked on by the staff have no ideal answers or where the nature and distribution of significant abilities or processes are unknown, the first way of determining change is the only one available. Where it is possible to define the goals to be achieved, the second method can be used, and, because of the availability of a defined goal, it provides the easier evaluation of change. Value has already been established by the definition of the desired goal. The first method makes no commitments as to the value of the determined change.

NATURE OF THE JUDGMENTS IN DETERMINING CHANGE

Five judgments are important in the determination of changes resulting from programs of in-service education. These judgments are: (*a*) the perception of the *presence* of change in relation to some continuum of behavior; (*b*) the determination of the *amount* of change which necessitates the quantification of observable differences in terms of some countable unit; (*c*) the determination of the *rate* of change or the quantity of change per unit of time; (*d*) the determination of the *direction* of change which requires some goal definition of a determined means-end relationship; and (*e*) the determination of the nature of the *relationship* that exists among changes.

Determination of Presence of Change. This problem has been discussed and, naturally, is the basis for all other judgments connected with determining the value of the change perceived.

As one moves from the questions of perceiving the presence of change to the ones of determining the amount, rate, and direction of change, the problem of valuing these aspects of change becomes more important.

Determination of Amount of Change. The amount of change can be determined only after some suitable unit has been developed. Usually simple units of experience serve this purpose. Thus, the number of times the leader of a problem-centered working group talks as compared with the number of contributions made by individual members of the group would be a simple index of amount of change. The value of this change would depend on the nature of the concept of leadership held. A decrease in the number of times the leader talked accompanied by an increase in the number of contributions by each member would be considered a desirable change from the point of view of one value, orientation.

It is difficult to add the common units of experience and reach any precise statement of amount of change. Most areas of desired change in programs of in-service education do not have standarized units developed for quantifying these changes. There are few scales available for evaluating the activities of in-service programs. Most evaluations of changes in problems and individual behavior will deal with rough units for counting and in many cases do not quantify the qualities being considered at all.

In common practice, however, we usually count the amount of change and make direct comparisons. This might be illustrated by observing and comparing changes in the co-operation of members of two groups of teachers working on curriculum problems. The presence of changes in the amount of five units of co-operation in the behavior of one group and three units of co-operation in the second group tends to suggest that five units of co-operation are better than three units. Very seldom do we ask whether errors in our observation and units for counting might not have produced this difference.

Determination of Rate of Change. A new aspect of this problem is revealed when further examination of the first group's five units of change in co-operation indicates that this amount of change occurred in a five-week period. The three units of change in co-operation of the second group, however, took place over a one-week period. Comparison of the amount of change with the time modifies our assessment of the two groups. The efficiency of the second group in modifying its behavior in the direction of co-operation seems to be superior. This is true only if certain assumptions are made. One is that both groups started at the same point in learning co-operation, which means that the amount of co-operation possible to be learned by group one was the same for group two. Rate of change, when one is already proficient in a skill or area of knowledge, tends to be very low. Rate of change tends to be relatively higher in the initial stages of learning. Group two might have just started trying to work co-operatively, and the assessment of the efficiency of three units of change in one week would have to be modified.

A second set of assumptions which need to be examined in valuing rate of change has to do with the relative significance or quality of the units of co-operation considered. In the case of group two, the evidence of co-operation may have been the number of times members of the group expressed their desire to "work together on our problems." In group one, the evidence of co-operation may have been the number of times the group was able to agree on a common problem and to utilize the resources of the group in working on it. It is likely that one unit of this kind of co-operation is worth many units of verbal expression of interest in working together.

If rate of change is going to be considered in valuing activities of in-service programs, thought must be given to the relative position of individuals, groups of teachers, and school systems on the continuum of behavior being considered. Frequently, however, this is not possible. A rough approximation of the level of development such as, "this is the third year their group has worked together" or "this is a group of experienced teachers, all of whom have had formal courses and workshop experience in child study," is all that can be known about the starting position of many groups or individuals. This, of course, makes judgments of the extent to which change has taken place less exact.

It is difficult to determine the relative positions of individuals or groups on a continuum of behavior or to compare with any accuracy their opportunities and motivations for change. It is, therefore, desirable to assess those changes that take place in the same individual or group over a period of time rather than making comparative judgments about rates of change in different individuals, school groups, or school systems.

Perhaps even more important than position on a line of possible development in evaluating relative amount and efficiency of change is the question of the relative worth of different behaviors on the same growth dimension. Is it more important for a teacher to know that the development of children tends to be continuous than it is to know that development is interrelated? Is it more important for a group of teachers to agree to get together every two weeks to work on ways to hold parent conferences than it is for them to spend time studying stenographic records and tape recordings of parent conferences? In answer to the first question, teachers may agree that these two generalizations about child development were equally important. In respect to the second, the judgment might be that the analyzing of records has a greater potential for improving parent conferences than the mere agreement to hold a meeting but that holding a meeting was a necessary first step to the making of the analysis. Granting the difficulty of finding comparable qualitative units for determining efficiency of change, it is important in any evaluation of change for the staff to consider this question of the nature and significance of the unit used. Seldom, however, will they ever be completely satisfied with what they can devise.

Determination of Direction of Change. Many of the problems of evaluation of change in programs of in-service education cannot be handled on the basis of knowing precisely where teachers and groups start or the comparability of units used in determining the amount and efficiency of change. Frequently about the only judgment that can be made is that "things are different from what they were," or "Marge is sure getting more acceptant of her children." Here, there is an awareness of change and, tied to this awareness, is some judgment as to direction. Teachers can compare two samples of handwriting and agree with great consistency that they are different in legibility and that one is more legible than the other. Yet, there could be little agreement as to the specific nature of this difference in formation of letters, degree of slant, and in the spacing of letters and words.

One of the most useful and valuable judgments regarding change, therefore, will be the dual judgment by an individual or group that change has taken place and that this change in behavior is moving in a certain value direction. All this judgment needs is a knowledge of the goal and the perception of direction of change. Viewed in this way, many evaluations of activities growing out of in-service programs can be made which will give direction and significance to what is being done without having to wait for the secondary judgments as to whether changes are being achieved to the greatest degree and in the most efficient way. Frequently, all we need to know is whether we are moving in the right direction. The rest can follow in good time.

Determination of Relationship among Changes: Another judgment important to make in evaluating change in programs of in-service education has to do with the relationship that exists among changes. Much of the behavior of teachers and school staffs as they work on their personal and professional problems is complex and is directed toward more than one goal at a particular time. The value of one kind of change is determined frequently by the relationship this change has to other desired changes. With children, for example, the value of changes in the number of words they can spell in the spelling class is determined by the relationship of this to the changes in the correct spelling of words they use when they write. Similarly, changes in the behavior of members of a group are related to each other and to their development of the group goal.

Three levels of judgment about the nature and relationship of changes can be made—each more important and difficult to make than the preceding one. The first is the perception of change based upon at least two observations separated in time. The second is the judgment that two kinds of change are seen to be related. Frequently this kind of judgment is verified or tested by methods of statistical correlation or by the testing of the significance of true differences. The third is the judgment that changes are causally related. Of course, this is the most important judgment of all to make about the relationship among changes because changes which are causally related to desired ends are more important and to be prized more highly than those which are not.

The test of causality is invariability of consequence. If one kind of change is invariably related to another kind of change, it is likely that there is a causal relationship between the factors producing these changes. This kind of relationship in programs of in-service education can be determined either by observing over a long period of time or by producing changes consciously in one area and then observing the nature of the changes that take place in other areas.

Evidence has been accumulating in the past few years that it is rarely possible to explain relationships in patterns of change on the basis of simple cause and effect. A much more useful concept seems to be that factors in human behavior are operating in complex patterns of dynamic interrelationship. Changes in one area or aspect of development account for changes in another area, and vice versa. Emotional problems frequently cause difficulties in learning to read. It is equally true that difficulties in learning to read cause emotional difficulties.

Nature of the Evaluation Process

The nature of the evaluation process is determined in part by the nature of the problems attacked in programs of in-service education and in part by the nature of changes desired. It is helpful, however, to examine briefly the necessary aspects of the evaluation process to see how they apply to the problems of evaluation of changes in programs of in-service education.

THE ROLE AND FUNCTION OF OBJECTIVES OR GOALS

Evaluation is usually defined as that process by which one determines how well he has achieved his objectives. Essential parts of this process have to do with the identification of the important objectives to be achieved, the definition of these objectives in terms of the behavior which would characterize them, the use of this behavioral definition in the development of the necessary appraisal instruments or observation devices, the observations and collection of data, the use of norms and standards to judge the adequacy of the behavior, and the making of the final decisions regarding value.

Objectives play the key role in the above series of activities. In programs of in-service education before evaluations can take place, there must be some definition of what purpose or goal is to be achieved or what problem is to be studied. If the program of in-service education has defined its purpose in terms of knowledges, abilities, and attitudes it desires to achieve, then the evaluation will necessitate specifying these attributes in behavioral terms and observing repeatedly to see if the behaviors have been acquired. If, however, the goals of an in-service program are in terms of identified problems, then the evaluation process starts by defining the essential parts of a problem important for both work and evaluation activities. In both cases, evaluation of change is dependent on the definition of the goals, either as problems to be studied or knowledges, skills, attitudes to be learned.

Definition of Goals. A behavioral definition of objectives or goals is difficult to make. All definitions, however, start from a consideration of what is essentially involved in whatever phenomenon is being considered. When this is known, all the other forms of definition can follow.

A group of teachers, for example, were struggling with the problem of defining "weather" or "climate" for both teaching and evaluation purposes. All efforts broke down until someone suggested that they define "weather" by describing its essential components—things which go together to produce weather. This effort to define produced three components of "weather"—temperature, moisture, and air mass and its movement. The test of this definition is the fact that through the control of temperature, moisture, and the movement of air, one can produce any kind of weather or climate he wishes. Having these three essential parts of weather, it was easy for the teachers to see what observations to make in order to produce the data for the evaluation of changes in weather with their children.

Another group of teachers was interested in studying and evaluating their own group work as a basis for helping their own students work together more effectively. Again there was difficulty in defining the knowledge, skills, and attitudes of group work. Long lists of specifics seemed to be unmanageable. Again, the suggestion that it might be better to define group work in terms of its important components seemed helpful. The teachers defined group work as including (a) the identification and definition of group goals, (b) the means by which the group goal is achieved, and (c) the interpersonal relationships among the members of the group. This definition served to get started, and some preliminary observations soon indicated that the category of interpersonal relationships needed to be broken down into (a) leadership functions (b) decision-making processes, and (c) individual status roles. Needless to say, there were further revisions as attempts were made to observe and identify the nature of the behavior of the group at these points and the changes which were taking place. Rather soon this group of teachers faced the question of whether they liked the direction in which some of their group activities were going, whether they had the kind of leadership they wanted, and whether one or two people should go on doing most of the talking and decision-making. This caused a discussion of the values to be obtained from group work and the relationship of the observed behavior to these values.

Many of Parker's guidelines in chapter v provide operational definitions of areas of behavior in programs of in-service education in which to observe and evaluate changes. Examples are: (a) people . . .

work on problems of significance to them, (*b*) people plan how they will work, (*c*) continuous attention is given to problem-solving processes, (*d*) simplest means for going from decision to action should be established, (*e*) appraisal is an integral part of the in-service education program. It is well to recognize the value orientation of these principles, namely, that it is important for the learner to be involved in all the critical decisions of his learning activities.

The evaluation of changes in programs of in-service education is based fundamentally on a definition of the essential components of the goals desired or of the identified problem. This definition is necessary in order to know what observations to make and what kind of data to consider and value. This definition is not made at one time and is usually under continuous revision. Major portions of this definition, however, have to be kept in use long enough to make enough observations to get evidence of change or of needed revision.

THE ROLE OF OBSERVATION IN THE EVALUATION PROCESS

All aspects of evaluation are based on the process of observation as a means for obtaining the necessary data for valuing and for making comparisons between what is observed and the desired goals. The process of observation involves a person (observer) who is looking at some situation in which people are dealing with the various problems of concern to them. Sometimes this observer uses some method for recording the data of his observations for future study and analysis. Much of our day-to-day, on-the-spot evaluating, however, is based on a continuous succession of unrecorded observations. Evaluations made on the basis of this kind of observing are heavily weighted by last impressions and are not based on evidence which can be checked and re-examined from a number of different points of view.

Observations are improved for evaluation purposes when (*a*) the behavior, problem, or area of activity to be observed is sharply focused; (*b*) repeated observations are made of given phenomena in the various situations in which it occurs; (*c*) a number of related observations are made of the various essential components of the problem or situation being observed; (*d*) more than one observation is made of a single phenomenon at one time; and (*e*) records are made of observations for the purpose of repeated study and examination.

Focusing the Observation. The process of defining the objectives to be achieved, or the problem to be attacked, helps focus the observations. When a school staff agrees that the language-arts program is to be studied, the definition of the language arts into its essential parts of speaking, listening, writing, and reading provides a basis for knowing the kind of activities to observe in the behavior of children and youth. Similarily, a group of teachers trying to study the classroom-teaching situation might well examine a number of running records of classroom activities in order to see what is important to watch in this complex dynamic situation. Discussion of the relative merits of concentrating attention on the teacher and his activities or on the behavior of children might result in actually observing teachers and children working together on their educational program. This would probably lead to a decision to watch the behavior of both the teacher and pupils as they organized their activities around and in relation to the problems, tasks, objects, and questions which served as the focus of attention for the classroom activities. In this way teachers, children, and educational tasks could be meaningfully observed.

Repeating the Observation. The evaluation of change is based on the perception of change through *repeated observations* of similar phenomena through time. Focusing the observation merely provides the essential conditions for repeating observations so that change can be determined. Each observation must be recorded or otherwise preserved so that comparisons of different observations can reveal the presence of changes. So, without a consistent focus for observations, without repeated observations, and without records of each observation, the evaluation of changes which have any significance and possibility of future use in the program of in-service education are impossible.

Achievement examinations given to children in the fall and again in the spring or tests of teacher-instructional practices given to teachers at two different periods in a program of staff work are forms of repeated observations used to determine change. The anecdotal records of the behavior of a child over a period of time, the records of the learning activities of a group of children working with their teacher over a period of a week, or the recorded observations of a chairman of a working group over a series of meetings would provide the basis for identifying and studying changes in behavior.

Broadening the Range of Observations. Much of the behavior observed in programs of in-service education is complex and interrelated. In studying group behavior, to count the number of times one individual talks without examining the verbal behavior of the other members of the group, or to observe the nature of the change in the group goal without checking the change in the role and status positions of individuals, is to fail to observe the related changes which bring meaning and significance to change in any one.

Again, the breadth or range of the observation to be made in a program of in-service education is determined by the definition, by the staff or appropriate staff groups, of the essential components of a problem or goal. Naturally, the staff will expect to revise their definition on the basis of greater knowledge about and experience with a problem area. The range of observations to be made is related to the range of things an individual or group considers important in the identified problem. Change in one should always be accompanied by changes in the other.

Broadening the Point of View of the Observation. The assistant superintendent, directors, and supervisors of the central office of a large school system were examining the services a central office staff provided to the educational programs of individual schools. After looking at these services from this point of view for a time, it was suggested that they could be examined also from the point of view of the school staffs using them. This additional observation of these services from another point of view brought out information which formed the basis for a proposed reorganization of the instructional services provided by the central office staff.

Confidence in the evaluation of change growing out of observations increases if two or more people agree on what they see. One elementary-school staff was checking the instructional goals they were actually trying to achieve in their teaching with individual groups of children. In addition to the check-sheet each teacher made out at the end of a lesson, the children in the same class made out a similar check-sheet on what they thought was being achieved.

Comparisons of these two important perceptions of what was happening in a given teaching situation led to serious thinking by the staff as to how purposes could be clarified and used in giving direction to the teaching-learning activities of a classroom.

Recording the Observation. The ideal record of an observation would capture its essential data, preserve its relationships, and yet be easier to use than the phenomena observed. It is possible to distinguish two broad categories of records: (*a*) those which are in effect primary records of the original activities or behavior, i.e., still, moving, and sound pictures; recordings of actual sounds, conversations, verbal activities of groups; stenographic records of classroom activities, both descriptive and verbal; anecdotal records of the behavior of children, teachers, and groups; notes, diaries, planning agenda, and minutes of formal group activities; and the actual performance records of behavior such as records of handwriting, stories of children, letters, work products of individual and group activities, etc., and (*b*) those records of behavior which grow out of standardized interviews, inventories, tests, scales, and check-lists. These standardized observations are different from the first in that they grow primarily out of definitions of the objectives or what the problem should include. They focus and categorize the observation into the defined component parts. In addition, the behavior observed is valued both in respect to its position on a value continuum and its degree of adequacy as normative behavior. The records of type (*a*) can be called records of uncategorized behavior as a way of distinguishing these records from those in type (*b*) which are usually categorized and are frequently scaled behavior.

Records of type (*a*) need to be categorized and translated to behavior continuums before precise determination of change and the valuing of this change can take place. A group of elementary teachers in La Grange, Illinois, were examining their teaching practices to ascertain the extent to which they were democratic. They studied a number of records of classroom activities and identified all the items of teacher behavior they could find. Each item was placed on a three-by-five card. These items were examined to make sure all duplicate statements of the same kind of behavior were eliminated. The remaining items were arranged on a continuum so that those judged to be most autocratic were on one end, those judged to be most democratic were on the other, and those considered neutral were in the middle.

These rough scales of autocratic-democratic behavior were used by the teachers to locate their general position on this scale. A neutral observer used the scale to identify the position of each teacher on it, and the pupils of each teacher used a modified version to judge what they believed their classroom atmosphere to be. After three months, these same observations were repeated, and the nature and direction of these changes were noted. This evaluation was followed by a re-examination of teaching practices and what could be done to increase their democratic qualities. This experience with the observation of democratic behavior became more meaningful as they were related to specific situations, such as passing in halls, conduct on playground, planning a unit with children, and organizing a classroom for school routines.

It is often unnecessary for teachers and groups working in programs of in-service education to be this precise in dealing with their records. It is possible to examine repeated records of uncategorized behavior and to identify the nature of the changes taking place in them on a more informal basis. This preliminary evaluation becomes more valuable, however, as the amount and the goal or value direction of these changes is determined.

THE ROLE OF PEOPLE IN THE EVALUATION PROCESS

In assessing the value of changes in the behavior of people in programs of in-service education, the different aspects of the evaluation process become clearer when the various roles played by people in this process are identified and examined. In the evaluation process a person may assume one or more of the following roles: (a) as the definer of the goals to be achieved, (b) as the individual who modifies his behavior in order to achieve the goal, (c) as the observer and recorder of the acts of the individual attempting to deal with a problem or to achieve a goal, (d) as the evaluator of the goal-seeking or problem-solving behavior, and (e) as the individual who acts on the basis of these evaluations to improve his behavior.

If the purpose of the in-service program is to improve the understanding and competency of all participants to deal with their educational problems and to contribute to the education of children and youth, then it becomes important that participants assume the different roles in the evaluation process as an integral and important part of their in-service activities.

Evaluations of changes in in-service programs move in this direction when self-evaluation is the dominant emphasis in all evaluations made. When the teachers, administrators, board members, and parents become active participants in evaluating the importance of changes in their educational thinking and behavior, then the maximum educational potential in the evaluation process is being achieved.

With this point of view in mind, it is important that the participants in a program of in-service education engage in the act of defining problems, of striving to deal with these problems more effectively, of observing evidence of change, of evaluating these changes as to direction and adequacy, and of using this increased understanding to modify their future behavior. When this kind of participation becomes difficult, as is the case when one is a member of a group and is trying to observe group behavior at the same time, the use of observers or observation devices helps the participants see themselves more efficiently. The use of a recorder for group discussion permits the group members to play back to themselves an observation of their own verbal behavior for study and analysis. This could also be accomplished by designating one member to act as observer during a period of group work and to report to the group on his observations. The important point is that it is difficult to observe one's own behavior at the same time one is striving to achieve some goal. These two functions get mixed up. Yet, this is the kind of dual effort that is important for any individual to learn in his efforts to modify his behavior in order to achieve a goal more effectively.

THE ROLE OF NORMS AND VALUES IN EVALUATION

The nature of norms or standards in the evaluation process is to provide a basis for determining what degree of accomplishment of the goal or objective is adequate at any particular time. There are few situations where the behavior of people or the solution to problems are made on an all-or-none basis. Norms provide a different valuing referent than objectives and values, and both are necessary for adequate evaluation.

It is important in evaluating programs of in-service education to make the norms for judging adequacy just as explicit as the hypotheses to be tested or the objectives to be achieved. The same observed behavior related to the same objective can be judged differently, depending upon the particular norm of adequacy that is applied.

Norm of the Task Itself. It is possible to identify some tasks which are sufficiently unitary to be completed on an all-or-none basis. With children, a word is not spelled correctly until it is complete, a ball is not hit with a bat until the event actually happens, a step is not taken until it has occurred. With teachers, it is possible to say that a report is not handed in until it is received on the principal's desk or that discipline is not being maintained until all children are quiet when the teacher speaks. In this approach to adequacy, the task to be accomplished or essential aspects of the task are defined so as to include the conception of adequacy. The evaluation problem is merely to observe the behavior in such situations and to judge whether it is present or not. Most of the evaluation that takes place in programs of in-service education will not have levels of adequacy so arbitrarily defined but will involve the more difficult task of determining whether the degree of accomplishment at the time was adequate.

Norm of the Experience of Others. In education most of our norms of behavior and achievement have been based on some measures of central tendency of a distribution of the accomplishments or judgments of an appropriate group of people. In programs of in-service education, however, there are few tasks of teaching and learning where the achievements of a sizable group have ever been recorded and tabulated. Even if available, this norm of distributed behavior is very difficult to use and apply meaningfully to individual teachers and school staffs. It should be pointed out, however, that we feel competent to use this kind of norm to judge the adequacy of the behavior of children.

Norm of the Capacity of the Individual. Another common position taken in determining adequacy is to judge the behavior as being adequate for a person in relation to his capacity to perform the task. Common measures of capacity in this sense are tests of mental maturity, appraisals of what is done now with what the individual has been able to do in the past, or estimates of the "task" potential or ceiling of the individual. These measures or estimates are used as a referent to compare present with past accomplishments and, on the basis of this norm, to judge them as to their adequacy.

Norm of What Is Socially or Educationally Desirable. Judgments of the adequacy of many of the professional roles of teachers and principals are strongly influenced by certain education and social expectations. A principal acting as leader or chairman of a faculty group has to meet one of these expectations and it does not make much difference whether he has made progress or is working up to his capacity or not. His performance is not judged relatively but on the basis of what other people perceive the normative behavior of principals to be in this situation. Teachers, like all people, develop model patterns of expected behavior which they apply to the other teachers, the children, and the parents, and then make value judgments about these individuals on the basis of this conception. Whether this "model" is *right*, in the sense that it represents the most efficient pattern of behavior for accomplishing the work of a teacher or principal, is not the question.

The recognition of the role and function of this kind of norm in evaluating persons and activities in programs of in-service education is extremely important. Several suggestions as to ways to improve its use may be helpful.

1. Make the expectations of social and educational adequacy as explicit as possible in operational or behavioral terms. The question here is not whether this norm is used but how it can be examined and consciously used to make evaluations constructive and educational. In many school staffs, it takes years for individuals to become aware of the codes of behavior that govern the status and success of people. These definitions can be made through the process of listing and organizing the behavior believed to be normative for a given professional or personal role. Similar procedures can be used for getting at how individuals perceive and value a particular problem or aspect of instructional practice.

2. Make comparisons among and between the various appropriate conceptions of actual and perceived normative behavior. This is of particular value in comparing methods and procedures of teaching—an area of behavior seldom examined by teachers and professional workers. One of the reasons for a lack of study in this portion of

educational practice is that the normative basis for making valuing statements as to what is good is usually hidden and personal. Yet, this area of activity represents a large portion of the time of most professional people. Evaluation procedures need to make it possible for the norm of social and educational expectancy to be recognized for the important role that it does play in our valuing of the many things we do and to get such definitions out in the open in order that they can be examined and constructively improved.

Norm of Use. An important conception of value which can be useful in evaluating change in programs of in-service education involves testing the importance of ideas and plans by seeing what happens when they are used to produce change. Most programs of in-service work do not operate within a comprehensive and adequately planned framework of evaluation procedures. Most try, however, to identify and use the products of the ongoing experience as a basis for improving future behavior. Generalizations are derived from present and past experience and then used to plan and direct future activities. If things get worse, the generalizing and/or applications of that generalizing probably were not good. If things get better, then there is some confidence that these processes are of value and that the program is on the right track.

In the use of this norm, it should be recognized that generalizations as to ideas, processes, and values are intermingled. Other norms need to be applied as well in making final value judgments. The value of this norm of use is that it permits this kind of multiple evaluation to take place and that it provides an opportunity for any level of sophistication in evaluation to develop.

Norm of Ends. Much of the previous discussion has to do with the evaluation of the goodness of means and the adequacy of development. It should also be recognized that the ends need to be appraised as to whether they are worth trying to achieve. The three common tests of ends have to do with their importance, their significance, and their cruciality.

The importance of an end is determined by its role and position in the program or field of knowledge that it represents. A problem for study in a program of in-service education is important if the products of the study of that problem will deal with many specifics and if these products will influence the direction of large portions of the program. As such problems become more comprehensive in their application and more pivotal in determining direction, their importance increases accordingly.

The significance of an end or problem is here used to indicate its personal importance to an individual or staff. A problem gains in significance if an individual perceives greater consequences for himself as a result of work on the problem and its resolution. An in-service education activity could have importance yet lack significance. Important problems, however, are more apt to be significant.

The perceived cruciality of a problem is determined by the degree to which something must be done about it *now* either because of its evident urgency or because it is the first step in a series of related activities. Cruciality is also related to the degree to which the people involved see a given goal as something about which they have confidence they can do something rather immediately. They see it as being both accessible and possible of accomplishment.

All of these tests of the importance of ends are necessary in programs of in-service education. The best goals or ends have importance in the sense of being comprehensive and pivotal, significance in the sense that people see important consequence for themselves in working on it, and cruciality in the sense that it is necessary to do something about them now.

In looking back over the tests for means and ends, it should be recognized that all tend to answer different kinds of value questions, and, thus, all or many can be used to get desirable evaluations of the same in-service program. This is the basis upon which multiple evaluations should be made.

Evaluations of Change in the Activities of Programs of In-service Education

The first three sections of this chapter have examined the nature of the activities and problems in programs of in-service education in which changes are usually desired, the ways in which change in problems and behaviors can be determined, and, finally, the various aspects of the evaluation process itself. This last section deals with a number of actual illustrations of the ways in which evaluations of change have been made in programs of in-service education. The first is an illustration of a school staff working on the problem of improving a language-arts program and the informal and continuous evaluation of the changes that were taking place. The second is an illustration of teachers observing and trying to understand children. The third is an illustration of attempts to evaluate changes in the total educational program.

EVALUATION OF EMERGENT CHANGES IN A PROGRAM
OF CURRICULUM STUDY

Many school staffs get into programs of curriculum study very much the same way the Fond du Lac, Wisconsin, staff did in its study of the language-arts program. Criticism of the language skills of students by upper-grade and high-school teachers, letters in the local newspaper regarding the poor spelling of girls hired as stenographers, questions asked in school board meetings regarding the quality of the language-arts program, and the interest of some members of the staff in actually studying and trying to improve the program, all culminated in the appointment of a faculty committee to study the problem.

This committee met, elected its chairman and secretary, and started to discuss what to do. One plan of attack suggested was to give tests in spelling, composition, and reading at the third, sixth, and tenth grades in the fall and again in the spring in order to determine the gains made in these skills over the school year. In this way, individual grade groups, schools, and grade levels could be identified as to amount of change taking place, and their relative position in respect to each other could be determined. Examination of the "good" programs and the "poor" programs could then be made in order to see the factors which tended to differentiate them. High relative gains in achievement during the year indicate the "good" programs, and low relative gains reveal the "poor."

Examination of this suggestion by the committee revolved around the following questions: Granting that this procedure would indicate the growth students would make in spelling, composition, and reading over this period of the school year, would this procedure provide means for knowing how the language-arts program should be reorganized and what instructional procedures should be changed? Would this procedure encourage the "poor" teachers and "poor" schools to improve their programs? And is relative change over a constant period sufficient to determine the value of instruction?

Tentative negative answers by the committee to these questions caused them to recommend that each individual school staff survey its present program of language arts and indicate what changes were needed to improve the system-wide program. This was done, and the committee spent a portion of a summer vacation summarizing these reports and developing a statement to be given at the "Teachers' Institute" in the fall. In trying to interpret what this survey showed and to draft their report, the committee discovered that they had to take a large number of value positions regarding the purpose for teaching the language arts, the relative importance of the functions of language, and the way in which effective learning can take place. They felt that a summary of practices without a statement of the nature of the ultimate goals of English instruction would leave the summary of practices without desirable directions.

The reporting of the survey of language arts with evaluations of the practices of individual schools to the total staff by the committee created considerable excitement, especially among the staffs of schools whose practices were criticized and whose value positions were challenged. The next result was a realization by the committee of the need for further study and help. Consultative help was obtained from the State Department of Public Instruction and from the state university, and meetings were held with different staff groups to discover next steps. As a result of these conferences, a three-year plan of work developed, involving the following activities: (a) an analysis of the social-studies activities to discover ways in which language was being used; (b) a study and summary of research and practices in teaching the writing, reading, speaking, and listening aspects of the language; (c) the development of a plan of staff organization which ranged from using individual school units as working groups to an over-all planning and co-ordinating committee for system-wide work; and (d) the development of instructional booklets for children on such topics as "Writing Letters," "So You're an Author," "Making an Outline," "Using a Telephone," etc. Naturally, these four major strands of staff activity did not occur at once but grew out of the continuous planning and evaluating activities of the language-arts committee and the various work groups.

It is not possible to document each step and each procedure of this program of staff study, but the implications of this experience for the problem of evaluating changes in programs of in-service education seem to be the following:

1. The major technique for determining change and for evaluation of its significance is the continuous use of the planning and evaluating processes by the participants in the in-service program.
2. The characteristics of this process, in this instance, were the teachers and committees looking at where they had been, seeing where they were at the present, and then trying to discover where they should go. Directions for future change grew out of this analysis of ongoing experience using such tests as: "Is this the best thing to do next?" "Will this help us improve our teaching?" "Will this actually change the experiences children are having in our classrooms?" "Will this bring the parts of our program into more meaningful relationship for children and teachers?" "Will this help us teach more efficiently?"
3. The most difficult part of this approach to evaluation of change was getting agreement as to positions of value regarding the language-arts program. It was relatively easy to agree upon general and over-all goals, more difficult to agree on ways to consider the nature and organization of the language arts, and even more difficult to agree on the importance, for example, of grammar and ways to teach it.
4. The presence of careful minutes, records of group work, memoranda on plans, evaluation sessions at regular intervals, regular use of questionnaires to staff, all provide means for examining progress and for assessing its values. The evaluating procedure used included discussion, study of records, analyzing, goal setting, judging, and planning next steps in light of this best thinking. The test of this thinking was its effectiveness in promoting the next series of activities. Things seemed to get better or worse; more or fewer individuals were active or interested; more groups got excited and more suggestions and ideas seemed to flow or interest dropped away and attendance at group meetings fell off. Signposts were looked for in all directions, and the major referents for the evaluation process were in the perception and personal judgments of the participants.
5. Most value judgments regarding procedures of staff work, the curriculum organization of the language arts, the development of responsibility and leadership in working groups, and the way to institute changes in the instructional program were complex and interrelated. These judgments were influenced by the prestige positions of people, the nature of the desired goals, the most effective way to make progress at the moment, the conceptions and value positions of the involved groups of people at that time, the hierarchical organization of the

school system, and the well-being of children and youth. Frequently the prestige factors and conceptions and value positions of teachers, lay groups, and administrators were more important in determining the value of changes than such factors as the ultimate goals of English instruction and the well-being of children and youth.

6. The staff was threatened by attempts to relate the evaluation of change to the prestige positions and professional roles of teachers and building groups. Staffs seemed more comfortable and willing to work when the evaluation of change was directed toward ways of working on educational problems, toward influencing the behavior of children, and toward the achievement of common objectives and values.

7. Evaluations of changes in knowledge and skills of children in the language arts seemed to be more useful in effecting changes in instructional practices when these evaluations came after, not before, objectives had been defined by the teachers and staff for such evaluations.

8. Most judgments of change were confined to direction of change. Few, if any, norms were available to determine adequacy of change.

UNDERSTANDING CHILDREN AND INSTRUCTIONAL PRACTICES

Because our attention is on the problem of change, only brief reference will be made here to a rather well-known in-service education program of child study and its implications for evaluation. The work of Daniel Prescott, in so far as field situations are concerned, is designed to help teachers perceive and understand the important developmental processes of a child growing up in a cultural and social setting. It was felt that this understanding would provide a teacher with a powerful tool for knowing how to work effectively with children.

The procedures used to study children include having each teacher observe a single normal child over an extended period of time. The record of these observations consists of a series of short anecdotal statements of the actual behavior of this child in the various situations in which he is active. This record of actual conversations and behavior is read and discussed to try to determine the motives behind the behavior, the factors operating to cause this behavior, the continuities of behavior that can be identified, the applications of scientific knowledge of children that can be made, and the implications of this increased understanding of a particular child for knowing other children and for improving instructional activities.

The analysis of this record is aided when a framework of important areas of development is used to check possibilities. One useful framework includes the areas of (a) physical and biological development, (b) growth in self-concept, (c) nature of peer-group relationships, (d) social and cultural factors, (e) intellectual and academic development, and (f) protective and adjustment mechanisms.

In many school staffs, this program of child study extends over a four-to-six-year period. The use of consultants and workshops are important aids and resources for this kind of in-service education.

The lessons of this approach for the problem of evaluating change are as follow:

1. The making of a series of consistent observations of a single person enables the sharp focusing of these observations and a consequent improvement in their accuracy. The repeated nature of these observations provides a base for the identification and valuing of change.
2. The teacher can play the role of the observer and recorder of the behavior without having to be the participant or a part of the situation at all times. The teacher can be the evaluator also without immediate threat to his own prestige and professional roles because he is watching children rather than observing himself. Yet the teacher, if he will, has an opportunity to see himself and his own value patterns in the behavior of the children he observes. The effect of any changes he makes in his own behavior can be observed in what this does for modifying the behavior of the individuals with whom he works.
3. Changes identified in the behavior record of children can often be evaluated in relation to known norms and behavior scales of child development and achievement. More norms are available here than in any other area of school work.
4. Personal and social values can be seen in the life experience of the individual being observed. The child can be seen using these values to give direction to his own behavior. The teacher, also, can use educational and social values to evaluate the direction and adequacy of the changes perceived in the record.
5. Predictions can be made as to future behavior and development as the basis of the trends and themes running through the behavior record. This illustrates the essential purpose of all evaluation—improved direction and control of future behavior. Products of such evaluations can be put into use immediately.
6. This practice of observing consistently, recording, and analyzing behavior as a basis for determining and evaluating change can be applied to many other problems and areas of activity in programs of in-service education.

EVALUATION OF CHANGE IN PROGRAMS OF EDUCATION

The third illustration of evaluating change is at the level of the total school program. Various means have been used to provide the data for such evaluation. The trend has been away from short-time surveys by "outsiders" to long-time efforts by the staff and their resources to study the educational needs of a program and to introduce changes designed to meet such needs. The thinking behind this trend has been influenced by the need to include the staff and the school communities in the evaluation and development process—in definition of goals, in working to achieve them, in observing behavior, in judging the direction and adequacy of development, and in using the results of such evaluations for future improvement.

Many devices have been used to identify and appraise practices in the evaluations of school programs. One common procedure, after listing the areas of school programs to examine, is to judge the adequacy of related practices in terms of a scaled definition. One common scale follows:

0—If practice does not exist in any extent, quality, or degree.
1—If practice exists to a small extent but (a) is found in a restricted amount, or (b) appears in some classrooms but is not typical of school as a whole, or (c) is of doubtful quality.
2—If practice exists to considerable extent, that is, (a) it is present in average amount, or (b) appears in enough classrooms to make it typical of school as a whole, or (c) is of fair quality.
3—If practice exists to a great extent, that is, (a) it is found in large amount, or (b) appears in enough classrooms to make it practically universal throughout school, or (c) is of excellent quality.[1]

The emphasis is on inclusion and adequacy of practices in the scale definitions. The values and goals which determine the quality of the practices are never explicitly stated.

Another procedure is to set up a continuum of practice with behavioral definitions at stated points. The observer can check the points of practice on this scale. Following is an example on "Use of Instructional Materials."[2]

1. South-wide Workshop on Elementary Evaluation, *Elementary Evaluative Criteria*. Vol. II. *Workbook*. Tallahassee, Florida: Florida State University, 1949.

2. Virgil E. Herrick, "Handbook for Studying an Elementary-School Program." Chicago: Department of Education, University of Chicago, 1943 (mimeographed).

1	2	3	4	5
Reliance is on text and workbook. Not many materials brought in. Few attempts are made to use the resources of the school and community.	A few books, magazines and pictures brought to school, but no conscious search for materials related to current problems and projects. Teacher is more alert than pupils in this area. Pupils not encouraged to bring in materials.		Both teachers and pupils are alert in bringing in materials related to work at hand. Skill is shown by both teacher and children in using resources to enrich learning experiences.	

The value of this procedure is that it identifies and differentiates practice yet allows the staff to examine the direction in which change is desired. This device enables the staff to distinguish values from behavior. This technique can be used to identify and appraise changes in school practices when observation and checks are made at different periods in a program of in-service education and the results of these appraisals compared. The advantages of this procedure are: (*a*) The points of observation tend to be focused, and their range tends to cover important aspects of an educational program; (*b*) a point in a continuum of practice can be identified. Some of the problems of the use of such instruments are: (*a*) The bases upon which judgments of the values of such practice are determined are not made explicit—in many cases the staff will want to determine these values for themselves. (*b*) Changes in practices are revealed by repeated use of such devices and are frequently difficult to relate to programs of activities in the school program itself.

It is very difficult to apply norms or scales to such evaluations, as few school systems have made such definitions of change in teacher behavior and educational programs. Again, the evaluation of the value *directions in* which changes are moving become the major judgments to be made.

Evaluations of change in over-all educational programs depend upon the following steps:

1. The identification of the important areas of the educational program to observe—objectives, subject areas, instructional practices, organization, materials and resources, etc., are common definitions.
2. The development of a continuum of practices in each area in order that present practices can be determined on the basis of adequate observations.

3. The repeated use of these instruments over a suitable period.
4. The comparison of the records of these different series of observations to determine the nature of the changes taking place and their directions.
5. The consideration of the personal, social, and educational values underlying these changes and the assessment of the values and desirability of such changes.
6. The development of plans of action to utilize the products of this evaluation for future development.

Conclusion

The sense of this chapter is that change is the dynamic aspect of all learning and development and that some kind of evaluation as to its direction, efficiency, and importance is always taking place. Such evaluations, however, become more useful when the goal referents for such evaluations are clear, when the observations of relevant behavior are focused, repeated, and recorded, when the judgments of the value of change go beyond their perception to their goal significance and their degree of adequacy, and when the products of such evaluations are used to influence future behavior.

This chapter urges the use of all the resources of our knowledge of evaluation and its techniques and procedures. The base, however, for this kind of development is the growing competence of teachers and staff members to make the emergent evaluations of their own ongoing professional behavior. The problem is to feed into this stream of evaluative behavior the helps and technical assistance available.

It is urged, finally, that while it is possible for individuals other than staff members to assume the major roles in the evaluation of change, the products of this evaluation are more likely to influence the future behavior and activities of the staff if its members have had an important part in the development of all aspects of this important process. A staff member of a school system grows in his understanding and sense of professional responsibility when he is able to judge the value of change and to test the significance of this value for his own personal and professional future.

CHAPTER XIV

Training in the Skills Needed for In-service Education Programs

MATTHEW B. MILES

and

A. HARRY PASSOW

The Nature of Training

TRAINING AS A PATH TO PROGRAM IMPROVEMENT

If the promise of in-service education as a means for change is to be realized in an educational system, obstacles must be anticipated and avoided or minimized. Developing, carrying out, and evaluating in-service education programs can be replete with difficulties and pitfalls. The responses to anticipated or existing program difficulties, however, frequently take the form of redoubled effort, puzzlement, or frustration, due chiefly to the lack of an analysis of the nature of the difficulties. Opportunities for training or self-development in the competencies needed for effectively implementing an in-service program frequently are not available to participants. Moreover, the idea of providing such training may not even occur to persons responsible for the program, partly because it is not apparent what the needed skills are and partly because people do not know how training of this kind can be organized and carried on. In addition, the demands of the ongoing program often prevent participants from taking time out for training when needed.

Schools have, however, on occasion, provided such training for the participants in an in-service education program. The following example[1] may serve to illustrate this feature of the in-service program and to clarify the authors' viewpoint toward training.

1. Stephen M. Corey, Paul M. Halverson, and Elizabeth Lowe, *Training Teachers for Discussion Group Leadership*. New York: Bureau of Publications, Teachers College, Columbia University, 1953.

A curriculum revision committee, the reading group, working in a suburban school system, arranged a half-day conference of the entire professional staff of 208. In addition to explaining the school's reading program, the planners wished to provide time for small groups to identify problems in the teaching of reading which were common throughout the system. Such groups would, of course, need intelligent discussion leadership.

Twelve group leaders were selected by peer nominations, but all of them felt that group discussion leadership required skills they did not have. Accordingly, a training session was set up for the group chairmen with the help of outside consultants. A subcommittee prepared a tape recording which illustrated eight common problems faced by discussion leaders, such as "starting the meeting," "handling conflict," and the like. Each problem was depicted in an episode on the tape; the content was what the planners felt might come up in a typical meeting during the actual conference.

At the training session itself, after an introduction, the episodes were played back, one by one. The group of leaders discussed the problem raised and how well or poorly the chairman on the tape handled it. When it seemed valuable, the group role-played certain episodes themselves and analyzed their own performance.

The training session was carefully evaluated, both immediately and after the reading conference, and the findings indicated that the training session had influenced the success of conference groups positively.

This chapter is based on the premise demonstrated in the foregoing example, namely, that providing needed training for participants when program difficulties are in the offing is not only desirable but essential, if a high level of performance on the part of participants is to be maintained. As such, the chapter is focused primarily on the improvement of *processes* through training and does not deal centrally with the *content* problems of in-service programs.

After discussion of the nature of training as the authors view it, the chapter will successively focus on the diagnosing of training needs, the role of the "trainer," organization for training, characteristic needs and illustrative training activities, and some problems associated with the evaluation of training.

The chapter is written for two groups of professional personnel:

those participating in in-service programs (e.g., teachers, principals), and those responsible for the initiation and maintenance of programs (e.g., curriculum workers, supervisors). The scope of the chapter does not, of course, permit a comprehensive discussion of specific training techniques and procedures, but guiding principles are presented and references are suggested for more detailed accounts.

A CONCEPTION OF TRAINING

The term *training* is upsetting to many school people, partly because it carries connotations of rote or mechanical learning, of a jack-booted figure with a whip (the "trainer"), or even of the struggles of parents and children over toilet behavior. However, we believe it is a useful term for the purposes of this chapter and that it can be profitably differentiated from the more general term, *education*.[2] *Training*, as the authors see it, has these characteristics:

a) *Concern with skill.* Training implies a focused concern on problems of *skill*—the tools which a person requires to bring intention into consonance with purposes. Skills do not, of course, exist in a vacuum of motives and values—but once a person or group has decided on a goal, then problems of "how to" become uppermost.

In the above illustration the teachers focused on the skills needed to lead a group discussion—especially as these skills were needed to insure the success of a particular kind of meeting. Furthermore, the training was focused on the improvement of *particular* skills, such as "handling conflict," rather than on chairmanship in general.

b) *Concern with whole-person learning.* Training, as we see it, implies a total person working to perfect particular skills. This working must be thought of as organismic—with cognitive, affective, and motoric elements integrated—rather than as primarily academic or verbal-intellectual.

In our example, the group chairmen who participated in the training session not only talked more freely about and *understood* more clearly the nature of conflict but they experienced the *feelings* (for example, helplessness, anger, rejection) that accompany attempts to reduce conflict. Also, they *acted* confidently in a specific conflict

2. A relevant discussion here is, "Can Leadership-training Be Liberal Education?" in *Adult Leadership,* II (June, 1953), 1. The point of view is similar to that presented here. The article also includes material on values underlying training.

situation—had actually to step in and do something as chairmen when members were disagreeing too sharply.

c) *Concern with practice.* Training, as we are using the term, implies opportunity for repeated performance of particular skills, with explicit, immediate feedback on the results of a particular try.

Discussion of tape-recorded episodes, some of which were role-played, gave the leaders in our illustration an opportunity to practice handling situations they were likely to meet and to see the effects of their own chairmanship.

d) *Concern with safe experimentation.* Effective training in our view implies a situation of at least partial irreality, where the normal consequences of failure do not ensue, where the "chips are not down" and the learner can be freed to experiment more thoroughly with his own behavior.

The illustrative training session was held prior to the real group meetings and provided this chance to test behavior and develop skills without fear of failure.

It is to be expected that some readers of the chapter will take exception to this general conception of training. However, we have tried to make it explicit to provide a background for the remainder of this chapter. We will discuss training for a wide range of skills: becoming more empathic toward other members of a group, analyzing unstructured data, reporting to others. Much recent work in the field of training has emphasized human-relations skills, as we have in this chapter. In school systems, research-relevant skills are looming as another important area, while some other skills, such as "producing film strips," fall into neither the "human relations" nor the "research" category. We shall draw illustrations of skill-training sessions from as many areas of in-service education as possible.

PLANNING FOR TRAINING

As Coffey and Golden suggest in chapter iv, training must be more carefully planned and staffed to the extent that the focus is on matters that are central to the person. Training in running an opaque projector is less threatening than training in effective decision-making, and the intrapersonal barriers to change are not nearly so formidable.

Moreover, the surrounding institutional system may vigorously affect planning for training. If operating standards of authority figures tend to focus heavily on "efficiency" and "getting the job done," as over "against" a sound emotional climate in the school, then the barriers to change in relatively central regions of individual teachers are even more difficult to cope with.

When someone begins talking of "central regions" and "intrapersonal barriers," a frequent reaction among school people is to avoid giving attention to these problems by terming them "therapeutic," just as difficulties in in-service programs are sometimes laid to the maladjusted nature of one or more participants or leaders. Widespread use of therapeutic experiences by teachers and administrators would be very desirable.[3] However, we believe that our American tradition of individualism tends frequently to encourage diagnoses of situations primarily in terms of personality functioning. ("He's hostile. . . . He's dominating the group.") Frequently ignored are socialscience findings indicating that forces in small groups, and in the institutional contexts of these groups, exert profound effects on behavior.[4] From this point of view, change in people is much more a function of change in small groups and formal organizations than we have usually realized.

Finally, it should be said clearly that while therapy and training overlap in some respects—for example, they both may deal with the more central regions of the self—they certainly do not coincide. Therapy is primarily concerned with defect or illness and cure. Training as we view it is most centrally concerned with lacks in the instrumental skills needed to accomplish desired goals, and it proceeds through practice and refinement of these skills.

Diagnosing Training Needs

Training cannot begin until someone has decided that someone (either the self or another) needs to do something better. The process of diagnosing training needs is crucial for the success of a train-

3. See, for example, Arthur T. Jersild and Kenneth Helfant, Education for Self-understanding. New York: Bureau of Publications, Teachers College, Columbia University, 1953.

4. For example, group decision was found to be two to ten times as effective as other methods (including a face-to-face interview) in getting mothers to follow through on use of new foods. See Kurt Lewin, "Studies in Decision," in Dorwin P. Cartwright and Alvin F. Zander, Group Dynamics, pp. 287–301 (Evanston, Illinois: Row, Peterson & Co., 1953); and Dorwin P. Cartwright, "Achieving Change in People: Some Applications of Group Dynamics Theory," Human Relations, IV (1951), 381–92.

ing program. Inadequate, coercive, or arbitrary diagnoses almost inevitably intervene to sabotage the training experiences based on them.

THE PROBLEM OF READINESS

A great deal has been written on reading readiness, and most educators are relatively comfortable with the concept and know how to act on it. Readiness for training on the part of in-service education personnel is at least as complex and important a problem, and one about which educators are usually much less clear. In general, our experience has been that training in respect to almost any kind of skill is quite unlikely to be successful unless certain conditions obtain both before and during the training.

Some motivation for change exists. Probably the most helpful form of motivation is dissatisfaction with one's *own* (as contrasted with someone else's) present *performance*. This general condition implies at once a willingness to focus on the self, to become ego-involved with concrete, *doing* activities that promise to reduce dissatisfaction. Such dissatisfaction is *relative* in nature, in the sense that an "objectively" successful supervisor may want to do something that represents an improvement for him.

However, people and institutions being what they are, motivations for change do not often appear in pure form. As Coffey and Golden suggest in chapter iv, while motivation for change may be primarily internal to the person and be a result of changes in aspiration or ideology, external crises or new demands in the social field, such as Parker's account of the school fire in chapter v, may also be operative. Too, motivation may very frequently be *reductive*[5] in nature—the desire to avoid the frustration of needs now being met, rather than *augmentative*—driven by the promise of need satisfaction, the accomplishment of personally significant, involving goals.

Finally, motivation for change is almost never clear and uncomplicated, especially where the changes involve more central regions of the self. Ambivalence and resistance before and during early stages of training, far from being contraindications for training, are probably more frequently a symptom that genuine involvement is taking place. In thinking about potential change, the individual has to have

5. *See* Douglas M. MacGregor, "The Staff Function in Human Relations," *Journal of Social Issues,* IV (Summer, 1948), 5–22.

internal conversations dealing with the potential consequences that lie ahead—gratifications such as confidence, adequacy, rewards from others; and discomforts such as time load, fears of failure, resentments of authority figures, strained relationships with peers.

We do not wish to imply that motivation for change must exist in full-blown form before training starts; proper training nearly always helps to increase motivation in early stages. Furthermore, some motivations may be latent, and "sensitizing" experiences[6] (where potential trainees become more fully aware of difficulties and problems they are encountering), may be helpful in clarifying and intensifying motivation.

Training needs become differentiated. Dissatisfaction in general cannot endure for very long as a basis for training. Training implies and requires focus, concern with "how to start a meeting" rather than "how to be a better chairman"; concern with "how to analyze unstructured data" rather than "how to do action research." This means differentiation—some before training starts, much during early phases of training. Particular skills must be located as being related to the resolution of the "tension system" or set of dissatisfactions within the individual, group, or institution involved.

Some training activity is perceived as a path to tension release. People cannot be thought of as ready for training if they have no perception that attending a particular type of training activity will give them promise of relief. Some proposed training activities, far from being a path to tension release, look to potential trainees more like a way to get more tense. People's feelings about tape recording and process observation of meetings, for example, either through anticipation or actual experience, are frequently apprehensive and negative.

Engaging in the training activity must not be seen as seriously jeopardizing membership in significant groups. The word "seriously" is used because training nearly always involves risk-taking and juggling of loyalties by people. However, a person must be relatively sure that being in the training activity will not mean that his rela-

6. For an account of such an experience, *see* Leland P. Bradford and Paul Sheats, "Complacency Shock and Retraining," in Kenneth D. Benne and Bozidar Muntyan, *Human Relations in Curriculum Change,* pp. 202–7. New York: Dryden Press, 1951.

tionship to other teachers, or other principals, or the teaching profession, or his superior will be permanently the worse for it. In addition, it is probably quite important that the generalized role prescriptions in the particular school system include engaging in training activity as justifiable, accepted, or even expected. Training goals and training procedures must, in effect, be sanctioned by both formal and informal organization if training is to be successful. If the tacit norms are, "Anyone who stays after school voluntarily is simple-minded," or "Admission of inadequacy means a black mark for you in *my* book," then readiness for training is reduced, to say the least.

DIAGNOSIS

The generalized conditions described above are probably most likely to be met when a reasonably cohesive, supportive group of peers already functioning with enthusiasm in the in-service program proceeds to analyze the difficulties and the blocks they face. If the group is already functioning, it means that training needs can be identified reasonably objectively in relation to the requirements of an agreed-on task, rather than as dimly seen inner needs of persons. If the group is supportive and cohesive, it is more likely that real feelings and problems can appear. The peer requirement is possibly less important than the underlying idea that the group's composition should not be such as to increase failure anxiety, make expressions of inadequacy unsafe, or jeopardize people's membership in significant groups. For some staffs and some problems, such a group which is diagnosing training needs encountered in an in-service program may cut across all levels of the hierarchy. Assuming underlying readiness for training, the existence of a clear, accepted task, such as preparing for a one-day teachers' institute or analyzing why the new social-studies guide is not being used, helps diagnosis considerably.

What is basically needed in such a diagnosis session is an atmosphere which is at the same time highly safe, that is, permits the expression of unpopular, uncertain, unlovely feeling relevant to the task and highly supportive of attempts toward change. Very often a situation of "irreality" such as that found in role-playing is productive of diagnostic insight, since it permits the expression of ordinarily inhibited feeling and encourages experimentation and change. The "action research" approach also appears to be unusually helpful in increasing safety, since reliance is on objective data, and in encouraging change, since scientific method is reasonably well accepted in our culture as a mode of change.

Diagnosis of training needs, then, is closely intertwined with individual, small-group, and institutional *readiness* to change. Diagnosis which results in subsequent productivity of training sessions must be a shared operation in a permissive setting, if genuine ego-involved training needs and not pseudo-needs are to be identified.

The Trainer Role

Such diagnosis and evaluation and, indeed, training itself will not ordinarily take place with regularity in a group working on the in-service program, as we have suggested in the introduction to this chapter. The diagnosis function and the training function are more likely to appear in in-service groups if some persons with appropriate skills are members of the group. Comments like these are needed: "I wonder why we take so long to make decisions?" "Are we blocked because we are concerned about how the interviews will go?" "Maybe we could practice scoring on some of the tests right now." "Do we have any evidence that staff meetings have improved since the new set-up started?"

This *trainer* role, with responsibility for helping members locate needed areas of change, devise learning experiences, and evaluate them, is distinguished quite clearly from the *chairman* role, which implies assistance to the group in task accomplishment. We have come to feel that there are some general identifiable characteristics of this role, whatever the content.

PERCEIVED HELPFULNESS

The trainer must be perceived as someone who is potentially and actually able to provide training assistance to the group.[7] This perception by group members, needless to say, must be held both initially and as training proceeds. However, it need not and should not block off members' perception that they themselves can increasingly supply training help.

7. See Irving Knickerbocker, "Leadership: A Conception and Some Implications," *Journal of Social Issues,* IV (Summer, 1948), 23-40.

From this point of view, the trainer may fill a variety of occupational roles—supervisor, teacher, outside consultant, curriculum co-
ordinator, elementary principal, and so on. The basic role requirement, however, is that the trainer be able to be recognized as a person capable of helping others grow and learn. Specific role-behaviors
can be learned by trainers in workshops, through observation of
other trainees and through practice.

FACILITATION OF GROUP DEVELOPMENT

The trainer needs to be continuously helpful to the group in facilitating growth of its members as a group toward cohesion, need-
meeting, and problem-solving.[8] It is probably true, for example, that
the trainer initially serves as a "model" from whom group members
learn the group standards of permissiveness, objectivity, and positive
orientation toward change. And as the group continues work, the
trainer needs to help the members make apparent the group-wide
changes which are taking place. The basic attitude of the trainer
needs to be one of *trust*—confidence in the group's powers to grow,
work, and develop. This attitude may communicate directly to
group members and influence activity immediately.

EXPERIMENTALISM

Since our knowledge of training is still at a relatively primitive
level, the trainer must be thoughtfully experimental about his role
and approach to training. The trainer's operations must be seen as
legitimate content for analysis by all group members, particularly
where training content is concerned with self-central matters. It also
means that heavy reliance in planning must be put on systematic
data on training outcomes—data gathered before, during, and after
training.

SHARING OF TRAINING RESPONSIBILITY

From one point of view, the trainer's chief job is to work himself
out of a job. That is, the trainer does all he can to help group members develop responsibility for diagnosing their own training needs,
planning training experiences, and evaluating them. Although it is
relatively easy for most trainers to indicate to groups that they do

8. *See* Matthew B. Miles, "Human-Relations Training: How a Group Grows,"
Teachers College Record, LV (December, 1953), 90–96.

not want to be responsible for a chairmanship, it is usually much more difficult for them to suppress the impulse to use the special skills they have in relation to training—whether these skills would be helpful in conducting a problem census, staging and analyzing role-playing, analyzing process problems, or helping to construct evaluation instruments. The trainer *does* have special competencies here, but he should not present them in a way that blocks member participation in the activities of the trainer role. This general characteristic of the trainer role assumes paramount importance for members of the training group who themselves will eventually stand in a training capacity toward others.

LIAISON WITH THE SURROUNDING ORGANIZATION

Just as the trainer must have membership in the group, he must also be perceived as having influence in the surrounding formal organization.[9] If the trainer is an outsider to the organization, he may find it necessary to make a special effort to become recognized as relating in some clear way to the structure.

We believe that these characteristics of the trainer role apply in general, although we have tended to phrase them in relation to content which is maximally central to the self—human-relations training. As training content moves away from the self toward matters carrying less feeling, careful trainer-role definition is probably less important but is still a feature of the relationship.

Organization for Training

DECISION-MAKING PROCESS

A wide variety of decisions about training have to be made: Who will come, where, when? What procedures, for what purposes? How and by whom these decisions are made will directly affect the success of training. Two aspects of decision-making are important here.

Sharedness of decision. To the degree that the training group and trainer share actively in the making of decisions about organiza-

9. See Herbert A. Thelen, *Dynamics of Groups at Work*, pp. 95–127 (Chicago: University of Chicago Press, 1954), for a discussion of administrative decision-making based on clarifying two potentially conflicting roles of the leader. The trainer role can be thought of in a parallel way.

tion, training will run better. This is primarily because such participation increases the "attractiveness"—possibility of need-meeting—of the group and makes it more likely that group membership will be a force for change in members. The reduction of secondary frictions and resistances, like those implied in the comment, "I never wanted to meet at 2:30 in the first place, but I didn't feel it was safe to speak up," is another by-product.

Clarity of decision areas. Maier[10] has pointed up the importance of clarity in respect to the areas where shared decision-making is possible and those where it is not. If the trainer feels that decision-making on certain areas in planning for training, such as time of day, physical arrangements, or procedures, should not be shared with the group, then it is much sounder simply to indicate this and free the group to work on problems about which its members can decide and do something. Pseudo-sharing in decisions which have already been made by the trainer, or by objective demands of the situation, is worse than time-wasting—it debilitates the trainer-group relationship rapidly.

TYPICAL DECISION AREAS

A variety of decisions usually have to be made about training within the context of a continuing in-service education program. Some of these can be reached in a split second—"Let's you and I meet afterwards to go over how to use the tape recorder"—and some can take hours—"Should we make this voluntary for the principals or not?" Effective training usually requires a good degree of consensus by a planning group in at least these seven decision areas:

Who will be trained? Who are the people involved, and on what basis will they appear—voluntarily, or as part of their regular job description? Are they all members of one working group, or do they come from many different levels of the organization and meet only during training sessions? Are they people who will, in turn, be training others—or is this primarily for their own benefit?

Time arrangements. How many sessions will there be? Will the sessions be held on or off school time? Will they be interwoven with other regular meetings or done in an intensive "time out"

10. Norman R. F. Maier, *Principles of Human Relations,* pp. 24–28, 198–99, 250–53. New York: John Wiley & Sons, Inc., 1952.

period? Is one lengthy session enough or should sessions be periodic over a longer time?

Physical arrangements. Will sessions be held at the school, at a central location, or in some "cultural island" setting away from the demands of the job? What room arrangements will meet training needs best? What audio-visual equipment should be available? What use should be made of existing laboratory, shop, art, and library facilities? Should existing facilities be altered or new ones developed specially?

Special roles needed. What differentiated jobs are required if training is to proceed as planned—chairman? inside or outside consultant? recorder? trainer? What do these roles demand, and how will people learn to perform them? What is being asked of people as they fill the *member* role? Does it have any special demands?

Content. Precisely what are the skills about which people are concerned? Are they sufficiently differentiated for good training to take place? How do we know that these are the "real" things training should focus on? (See the following section on training needs for additional comment on problems of determining content.)

Procedures. Effective training requires a generalized, cyclic procedure something like this:

a) Location of problems, dissatisfactions
b) Selection of new possible behaviors (action hypotheses) to reduce dissatisfaction
c) Practicing new behaviors
d) Getting feedback (evidence) on results
e) Generalizing, integrating, and reapplying insights
f) Locating new problems

Given this general outline, what specific procedures are needed to meet particular needs? Should the group work as a whole? in subgroups? tutorially? How can we locate real problems? Should role-playing be used? actual situations? How much practice is needed before we analyze results? Will a lecture help in generalizing? How can we work it so people can hear criticisms without getting defensive? These questions are many and complex, and here the trainer can be maximally helpful in playing the role of technician or methodologist in setting up learning situations.

Evaluation. How can we be relatively sure about what the training is accomplishing? What data should we gather before, during, and after the sessions? and how do we go about it? Who is responsible for this—the trainer? someone outside the group? all group members?

Although listing these decision areas suggests a structured, preplanned session, training may also take place as an integral part of an ongoing situation. In a situation where a group stops its work in order to acquire skills needed to overcome certain obstacles it faces, decisions about many areas (who? when? where?) are already made, and the group may move quickly into the planning of training experiences.

Training Needs and Illustrative Activities

INTRODUCTION

As Hass and Richey have indicated in chapters ii and iii, in-service programs are of many types—some group-based, others concerned primarily with individual activity. Some aim directly at a specific aspect of the instructional program, others are attempting to broaden participants' general education or competencies as a means to change. Some take place in the context of a large-scale overhaul of the curriculum; others are relatively isolated from the main stream of curriculum change.

The approach of this yearbook has tended to emphasize group activity as the basic mode of in-service education. But in-service education is *more* than getting a group of teachers, administrators, staff members, parents, citizens, or students together. The failure of many in-service education programs has been closely related to failures in supplying the many and varied skills which a good program needs to maintain itself.

THE SKILL DEMANDS OF IN-SERVICE PROGRAMS

The skills or tools most appropriate to in-service education programs are numerous. For example, the skills needed by a third-grade committee in studying ways to improve their own program in teaching reading differ somewhat from those needed by an elementary-school staff engaging in an art workshop. These, in turn, are different from the array of skills needed by two teachers in visiting another school, those of a junior high school committee deciding on a new reporting system which will improve articulation, and those of a science teacher looking for ways to help gifted children.

To emphasize this diversity, we are listing below some of the varieties of focus and procedure that characterize in-service education programs.

Foci of attention. Programs differ widely in what they are set up to do, even though the general purposes are professional and system growth. Committees and activities may be:

a) Task-centered—working on a particular, limited job such as the revision of a report card or making a report to the community or board.

b) Idea-centered—focused on the clarification of concepts, or philosophy, such as a committee preparing a preliminary statement on social-studies objectives for the local elementary program.

c) Problem-centered—not centered on a *particular* problem but on using the methodology of identifying, refining, and working toward solutions of many different problems. Many grade-level groups and departments operate this way, as do action research study groups.

d) Production-centered—focused on the preparation of particular instructional materials or equipment: kindergarten teachers making new play equipment; teachers preparing a language-arts guide.

e) Skill-centered—focused on the development of skills needed in teaching or administration: an art workshop for elementary teachers; a leadership-training group for principals.

f) Policy-centered—focused on the development of general guides to action: a representative group surveys parents, teachers, and administrators and submits a draft of a statement on P.T.A. fund-raising activities relevant to the school program.

g) Appreciation-centered—focused on the general education of participants: a graduate course in philosophy of education; credit for travel during the summer; music appreciation series.

Procedures. The procedures of in-service programs vary at least as widely as do their foci of attention. Some examples:

a) Surveys—a high-school staff engages in a follow-up study of graduates; a curriculum-consulting service helps a committee gather data on English offerings.

b) Study groups—six junior high school teachers engage in intensive child study; part of a high-school staff does action research on student leadership problems in the co-curriculum.

c) Workshops—interested junior high teachers spend a day on problems of remedial reading which they have identified.

d) Clinics—supervisors in a large county system get together periodically to analyze case problems which members face in supplying help to schools; experts supply special knowledge.

e) Institutes—all the teachers in a county meet for a day to become acquainted with techniques of action research.

f) Curriculum revision groups—a committee meets for a year to produce a new language-arts guide for Kindergarten-Grade III; departmental chairmen in a junior high school prepare resource material for the new English–social studies fusion.

g) Visitations—three teachers are released to visit the regional high school in the next county; two elementary teachers take turns visiting each other as they experiment with grouping.

h) Academic work—teacher gets in-service credit for graduate course in urban sociology; principal has leave of absence to complete doctorate.

Such complexity can only suggest the variety of skills for which training conceivably might be desirable. Below, we suggest some recurrent or characteristic training needs. Following each need are outlined illustrative training activities with which, for the most part, the authors have had direct and successful experience.

RECURRENT NEEDS AND SAMPLE ACTIVITIES

Convenience suggests three major families of training needs encountered in in-service programs: those concerned with group operation; those dealing with techniques of research and evidence-getting; and a miscellaneous category including workshops, conferences, and related activities.

Effective group operation. Needs in this category are usually rather compelling, even though frequently quite undifferentiated, and do much to hamper in-service growth. These needs arise partly from individual personality, as in the case of extreme anxiety in the face of an unstructured group meeting; partly from immediate small-group factors, such as the fact that members are not really listening to each other and decisions have to be remade constantly; and partly from general subcultural factors, such as middle-class anxiety about the expression of hostility. Such training needs often are associated with considerable feeling on the part of members, and good training of necessity deals with feeling as basic content. What is frequently overlooked, however, is that new cognitive material is perhaps equally essential—group members need to learn about group standards, about systematic problem-solving, about reference groups, even about Lewin's "quasi-stationary equilibria." Finally—and this is central to training as we have defined it—there must be repeated opportunities for diagnosis, practice, and evaluation of skills. These skills must be "whole-person" in nature—that is, they require the actor to integrate feeling, thought, and overt action so that the outcome in a group setting is optimal.

Below are listed some training needs which in-service groups frequently have in relation to group operation. One or two illustrative training activities are described in each need. Many different types of activities can be used, of course, to meet a given need. Some criteria for selecting training activities are suggested on pp. 359–61.

It may be helpful to say that the activities listed here have not, to our knowledge, been widely used in schools. Our own experiences with them suggest that they have considerable potential, however. The discussion here must necessarily be sketchy. For more complete discussion, the interested reader is referred to the references cited in the following paragraphs.

a) Agenda-building, goal-setting: Use of group as "laboratory" for self-study, with time taken out to analyze difficulties in reaching decisions about agenda and to plan experimentation into new procedures.[11]

b) Effective chairmanship: Rotation of chairman role through the group, and analysis of chairman behavior. Use of prerecorded tape to initiate discussion and role-playing of problem incidents requiring chairman action.

c) Overcoming frustration, reducing confusion, alleviating low morale. Use of group as laboratory; analysis of blockages. Discussion of resource material on methods of group diagnosis of difficulties.[12]

d) Increasing member sensitivity to feelings and perceptions of other members: Perception-check exercise in which each member estimates

11. For illustrative discussion of this and other training activities, *see* A. Harry Passow, Matthew B. Miles, Stephen M. Corey, and Dale C. Draper, *Training Curriculum Leaders for Cooperative Research,* pp. 22–26. New York: Bureau of Publications, Teachers College, Columbia University, 1955. Many of the specific examples not footnoted below come from this publication.

12. For example, Leland P. Bradford, Dorothy Stock, and Murray Horwitz, "How To Diagnose Group Problems," *Adult Leadership,* II (December, 1953), 12–19.

each other member's view of an issue facing the group; results are collated and analyzed.[13]

e) Process analysis: Practice of the process-observer role with group analysis of observer's performance.[14] Also, establishing "ground rule" that any member may initiate process analysis at any point during meeting.

f) Orientation of new or absent members: Study session in which "orientees" and "orienters" plan together how orientation will be done, carry it out experimentally, and evaluate it carefully.

g) Handling conflict and disagreement: Cognitive discussion of the nature of conflict. Use of a previously tape-recorded episode; several successive members try ways of resolving conflict; analysis.

h) Dealing with "problem members"—monologists, withdrawers, non-goal-directed members: Analysis of process in group to discover what features are evoking difficult behaviors. Role reversal, where "problem members" exchange places with other group members to increase insight and empathy. Use of "alter ego" technique, where unvoiced thoughts and feelings are spoken by another member.[15]

i) Problem-solving: Presentation and discussion of material on steps and stages of problem-solving.[16] Tape recording of group discussion, then listening to tape with recurrent stops for analysis and clarification of problem-solving procedure.

j) Decision-making and follow-through: Stopping after decision has been reached, with each member writing down his perception of decision; comparison and analysis. Record-keeping on follow-through on decisions.

k) Evaluation: Construction and use by group of post-meeting reaction sheets to assess member reactions to a meeting.

Research and inquiry. Needs in this category are frequently less compelling than those in the "effective group operation" category, partly because they stem less directly from involvement in a face-to-face situation. Even so, some training experiences have suggested that the term *research* is threatening to many school people and

13. Passow *et al., op. cit.,* pp. 36–38.

14. *See* Jack R. Gibb, Grace N. Platts, and Lorraine F. Miller, *Dynamics of Participative Groups,* pp. 31–43. St. Louis: John S. Swift Co., 1951.

15. Margaret E. Barron and Gilbert K. Krulee, "Case Study of a Basic Skill Training Group," *Journal of Social Issues,* IV (Spring, 1948), 10–30; also Chris D. Argyris, *Role-Playing in Action.* New York State School of Industrial and Labor Relations, Bulletin No. 16. New York: Cornell University, 1951.

16. John Keltner, "Decision-making through Problem-solving," in *Proceedings, First Annual Human Relations Training Laboratory,* pp. 24–33. Austin, Texas: University of Texas, 1955.

evokes expressions of inadequacy as well as attempts to escape from participation in experiences perceived as research-oriented. The rapid growth of the "action research" movement, however, suggests that the appeal of fact-finding and experimentation by persons themselves involved in the implications of findings is considerable.

The training needs in this area are probably numerous and closely intertwined with the "group operation" needs, since much action research is co-operative in nature, with teachers, supervisors, or principals working to solve problems together. We have insufficient experience as yet in the problems of training for research to have a clear idea of the most characteristic needs experienced by school persons as they work in a research way on practical problems. The general nature of research, however, suggests some for which we describe training activities below.

a) Clarification of over-all research process: Lecture with visual material;[17] sequential analysis of a case study of an action research project.

b) Doing "library" research (locating, synthesizing, generalizing, interpreting): Direct instruction from librarian or other resource person. Practice in locating materials on a given topic. Comparison of independent summaries by group members of the research on a problem.

c) Problem identification: Role-playing skit of group attempting to define research problem; commentator stands at side to make interpretive comments about the process. Tape-recording may be used similarly.

d) Creative hypothesizing: Use of "brainstorming" sessions, in which, after a problem area is agreed on, the ground rule is set that suggestions for solution or hypotheses must not be criticized but merely listed rapidly on the board; followed by analysis of features making for effective and ineffective hypothesizing.

e) Evidence-getting techniques:

　1) Questionnaires and inventories: analysis of particular questionnaires to bring out underlying principles; practice in construction of instruments to get answers to particular questions.

　2) Projective techniques: analysis of particular protocols such as unfinished sentences or picture stories by individuals separately; comparison- and generalization-drawing.

　3) Interviews and conferences: tape-recording of sample interviews, analysis and rating of effectiveness by listeners.

17. "Curriculum Change as Action Research," in Smith, Stanley, and Shores, *Fundamentals of Curriculum Development,* pp. 641–45. New York: World Book Co., 1950.

4) Behavior observation: half of group role-plays a meeting; other half observes in pairs, using specific instruments; data are shared and analyzed, reliability and validity of observations are checked.

f) Analysis of data:

1) Unstructured material: practice in subgroups on data previously gathered by group in its own meetings; sharing of generalizations.[18]

2) Prequantified data: practice in identifying and using statistical measures to provide answers to the questions.[19]

g) Interpretation of analyzed data: Presentation of complex, processed data such as education journal article with final conclusions removed, individual interpretation-making, comparison, analysis of differences. Or: group members take the *Interpretation of Data Test*[20] and score results.

Other training needs. Inspection of and experience with a number of in-service programs suggests a variety of additional activities for which training may be appropriate. These are not easily classifiable into either the "group" or the "research" category.

a) Planning workshops and conferences: Use of resource material[21] to aid in planning. Group of persons responsible for conference-planning, such as a central office staff in a county, plan, execute, and evaluate an actual model conference to test and improve their skills. Several members attend university clinic on workshop planning and return to provide training for others.

b) Consultation, approached either from consultant or consultee point of view: Skits showing characteristic problems consultants face.[22] Cognitive discussion of the nature of the consultant role.[23] Practice of consultative skills and analysis of characteristic difficulties encountered, with the contributions of consultant and consultee analyzed

18. See Matthew Miles and Stephen M. Corey, "The First Cooperative Curriculum Research Institute," Appendix B, in *Research for Curriculum Improvement.* 1957 Yearbook of the Association for Supervision and Curriculum Development. Washington: National Education Association, 1957 (in press).

19. *Ibid.*

20. Part of *General Education Series.* Upper Level, for Grades XII–XIV. Princeton, New Jersey: Co-operative Test Division, Educational Testing Service.

21. Robert A. Luke *et al.,* "Conferences That Work," *Adult Leadership,* II (May, 1953), 2–24, 28, 32 (seven articles on planning and running conferences); Richard Beckhard *et al.,* "Improving Large Meetings," *Adult Leadership,* I (December, 1952), 2–29 (ten articles on this topic).

22. Ernestine Bowen and Barry Levin, "The Consultation Role and Process," *Proceedings, First Annual Human Relations Training Laboratory, op. cit.,* pp. 132–36.

23. Douglas M. MacGregor, *op. cit.*

through role-playing soliloquies. Experimentation with different patterns of consultant use—from "inside" the system, from "outside," having consultant come to meetings, having consultant as leader of "guided tour" when school-community relations are being studied—and comparative evaluations of effectiveness. Many of these suggestions also apply to learning of the trainer role. The importance of opportunity for *practice* of roles like those of consultant and trainer is great. One attempt to teach trainers to conduct role-playing by explanation failed until they had an opportunity to role-play the conducting of role-playing.[24]

c) Visitation: Practice in observing a classroom, refinement of observing skills. Role-playing of interview situations.

d) Demonstration of teaching methods: Use of role-playing as a "dry run" for a demonstration; performance is critiqued and re-played until members are satisfied. Use of "listening teams," each watching for a selected aspect of demonstration.

e) Production of materials, such as audio-visual aids, courses of study, or resource guides: Direct instruction and practice. University or college training for one member who returns and serves as resource person, developing an audio-visual workshop or clinic.

f) Improved communication skills:

1) Reading: local reading consultant brings in speeded-reading equipment for weekly sessions for an interested group of teachers.

2) Writing: local university offers field course and sends instructor to school system weekly for a semester.

3) Speaking: playback and critique of tape-recordings.

4) Reporting: group of kindergarten teachers, planning a presentation to the school board on admission age, do "dry run" and revise approaches and personnel until they are comfortable with the result.

CRITERIA FOR SELECTING TRAINING ACTIVITIES

Planning and conducting helpful training activities is never easy or simple, and this skeletonized list of training needs and activities can only be illustrative. For the reader who is interested in organizing the diversified experiences suggested above, and in deciding which activity best meets needs he sees in his own in-service program, we are suggesting some selection criteria.

a) *To what extent does the proposed activity in fact have characteristics which make it a training activity?* This preliminary assess-

---

24. *See* Alex Bevalas in "Some Comments on the Uses of Role-Playing," in Benne and Muntyan, *op. cit.,* p. 247.

ment is important, and the proposed activity should be checked against the features discussed above under "A Conception of Training."

b) *To what extent does the training activity aim at remedying shortcomings which members have in the in-service program?* Learning better behavior in the training group is not enough. Members in training have to improve in the skills they need to do a better job in the program, or the training is not much good.

Real shortcomings, real problems have force behind them; training activities which are built on ego-involving problems have considerable urgency. Sometimes real problems are too compelling, and it is useful to construct an unreal situation which is somewhat more secure. But even here the approximation of important concerns is desirable.

c) *To what extent does the training activity encourage a constant interplay between the job situation and the training group?* Good training requires that members constantly test what goes on in the in-service program against the events of the training situation, and vice versa. If the training is seen as all "theory" and the job as all "practice," not much job improvement will result. The same is true if the job is "impossible" and the training group is "wonderful." If trainees learn things in the training group which they plan to apply when the time is "right," that time may never come. The tie-in between training and program must be direct, and the links between "what we just did here," and the "meetings with the supervisors I have next week" must be made explicit.

d) *To what extent does the training activity support on-the-job experimentation?* Training is not much help unless members feel that they can try out new ideas in the setting where the problems which stimulated the training arose. Experimentation in the training group is easy; everyone is supportive and there to learn. But experimenting when the "chips are down" is more difficult. Yet improvement can only come about if members feel secure enough to try things out in the in-service program itself. A good training activity includes a chance to get the help of the training group at diagnosing situations on the job that need changing.

e) *To what extent does the training activity give promise of helping members with more than one aspect of their behavior?* Effective in-service work is complex. Training activities should be focused, specific, and concrete, but they should not encourage members to believe that effective operation in an in-service program is an over-simplified dream, or that panaceas are readily available. A given training activity should probably focus rather narrowly, but its place in a sequence of training activities should be such as to round out the picture, show the whole situation, assist the member in many different aspects of his task.

 f) *To what extent does the training activity contain provision for its own evaluation and self-correction?* Unless members can discuss and criticize training activities, it is very difficult to improve them. Such evaluation also helps to uncover new training needs for the future. In addition, some members may be in a position to conduct training themselves and can gain ideas from a discussion of "how well this went."

Evaluation of Training

The problems encountered in evaluation of training for the specific skills needed for an in-service program do not differ in kind, of course, from those arising in evaluation of the program as a whole. The reader is referred to chapter xiii for an analysis of general program-evaluation problems.

DIFFICULTIES

It may be helpful here to discuss some of the special problems that arise during evaluation of training, whether this evaluation is "reconnaissance" or steering research carried on during the training activities to help in replanning them, or "assessment" research designed to get at over-all effects of training.

To the degree that training is concerned with matters central to the self, evidence-getting is technically difficult. Few standard measures exist in the area of effective group operation, for example, and "home-grown" measures have to serve. Furthermore, it is difficult to get practical controls which will help a trainer discover with some certainty whether the training experience actually did the trick or whether other features in the school system exerted forces for change at the same time. In any ongoing, highly interdependent social system, it is difficult to get data on performance without influencing the situation and so distorting the data. The pressures of the school organization influence data-production considerably: responses to a questionnaire item for teachers asking, "How helpful did you find the principals' workshop in terms of the way your principal works with you?" must inevitably be influenced, distorted, and perhaps even blanked out by the quality of the principal-teacher relationships in the system. An added obstacle to effective evidence-getting is the multiple causation of human behavior in an organization; determining the effects of a particular training experience is very difficult, indeed.

Beyond technical difficulties, a second major problem is that of the threat ordinarily associated with evaluation, which is particularly evident where central-to-the-self concerns are the content of training. A wide range of defensive behaviors—flight, rationalizations, and hostility—appear frequently, even when much thought has been given to evidence-getting. Defensiveness is not limited to group members and may even be more acute on the part of trainers.

To the extent, however, that planning for evaluation has been included as part of the training experience, such that evaluation of training can take place initially in the safe, supportive atmosphere of the training group, these reactions are less likely to hamper evaluation. Training-group standards of permissiveness and objectivity also help here. The other major value of this approach certainly lies in the active involvement of all those concerned with the training in its evaluation.

EVALUATION METHODS

The basic criterion for evaluation of training, of course, must be, "Is the difficulty or reason for initiating training in the first place being lessened or removed?" Much evaluation can be highly informal and matter-of-fact: "How much has our reading speed improved since we started the workshop? Does the tape recorder get tangled up any less frequently after our session last week? Do we still have snags in how to process the sociometric data, or are things going smoothly now?" Other evaluation must be more formal, complex, and affect-laden: "What perceptions of supervisors do the elementary teachers have *now* in relation to their consulting behavior? What is the percentage of follow-through on committee decisions during the last month? Are we any better in conducting role-playing with our core classes than we were last November?"

Evaluation methods must be designed carefully in relation to the whole organizational structure in which training is taking place. Just as training starts with a difficulty, imbalance, or dissatisfaction in part of the system, some features of the training program, while reducing the immediate difficulty, may tend to bring about imbalance in the surrounding system. For example, when some teachers are released to see a film on leading a discussion group, the teachers who are not released may begin to worry about their relationship to the principal or to the curriculum director.

Immediate evaluation methods. Several devices have seemed useful for getting immediate data on the success of training:

a) Oral evaluation. Assuming a relatively permissive atmosphere, oral evaluation while training is in process and at the end of sessions can usually be quite helpful. It is not, of course, helpful in assessing longer-term results of training, but, in the absence of better instruments than are now available, it is probably better than anything except direct observation of members in operation "on the job." Oral evaluation also has the advantage of being interactive, and so evaluative comments often go deeper and stimulate latent ideas.

Oral evaluation suffers the disadvantage that the action of the moment sometimes leads to such aftereffects as the "golden glow" and the "black cloud." However, the value of oral evaluation as evidence may be enhanced considerably by having a series of guidelines or aspects of the training experience on which there is agreement to have careful discussion. Given permissiveness, the accuracy and completeness of data which can be gathered through oral evaluation on an immediate situation are substantial.

b) Post-meeting reaction sheets. These much-used P.M.R. sheets have both values and disadvantages. If inhibition of feeling or incomplete participation patterns exist in the group, opportunity for each group member to have his say on paper, unimpeded by faster-talking members or problems of deviance from group standards, may be essential for getting good evidence. P.M.R.s also probably permit of more thoughtfulness and thoroughness, minute for minute and group member by group member, than does oral evaluation.

P.M.R.s have disadvantages. Many people express themselves least easily in writing. If there are really strong inhibitory forces, these will extend to responses even on unsigned P.M.R.s. Many training situations really do need interactive and not individually oriented evaluation. Too, preconstructed P.M.R.s often miss the real training points of a session.

The idea of building a P.M.R. at the close of a session, with members agreeing on the questions to which answers should be written, combines the values of oral and written evaluation and minimizes some of the disadvantages. It also introduces another important dimension; group members are much more heavily involved in the planning of data collection and may be equally concerned with summary and analysis of the results.[25]

Signing or not signing P.M.R.s seems to make much less difference than people expect it will. As with tape-recording, the anxiousness with which the issue is presented makes much difference. The basic issues are: (*a*) who will see P.M.R. results, and (*b*) for what purpose? If these are clarified (preferred answer to *a*, "all of us"; preferred answer to *b*, "to improve our sessions, as well as sessions of other similar groups") then the use of the P.M.R. in general—of which the "signing" issue is really a symptom—is clear, and better evidence is assured.

c) Observation of behavior in the training session. A third source of immediate data, assuming that training sessions are working on concrete skills in training settings roughly analogous to the work setting, is observation of what members are doing, right here and now. This approach has serious limitations.

However, if the assumptions of (1) behavioral continuity between training and job, and (2) reasonable similarity of training and job situations are met, then observation of training-group behavior can be a fruitful source of data. What this means is: If Miss Walker is unable to stay "on the beam" in a training group discussion, then she probably, but *not* inevitably, will have the same difficulty in the in-service group with which she is working. Correlatively, if Mrs. Martino develops a good feeling for building categories in some open-end data during a practice session, then she probably, but *not* certainly, can cope with the unstructured material her in-service group is just now plowing through.

Increasing the accuracy of prediction from training behavior to job performance is, and has been, a problem of major concern to educators and psychologists for years. The difficulty of the problem is often increased because training situations are different from job situations in procedures, in the amount of "irreality," and even in content discussed. The quality of evidence obtained through observation of members in training sessions can be enhanced considerably if members discuss differences and similarities between training and "job,"

25. See Passow *et al., op. cit.,* pp. 88–89.

as well as exploring specific barriers and obstacles to behaving in new ways as a result of training.

Follow-up evaluation methods. Some other general methods appear to have value for gathering data on the effects of training some time after sessions end.

a) Questionnaires and inventories. The advantages of some sort of pencil-and-paper response procured some time after training are roughly parallel to those of written P.M.R.s immediately after training. Questionnaires and inventories have the added advantage of the relatively systematic planning and coverage that a good instrument involves. Hypotheses of an "explanatory," as contrasted with a purely summary-descriptive, nature can be tested, as, for example, "Did people with the strongest initial interest tend to feel they learned the most?"[26] The resulting data can be used to get answers to questions formulated before any training sessions are held.

Questionnaires and inventories share the disadvantages all pencil-and-paper items have in facing the realities of behavior and trying to get verbal correlates of it. This is more acutely true to the degree that training deals with nonperipheral matters.

The use of an inventory or questionnaire after training, optimally speaking, should imply the existence of preresponses on the same instruments. Recollected "before" responses are useful and serve to discriminate among group members quite well, but—accomplishment-needs being what they are—may show differences where performance or a pre-post measure would show none. A further refinement is to gather responses on the same instrument from co-workers who did not attend the training sessions. This cuts out "practice effect" on the instruments even though this cannot be easily separated from the inevitable disagreements between co-workers and training-group members.

A final suggestion is that such co-workers can be asked to react to the inventory or questionnaire either in terms of (*a*) their estimate of the change or growth in the trainee, or (*b*) in terms of the way they think the trainee would answer. These responses supply a kind of validity check for trainee responses or can be used as an additional criterion of trainee change.

b) Interviews. Talking with group members or co-workers some time after training, either individually or in groups, gets helpful and thorough data—again the more valuable because a systematic pre-planned set of questions can be answered by careful inquiry. Inter-

26. See Passow *et al., op.. cit.*, pp. 156–58, for an account of sixteen such explanatory hypotheses tested following a series of training conferences.

views share the advantages and disadvantages of oral evaluation suggested above. They take practicing if they are to get evidence that can be counted on; and careful recording is important. The processing and analysis of interview data is extremely time-consuming. An added advantage, however, is that most people are not ordinarily listened to very much in our culture, and interviews are not only ego-involving but fun (and even flattering) for the interviewee—so data are easier to get.

c) Observation of behavior in the in-service program. We have saved until last the evaluation method that most people find most effective for judging the consequences of training for in-service program skills. The basic question is: Are members doing any better what they originally were worried or concerned about? From this point of view, members, the trainer(s), and co-workers not involved in the training are all looking at in-service performance with a keenly pragmatic eye to see whether the program is going any more smoothly.

Two general considerations may be mentioned here. The question of what "works" is not as easy as it looks, since immediate "successes" often turn out to have hidden snags in them, and long-term improvements are sometimes only barely evident in an in-service situation today. Furthermore, if the original diagnosis of the training problem was partial or incorrect, then it is optimistic to expect the problem to dissolve or disappear completely after training.

A second consideration is that any problem is a problem to some people and not a problem to some others. This means that adequate assessment through observation of the in-service program and the way people perform in it must be undertaken by as many different kinds of people as are disturbed because of the problem. Different perceptions must be shared, compared, contrasted, and analyzed to sift out the genuine effects of the training experiences.

Concluding Statement

We believe that in-service programs can be aided measurably through attention to the improvement of the kinds of skill needed by participants. This means that the need for acquiring particular skills must become recognized, that participants and planners must be willing to take time out for training, that inventiveness during the planning stages must be central, and that efforts to secure data on the effectiveness of the training must be made.

We have a generalized hypothesis which, in our view, needs wider testing: *If* program planners and participants give careful attention to locating gaps in the teacher's preparedness for instructional services, to planning and carrying out meaningful training experiences, and to research on the effects of the experiences, *then* the in-service program will go deeper and farther, and educational experiences of boys and girls will be improved.

INDEX

Index

371

INFORMATION CONCERNING THE NATIONAL SOCIETY FOR THE STUDY OF EDUCATION

1. PURPOSE. The purpose of the National Society is to promote the investigation and discussion of educational questions. To this end it holds an annual meeting and publishes a series of yearbooks.

2. ELIGIBILITY TO MEMBERSHIP. Any person who is interested in receiving its publications may become a member by sending to the Secretary-Treasurer information concerning name, title, and address, and a check for $6.00 (see Item 5).

Membership is not transferable; it is limited to individuals, and may not be held by libraries, schools, or other institutions, either directly or indirectly.

3. PERIOD OF MEMBERSHIP. Applicants for membership may not date their entrance back of the current calendar year, and all memberships terminate automatically on December 31, unless the dues for the ensuing year are paid as indicated in Item 6.

4. DUTIES AND PRIVILEGES OF MEMBERS. Members pay dues of $5.00 annually, receive a cloth-bound copy of each publication, are entitled to vote, to participate in discussion, and (under certain conditions) to hold office. The names of members are printed in the yearbooks.

Persons who are sixty years of age or above may become life members on payment of fee based on average life-expectancy of their age group. For information, apply to Secretary-Treasurer.

5. ENTRANCE FEE. New members are required the first year to pay, in addition to the dues, an entrance fee of one dollar.

6. PAYMENT OF DUES. Statements of dues are rendered in October for the following calendar year. Any member so notified whose dues remain unpaid on January 1, thereby loses his membership and can be reinstated only by paying a reinstatement fee of fifty cents.

School warrants and vouchers from institutions must be accompanied by definite information concerning the name and address of the person for whom membership fee is being paid. Statements of dues are rendered on our own form only. The Secretary's office cannot undertake to fill out special invoice forms of any sort or to affix notary's affidavit to statements or receipts.

Cancelled checks serve as receipts. Members desiring an additional receipt must enclose a stamped and addressed envelope therefor.

7. DISTRIBUTION OF YEARBOOKS TO MEMBERS. The yearbooks, ready prior to each February meeting, will be mailed from the office of the distributors, only to members whose dues for that year have been paid. Members who desire yearbooks prior to the current year must purchase them directly from the distributors (see Item 8).

8. COMMERCIAL SALES. The distribution of all yearbooks prior to the current year, and also of those of the current year not regularly mailed to members in exchange for their dues, is in the hands of the distributor, not of the Secretary. For such commercial sales, communicate directly with the University of Chicago Press, Chicago 37, Illinois, which will gladly send a price list covering all the publications of this Society. This list is also printed in the yearbook.

9. YEARBOOKS. The yearbooks are issued about one month before the February meeting. They comprise from 600 to 800 pages annually. Unusual effort has been made to make them, on the one hand, of immediate practical value, and, on the other hand, representative of sound scholarship and scientific investigation.

10. MEETINGS. The annual meeting, at which the yearbooks are discussed, is held in February at the same time and place as the meeting of the American Association of School Administrators.

Applications for membership will be handled promptly at any time on receipt of name and address, together with check for $6.00 (or $5.50 for reinstatement). Applications entitle the new members to the yearbook slated for discussion during the calendar year the application is made.

5835 Kimbark Ave.
Chicago 37, Illinois

NELSON B. HENRY, *Secretary-Treasurer*

i

PUBLICATIONS OF THE NATIONAL SOCIETY FOR THE STUDY OF EDUCATION

NOTICE: Many of the early yearbooks of this series are now out of print. In the following list, those titles to which an asterisk is prefixed are not available for purchase.

iii

POSTPAID
PRICE

Distributed by

THE UNIVERSITY OF CHICAGO PRESS, CHICAGO 37, ILLINOIS

1959